S0-BYQ-019

THEMES IN DRAMA

Themes in Drama is a journal which brings together articles and reviews about the dramatic and theatrical activity of a wide range of cultures and periods. The articles offer original contributions to their own specialized fields, but are presented in such a way that their significance may be readily appreciated by non-specialists.

Editorial Advisory Board

DENNIS BARTHOLOMEUSZ, Senior Lecturer in English, Monash University
EDWIN EIGNER, Professor of English, University of California, Riverside
MARTIN ESSLIN, Professor of Drama, Stanford University
INGA-STINA EWBANK, Professor of English, University of Leeds
JOHN FLETCHER, Professor of Comparative Literature, University of East Anglia
WILLIAM O. HARRIS, Professor of English, University of California, Riverside
PETER D. HOLLAND, Lecturer in Poetry and Drama, Trinity Hall, Cambridge
MILTON MILLER, Professor of English, University of California, Riverside
H. B. NISBET, Professor of German, Sidney Sussex College, Cambridge
ANN SADDLEMYER, Professor of English, University of Toronto
S. SCHOENBAUM, Professor of English, University of Maryland
MICHAEL J. SIDNELL, Professor of English, University of Toronto
JOHN WEIGHTMAN, Emeritus Professor of French, Queen Mary and Westfield College, University of London

SUBSCRIPTIONS The subscription price to volume 14, which includes postage, is £42 (US $75.00 in USA and Canada) for institutions, £24.00 (US $47.00 in USA and Canada) for individuals ordering direct from the Press and certifying that the annual is for their personal use. Airmail (orders to Cambridge only) £7.00 extra. Copies of the annual for subscribers in the USA and Canada are sent by air to New York to arrive with minimum delay. Orders, which must be accompanied by payment, may be sent to a bookseller, subscription agent or direct to the publishers: Cambridge University Press, The Edinburgh Building, Shaftesbury Road, Cambridge CB2 2RU. Payments may be made by any of the following methods: cheque (payable to Cambridge University Press), UK postal order, bank draft, Post Office Giro (account no. 571 6055 GB Bootle – advise CUP of payment), international money order, UNESCO coupons, or any credit card bearing the Interbank symbol. Orders from the USA and Canada should be sent to Cambridge University Press, 40 West 20th Street, New York, NY 10011–4211.

BACK VOLUMES Volumes 1–13 are available from the publisher at £40.00 ($75.00 in USA and Canada).

Themes in Drama

An annual publication

Edited by James Redmond

14

MELODRAMA

Themes in Drama

Edited by James Redmond, Department of Drama, Queen Mary and Westfield College, University of London, Mile End Road, London E1 4NS.

MELODRAMA

LIBRARY

Published by the Press Syndicate of the University of Cambridge
The Pitt Building, Trumpington Street, Cambridge CB2 1RP
40 West 20th Street, NewYork, NY 10011–4211, USA
10 Stamford Road, Oakleigh, Victoria 3166, Australia

© Cambridge University Press 1992

First published 1992

Printed in Great Britain at The Bath Press, Avon

A catalogue record for this
book is available from the
British Library

ISSN 0263–676x
ISBN 0 521 41958 1

PN
1912
M456
1992

Contents

Contributors

Victor Castellani, *University of Denver, Colorado*
Halina Filipowicz, *University of Wisconsin, Madison*
Eileen Fischer, *The City University of New York*
Robert F. Gross, *Hobart and William Smith Colleges*
Ira Hauptman, *University of California, Riverside*
Gabrielle Hyslop, *University of New England, NSW*
Joel H. Kaplan, *University of British Columbia*
Robert C. Ketterer, *University of Iowa*
Bruce A. McConachie, *College of William and Mary*
J. Paul Marcoux, *Boston College*
Jeffrey D. Mason, *California State University, Bakersfield*
William R. Morse, *College of the Holy Cross, Worcester, Massachusetts*
Susan Painter, *The Roehampton Institute, London*
Denis Salter, *McGill University*
William Sharp, *Emerson College, Boston, Massachusetts*
Roxana Stuart, *Adelphi University*
Gary Westfahl, *University of California, Riverside*
Elizabeth Hale Winkler, *Texas Tech University, Lubbock*

Illustrations

Everything to do with Dionysus: *Ur*drama, Euripidean melodrama, and tragedy*

VICTOR CASTELLANI

The Athenian playwright Euripides, although called by Aristotle the 'most tragic' of tragedians, has received his share of criticism for sometimes not being tragic *enough*, for having written during the 420s and especially the 410s BC plays that are nominally tragedies, are nowadays often called 'romances' or even 'comedies', and are actually *melodramas*, in part or *in toto*.[1] Such sequences as the prologues and first episodes of his *Andromache* and *Heracles*, as well as entire plays like his *Children of Heracles*, *Iphigenia among the Taurians*, and *Helen* show several or all of the following characteristic features of melodrama: a villainous and smug bully, a woman or women in distress, a child or children in mortal danger, and an unexpected rescue whose agent is either a rejuvenated old person or a person presumed dead or otherwise lost forever. Such business, feel some critics who admire classic Sophoclean tragedy, is *Euripidean degeneracy*.[2] Or at least it is *philanthropos*, what Aristotle names the 'humanly satisfying' mood at its happy cadence, even as he denies that it is properly 'tragic'.[3] I submit, however, that melodrama of this sort has as venerable an ancestry as 'pure' tragedy and comedy – that, in fact, all three of these theatrical genres, and the Attic satyr play, too, share a common origin in the dramatic myth of drama's patron god. This is what the present paper endeavors to explain, historically and with regard to Euripides' *œuvre* taken as a whole.

First let us consider for a moment what one may call the *dramatic* origin of drama in Greece, in ritual re-enactment of the homogeneous stories of young Dionysus that tragedy's choral parent the dithyramb-song evidently celebrated.[4] Let me rehearse those stories for the reader who may not be familiar with them.

As a baby, as a boy, and as a youth the son of Zeus and Semele suffered persecution from his stepmother Hera, and also from a series of non-Olympian heavies. Not only did he himself suffer (imprisonment, murderous pursuit, various kinds of symbolic death, indeed even tempor-

* A draft of this paper was read at the *Themes in Drama* International Conference held at the University of California, Riverside, in February 1990.

ary death, by dismemberment), but so did also his female nurses, viz. his lightning-slain mother's sisters and/or other women who looked after him in his infancy. His helpers also include friendly old men, whether Nereus, the Old Man of the Sea, as implied by the Homeric *Iliad*, or his maternal grandfather old Cadmus and the ancient priest-prophet Tiresias, both of whom we know from Euripides' unquestionably tragic *Bacchae*. His rescuer is sometimes his divine brother Hermes, sometimes a kindly human being, but most often himself, by a sudden outburst of supernatural power that his persecutor did not suspect he possessed. When he himself reacts, he typically drives his enemy mad, making him directly or indirectly self-destructive. Lycurgus, in some accounts, chopped off his own leg (thinking it a vine-stock); Pentheus, whom we know both from the *Bacchae* and from reconstruction of an earlier treatment of the myth by Aeschylus, goes gleefully to a grisly death. For Lycurgus, Pentheus, Proetus, and the god's other royal human foes, the outcome is catastrophic – a wholly 'tragic' one if we look at the action from their point of view. *From Dionysus' eye-view, on the other hand,* and from that of his aunts and his nymph-allies, *the shape of the action is melodramatic.* The evolution of tragedy more or less as we understand it (that is, centering on a mortal hero who suffers death or other disaster after colliding with divine power) seems, therefore, to depend upon a shift of perspective. The poets moved their focus, and all or almost all of their sympathy, from heaven to earth, from gods and gods' friends to mortal demigods and other *mortal* persons opposed in some way, by defiance or by mistake, to those gods.

One might expect to trace this reversed perspective to Homer, or at least to the prototragic *Iliad*, whose humanism and whose disparagement of the Olympians needs no demonstration here. Trace it we can, even in the Homeric epic's very condensed reference to the 'Bacchic melodrama'. Homer's Diomedes, a stubbornly un-tragic foil to Achilles, is the one who tells the story of Lycurgus in Book VI (129–40). I don't want to fight you if you are a god, the young Achaean hero says to an unknown opponent, for

> not even Dryas' son, mighty Lycurgus, lived long, who strove with heavenly gods. He once upon a time chased the nurses of mad Dionysus down sacred Mount Nysa, and they all threw their wands to the ground, smitten by the ox-goad of murderous Lycurgus. Dionysus in fright dove below the wave of the sea, and Thetis welcomed him, terrified, to her bosom, for a mighty trembling took hold of him at the man's violent pursuit. At this man then the easy-living gods were angered, and the son of Cronus made him blind; nor did he live long, since he was hated by all the immortal gods.

Diomedes now reiterates that he would not want to fight gods. This earliest literary account of Dionysus presents a rudimentary (and unmotivated) tragedy of Lycurgus, a pattern that Diomedes himself will avoid repeating; but the same tale also presents a (better motivated) *melodrama*, describing the danger and stating, and restating, the fear of the god's nurses and of the god himself before the latter's rescue and their pursuer's punishment.

Centuries later Athenian *tragoidia*, we know, following the Homeric and Archaic lead, assumed a fundamental *human* focus and dealt sympatheticly with *human* catastrophes, whether inherited from the older poetic tradition or freely adapted or wholly invented. (Indeed to call the *Iliad* 'tragic' at all is to commit a wise anachronism!) In any case, both of the earlier Athenian tragedians are in one sense or other clearly 'Homeric'. Well known are both the great debt to Homer that Aeschylus himself evidently acknowledged and the intimate kinship with the Iliadic Homer that Sophocles displayed in every play (whose protagonists are all variations on epic Achilles).[5] Whether with an optimistic view about the justice of his protagonist's sufferings (Aeschylus) or a more ambiguous one (Sophocles), a successful tragedian at Athens until well past the middle of the fifth century would dramatize plenty of such suffering *where the sufferers were persons who somehow challenged a god or the gods*. Not the anguish of a challenged god, but rather the terrible punishment of the challenger, is thus usually central to *muthos* and *pathos* alike, to plot and to emotional content, of a tragedy. Departures from this pattern, moreover, seem to have been very few; for to arrange such a happy outcome as the reconciliation between the supreme god Zeus and the pro-human divinity Prometheus, ending a (reconstructable) trilogy in which Aeschylus has concentrated attention on the latter, on Prometheus, is really not to depart from the pattern but to enrich it, and to mitigate Olympian harshness as a theologizing poet and his pious audience might wish to do.[6] A more important departure in Aeschylus concerns the last play of another trilogy, the *Eumenides*, where the anguish of offended deities, the Furies who avenge matricide, is explored at great if unpleasant length. Their human antagonist Orestes and his immortal patron Apollo bespeak a kind of arrogance that makes the dread goddesses themselves perhaps a bit sympathetic to the audience, and certainly sympathetic *within the play* to the audience's esteemed protrectress Athena. By a denouement that satisfies them (and completely ignores Orestes and Apollo, both long since gone) the playwright in effect takes the goddesses' side against criminal humans, and appears to be more concerned about the many guilty homicides than about an occasional and extraordinary innocent one. We find only a few features of Dionysus-type melodrama here (outrage to divinity, Phoebus Apollo's outrage to the female, possibly the Furies' rejuvenation at the end); but we find even less 'tragedy' as that word is commonly understood, above all as Sophocles' subsequent practice implies its definition.

It took the maverick Euripides to return to melodramatic matter, in many plays, and to melodramatic form, after fashions that we shall now examine and with doubts about which I shall speculate below.

We may begin with Euripides' special humanism within Hellenic humanism, or, to name it differently, with his peculiar *humanization*. Everyone knows how he brought the great personages of Bronze Age legend down to all-too-human levels. Aristophanes' complaints about kings and heroes in rags, in tears, and in sophistries are very familiar and very telling.[7] Familiar, too, is Sophocles' reported diagnosis. 'I make such [persons] as *should* be made', his older rival is said to have said, 'while Euripides makes them as they *are*'.[8] What has apparently not been so well appreciated is how the same Euripides brings *divine action*, the type identi-fied above as Dionysiac melodrama, down to the human level, where mortal women and girls, where mortal babies, suffer the threats of mortal persecutors who play for keeps. Indeed he does this quite often, not only in those five plays already mentioned which either open with or consist of melodramatic events.

A survey of other occurrences in Euripidean drama of deadly scoun-drels, women and children in distress, surprise rescues and the like will be instructive before we look closely at more complete melodrama in *Andromache* and *Heracles*, *Children of Heracles*, the earlier *Iphigenia*, and *Helen*.

The undated but probably early satyr play *Cyclops* has only one of the elements I am concerned with, the one-eyed brute of the epic tradition. There is no woman at all, no child. The *Alcestis* of 438 BC, on the other hand, although we should perhaps not name the result melodrama, has all or most of its chief elements: (1) Thanatos, 'Death' personified, is the dastard who actually kills Alcestis (though of course she does not *stay* killed); (2) not only is she herself in danger, but (3) so are her children, who will not be raised well after her death, whether they have no mother at all or (worse, in Greek thinking) they get a step-mother upon the remarriage of Alcestis' husband Admetus. There is no rejuvenation in this play (unless perhaps in some liveliness on the part of Admetus' old father Pheres), but it ends, of course, with (4) Alcestis' resurrection, which the miraculous intervention of (5) Heracles brings about. Nevertheless, I would not classify this somewhat melodrama-like play as a melodrama.[9]

Turning to Euripidean tragedies proper, we find in the *Medea* (431 BC) and the second, surviving *Hippolytus* (428) both a woman and her children in very grave distress indeed, though in neither play does rescue ensue. The children in the earlier of these plays, the woman Phaedra in the later, perish. In *Medea* we may further note a fleeting suggestion of the villain-king in Creon, who does *not*, unluckily for himself, treat or seriously threaten Medea and her little boys with melodramatic violence (our expectation of which he notably frustrates); he spares them all, so that, by a harsh irony, she herself can kill her and Jason's sons. The danger to Phaedra and her children in *Hippolytus* is rather different. Her persecutor is a goddess, Aphrodite, whose manipulation of Phaedra's feelings (Phaedra lusts for her stepson Hippolytus) does not inevitably entail death for the unhappy woman, but the gravest possible dishonor – and, if she is dishonored, dishonor for her young children as well (whom her husband Theseus might well disown). Medea saves herself (in her twisted thinking) by killing her sons; Phaedra (distraught, but thinking more clearly) saves her children by killing herself. Neither outcome, however, completes the pattern of melodrama.

Euripides' *Suppliants*, probably written about the same time as the two more famous (and better) works just discussed, has a whole chorus-ful of women in distress and, apparently with them, children.[10] They are all the widows and orphans of the seven heroes who have attacked and fallen at Thebes shortly before the play begins. Their nasty enemy is Creon of Thebes, who refuses to return the heroes' bodies for burial and threatens to apply force even against their unarmed widows should they enter Theban territory. Through his herald he demands that the Athenians expel old King Adrastus of Argos, who supported the attack and lost two sons-in-law when it failed, and who now leads the effort to bury the fallen. For all of the bereaved and threatened a rescuer is at hand. The suppliants' champion is Theseus of Athens. Whether Adrastus can be said to be rejuvenated or not, he is protected, honored (though not without some sharp criticism of his disastrous war policy), and satisfied as the good Theseus takes up the Argive cause, at first diplomatically, then militarily, and fights a holy second battle near Thebes to recover the bodies of those who fell in the unholy first one. The end of this unusual play does not resemble melodrama at all, however, occupied as it is with mourning for the dead, promise of revenge in the future, and an alliance struck (at the goddess Athena's behest) between Argos and Athens.

Two very unpleasant plays written probably about ten years apart, the earlier but undated *Hecuba* and the *Trojan Women* of 415 BC, deal with similar matter: the brutal aftermath of the Trojan War. Women and children fear and suffer atrocities from which there is now no one to rescue them. The villains are the victorious Greeks in general, though individual Greek chiefs bear special responsibility – Agamemnon and Odysseus above all, on stage in *Hecuba*, behind the scenes in *Trojan Women*. The former play has a bitter complication in the vindictive attack by Hecuba against not only Polymestor himself (who treacherously murdered her last surviving son, the boy Polydorus) but also Polymestor's own innocent small children. Victim here has become villain, by a shocking reversal such as Euripides' audience had seen already in *Medea* (and would see again). This, of course, is not melodrama but moral degradation, at once pathetic and appalling. Euripides' concern with suffering innocents, with female and young victims of kings' brutality nevertheless continues in both these plays.

Probably written sometime between these two, the *Ion* is much more a melodrama, and contains a very neat irony by which a young divine child (the title character, Ion, son of the Athenian princess Creusa by the god Apollo) nearly meets death at the hands of his own mother, who does not, of course, know who he is. To the extent that this play – of near-catastrophe survived – has a villain, it is Apollo.[11] The brilliant god – and rapist – has caused much grief to Creusa, who believes that the child she bore the god fifteen or so years ago is dead, and who now fears that her mortal non-Athenian husband's bastard son (what she believes Ion to be) will prevent any child she may yet bear from succeeding to her father's kingship of Athens. She tries to kill Ion and fails; then *he* seeks to catch and kill *her*, for punishment. Another irony makes Apollo also the rescuer. One of his significant birds forestalls Creusa's attempt to poison the boy; but then his altar protects her from retaliation, and his priestess facilitates a recognition between mother and son. Furthermore, Creusa's rather dim-witted husband Xuthus experiences a kind of rejuvenation, while Creusa's abandoned baby, long presumed dead, comes surprisingly, if at first con-fusingly, back to life in Ion. The central and emphatic ambiguity about Apollo, who seems rather insensitive than evil, is all that might prevent our classifying this play as a true melodrama, for it had a profound influence upon fourth-century Athenian *comedy* (whose plots are often distinctly melodramatic, with or without a personal villain).[12]

Two plays from near the end of Euripides' life also show ironic displace-ment of melodramatic elements. *Orestes* (408 BC) makes the divinely appointed matricide Prince Orestes into the villain-figure, who attempts to kill a woman (his aunt Helen), and who takes a girl (cousin Hermione) hostage under a very real threat of death. *Iphigenia at Aulis* (produced posthumously in 406 or 405), on the other hand, makes King Agamemnon into the deadly enemy of a mother and daughter who are none other than his own wife Clytemnestra and his dear first-born child Iphigenia. In both these late plays a mortal would-be rescuer fails. Menelaus in *Orestes* tries to save first his wife, then his daughter; in *Iphigenia* Achilles comes to admire, perhaps even to love Iphigenia, and offers to defend her against her sacrificers. Thereafter, however, a divine rescuer *ex machina* succeeds (respectively Apollo and, in *Iphigenia*'s lost original ending, Artemis). In both, too, an old man is futilely allied with the embattled mother-daughter pair (Helen's step-father Tyndareus and Clytemnestra's ancient slave); and in both the 'rescue' is not completely satisfactory. At the *Orestes*' end Helen is not dead, but Menelaus does not get her back either (she goes to Olympus); while Hermione *is* spared, but Menelaus must marry her to the same Orestes who nearly slew her! Nor in the reconstructed ending of the posthumous play is Iphigenia sacrificed, although to her parents she is forever lost (having been snatched away to serve Artemis among the distant, savage Taurians). In these two plays of the playwright's oldest age, therefore, melodrama combines with bitter disappointment. Melodramatic elements are many of them there; so indeed is an ostensibly 'happy' ending. Justice, however, does not seem to have been done, for the guilty (Orestes and Agamemnon) seem to prosper.

What happens in the *Bacchae* (produced the same year as *Iphigenia at Aulis*) we shall see below. For the moment, before we pass to the purest Euripidean melodrama, let me remark that *only two* of the surviving plays seem to have either no melodramatic features at all, or such features so attenuated as to resist even the most determined effort to make them consistent in this respect with all the rest: *Electra* (probably 410s BC) and *Phoenician Women* (around 410). The former does present an old man, a slave, who experiences at most a rejuvenation of murderous loyalty to the family of his late master Agamemnon; the woman Electra's life is threatened more in her paranoia than in her reduced but comfortable circumstances, and the only endangered child here is the figment of the princess's diseased imagination. In *Phoenician Women*, on the other hand, we have a genuine villain in Eteocles; but the mother and child this shameless, professed tyrant terrorizes are his own mother Jocasta and Jocasta's other son, his own grown brother Polyneices. Electra, of course, is 'saved', by her brother, though for no life happy ever after; in contrast, Jocasta kills herself over the dead bodies of both her sons, and old Oedipus prevents nothing, laments all. No melodrama ever really starts up in either play; features that might have been or become melodramatic prove to be merely pathetic or pessimistic instead.[13]

We begin treatment of the real, complete Euripidean melodramas with the play-long specimens thereof, in *Children of Heracles* (undated, possibly pre-*Medea*), *Iphigenia among the Taurians* (420 to 415), and (from the year 412) *Helen*.[14]

The early *Children of Heracles* casts as potential victims of the same villainous King Eurystheus of Argos who had made Heracles' own life miserable the younger sons and daughters of the late hero, his mother Alcmene, and an improbably old and decrepit nephew of his, Iolaus. Dastardly Eurystheus has sent his despicable herald Copreus all over the Greek world, and onto the scene of this play (in Attica), demanding that no foreign state shelter Heracles' family, whom Eurystheus wants to arrest and eradicate. Copreus even roughs up Iolaus and seizes a Heraclid boy or two on stage before a chorus of old Athenians intervene. In fact Athens alone, led by two sons of Theseus, will stand up to Argos' ten-thousand-man army (and that only after, in obedience to an oracle, one of Heracles' daughters offers herself for sacrifice to Persephone). The Athenians win a battle against the Argives in which Iolaus, miraculously rejuvenated, captures Eurystheus – and sends him alive to old Alcmene, who insists, against all the conventions of Greece and against Athenian scruples, upon putting her life-long enemy to death. This grim ending foreshadows Euripides' plotting in two later plays where melodrama goes awry as we shall see below. Note for the moment that all the characteristics of Dionysiac melodrama are here, including suspense (when the Argive herald attempts violence in the prologue, when the oracle's requirement is made known, and when a dangerous battle is to be joined) and the most explicit possible rejuvenation. There is even a distinct suggestion that the great Theseus comes back to life in his heretofore undistinguished sons.[15]

Now let us look at a pair of more famous melodramas, the earlier *Iphigenia* (surnamed *among the Taurians*) and the brilliant *Helen*. In both of these unusual, non-tragic tragedies a hero (Iphigenia's brother Orestes, Helen's husband Menelaus) and a noblewoman (the title character herself) are in grave danger from a truly barbaric barbarian king (respectively Thoas the Taurian and Theoclymenus of Egypt). Orestes may be a victim for the Taurians' cult of Artemis, to serve which Iphigenia will be forever detained if her brother does not take her home to Greece; Theoclymenus may kill Menelaus in order to widow Helen, whom the Egyptian then expects to marry. In both plays, moreover, a chorus of Greek women, who conspire with the Greek protagonists, risk savage punishment thereby. Only in the *Helen*, however, is the theme of endangered child present, affecting Hermione, who will be both orphaned and disgraced if her parents Mr and Mrs Menelaus do not return to Greece and tell the astounding truth about Helen's virtue. (In this version of the myth Helen did not go to Troy, but only an image of her that Hera maliciously made.) The *Helen*, too, has a rejuvenation of sorts, in that the bedraggled and despondent Menelaus is cleaned up, given a new suit of clothes, and restored, by the real Helen, to self-esteem. In both these plays a false notion that the endangered man has died contributes toward his rescue from actual death and his eventual return to home and kingdom in Greece; in both there is nice suspense, immediately before the protagonists' recognition and later, when the success of a daring deception is thrillingly uncertain. Finally, in both plays the non-Greek villain is frustrated and angered, but suffers no personal harm (though some of his subjects may be killed during the little battle that a messenger announces to each king); and the plays end with divinities appearing *ex machina*, the Dioscuri in *Helen*, Athena in *Iphigenia*, to place a divine seal of approval upon the escapes that the clever Greek heroes and especially clever heroines have contrived. The good and the Hellenic prevails, therefore, in these plays, relatively unclouded by the intrigue that it had to use against the violent and the barbarous; and, in both cases, the harsh Trojan War and its even harsher aftermath is mitigated by the happy outcome – by a happy homecoming for two scions of the great Atreid dynasty. This final happiness may well be escapist, as some critics have supposed, departing as it does from Euripides' more typical bitterness and irony.[16]

Euripidean bitterness and irony are perhaps nowhere more apparent than in two plays that open with a melodramatic sequence whose happy end the rest of the play brutally reverses. The *Andromache* is surely the earlier of this pair, dating probably to the early-to-mid 420s, fifteen years or so before the other, the *Heracles* (also known as *Heracles Mad*).

The former opens with mortal danger both to Andromache, Trojan Hector's widow, and to the infant son she has borne to her Greek master Neoptolemus (Achilles' son). In Neoptolemus' absence the despicable Menelaus of Sparta is using violence, threats of violence, and cruel deception against them. Menelaus, humoring his spoiled-brat of a daughter Hermione, who is now Neoptolemus' lawful wife, wants to rid her of a rival for the hero's affections (and a rival who has also given him a son, what Hermione herself has been unable to do – because, she says, of Andromache's oriental magic). In the first parts of the play the Spartans have gotten control of 'enemy' mother and child and are ready to murder them when old Peleus, Neoptolemus' grandfather, arrives and, with a vigor that confounds Menelaus, rescues his grandson's concubine and his own baby great-grandson. So far, so good; we see melodrama plain and pure. Andromache and the baby are saved. Menelaus is routed, Hermione is driven to attempted suicide (in fear of what her husband Neoptolemus may do when he learns of the Spartan plot). But suddenly, as the audience will begin to feel somewhat sorry for the deserted princess-brat Hermione, her cousin Orestes appears, offers to 'rescue' *her* from the offended and dangerous Neoptolemus, and elopes with her, already having set a deadly and successful ambush for Neoptolemus at Delphi (as we learn later). Humanly satisfying melodrama gives way to a kind of parody of itself, therefore, and good old Peleus is devastated. The improbably happy future that Peleus' ex-wife, the sea-nymph Thetis, thereupon reports *ex machina* offers a modicum of solace both to Peleus (who will soon report to Elysium) and to Andromache (who will marry a surviving Trojan brother-in-law). We nevertheless miss human, 'philanthropic' satisfaction. For the gallant Neoptolemus has been impiously assassinated, and, worse, the 'bad guys' evidently will live quite happily ever after, enjoying wealth, kingship, and even honor in southern Greece.

The *Heracles* is yet more depressing. The melodramatic opening, like the opening of the *Andromache* Euripides' own invention, sets up as victims Heracles' wife Megara, their three little sons, and Amphitryon, the hero's aged father, all of whom the murderous Lycus intends to kill this very day. Lycus has already assassinated Megara's father, King Creon of Thebes, and her brothers; has usurped the Theban throne; and wants to finish the nasty job by killing off the late king's daughter and grandsons. (Amphitryon is presumably an embarrassing witness, who must also be liquidated.) After a few hundred lines demonstrate Lycus' dastardliness and the goodness of his victims, the latter exeunt into Heracles' house to dress for their execution. The chorus sing a eulogy of Heracles, who, they believe, will never return from his attempt to fetch Cerberus from the House of Hades. Return he does, however, just as his family emerge sadly from their home on their way to die. Informed of the crisis, he sends his wife and sons back inside, where they will be bait to lure Lycus into a deadly ambush. The ambush succeeds, of course; but then Heracles, by explicit divine intervention, is driven mad, hallucinates a journey to Mycenae, and further hallucinates a violent attack upon his cousin and persecutor Eurystheus, who has sent him on (and intended to destroy him by) all his famous Labors. He kills persons whom he believes to be the wife and children of Eurystheus, but who are really his own; and menaces Amphitryon, imagining him to be Eurystheus' father, when his divine patroness Athena at last knocks him unconscious. Interesting though the sequel is (Heracles contemplates suicide, but is taken instead to Athens by his friend Theseus), we have seen enough: the sweet solution of a melo-dramatic action turned as sour as it can possibly be, with the 'good guy' doing the same evil as the 'bad guy' he has frustrated. Critics are anything but unanimous about the meaning of this shocking turn of events – which probably has much to do with meaning (in the sense of 'intention') and meaninglessness (in all senses).[17] We may nevertheless note here that Euripides seems in this play to examine the effects of 'good' violence upon its 'good' perpetrator, who tragically fails to know when and where to end it, becoming in the end more terrible than his villainous enemies. For his enemies at least *treated their enemies badly*, keeping one of the chief com-mandments of ancient morality; while he *failed to treat friends well*, violating the only even more important commandment. Moreover, the hero's kill-ing power here turns not against villains who become sympathetic (like Polymestor in *Hecuba*, for example), but rather against loved ones, sympathetic from the start, whom he can no longer distinguish from enemies. Perhaps the very categories 'enemy' and 'friend' must be held in abeyance? (Both Euripides and his contemporary Sophocles are often concerned, almost obsessed with this problem.[18]) In any case, by this play, as elsewhere, our poet suggests that there may be no easy way to respond to criminal violence, and maybe no way at all that does not itself entail criminal guilt.

Finally we have the posthumous *Bacchae*, a play written during

Euripides' self-imposed exile from Athens but brought and produced there after his death in Macedonia. Its familiar plot is the substance of the 'original' Dionysiac melodrama described at the outset: a grim persecutor, King Pentheus of Thebes, harshly threatens and attempts to punish not only Dionysus himself (in disguise as an Asiatic priest of the Bacchic cult), but also women under his influence (both Asiatic, in the chorus, and Theban), babies suckled by those Theban women, and two silly but harmless old men (Pentheus' own grandfather, whom he reproaches, and the prophet Tiresias, whom he bullies). And yet bad though Pentheus is, his divine cousin is worse. (Dionysus and Pentheus *are* cousins, sons of sisters, and should resemble one another in physical appearance as well as in brutality.) As in the *Heracles*, madness is a divine weapon. Here, though, it is at once the means to a 'happy' ending, destroying the Evil King and rescuing his intended victims, and itself an atrocity. Let me remind you what happens: Dionysus confounds Pentheus' thinking, which becomes a mixture of persecutorial hatred and imitative curiosity concerning the maenad women on the god's sacred mountainside. The crazed young king dresses as a Bacchant to 'spy' upon the real Bacchants, is spotted, is recognized as a spy (but not as her son/their nephew) by his mother and two of his aunts, and is torn to pieces. The dotard Cadmus is now quickly sobered, and helps bring his daughter Agave, Pentheus' mother, to her senses. The 'melodrama' here is uniquely and devastatingly tragic. Not only have the rescuer and the defeated 'villain' lost and gained sympathy, respectively, by the sort of peripety of sympathies Euripides had been contriving since his *Medea* and probably even earlier,[19] but *the process of deliverance itself* (and not a separate, ensuing punishment of the persecutor) *has become hideous*. Not its subsequent effect, therefore, but rather the *essence* of resistance-and-rescue, examined, appears morally and intellectually wanting. For a god, as Cadmus eloquently complains toward the end, ought to know and to do better than a mortal; and yet Dionysus has proven superior to his pathetic lookalike Pentheus only in ingenuity, and in irresistible violence of his own, not in moral quality.

It is now time and place to draw conclusions. The dramaturge Euripides for plots and plot-parts again and again, early and late in his career, took up and renovated the very ancient Dionysiac melodrama, its scenario, its characters (less only the god himself), and its happy ending in which good prevails and evil is frustrated. Sometimes the ending appears happy, however bitter-sweet the antecedents (as, for example, in the first *Iphigenia* and the *Helen*). Other times the happy ending gives way to something less satisfying, even to the repugnant vindictiveness of the rescued that we see in *Children of Heracles*. The playwright also explored and deplored the effect of even 'good', rescuing violence upon its worker, as in the *Heracles*, whose ending is happy for no one on earth. And finally, at the very end of that career, putting the god Dionysus back into the scenario and composing, in *Bacchae*, a human tragedy from the matter of a divine melodrama, he equates aggressive, persecuting violence to the defensive, resisting violence that *should* be morally finer. He thereby rejects the attitudes and moods both of high-classical tragedy, which makes defiance of Olympus somehow grand, and of melodrama, which casts a rosy light upon gods' effectiveness against an evil that is not themselves.

NOTES

1 H. D. F. Kitto, for example, in *Greek Tragedy: A Literary Study*, 3rd edn (London: Methuen, 1961), places several of the works to be treated here in chapters entitled 'New Tragedy: Euripides' Tragi-Comedies' (pp. 311–29, on *Alcestis*, *Iphigenia among the Taurians*, *Ion*, and *Helen*) and 'New Tragedy: Euripides' Melodramas' (pp. 330–69, on *Electra* and *Orestes*). Albin Lesky, *Greek Tragic Poetry*, trans. M. Dillon (New Haven and London: Yale University Press, 1983), groups a number of Euripides' dramas as 'tyche plays' (that is plays of chance or coincidence) and further calls them *'pièces roses*, which can only be called tragedies in the ancient sense of the word' (p. 392).

   D. J. Conacher, *Euripidean Drama: Myth, Theme and Structure* (University of Toronto Press, 1967) classifies *Ion*, *Helen*, and *Iphigenia among the Taurians* as 'Romantic Tragedy' and treats them after five other sorts of Euripidean tragedy, before 'Satyric (and Pro-Satyric) Drama'.

   Others have called some of these plays 'comedies' outright. Bernard Knox, *Word and Action: Essays on the Ancient Theater* (Baltimore and London: Johns Hopkins University Press, 1979), has a chapter on 'Euripidean Comedy' (pp. 250–74, namely *Iphigenia among the Taurians*, *Helen*, and *Ion*), which appeared earlier in A. Chase and R. Koffer, eds., *The Rarer Action: Essays in Honor of Francis Fergusson* (New Brunswick: Rutgers University Press, 1970), pp. 68–96. See also J. Michael Walton, *The Greek Sense of Theatre* (London and New York: Methuen, 1984), whose discussion 'Euripides: The Comedies' takes in not only the satyr play *Cyclops*, but also *Alcestis* – which was presented in the place of a satyr play – and *Iphigenia among the Taurians*, *Ion*, and *Helen*.

2 Conscious admirers (rather than apologetic defenders or explainers-away) of the melodramatic tendency in Euripides' work have been rather few.

   Anne Pippin Burnett, *Catastrophe Survived: Euripides' Plays of Mixed Reversal* (Oxford University Press, 1971) regards a number of plays as together a justification of the Olympian gods: *Alcestis*, *Iphigenia among the Taurians*, *Helen*, *Ion*, *Andromache*, *Heracles* and *Orestes*.

   Cedric H. Whitman, *Euripides and the Full Circle of Myth* (Cambridge, MA: Harvard University Press, 1974), p. 142, after chapters on each of these three plays writes that 'It is a matter of taste whether or not one chooses to regard the achievement of the *Iphigeneia*, *Helen*, and *Ion* as the climax of Euripides' development.' He argues for the affirmative, by relating 'tragic action, so filled out' [by the realized possibility of salvation] to 'the full sweep of myth as principle of order and as the life history of the world'.

More specific to theatrical effect within the Athenian context is Ann Norris Michelini, *Euripides and the Tragic Tradition* (Madison: University of Wisconsin Press, 1987), whose exposition of Euripidean dramaturgy as a whole allows quite happily for 'melodrama' – on which she has a short Appendix A (pp. 321–3).

3 I offer a literal translation of *Poetics* 1452b30–1453a4, on the nature of tragic denouement: 'In the first place, one must not make morally good persons [*tous epieikeis*] change from good fortune to misfortune, for this inspires neither pity nor fear but rather appals; nor bad persons [*tous mokhtherous*] change from misfortune to good fortune, for this is the most untragic of all, having nothing of what it ought to, since it is not pitiful, fearful, or *philanthropos*; nor, on the other hand, should an exceedingly evil person [*ton sphodra poneron*] pass from good fortune to ill, for, although such a construction has the *philanthropos* quality, it has neither pity nor fear.'

4 On the Dionysiac origins *and continuing connections* of drama in general, and of tragedy in particular, see Harald Patzer, *Die Anfänge der Griechischen Tragödie* (Wiesbaden: Franz Steiner, 1962), especially pp. 120–33 on 'Urtragödie'. Albin Lesky, *Greek Tragedy*, 2nd edn, trans. H. A. Frankfort (London: E. Benn and New York: Barnes & Noble, 1965), pp. 1–24, qualifies Patzer, though he is in substantial agreement on the main features of the prehistory of this theatrical genre.

Many details and a much more comprehensive discussion, involving all the ancient Greek dramatic forms, may be found in Francisco Rodriguez Adrados, *Festival, Comedy, and Tragedy: The Greek Origins of Theatre*, trans. C. Holme (Leiden: Brill, 1975), which supplements the classic but no longer definitive A. C. Pickard-Cambridge, *Dithyramb, Tragedy and Comedy*, 2nd edn rev. by T. B. L. Webster (Oxford University Press, 1962).

5 This is the thesis of Cedric H. Whitman, *Sophocles: A Study in Heroic Humanism* (Cambridge, MA: Harvard University Press, 1951), to which his *Homer and the Heroic Tradition* (Cambridge, MA: Harvard University Press, 1958), principally about the *Iliad* and its heroes, was the almost inevitable sequel.

See also Bernard Knox, *The Heroic Temper: Studies in Sophoclean Tragedy* (Berkeley and Los Angeles: University of California Press, 1966), pp. 50–3.

6 I assume that the extant *Prometheus Bound* and the play of this name authoritatively ascribed to Aeschylus in the manuscript list of his plays are one and the same. The case against Aeschylean authorship is ingenious and interesting but not compelling; see C. J. Herington, *The Author of the 'Prometheus Bound'* (Austin and London: University of Texas Press, 1970).

The play and the trilogy must be very late; the play itself seems to reflect influence of Sophocles (whose first production was in 468 BC); the outcome of the trilogy, on the other hand, must have been a rejection of the unyielding, tragic 'humanism' of Sophocles. The optimism of the whole, at the end of which Zeus and Prometheus are reconciled through Zeus' mortal son Heracles, and the celebration of technological progress that even the unhappy but also non-final *Prometheus Bound* includes, may owe something to the earliest stages of the

Sophistic. We must be careful, however, not to assume that Aeschylus (or whoever wrote the surviving play) can only have derived 'sophisticated' attitudes and ideas from and after the Sophists, for the Athenian playwrights themselves were intellectual *leaders*, whether in progressive movements (Aeschylus and Euripides) or in humane reaction (Sophocles), *philosophers*, albeit non-systematic pre-Socratic ones (like the poets Xenophanes and Empedocles), whose medium and whose platform were the most prestigious and powerful ones available in the fifth century, tragedy and the Theatre of Dionysus at Athens.

7 See especially the long sequence about heroes' rags in Acharnians, 383–480. Aristophanes' 'Aeschylus' (and, most readers believe, the comic poet himself) complains of Euripides' de-heroization of heroes in the *Frogs* as well, in the magniloquent and contemptuous vocatives of address to his rival: *o stomuliosul-lektade kai ptokhopoie kai rhakiosurraptade* ('O gossip-compiler and beggar-maker and rag-patcher', 841–2).

8 Quoted in Aristotle *Poetics* 1460b34. Note the Olympian aloofness of Sophocles, who, like Homer, contrasts ordinary human beings 'such as *mortals are now*' (*Iliad* v, 304 and *passim*) to the mighty heroes of old, but not 'such as *we are*'!

9 I have argued elsewhere ('Notes on the Structure of Euripides' *Alcestis*', *American Journal of Philology*, 100 (1980), 487–96) and still believe that this play is rather a spliced tragedy-and-comedy, such, in fact, that we find in it all four categories of Greek Dionysiac drama: melodramatic material, arranged in a tragicomedy, and performed rightly in place and in the spirit of a satyr play.

10 That this play had an unusual 'secondary chorus' of boys to represent the orphaned sons of the heroes fallen in the attack on Thebes is now generally accepted. See Christoher Collard, *Euripides Supplices* (Groningen: Bouma's Boekhuis, 1975), vol. I, p. 19.

11 Admirers of Euripidean melodrama somewhat surprisingly also admire Apollo, for his divinity if not for his sensitivity; see Burnett, *Catastrophe Survived*, pp. 101–29, in particular pp. 125–9; and Whitman, *Euripides*, pp. 100–1; compare Felix M. Wasserman, 'Divine Violence and Providence in Euripides' *Ion*', *Transactions of the American Philological Association*, 71 (1940), 174–86.

Malcolm Heath, *The Poetics of Greek Tragedy* (Stanford University Press, 1987), pp. 54–6, defends Apollo without the theology.

Most readers, however, will probably not exonerate Apollo, however bright the future that awaits his long-abandoned 'wife' and son, agreeing with D. J. Conacher, *Euripidean drama*, p. 279 that 'shadowing the golden Apollo of Creusa's glorious "mythological" picture and the (politically) all-provident one of Athena's epilogue is the background impression of a rather furtive, shabby, and inefficient god, which leaves its mark even when the official defence has rested'.

12 Slave-dealers, brutal mercenary soldiers, and even nasty old fathers were the common 'bad guys' in Middle and especially in New Comedy. Middle Comedy also used mythological characters and stories, very often the same ones that Euripides' melodramas had treated: Anaxandrides wrote a *Helen*, while Eubulus wrote an *Ion* and also an *Auge* (presumably based upon a lost tragedy

of the same name by Euripides that we know to have been quite melodramatic).

Albin Lesky, *History of Greek Literature*, 2nd edn, trans. J. Willis and C. de Heer (New York: Thomas Crowell, 1963), p. 660, observes how tyche (the same factor that he finds very important in Euripides' non-tragic 'tragedies') is the dominant force, appearing even once or twice as their prologist, in later Greek comedy. Recognitions, typically just in the nick of time and surprise reversals, both usually involving a woman and/or a child, are essential plot mechanisms, whether or not the woman/child has to be rescued from some villain.

13 In the *Phoenician Women* Creon's son, Menoeceus, for example, could have become a very different sort of victim than he did. No one beside the god Ares (as reported by Tiresias) threatens his life, neither his otherwise despicable cousin Eteocles nor his father Creon; he bravely accepts his sacrificial death, and even deceives Creon in order to suffer it.

It is amusing to note that some critics have treated the *Electra* among 'melodramas', Kitto, *Greek Tragedy*, for example. This is no mistake if we look only to the tone of one or two passages (almost entirely in speeches or dialogue of the paranoiac title character), especially to the expectation *Electra* creates of melodramatic villains in Clytemnestra, who is a conscience-stricken wretch, and Aegisthus, who turns out, however, to be a friendly and courteous person!

14 I limit the discussion to surviving plays. Quite a number of the lost ones about which we know more than just their titles certainly had a plot and cast of characters entirely melodramatic, through to the rescue of an embattled heroine (an Alcmene, an Alope, an Andromeda, an Antiope, an Auge, a Danae, a Hypsipyle, a Melanippe, or the like) or the last-minute salvation of an endangered hero (e.g. Alcmaeon, baby Orestes, Peleus, Theseus); some of these 'tyche tragedies' (as Lesky would term them) and others as well, ended with the punishment of a nasty tyrant or of one of Euripides' horde of evil women (Althaea, Astydamia, Ino, Medea and Phaedra in other plays beside the ones extant, Stheneboia).

15 See *Children of Heracles* 205–46. Iolaus reminds Demophon, who does all the talking for both sons of Theseus, of their father's blood relationship to Heracles (207–12), of Theseus' and Heracles' joint expedition against the Amazons (215–17), and of Theseus' resurrection by Heracles from the depths of Hades (218–19); in reply Demophon acknowledges the obligations of kinship and *patroian kharin*, 'a paternal debt of gratitude' (240–1) that are the central reason for his desire to help the children of Heracles.

That the two sons of Theseus have been allotted kingship, but have only their father as a claim to fame, Iolaus suggests earlier, at 34–6 in the prologue, and the chorus of old Athenians seem to confirm by calling their king 'a noble father's child, Demophon son of Theseus' (115).

16 That some irony remains is nevertheless clear; see Philip Vellacott, *Ironic Drama: A Study of Euripides' Method and Meaning* (Cambridge University Press, 1975), pp. 127–52, on the figure of Helen 'of Troy' in several of Euripides' plays. He addresses the consequent huge irony of the *Helen*, which exonerates

her of all the vilification heaped upon her elsewhere (save at the very end of the *Electra*, where her divine brother Castor also tells the story of Helen in Egypt).

17 On the harshness of the playwright's 'lesson' in this play about divine power and human frustration see William Arrowsmith's introduction to his translation in D. Grene and R. Lattimore, eds., *Euripides II: Four Tragedies* (University of Chicago Press, 1969), pp. 44–57; and Michelini, *Euripides and the Tragic Tradition*, pp. 231–76.

18 Whole plays turn upon the confusion of 'friends' (*philoi*) and 'enemies' (*ekhthroi*), notably Sophocles' early *Ajax* and *Antigone* and his late *Philoctetes* and *Oedipus at Colonus*, as well as Euripides' own *Medea* and *Electra*.

19 In the first, lost *Hippolytus*, for example; see the efforts to reconstruct this play, with a Phaedra initially much less sympathetic than the 'same' character in the extant play, but who evidently ends pathetic, in T. B. L. Webster, *The Tragedies of Euripides* (London: Methuen, 1967), pp. 64–71 with further bibliography in its footnotes.

Desire and the limits of melodrama*

WILLIAM R. MORSE

In what follows I would like to reflect on the recent renaissance of critical interest in melodrama, and its place in modern culture, in light of contemporary advances in our understanding of culture and discourse. As one whose love of drama grew out of my encounter in college with Shakespeare, I have always had a soft spot for the raw theatricality of melodrama, and this has been reinforced by an identification with my own working-class and populist upbringing. I suspect that the attraction many of us feel to melodrama is reflected in our tendency to respond to such a comment as Eric Bentley's in his well-known defense of melodrama:

> The tears shed by the audience at a Victorian melodrama ... might be called the poor man's catharsis, and as such have a better claim to be the main objective of popular melodrama than its notorious moral pretensions ... Once we have seen that our modern antagonism to self-pity and sentiment goes far beyond the rational objections that may be found to them, we realize that even the rational objections are in some measure mere rationalization. Attacks on false emotion often mask a fear of emotion as such. Ours is, after all, a thin-lipped, thin-blooded culture.[1]

Bentley here shows a sympathy with popular culture that speaks immediately to the popular resistance to 'highbrow' literary standards, even as he subtly evokes the cultural establishment, ready to explain away and dismiss popular culture's most enduring predilections, in terms sure to appeal to any populist audience.

But there is also a problem here, for the same upbringing has made me receptive to that political strain of poststructuralist theory that has resolutely analyzed literature as an element of culture, inveterately inscribed within culture's material structures and modes of producing significance and meaning. Notwithstanding the widespread identification many of us make of melodrama[2] with populism and the interests of the great body of common society alienated from 'high culture' (as it tends to conceive of itself), any materialist analysis of the nature of melodrama as

* A draft of this paper was read at the *Themes in Drama* International Conference held at the University of California, Riverside, in February 1990.

historically constituted raises doubts about its social role and efficacy. Simply put, does not melodrama, because articulated within the dominant essentialist discourse,[3] primarily provide escapist controls that support and solidify the political status quo? If the central characteristic of the melodramatic is attention to and recognition of the human passions, as Bentley suggests, how can that preoccupation ever bear fruit within a rationalist discourse of analysis and reference that systematically derogates passion in favor of abstract knowledge? From a cultural materialist perspective, a revaluation of melodrama would require the emergence of new discourses that decentered the figure of 'man' as a universal and unchanging nature whose essence is immaterial consciousness, and a return of that consciousness from its 'objective' exile beyond the world to its natural home within mutable nature and the material conditions of its existence, which is also to say within, not beyond, language itself. Poststructuralist criticism suggests the paradox that in the context of the bourgeois culture that has given rise to the genre of melodrama itself, Bentley's valorization of human desire can never be achieved.

Contemporary criticism's chief achievement has perhaps been to implement a deconstruction of the West's dominant discourse, and from it we have learned that we need to accept a radical inversion of liberal humanism's privileging of individual over culture and language; far from being the aggregation of its constituent individual members, it now becomes clear that a culture dynamically generates in history the forms of individuality and identity that it inscribes within its particular members, and 'man' is not the authorizing source of its discourse, but rather its creation, its effect. Since the time of Galileo's deployment of the telescope, western consciousness has striven to become the disembodied observing subject, accruing knowledge of an objectified world distanced from itself at the far end of the observing instrument, and the dominant modern concept of 'man' is the monument to this project, that one privileged entity not of the world, assumed to be knowing rather than a material object to be known. Thus in its pursuit of the 'advancement of learning', the prize of worldly power over nature, the individual has been alienated from its own material nature.

The theatrical community knows very well, of course – from the challenges of fundraising if nothing else – that within modern western culture drama has long occupied a peripheral, isolated position. In this regard the critical fate of melodrama can be seen as merely one extreme case of all art: rational discourse peripheralizes art generally, and in response those invested with leadership of and responsibility for the peripheral system seek to redress their isolation by distinguishing between 'high culture' or 'real' art and those lesser forms seen as more deserving of the dominant culture's contempt. But the derogation of drama generally and melodrama in particular can now be seen to be inevitable, for in a discourse of rational analysis and essentialist referentiality that accepts a simple positivist relation between consciousness and quotidian reality, that understands language as a simple tool of the individual rational consciousness, drama and indeed art can occupy only a subsidiary ghetto of significance, carefully isolated in terms of 'aesthetics' and 'taste'. In recognizing the inherent devaluation of desire and imagination within this discourse, we must recognize the difficulty, and very possibly the futility, of any attempts to revaluate the production of art, and certainly the value of melodrama, within its practice.

Exactly because he writes at the emergent moment of modern discourse, Shakespeare can provide a useful point of comparison for clarifying the place of melodramatic theatre (and the melodramatic impulse generally) within that discourse. Shakespeare's particular adaptation of the romance tradition to Renaissance tragicomedy clearly reveals a love of what we would now call melodramatic theatre – his late plays are full of passions, journeys, spectacular events, extremes of stock characterization, and utterly improbable surprises. Just as melodrama has suffered the scorn of high culture for this poetic, much of the criticism that Shakespeare's work received before the advent of romantic bardolatry focused exactly on this supposed 'pandering' to the popular expectations of his audience. Ben Jonson, applying his neoclassic standards, was contemptuous of these 'moldy tales', fables as antic as they were 'antique', and later Samuel Johnson found himself absolutely at a loss to appreciate their aesthetic nature from the perspective of the Enlightenment. For instance, Shakespeare opens his first romance, *Pericles*, with an induction spoken by the archaic ghost of the fourteenth-century poet John Gower:

> To sing a song that old was sung,
> From ashes ancient Gower is come,
> . . .
> If you, born in those latter times,
> When wit's more ripe, accept my rhymes,
> And that to hear an old man sing
> May to your wishes pleasure bring,
> I life would wish, and that I might
> Waste it for you like taper-light.
>
> (I, Cho. 1–16)[4]

The subtle drawing of attention to the self-conscious naiveté of the play is typically Shakespearian in its ironic self-deprecation, a challenge to the sophisticated to enter into and try to appreciate the specific virtues of such unsophisticated drama. Gower proceeds immediately to tell the tale of the incestuous affair of Antiochus the Great and his 'buxom, blithe' daughter, and the murderous riddle by which Antiochus prevents any suitor's claim from disrupting the arrangement, and we are off on a story rife with sea voyages, mysterious knights, lost treasures, and amazing reunions. Whatever the qualms of sophisticated Englishmen about such unsophisticated theatre, the melodramatic elements played so well that for the next century these plays were among Shakespeare's most popular.

But of course we have come to appreciate that the plays are marked throughout with a highly wrought *control* of these melodramatic elements; as David Young puts it,

> The primitivism of these plays is surely deliberate. It seeks our attention and invites our participation ... An atmosphere of double consciousness is thus evoked. On the one hand we share the wonder, delight, and mystery of these old stories and fabulous moments; on the other, simultaneously, we see them from a sophisticated perspective, aware of their peculiarities and limitations.[5]

Thus the melodramatic event takes its place in that 'metadramatic' aesthetic that has recently become such a prominent feature in Shakespearian interpretation.[6] The dramatist establishes a congruence between, on the one hand, the imaginative and melodramatic elements of his drama, which is to say their least mimetic or realistic elements, and on the other the epistemological issues raised by the play's thought, particularly the constructedness, the cultural contingency, of the play's 'meaning'. Shakespeare's embrace of the melodramatic thus becomes an aspect of his ongoing critique of rationality and the emergent essentialist discourse.

Whether this emergent signifying system is conceived in terms of an episteme, a discourse, or an ideology, there is a developing consensus that the Renaissance was the historical site of a radical shift in our culture's habitual mode of address to the world, from a medieval system of analogical understanding to the modern stance of objectified analysis, and that this shift in discourses was intimately associated with the rise of both modern science and capitalist structures of social organization.[7] Shakespeare writes at the historical moment when skepticism has thrown the old order into doubt, 'all coherence ... gone', yet before the new discourse has established its hegemony. Within the canon we see the decline of 'custom' and tradition enacted repeatedly – from the dethronement of Richard II to the murder of old Hamlet to the exile of Cordelia – and in its stead the rise of the 'new man', the paragon of rational calculation and self-interest: Claudius, Edmund, Octavius. What all of these figures of the new age share is an active self-conception of rational independence, objectified isolation, an assumption of personal control of the neutral tool of a referential language, and a Hobbesian self-interest in the war of all against all that society is now seen as being. Thus both the old and the new discourses are present in tense suspension, one residual and one emergent, yet neither exercising hegemony. Their conflict foregrounds each, makes each available to recognition and analysis, and this is the source of the particular range and richness of Shakespearian (and Renaissance) drama.

Shakespeare's works thus appear at a momentous juncture in the development of western culture, a moment when, to use Williams's formula of residual, dominant, and emergent cultures,[8] the dramatist can consciously see his production as a field upon which are played out many of the ideological tensions of the day. Exactly because the new essentialist discourse has not yet firmly established its own hegemony, it is not yet necessary that the discourse be 'deconstructed', as must happen in our own day from within the discourse. Because it remains yet one of several emergent possibilities, it is still available to conscious recognition, to formal presentation and debate, and this critique is enacted in play after play. This is the epistemological context of the melodramatic elements in Shakespearian tragicomedy, and it makes of these elements something more than merely aesthetic events: insofar as they are associated with the metaphorical, metamorphic aspects of language and the synthesizing imagination, they become representative of the meaning-making function of language, a function crucial to human cognition but displaced and repressed in the new rationalist discourse.

How does Shakespeare set melodramatic incident at odds with the growing impulse of Renaissance discourse to center and validate independent individual identity, using such incident as one means of undermining this impulse? Let me briefly return to the example of *The Winter's Tale* to try and substantiate my general point. The play is clearly constructed on the new tragicomic model of the Renaissance, with a three-act tragedy in which Leontes' jealous affection recalls *Othello* followed by two acts of pastoral romance that, by restoring to life Leontes' innocent queen, produce reconciliation and a magical peripety.

The modern critical tradition, as we would expect, has generally been much more comfortable with the opening acts of the play, for there we have what, with some interpretative manipulation, can be taken to be a drama built on a modern, centered 'subject' in the person of Leontes. Although he (unhappily to the modern critic) partakes to some degree of the stock characterization of the jealous husband, the realism and particularity of his passion suggest at times to a modern audience that they are encountering 'the thing itself'; thus the character can plausibly be taken to be a realistic and mimetic rather than deliberately artificial representation. In Leontes' famous apostrophe to 'affection' or passion, here specifically his jealousy, we see at work in the dense congestion of the

lines, with their logic wrenched by Leontes' own passion, the new realistic
aesthetic at its best:

> Affection! thy intention stabs the centre.
> Thou dost make possible things not so held,
> Communcat'st with dreams (how can this be?),
> With what's unreal thou co-active art,
> And fellow'st nothing. Then 'tis very credent
> Thou mayst co-join with something, and thou dost
> (And that beyond commission), and I find it
> (And that to the infection of my brains
> And hard'ning of my brows).
>
> (I, ii, 138–46)

But beyond its relative realism, in the internal contradictions of Leontes'
thought here Shakespeare creates a tool by which rationally to question
the whole enterprise of human rationality, for it is hard not to generalize
upon the ways in which we see the affective Leontes destroying his own
claims to rationality. Rather than analyze these lines in detail, I will
simply offer them as indicative of the new element of realism in Renaissance drama proleptic of the emergent discourse: here is a subject who
speaks on the assumption that his words refer directly and unproblemati-
cally to reality.

How seriously are we to take this subject *qua* subject? How mimetic or
realistic is the representation meant to be? Let us contrast this apparently
coherent and realistic subject with some of the later events of the play.
Leontes' passion culminates, is distilled in a position unambiguously evil:

> This brat is none of mine.
>   . . .
> Hence with it, and together with the dam,
> Commit them to the fire!
>
> (II, iii, 93–6)

The action of jealousy itself climaxes with the reading of the oracle at the
conclusion of Hermione's show trial:

> Hermione is chaste, Polixenes blameless, Camillo a true subject, Leontes a
> jealous tyrant, his innocent babe truly begotten, and the King shall live
> without an heir, if that which is lost be not found   (III, ii, 132–6)

Not only is any inclination of an audience to perceive the characters as
realistic forcefully undercut by the stock characterizations of the language
of the oracle, but Leontes himself, in his reactions following this revelation, will take on a different attitude to his own character, showing little
subsequent inclination to conceive of his personal identity in such centered and independent terms.

What of that most famous of Shakespearian stage directions, for Antigonus to 'exit pursued by a bear'? Once again, a character who in the first

1 Leontes: 'Let no man mock me, For I will kiss her' (v, iii). Engraved by R. Threw from the painting by William Hamilton, RA

acts has been portrayed in relatively realistic terms that create an effect of centered individuality is reduced to the most impersonal of roles; we might well say that the centered characterization of Antigonus is itself devoured by the most melodramatic bear.

And of course the play ends with Shakespeare's most wonderful *coup de théâtre*, Paulina's statue of the 'dead' Hermione that is brought to life by the faith of her stage audience. Paulina's imaginative creation of a reconciliation scene so thoroughly interpenetrated with 'art' and 'reality' depends upon her imaginative participation in the cyclical rhythms of 'creating nature' itself. Whereas a modern audience expects to discover Hermione '*like*' a statue, similitude being the most that life and art can logically share, Shakespeare carefully and even insistently maintains the dual reality of the object as statue *and* living queen. Priority is denied to either by both Shakespeare's onlookers and Shakespeare's art (and certainly too by the theatre audience for a long and wonderful spell). In this heightened moment of intense theatricality, Hermione is no longer merely 'metaphorically' a statue, but 'metamorphically' so. All pretense that the meaning of the scene might lie in a simple referential relation between perception and reality, that the role of language in the scene was to record a meaning already existent, is effectively destroyed as the melo-dramatic spectacle of the moment impresses its vital power upon us.

How comes it that such theatricality has generally found so little appre-ciation in formal criticism? We should not be surprised to discover that the criticisms of Shakespearian tragicomic practice in his own day and the centuries following are closely associated with a neoclassic aesthetic of mimetic, referential realism, for seventeenth-century neoclassicism is one component of the new discourse, and senses in Shakespeare's poetic a primal antagonism to its hegemony. Not only is Shakespeare's poetic not understood from such a perspective; it remains absolutely *necessary* ideolo-gically that it not be understood. Shakespeare's problematizing of a referential conception of language, in which the melodramatic elements of his poetic serve a crucial role, directly threatens the new discourse. By revealing the metaphorical roots of even the most resolutely rational dis-cursive language, Shakespearian drama dangerously decenters 'man' as a coherent subject prior to and therefore independent of the language, the culture, of which he sees himself an autonomous part.

Melodrama on the other hand, whether as a theatrical genre in itself or an element of drama generally, has had no privileged perspective on the dominant rational discourse; its roots in and continuing association with the romantic movement tie it inextricably to the essentialist discourse of the subject that I have been discussing. Indeed, romantic subjectivity might be considered the ultimate refinement of this discourse (even as it also reveals most starkly, in its dual loyalty to a subjectivity that is conceived of as centered in consciousness and yet is experienced in desire, the internal contradictions of the discourse). Melodrama is the popular art of a culture adrift on a vast deep for which its rational conceptuality has no name, no place. And while the culture is forever drawn to this alienated reality beneath and beyond rational consciousness as if to its own birthplace, it simultaneously senses danger and dark corners, forces that, even if they cannot be denied, are too subtle, too pervasive to name, too powerful to risk recognizing. Thus the ambiguous cultural function of melodrama has been the deictic gesture, suggesting in some sense the dark absence of desire from the dominant discourse while carefully circum-scribing that recognition, dismissing it exactly in its very 'popularity'.

In his fine analysis of the constitutive poetic of nineteenth-century melodrama, *The Melodramatic Imagination*, Brooks focuses on this melo-dramatic power to suggest the reality of a world beyond representation, a world in which virtue exists as virtue, citing exactly melodrama's deictic function (even to the centrality of muteness and hence gesture in its figurations) in developing his concept of the 'moral occult'. Moreover, he makes a large and well-substantiated claim for revaluating the cultural significance of this melodramatic enterprise: we must

recognize the melodramatic mode as a central fact of the modern sensibility
... in that modern art has typically felt itself to be constructed on, and over,
the void, postulating meanings and symbolic systems which have no certain
justification because they are backed by no theology and no universally
accepted social code ... there is a desperate effort to renew contact with the
scattered ethical and psychic fragments of the Sacred through the representation of fallen reality, insisting that behind reality, hidden by it yet indicated
within it, there is a realm where large moral forces are operative ... The
melodramatic mode can be seen as an intensified, primary, and exemplary
version of what the most ambitious art, since the beginnings of Romanticism,
has been about.   (pp. 21–2)

The basis of this revaluation becomes clear in his discussion of melodrama
as 'the dilemma of the moral sentiment itself, seeking to say its name' (p.
42), and later his definition of melodrama as 'the expressionism of the
moral imagination' (p. 55). In the moral vacuum following upon the
extended process of 'desacralization' that culminates in the French
Revolution, such forms manifest the culture's need for moral coordinates,
and suggest the centrality of the melodramatic in meeting those needs.

Brooks, in elaborating Bentley's suggestion that 'melodrama is the
Naturalism of the dream life' (p. 205), goes on to validate the melodrama
by associating it with the unconscious:

> Melodrama partakes of the dream world ... and this is in no wise more true
> than in the possibility it provides of saying what is in 'real life' unsayable ...
> Desire triumphs over the world of substitute-formations and detours, it
> achieves plenitude of meaning.   (p. 41)

Thus the appeal of melodrama stems from our unambiguous unconscious
identification with the manichaean moral structures of the mode, and
melodramatic rhetoric, with its figures of hyperbole, antithesis, and
oxymoron – 'those figures, precisely, that evidence a refusal of nuance and
the insistence on dealing in pure, integral concepts' (p. 40) – 'breaks
through everything that constitutes the "reality principle", all its censor-
ships, accommodations, tonings-down' (p. 41).

All this accords with Brooks's perception that the individual has
become for modern culture the only possible bearer of authority, that 'the
entity making the strongest possible claim to sacred status tends more and
more to be personality itself' (p. 16). The rhetoric of melodrama is seen as
the vehicle of a fullness of self-expression, of 'saying the self ... through
moral and emotional integers' (p. 38), and the melodramatic action can
be abstracted as a process of 'self-nomination' that, in bursting through
the occlusions and misnamings of evil, must ultimately establish the oneness of identity via identification with the moral occult.

Brooks here lays bare the ground of the melodrama in the essentialist
subject of modern discourse. But before we address the language by which
melodrama thus explicitly inscribes its characters and strategies of signifi-

cation within this discourse, we should note the implications of Brooks's comments on psychology. For in attempting to redeem the melodrama by positing for it a disruption of consciousness, repression, and the reality principle, what is revealed is emphatically *not* the unconscious as understood by Freud, and certainly not Lacan's linguistic unconscious, but on the contrary a transcendental identity in which 'desire triumphs over the world of substitute-formations and detours, [and] achieves plenitude of meaning', or 'full states of being' (p. 41), in short an identity grounded in the primal return to a lost oneness with immanent meaning. The inappropriateness of this valuation is obvious the moment we recognize in this fully integrated oneness a residual valorization of that very transcendence that is Brooks's critical object of attention. If in psychoanalytic theory the unconscious is the source of phantasy and thus imaginative production, this unconscious, so far from being the site of any 'plenitude of meaning', must be understood as a *process*, and a process of ongoing 'interaction multiply determined or overdetermined between different levels and mechanisms in the psyche'.[9]

From the psychoanalytic standpoint, then, it is precisely the *under*determined nature of melodrama and our 'monopathic' experience of it[10] that would seem most interesting, and this only highlights the need for a historically determined analysis of it. But Brooks himself provides such an analysis in his main line of attention to the cultural crisis of the Revolution and desacralization, and the essentialist subject of modern discourse lies at the very center of the analysis: the figural and rhetorical representation of the 'integer of the self' confirms that 'the melodramatists refuse to allow that the world has been completely drained of transcendence' (p. 22). The melodramatic project within modern culture is nothing less than the *deferral* of any confrontation of the individual with the abyss, so that we should not be surprised by Charles Nodier's comment on Pixérécourt's plays that 'I have seen them in the absence of religious worship, take the place of the silent pulpit' (translated and quoted by Brooks, p. 43). Whatever the details of any particular embodiment of the genre, Brooks sees finally that melodrama must be conservative, for if, as in comedy, the plot is structured by blockage and the overcoming of this blockage, the blockage is not of eros as in comedy, but 'much more virtue's claim to exist qua virtue', that is, the blockage is of immanent moral categories, and the peripety brings not a new society 'but rather a reforming of the old society of innocence, which has now driven out the threat to its existence and reaffirmed its values' (p. 32).

Of course, however conservative the formal imperatives of the genre, in actual practice melodrama has come to be associated with the populist political views of its mass audience. Frank Rahill notes over the course of the nineteenth century 'the growing practice of making heroes of common folks and villains of the highborn', and notes Sir Walter Scott's reprehension of the practice of melodramatists 'as a groundwork of a sort of intellectual Jacobinism', as well as his quoting of Coleridge's assertion that such melodrama consisted 'in the confusion and subversion of the natural order of things'.[11] Indeed, the evil capitalist has never lost his position of preeminence in the melodramatic pantheon of villains. But the relative failure of the melodrama to effect fundamental change in the culture's political and economic structures despite its widespread adaptation to socialist and communist causes is striking.

That 'bourgeois' melodrama has been so prominent a part of radical drama since the 1840s is only apparently paradoxical, for in fact the failure of leftist political movements to challenge the power of the dominant ideology is coming to be seen as a product of their own participation in the discursive practice of modern discourse. Even while Marx and Engels elaborate a theory of the historical contingency of culture and the individual, their attempt to valorize that theory via a claim to scientific objectivity tends to reinscribe the theory within the practice of the authorizing subject, creating opportunities for a process of incorporation or cooptation of the emergent discourse.[12] When we begin to conceive of communism (from the perspective of the dominant ideology) as a demonized inversion of that ideology, generated by the dualizing generative practices of modern discourse, then 'socialist melodrama' becomes less paradoxical, and the distinctions between 'bourgeois' and socialist literature less significant.[13]

We might understand the subversive limits of melodrama better if we conclude with some consideration of a distinct theatrical practice, that of Bertolt Brecht. I mention Brecht in the context of melodrama with some trepidation, of course, given his emphatic repudiation of the genre. But as with everything in Brecht, the reality of his work lies rather athwart his pronouncements, and his actual use of melodramatic elements is both extensive and significant. Even the most political, relatively the most Marxist of his works remain deeply grounded in the emotive force of personal predicament, and in images of vulnerability and suffering drawn directly from that tradition. His intellectual message is never so distinct from this emotive power as he tended to suggest in his theoretical pronouncements, and indeed if the intellectual does in fact give his work its distinctive hard edge, this ideological edge draws blood only when powered by the engine of empathy and identification.

Still, my immediate point lies in asking how his expressionist and ideological backgrounds shape a theatre more truly radical than even the most orthodox of realist Marxist melodrama, and the most immediate answers are an anti-realist theatrical aesthetic, and an anti-individualist and anti-sentimental ideological position. Leaving aside the explicitly theoretical Marxist commentary, Brechtian drama is still informed by a vital and energetic refusal to indulge the individual and subjective aspects of modern characterization: his art not only announces its theatricality at every turn, but actively seeks to elicit in his audience a questioning of the very nature of representation, and thus of the occlusions of realism. Constantly we see the apparent unity of the theatrical experience deliberately fragmented in ways that suggest, even recreate, the socialpsychic fragmentation of modern culture beneath its totalizing representations. Without glossing over the inconsistencies of his theory of 'epic theatre' and its central strategy of *Verfremdung* or alienation, we still find in the practice a foreshadowing of poststructuralism's deconstruction of the modern discourse of the subject as he fractures the solid appearance of the 'real', whether at the level of stage illusion, social conditions, ideology, or human nature, and thereby struggles to awaken in his audience a consciousness of the contingency of the human situation.

Brecht was a lifelong student of Renaissance drama in an age when its status was still seriously devalued (his reactions being as complex and contradictory as those to melodrama), but his fascination with Renaissance drama is not surprising in light of his theatrical preoccupations.[14] As I suggested earlier, that theatre's skeptical interrogation of the simple referentiality of language, of the real possibility of any objectified knowledge, and thus of a unified and integrated individual identity – in short, of the independence and transcendence of consciousness over material reality – makes this body of work as well a storehouse of both ideas and dramatic technique for Brecht. I cannot help noticing that Shakespeare practiced 'distancing' as insistently as did Brecht: his engagement with the genre of romance itself might be considered a fully elaborated example of Brecht's theory. But more to my immediate point, for each playwright the practice was motivated by a desire to penetrate the 'realistic' representations of a discourse centered on the essentialist subject. And beneath this representation, far from the transcendental reality of the 'immanent self', the 'moral occult', each found the open play of historical contingency. Thus it is that Brecht and Shakespeare can help to provide us with complementary historical perspectives from which to consider at least tentatively the counterproductive ideological status of the melodrama.

Can melodrama effectively awaken its audience to Bentley's primal world of human passion and desire beyond the pale of reason? Or does it, by parodying the complexity of this alien reality and reducing it to the terms of dominant rational discourse, 'domesticate' and coopt it? In truth, the genre has remained ideologically counterproductive exactly because it *is* popular, for mass culture is a constituent element in the continued reproduction of the dominant discourse, and, far from being an independent and competing locus of signification, functions dialectically to define and ratify high culture, thereby consolidating the cultural hegemony (in both its senses) of exactly those classes whose taste supporters of a more melodramatic theatre generally reproach. In fact, accepting a debate in terms of 'taste', of aesthetic preferences, is one way in which defenders of the melodramatic prejudice their position before ever launching a struggle for independent signification, because the concept of 'taste' is itself deeply interwoven with those conceptions of individuality and the subject that serve the dominant culture. However much we might wish to revaluate and valorize passion, action, spectacle, and sensibility as crucial elements in the significance of the dramatic experience, the discourse within which we articulate these desires has already and intrinsically defined such values as peripheral. However popular the melodramatic continues to be in all the areas of popular culture, such success can never redefine the peripheral status of desire within the dominant discourse, nor alter the fact that as a signifying practice it now regularly and ostentatiously functions to derogate the very aspects of human nature that Bentley valued.

NOTES

1 *The Life of the Drama* (New York: Atheneum, 1964), p. 198.

2 Given at least three widespread applications of the terms 'melodrama' and the 'melodramatric', let me immediately clarify my usage in what follows. Most narrowly the term is generic, and properly applied to that dramatic species first practiced by François-Réné Pixérécourt on the boulevard du Temple during and after the French Revolution: 'a dramatic piece characterized by sensational incident and violent appeals to the emotions, but with a happy ending' (*OED*). Because of the vital impact of the genre on romantic and postromantic literature as well as modern culture generally, the term is often applied as an adjective; thus Peter Brooks focuses his study of the nineteenth-century novel on 'the melodramatic imagination'. Finally, Bentley sees in the melodrama a fundamental mode of human perception and the key to the dramatic impulse itself, and therefore extends the term to become a universal potential of all theatre. Because I am interested in a broadly cultural critique of the melodramatic, including Renaissance analogues, I will be using the term in each of its senses, while agreeing with Brooks that 'the adjective "melodramatic" will take on greater critical force, greater definitional use, if we can refer back from it to a relatively well-characterized set of examples under the head of melodrama' (*The Melodramatic Imagination*, New Haven: Yale University Press, 1976, p. xi).

3 While pursuing what I take to be one of the broadly unifying concepts of poststructuralism generally, the terms of the following argument are more specifically those of cultural materialism as practiced by Raymond Williams, especially in his *Marxism and Literature* (Oxford University Press, 1977), and more recently Jonathan Dollimore in *Radical Tragedy* (University of Chicago Press, 1984).

4 References are to *The Riverside Shakespeare*, ed. G. Blakemore Evans (Boston: Houghton Mifflin, 1974).

5 *The Heart's Forest* (New Haven: Yale University Press, 1972), p. 106.

6 Since the publication of his seminal *Shakespearian Metadrama* (Minneapolis: University of Minnesota Press, 1969), James L. Calderwood has remained the most prominent exponent of the metadramatic element in Shakespeare's work, his preoccupation with the self-reflexive aspects of the drama. Michael Shapiro provides a convenient overview of the main strains of the practice in 'Role-Playing, Reflexivity, and Metadrama in Recent Shakespearean Criticism', *Renaissance Drama*, n.s. 12 (1981), 145–61.

7 Besides Dollimore, see especially Timothy Reiss, *The Discourse of Modernism* (Ithaca: Cornell University Press, 1982), the fullest investigation now available of Foucault's concept of 'epistemic rupture' as it applies to the Renaissance and the emergence of modern culture.

8 See in particular *Marxism and Literature*, pp. 121–8.

9 Anthony Easthope, *Poetry and Phantasy* (Cambridge University Press, 1989), p. 9 (italics his).

10 While Brooks cites Heilman's theory of a 'monopathy' as 'the kinds of need that give rise to, and the kinds of experience and satisfactions afforded by' the melodramatic structure, he overlooks Heilman's crucial qualification of the monopathy as a '*quasi*-wholeness', by which he means 'the *sensation* of wholeness that is created when one responds with a single impulse or potential which functions *as if* it were his whole personality' (Robert B. Heilman, *Tragedy and Melodrama*, Seattle: University of Washington Press, 1968, pp. 84–6, italics mine).

11 *The World of Melodrama* (University Park: Pennsylvania State University Press, 1967), pp. 155, 156. Scott's comments are from his 'Essay on the Drama' (London, 1887).

12 For a detailed analysis of Marx's claims to the objectivity of scientific materialism see, for example, Williams's chapter on 'Ideology'; for a review of the debate, Easthope's on 'Ideology and the Unconscious in Literature'.

13 As early as 1948 Wylie Sypher glimpsed from a literary perspective the limited radicalism of Marxism, in an article on 'Aesthetic of Revolution: The Marxist Melodrama', *The Kenyon Review*, 10, no. 3 (Summer 1948), 431–44. Sypher recognized the structure of *Das Kapital* to be essentially one of 'the archetypal 19th Century melodrama' (p. 438), his thesis being that 'the melodrama is a characteristic mode of 19th Century thought and art' (p. 433), that its central structural feature is dualism, 'the oversimplification into polarities and oppositions' (p. 435), and that despite its theoretical commitment to a dialectic that would subvert such dualism, Marx was unable to escape the dominant aesthetic form of the culture. If, theoretically, revolution is historically conditioned, in its formal elaboration it becomes melodramatic gesture: 'the dialectic is no longer a philosophical tactic; it is a program and Marx is writing the last episodes . . . the free laborer confronting the capitalist' (p. 440).

14 For a vivid discussion of Brecht's conscious and unconscious 'complex parody' of the Shakespearian drama, see Helen M. Whall, 'The Case is Altered: Brecht's Use of Shakespeare', *University of Toronto Quarterly*, 51, no. 2 (Winter 1981/2), 127–47.

The perils of Dido: sorcery and melodrama in Vergil's *Aeneid* IV and Purcell's *Dido and Aeneas**

ROBERT C. KETTERER

Vergil's account in *Aeneid* IV of the disastrous love affair between the Trojan hero Aeneas and Dido, the queen of Carthage, lends itself readily to dramatic adaptation. Its own style and structure are obviously dramatic: as has long been recognized, it owes much to Greek tragedy,[1] and its romantic and heroic elements have strongly attracted writers from Ovid to Berlioz.

In 1689 Nahum Tate, soon-to-be poet laureate of England, adapted this action for an hour-long musical entertainment to be performed by the 'young gentlewomen' of a Chelsea boarding school. The music for the piece, titled *Dido and Aeneas*, was set by Henry Purcell, and the production was probably choreographed by Josias Priest, a professional dancer who ran the boarding school.[2] It was one of the first English sung-through operas, and is still regarded by many as the most successful.

The story it tells of a woman who falls in love with a visiting adventurer, only to be abandoned and die because of violated honor and a broken heart, contains plenty of opportunity for melodramatic treatment. A *Dido, Queen of Carthage* by Christopher Marlowe (before 1594) had indeed indulged in emotional excess, especially during the death scene, as had Tate's own earlier adaptation of the story titled *Brutus of Alba; or, The Enchanted Lovers* (1678).[3] But critics have generally been at pains to assert that the Vergilian original and the operatic adaptation by Tate and Purcell are genuine tragedy, and not melodrama. For example, the classical scholar Eduard Norden says: 'The key of Dido's scene [in Book VI] is not tuned to sentimentality, but to heroic grandeur and tragic ethos (as is generally the whole of Dido's drama).' Kenneth Quinn believes that *Aeneid* IV is a 'perfectly contrived synthesis of tragedy and epic'.[4] As for the opera, music historian Ellen Harris argues that it is a perfectly conceived Aristotelian tragedy. Joseph Kerman believes the chorus exhibits Sophoclean growth and development, and Robert Moore says, 'Dido is always a great queen and never a Lydia Languish.'[5]

* A draft of this paper was read at the *Themes in Drama* International Conference held at the University of California, Riverside, in February 1990.

As a supplement to such views, I want to observe how Vergil, and Tate and Purcell after him, made use of what we would now call melodramatic situations and effects, specifically by their inclusion of sorcery as a melodramatic element in the story. I do not mean to suggest here that the *Aeneid* is the only source for the opera (it is clearly not), but rather that an examination of the two ways of telling the story helps with the interpretation of both.

I state first my assumptions about melodrama as a critical category and the relation of melodrama to tragedy. To begin with, melodrama is simplistic where tragedy is complex. Ultimately this relates to the hero's approach to his or her world: a melodramatic hero 'responds with a single impulse or potential which functions as if it were [the character's] whole personality'.[6] There is no confusion of good and bad in this universe; lines are clearly drawn.

Second, melodrama relies on outside forces to challenge the hero or heroine, where in tragedy, to paraphrase Walt Kelly, 'We have met the villain and he is us.' These outside forces may be other people or even nature itself; hence, for example, nineteenth-century melodrama's use of the storm as a sign of adversity.[7]

Third, the outcome of the struggle need not be happy. Though typically stage melodrama ended on a positive note, Heilman observes also the existence of a 'literature of disaster' which plays on the pleasure to be had from 'going down fighting' and the subsequent good cry for the audience. 'There are actually emotional compensations ... in being defeated or overwhelmed or victimized. One can find an affirmative pleasure in the relief from tormenting uncertainty, ... or can even welcome death.'[8]

Finally, melodramas exploits sensational effects to heighten emotion. This may include music, stage effects or exaggerated rhetorical and poetic devices.

Sorcery and the supernatural readily take on these characteristics of melodrama. Witches are generally associated with purely evil (or sometimes purely good) elements in the universe, and demand a comparatively simple reaction from the audience. They are furthermore a source of dramatic tension, posing danger not just from outside the protagonist, but even outside the usual categories of rational experience. They are by nature sensational, and so the supernatural remained a standard element in Gothic melodramas. The witch scenes from Shakespearian plays continued to be produced in the popular theatre of the eighteenth and nineteenth centuries long after the plays as a whole had lost popular favor.[9]

Literature of the early Roman empire regarded witches with fascinated horror, and the more extreme activities which popular imagination credited to them were exploited by poets and story-tellers. Medea in particular becomes a paradigmatic witch-figure for the poets, and special interest was paid to black magic connected with love charms.[10] Vergil himself, in *Eclogue* viii, lines 64ff., wrote a shepherd's charm to recall a straying lover, with the help of herbs received from a werewolf who could raise the dead.

In the seventeenth century, Tate and Purcell were also working with a popular literary convention. They had available to them Davenant's expansion of Shakespeare's witches in *Macbeth* (1661), as well as Shadwell's *Lancashire Witches* (1681), and others.[11] Tate himself had used a witch and her coven in *Brutus of Alba* to cause the queen's destruction. Thus we can observe that both in imperial Rome and in England of the seventeenth century, literature regarded the more lurid details imagined about witches as ready material to create a conventional melodramatic villainess.[12]

Let us now turn to Vergil's story and the sorcery there. By line 296 of Book iv, Dido has learned that Aeneas is leaving Carthage to continue his search for Italy.[13] A sarcastic directive from Jupiter, delivered by Mercury, has told him to move on, in accordance with divine plan. To this point in the poem Dido has fulfilled Aristotle's prescriptions for a tragic figure (*Poetics* 1452b, 1454a). In Book i, as successful founder and ruler of Carthage, she was 'extraordinarily beautiful' (line 496), like the goddess Diana with her train (lines 498–504), 'happy' (lines 503), and even 'most happy' (line 685). But when Venus and Cupid cause Dido to fall in love with Aeneas to protect him against the enmity of Dido's patron Juno, she becomes 'unhappy' (*infelix*, 1.712, 749, iv.68, etc.), 'scarcely sane' (iv.8), and like a wounded deer (iv.69–73). The famous scene in the cave where Dido violates her pledge of faith to her dead husband Sychaeus and the lovers consummate their desire during a storm is marked by Vergil as the Great Error: 'Ille dies primus leti primusque malorum / causa fuit ...' ('That day was first the source of her ruin, and of her evils', lines 169–70).

But a genuinely tragic Dido creates problems. The *Aeneid* is Aeneas' poem, after all; if Dido is a tragic heroine, if she usurps both our attention (which she does, temporarily) *and* all our sympathy, what are we to think of Aeneas? Many discussions have suggested that such a usurpation is part of the point, and that Dido's pain qualifies Aeneas' (and Rome's) final victory.[14] But the arguments which follow suggest that Vergil does not allow Dido's tragedy to dominate the end of the book, and instead complement observations that, through allusion and verbal echo, Vergil has associated Dido with the dangerous figure of the witch.

Previous scholars who have felt that pity for Dido's suffering is not the primary effect of Book iv focus their criticism on the moral disgrace into which Dido falls by breaking her vow to her dead husband Sychaeus and violating her chastity. They furthermore point out that her fall is due to

the reassertion of Aeneas' duty and destiny over the forces of destructive
chaos with which Dido is allied.[15] These observations are valid enough,
but they dwell on issues that sway sympathy from Dido intellectually, not
emotionally. As Aristotle indicated, any tragic figure will make mistakes,
and so become tragic; the mistake is human and so our sympathies remain
with the tragic figure. It was certainly true that Vergil's Roman audience
could read sympathetically of Dido's pain, despite her misbehavior:[16]
Ovid wrote the following to Augustus in defense of his own erotic poetry.

> et tamen ille tuae felix Aeneidos auctor
>   contulit in Tyrios arma virumque toros,
> nec legitur pars ulla magis de corpore toto,
>   quam non legitimo foedere iunctus amor.

(Certainly the blessed author of your *Aeneid* brought his 'arms and the man' to
a Punic bed, and no part of the whole poem is read more than that love affair
joined in illicit union.)   (*Tristia* 2.533–6)

Read in isolation, the book is indeed a story of Dido's broken heart. To
give emotional distance from Dido, then, and return the *Aeneid* to Aeneas,
Vergil had to counter that sympathy. He did so by employing the
melodrama of sorcery.

The process begins during the quarrel with Aeneas, or perhaps shortly
before. Dido is 'bereft of mind', 'inflamed', and rages throughout the city
like a wild devotee of the god Bacchus (lines 300–3). (Again a tragic
reference, but an extreme one: she is like Agave from the *Bacchae* who tore
apart her own son Pentheus.) Her mood swings dramatically. She is
capable of sentimental pathos: 'si quis mihi parvulus aula / luderet
Aeneas qui te tamen ore referret, / non equidem omnino capta ac deserta
viderer' ('If there were some little Aeneas, playing in my hall, who'd still
recall you in his looks, I wouldn't then feel completely taken and
deserted', lines 328–30). She is equally capable of frightening anger: 'heu,
furiis incensa feror!' ('Oh, I am swept away in flames of fury!', line 376).
Both the reference to Bacchants and the wild swings of emotion are typical
in ancient descriptions of women scorned in love and beyond reason. Hers
is not the divided mind of a tragic figure, but the irrational behavior of a
lover.[17]

After Aeneas rejects a final plea made by Dido's sister Anna, the poem
moves Dido psychologically towards the underworld and death. Nature
itself seems to conspire against her as she is visited by a series of gruesome
omens: holy water turns black and sacrificial wine to blood; at night she
hears ghostly voices of her first husband in his shrine; an owl sings
funereal songs on her roof; she is visited by frightening dreams of Aeneas
(lines 450–73).

Dido therefore begins to employ magic in order to control the dark powers that terrify her. She tells her sister that she has enlisted the help of a priestess from the Garden of the Hesperides, a place mythically associated with magic, love and the afterlife.[18] This priestess is a mistress of the black arts, who can relieve the mind of its cares and, more importantly, can place cares on others (lines 487–8); she can perform spectacular supernatural feats, such as changing the courses of rivers and heavenly bodies, and calling up the dead. 'You'll see the earth groan under her feet, and oaks descend the mountainside', Dido tells Anna (lines 490–1). On the advice of this priestess, Dido directs Anna to build a pyre in an inner court of the palace, and place on it her 'marriage' bed, and with it a sword and other mementos left by Aeneas. Dido and the priestess hang funeral wreaths on the pyre, and also place an image of Aeneas with the other paraphernalia. They then perform an elaborate magical rite, calling on the powers of the underworld – Erebus, Chaos, and triform Hecate (lines 510–11) – and sprinkle on the appropriate infernal ingredients – water from Avernus, meal, and noxious herbs appropriately gathered. They seek out a *hippomanes*, a lump of flesh supposedly taken from the forehead of a newborn foal and thought to have magical powers.[19]

All of this, Dido tells Anna, has been recommended 'to return him to me as a lover, or free me from loving him' (line 479). She appears no longer to be struggling internally with herself, but attempting to enlist dark, outside powers to her side and make the world do her will. A remark to her sister Anna indicates that she knows she has gone into forbidden realms (lines 492–3): 'Testor, cara, deos et te, germana, tuumque / dulce caput, magicas invitam accingier artes' ('I call to witness you and the gods and your sweet person, dear sister, that I undertake the magic arts unwillingly'). The effect of her associating herself with magical arts connected with the underworld at this point puts her in the simpler and more sensational world of melodrama.

Of course, Dido's explicit statements to Anna about the purpose of the pyre and associated rites hide her real intentions. As Vergil makes quite clear (lines 474–6, 500–1), she means these arrangements not as a love charm, but for her own funeral. Hence her statement that 'it will free me from loving him', has a meaning that Anna does not understand. But, as A.-M. Tupet has pointed out, something else even more sinister is going on.[20] Observing that the rites Dido performs with the priestess are not after all those used in a lover's charm, she points out that in fact they are the beginnings of an elaborate curse ritual which Dido will complete as Book IV comes to its end. According to Tupet, an ancient curse ritual includes preparatory rites, the speaking of the curse itself, and then a sacrifice. The preparatory rites have been performed with the priestess; when Dido subsequently observes Aeneas' fleet putting out to sea, she flies once again into a rage, and, invoking the Sun, Juno, Hecate and the avenging Furies, she pronounces a curse on Aeneas, his family, and his race (lines 584–629). Not only does she call for disastrous events which will be fulfilled in Italy in the second half of the poem, but invokes a Carthaginian avenger, who every Roman would know came in the historical person of Hannibal.

Having uttered the curse, Dido then mounts the pyre, pronounces her own eulogy, and ends her life with Aeneas' sword. Thus, as Tupet points out, Dido has duly performed the complete ritual, pronouncing the curse and with her suicide performing the final sacrifice.[21] She thus gives a terrible unity to the book, and her magic rites and curses take on a very real power, for we know, if Dido herself does not, that they will be fulfilled by legend and history.

Dido's increased power is indicated by her changing relations with the weather, another outside force which we noted was favored by modern writers of melodrama. Dido began as a passive victim of storms, as we all are: a storm arranged by Juno sent Aeneas to her coast in the first place. Another storm sent by Juno and Venus marked 'the first of her ruin' in the cave with Aeneas. But as her rage at Aeneas' perceived betrayal mounts, she begins to create her own storms. She is likened metaphorically to a storm at lines 437–49, as Aeneas' refusal to be moved by Dido and Anna's pleas is compared to a deep-rooted tree standing against buffeting winds. Then the storm becomes real. Dido's last words were, 'Hauriat hunc oculis ignem crudelis ab alto / Dardanus, et nostrae secum ferat omina mortis' ('Let the cruel Trojan on the sea drink in with his eyes this funeral fire, and take with him the omens of my death!', lines 661–2). At the beginning of Book v, as Aeneas looks back uncomprehendingly from his ship at the rising smoke of Dido's funeral pyre, he does carry the omens of her death with him and the metaphorical storm of her rage becomes real: 'Olli caeruleus supra caput astitit imber / noctem hiememque ferens et inhorruit unda tenebris' ('The blue-black rain cloud stood over his head, bringing night and storm, and the shadowy waves bristled', v.10–11). Her anger and her curse follow him and will affect his life beyond her death.[22]

Vergil has thus turned Dido from tragic heroine to a melodramatic villainess, according to the terms which I have already specified. She transcends her role as tormented and tragic victim, allies herself with the powerful (and melodramatic) figure of the evil sorceress, and, through the use of outside supernatural powers, imposes her will on the world.[23] Her use of dark powers of destruction connects her thematically with the destructive elements in the poem: primarily with Aeneas' bitter enemy Juno, who raised the storm that blew Aeneas to Carthage in Book I;[24] and secondarily, the Fury Allecto from the underworld, who at Juno's instigation in Book VII will stir up the wars in Italy.[25] Vergil thus diminishes sympathy for her and places her in the position of someone to be escaped, rather than pitied.

It cannot be denied that she still excites pity in spite of all this. The good and compassionate woman of Book I is occasionally visible at the last minute, as she debates whether she might go with him (lines 534–52), and in her last words, as she addresses the arms and bed of Aeneas tenderly (line 651). But as we have seen, dramatic swings of mood are typical of the lover in the final stages of madness, and Mercury's warning (lines 569–70) that a woman is 'varium et mutabile semper' becomes true in Dido's case.

Vergil also counteracts the momentary pathos with a final distancing device. He describes Dido's last moments with melodramatic excess: she does not die instantly or simply, but lingers, as Anna sobs over her, and her wound whistles air (lines 685–9).[26] Juno must finally take pity on her favorite-turned-victim, and sends Iris to end the agony:

> Ergo Iris croceis per caelum roscida pennis
> mille trahens varios adverso sole colores
> devolat et supra caput astitit. 'hunc ego Diti
> sacrum iussa fero teque isto corpore solvo':
> sic ait et dextra crinem secat, omnis et una
> dilapsus calor atque in ventos vita recessit.

(On saffron wings the dew-glittering Iris glides / along the sky, drawing a thousand shifting / colors across the facing sun. She halted / above the head of Dido: 'So commanded, / I take this lock as offering to Dis; / I free you from your body.' So she speaks / and cuts the lock with her right hand; at once / the warmth was gone, the life passed to the winds.)   (lines 700–5; trans. Mandelbaum)

This last moment is superficially pathetic and moving, the rainbow ending Dido's personal 'storm' which so buffetted Aeneas. But as W. R. Johnson has pointed out, the sudden and uncharacteristically compassionate appearance of the forces of Chaos – Juno and her messenger Iris – has the effect of upstaging Dido. Iris' colors are bright, as Johnson points out, but also *varius*, 'shifting', and the signification of her appearance sinister.[27] In *Iliad* XVII.547–52, Athene descending to battle is like a 'dark-gleaming' (*porphureën*) rainbow, which is a 'portent of and sign of war, or of wintry storm' (trans. Lattimore). In Euripides' *Herakles* (lines 822–73), Iris had served as a transmitter of Hera's malice bringing Madness to Herakles and causing him to kill his children.[28] In Book V of the *Aeneid*, Iris is an agent of Juno's destruction, when she is sent to burn Aeneas' ships. There at line 609 the description of her bright colors ('viam celerans per mille coloribus arcum') recalls the passage at IV.701 ('mille trahens varios adverso sole colores').[29]

Hence, Dido's curse has worked: she has bent the cosmos to her will, and brought the forces of destruction to her side. The rainbow is also a

Homeric portent of the storm which will immediately overtake Aeneas, as well as the bitter wars he will fight in Italy, and the Carthaginian avenger who will appear in the future. We are finally reminded by Dido's death of the melodramatic villainess she has become, not the woman she wished to be.

Nevertheless, the sense of pity for Dido can dominate when the story is taken in isolation from the wider context of the *Aeneid*, and subsequent literature could treat her very sympathetically. Ovid began the process in his *Heroides* VII (Dido to Aeneas). There he created a pathetic, heartbroken heroine, but did so in part by excising the sorcery and curse. Instead, he used the theme of sorcery and curse in *Heroides* VI (Hypsipyle to Jason), where the heroine describes her rival Medea as a classic witch, and goes on to curse her in terms much like Dido's curse on Aeneas.[30] Despite his remark in *Tristia*, Ovid clearly felt the alienating effect of the sorcery that Vergil's Dido practiced, and so removed it from Dido to a context more appropriate for his purposes.

Tate and Purcell made a similar choice in creating *Dido and Aeneas*.[31] In the opera the black magic is employed solely by a Sorceress and her coven, who are substitutions for all the divine and supernatural elements in the *Aeneid*. Dido does not practice sorcery, and does not even meet the witches. In consequence, the effect of the witchcraft (and so of the melodrama) is entirely different in the opera than it was in Vergil's poem.

In act I of the opera, Dido is moved by cheerful assurances from her confidante Belinda (who takes Anna's role), and from her court, to accept Aeneas' suit. Aeneas is the active pursuer, and evidently not motivated by anything other than his own desire. Act II then opens in the cave, but it is not the trysting place of Vergil's lovers. Instead it is a meeting place for the witches. In a manner standard to English witches at least since *Macbeth*, the Sorceress summons her cohorts:[32]

> Wayward sisters, you that fright
> The lonely traveller by night.
> Who like dismal ravens crying,
> Beat the windows of the dying.
> Appear at my call, and share in the fame
> Of a mischief shall make all Carthage flame.

The Sorceress's threatening F minor key is answered by her assistants – two enchantresses and a chorus – who express their willingness in a cheerful F major, singing, 'Harm's our delight, and mischief all our skill.' The Sorceress then continues in her F minor:

> The Queen of Carthage, whom we hate,
> As we do all in prosperous state.
> Ere sun-set shall most wretched prove,
> Deprived of fame of life and love.

In recitative the Sorceress explains her plan to send Aeneas on his way: Aeneas and Dido are in the field hunting: the Sorceress will send her 'trusty elf', who, 'In form of Mercury himself, / as sent from Jove shall chide his stay, / And charge him sail tonight with all his fleet away.' A reminder to Aeneas of his destiny will apparently send him running, and leave Dido 'ruined ere the set of sun'. As a nasty additional trick, two of the enchantresses resolve to stir up a storm 'To mar their hunting sport, and drive 'em back to court.'

A second-act hunt and dance is indeed interrupted by the storm, and the 'trusty elf' disguised as Mercury appears:

> *Spirit.* Stay Prince and hear great Jove's command,
>   He summons thee this night away.
> *Aeneas.* Tonight?
> *Spirit.* Tonight thou must forsake this land,
>   The angry god will brook no longer stay,
>   Jove commands thee waste no more
>   In love's delights those precious hours,
>   Allowed by the almighty powers,
>   To gain th'Hesperian shore
>   And ruined Troy restore.

This is delivered to flourishes of A minor chords that contrast abruptly with the D major key of the previous chorus ('Haste, haste to town', 27:1–22), and signify both villainy and disaster. As the Sorceress foresaw, Aeneas crumbles instantly and agrees to go, despite his anxiety about how the Queen will take the news.

The sorcery of *Aeneid* IV has thus been completely transformed. The witches' plot replaces the divine machinations of Juno and Venus, the subsequent message from Jupiter delivered by Mercury, and Dido's black magic. The melodramatic sorcery is shifted entirely to the villainesses: these enchantresses are motivated purely by their malice[33] – 'The Queen of Carthage whom we hate / As we do all in prosperous state' – and stand in simple opposition to the cheer and prosperity of the court, expressed by Belinda's sentiment in act I, when she sings, 'Shake the cloud from off your brow ... / Empire growing, / Pleasures flowing / Fortune smiles and so should you.' As in the *Aeneid*, the introduction of sorcery results in a simplification of motive, but in this case, that simplification comes from outside Dido, not from within. The witches are the source of a melodramatic conflict, a single-minded outside force challenging the heroes. Their malicious but rather pointless storms replace those raised by Vergil's Dido that became the storms of history. The enmity of Juno with its cosmic significance has been modulated here to simple, rather trivial evil.

In addition, they are also exploited for melodramatic spectacle. Opera of the day required what the French called *le merveilleux*, an elaborate

combination of chorus, ballet and scenic effects which often as not overwhelmed whatever plot there may have originally been. In England there
was no indigenous operatic tradition, but the English had been entertaining their royalty with masques, equally gaudy and even more plotless
combinations of pomp and music. Consequently, when Purcell and Tate
came to write their opera, they could hardly have conceived it without
some element of spectacle.[34] With witches such popular figures in the
Restoration theatre, it was a natural step to expand Vergil's magic to
encompass these witches who provide the necessary spectacle and
dance.[35]

     Act III returns to the happy emotional simplicity of the court in act I: a
singer who appears to be a Trojan sailor encourages the other Trojans
with a cheerful B flat major hornpipe to abandon their Carthaginian
sweethearts, 'With vows of returning, / But never intending to visit them
more.' Curtis Price has made a good case for following the Quarto of 1700
that indicates the 'sailor', whose part was scored for a soprano, is actually
the Sorceress in disguise.[36] In such an assumed role she completes her
work by getting the sailors to desert their own lovers, just as Aeneas is
about to abandon Dido. The putative sailor then strips off her disguise,
and there is some final gloating, followed by an eerie celebratory dance led
by 'Jack of the Lanthorn'. The scene has remained in the B flat major key,
emphasizing the success of the witches' plot.[37]

     The witches, then, dominate the central portion of the opera with their
villainous doings. They provide a simple dichotomy between good and
evil, and perform it to appropriate flourishes of minor chords with a gusto
that anticipates the villains of the later melodramatic stage.[38]

     The first and last scenes of the opera, on the other hand, belong to Dido.
She expresses her initial anxieties in the first, and in the last dies after
sending Aeneas packing. Despite the protestations of Robert Moore, the
Dido created by Tate's libretto certainly *could* be a 'Lydia Languish'. In
her first aria she actually dwells for eleven bars (3:28–39) on the thought,
'I languish till my grief be known.' (Seven of those bars are devoted to the
phrase 'I languish'.) She is depressed by her unspoken and unspeakable
love for Aeneas, but offers no political or ethical explanation. She seems
merely distressed at the prospect of romantic involvement. Her only two
lines in act II ignore Aeneas altogether, as she points out that they are
being overtaken by a storm and precipitates a return to town. Her rejection of Aeneas and subsequent death in act III appears to be based on
nothing more than his having thought of leaving, and she is finally
mourned by putti who 'droop' over her tomb. She might easily fit into the
melodramatic worlds of the court and the witches.

     But Purcell's music picks up certain phrases in Dido's text and expands
upon them musically to make her experience a tragic one.[39] As we have

seen, the sentiments of the court and the witches, though at times expressed in more elaborate musical terms, are emotionally simplistic, calling for either a positive or negative response. In contrast, Dido's aria in act I 'Ah, Belinda, I am press'd / With torment' (3:1–67), in which the voice struggles without success to unify with the ground bass. It is an expression of the profound anguish caused by the passion which she knows is forbidden her by fate and duty.

Again, at the end of the opera, when Dido realizes that her acceptance of Aeneas' advances was a mistake, she rejects him utterly, and the music makes clear that she remains true to her own deepest convictions about herself and her position as queen. The libretto here may tempt us to dismiss her reactions as neurotic and hysterical,[40] when having rejected Aeneas for the mere thought of leaving, she says,

> Away! (*Exit Aeneas*)
> To death I'll fly, if longer you delay.
> But death, alas, I cannot shun,
> Death must come when he is gone.

But Purcell's music returns her emotions to the agony of 'Ah, Belinda . . .'. The line 'To death I'll fly, if longer you delay', is muffled by an angry contrapuntal duet between Dido and Aeneas (35:52–4), which ends with Aeneas' exit on Dido's dismissive full cadence, 'Away, away!' Then the lines 'But death, alas, I cannot shun . . .' begin a new movement that will continue uninterrupted to the end of the opera. The words are sung slowly and simply, ending on a half-cadence that leads into the hymn-like chorus, 'Great minds against themselves conspire, and shun the cure they most desire' (36:1–13). The chorus has finally understood Dido's tragic predicament, and moved from the melodramatically simple world it inhabited in the first act. Its grave G minor round on these words brings our understanding along with theirs, and moves to the mood of Dido's final aria in G minor, 'When I am laid in earth'. As in 'Ah, Belinda . . .', the tormented voice, soaring over a simple but relentless ground bass, expresses the emotions of a woman tormented both by her own errors and by her continuing passion for Aeneas. There is no shift from a tragic role to a melodramatic one for Purcell's Dido as there was with Vergil's.

How, then, is one to reconcile the two strains of the opera, the tragic and the melodramatic? It appears that the melodramatic world of this opera is peopled not only by the witches, but by all the individual characters on stage *except* Dido; it acts as both the cause of, and dramatic foil for, Dido's tragedy. Dido herself lives in a more reflective world than either Belinda or Aeneas – she is aware from the beginning of the most salient argument against the affair: 'Fate forbids what you pursue', she sings pointedly to the love-struck Aeneas. Yet when she has given in and then finds herself abandoned, she returns to her militant virtue: 'No repentance shall reclaim / the injured Dido's slighted flame.' Finally in death she blames no one: 'When I am laid in earth may my wrongs create / No trouble in thy breast, / Remember me, but ah! forget my fate.' Belinda, by contrast, can only assure her sister that everything will be all right. Aeneas, under the pressure of his passion, makes foolish claims about his ability to withstand the demands of Destiny, and then, having announced that he will go, fails even to stick by that decision. 'Let Jove say what he will, I'll stay', he tries. But Dido knows better. It is therefore Aeneas who is 'varium et mutabile semper', and the witches must deal with him in this opera, not with Dido. She dies because she finally does not fit in the simpler melodramatic world inhabited by the rest of the characters.

A last look at the death scenes confirms the difference with the Vergilian original. As we saw, Vergil's Dido, having moved onto a more simplistic emotional level, could finally be upstaged by her own historical role and by her divine patrons; melodrama balanced tragic feeling and returned the poem to Aeneas. In the opera, on the other hand, Aeneas remains a virtual non-entity, while Dido's final sentiments carry her court and the opera with her; the music of the closing chorus and dance are really extensions of Dido's final aria, both in mood and key. As Kerman says, 'Dido's agony softens and deepens outward towards the audience through the mourning community on the stage.'[41] With her request, 'but ah! forget my fate', Dido has seized the play back from the witches, and confronted the enemy within herself. We remember who *this* Dido wished to be, not what the forces of evil wanted for her, and thus the tragic feeling in the opera eclipses the melodramatic.[42]

NOTES

1 See, for example, N. W. De Witt, 'The Dido Episode as a Tragedy', *The Classical Journal*, 2, no. 7 (1907), 283–8; A. S. Pease, *Publi Vergili Maronis Aeneidos Liber Quartus* (1935; repr. Darmstadt: Wissenschaftliche Buchgesellschaft, 1967), pp. 8–11; K. Quinn, *Latin Explorations* (New York: The Humanities Press, 1963), pp. 29–58; P. Hardie, *Virgil's* Aeneid: *Cosmos and Imperium* (Oxford University Press, 1986), pp. 268–9.

2 E. T. Harris, *Henry Purcell's* Dido and Aeneas (Oxford University Press, 1987), p. 4 and pl. 2. This is the most complete single study of the opera available. Musical analyses of the opera in this paper are based on those of Harris in her ch. 6, 'Musical and Dramatic Structure', pp. 69–81, and ch. 8, 'Ground Bass Techniques', pp. 107–19.

3 For this judgement on Marlowe, see R. B. Heilman, *Tragedy and Melodrama* (Seattle and London: University of Washington Press, 1968), p. 171; on the finale of Tate's *Brutus*, see C. Price (ed.), *Purcell*, Dido and Aeneas: *An Opera*

(New York and London: W. W. Norton, 1986), p. 39. All references to the libretto and score of *Dido and Aeneas* come from this Norton Critical Score (referred to hereafter as Price, *Dido*). For the relationship of *Dido and Aeneas* to *Brutus of Alba* and other sources, see Price, '*Dido and Aeneas* in Context', in Price, *Dido*, pp. 3–4; R. R. Craven, 'Nahum Tate's Third *Dido and Aeneas*: the Sources of the Libretto to Purcell's Opera', *The World of Opera*, 1, no. 3 (1978–9), 65–78; and Harris, *Henry Purcell's* Dido and Aeneas, ch. 3, pp. 20ff. and ch. 4. Harris and Craven argue convincingly that Tate was working closely with *Brutus* as he was composing his opera libretto, but it is equally clear that the opera is no more a simple condensation of *Brutus of Alba* than it is of the *Aeneid*, and it must stand on its own as a dramatic creation.

4 E. Norden, *P. Vergilus Maro: Aeneis Buch VI*, 2nd edn (Leipzig: Teubner, 1916), p. 253, on line 455; K. Quinn, *Virgil's* Aeneid: *a Critical Description* (Ann Arbor: University of Michigan Press, 1968), p. 135.

5 Harris, *Henry Purcell's* Dido and Aeneas, pp. 41–2; J. Kerman, *Opera as Drama*, rev. edn (Berkeley and Los Angeles: University of California Press, 1988), pp. 43, 44; R. E. Moore, *Henry Purcell and the Restoration Theatre* (Westport, CT: Greenwood Press, 1961), p. 50.

6 Heilman, *Tragedy and Melodrama*, p. 84. This book is the basis for most of my premises, but I have also used H. D. Kitto's *Greek Tragedy*, 3rd edn (London: Methuen, 1961) in addition to the others mentioned in notes 7 and 8 below.

7 E. Bentley, *The Life of the Drama* (New York: Athenaeum, 1967), p. 202.

8 *Tragedy and Melodrama*, p. 86. See also M. Booth, *English Melodrama* (London, Herbert Jenkins, 1965), pp. 154–5.

9 Booth, *English Melodrama*, pp. 61–2.

10 E.g., Horace, *Epode* 5 (a child sacrifice to obtain material for a love philtre) and Satire 1.8 (a witches' nocturnal gathering); Propertius IV.5 (witchcraft and love); Petronius, *Satyricon*, sections 61–2 (a werewolf) and 131 (a spell against impotence); Lucan, *Bellum Civile*, VI.413ff. (general description of witches and a necromancy). Medea appears in Ovid, *Metamorphoses*, VII.1–403 and Seneca, *Medea*, 670ff.; she is described as a witch and/or held up as an example in Horace's *Epode* 5, and Ovid, *Heroides* VI.83–94.

11 On the sources of witches in *Dido and Aeneas*, see references listed in note 3 on the opera's sources. Thomas Shadwell gives a cynical contemporary opinion about the use of witches for spectacle in plays in his 1681 introduction to *The Lancashire Witches*. See M. Summers (ed.), *The Complete Works of Thomas Shadwell* (London: Fortune Press 1927), vol. IV, pp. 100–1.

12 Shadwell, ibid., saw virtually no difference between ancient and Restoration witchcraft. At the end of the introduction to *The Lancashire Witches* he wrote, 'I have but one thing more to observe, which is, that Witchcraft, being a Religion to the Devil, (for so it is), their charms upon several occasions being so many offices of the Witches Liturgy to him, and attended with as many Ceremonies as even the Popish Religion is, 'tis remarkable that the Church of the Devil (if I may catachrestically call it so) has continued almost the same, from their first writers on this subject to the last. From *Theocritus* his *Pharmaceutria* [see below, note 17], to *Sadducismus Triumphatus* . . .'

13 Citations of the *Aeneid* are from R. A. B. Mynors (ed.), *P. Vergili Maronis Opera*

(Oxford University Press, 1969). Unless otherwise noted, translations are my own.

14 This view of the *Aeneid* (and the more positive view against which it reacts) is described by W. R. Johnson, *Darkness Visible: A Study of Vergil's* Aeneid (Berkeley: University of California Press, 1976), ch. 1, with references in note 10, pp. 156–7. The most succinct statement of the darker view is by W. Clausen, 'An Interpretation of the *Aeneid*', *Harvard Studies in Classical Philology*, 68 (1964), 139–47. From a somewhat different perspective: R. O. A. M. Lyne, *Further Voices in Vergil's* Aeneid (Oxford University Press, 1987), pp. 45–9; and R. C. Monti, who describes Dido as the perfect Roman dynast, whom Aeneas wrongs because of his own insufficient attention to the requirements of *fides* and *pietas*. (*The Dido Episode and the* Aeneid: *Roman Social and Political Values in the Epic*, Leiden: E. J. Brill, 1981, especially pp. 68–9, 76–9.)

15 V. Pöschl, *The Art of Vergil: Image and Symbol in the* Aeneid, trans. G. Seligson (Ann Arbor: University of Michigan Press, 1962), pp. 60–91; B. Otis, *Virgil: A Study in Civilized Poetry* (Oxford University Press, 1964), pp. 93–5; Quinn, *Virgil's* Aeneid: *A Critical Description*, ch. 4; R. Hornsby, *Patterns of Action in the* Aeneid (Iowa City: University of Iowa Press, 1970), pp. 96–7, 100; Hardie, *Virgil's* Aeneid: *Cosmos and Imperium*, pp. 267–85. Most of these believe that Dido is tragic, but would agree with Pöschl's assessment that, 'Through fate, grief and sorrow, Aeneas takes part in the world's unhappy turbulence, but he never sinks into it' (p. 91). F. Cairns, *Virgil's Augustan Epic* (Cambridge University Press, 1989), pp. 56, 129–50, shows Vergil's use of the Roman elegiac tradition to characterize 'Dido's love for Aeneas as wrong, and as destructive in tendency, while preserving the reader's sympathy' (p. 149). The evidence in this paper suggests a more critical view, closer to Hornsby's statement that to look on Dido's story as a tragedy 'is to distort its significance by a false emphasis' (p. 100).

16 Imperial Rome's passion for erotic and emotional poetry is demonstrated by S. Farron, 'The Sentimentality, Romanticism and Emotionalism of the Ancient Greeks and Romans, with Specific Reference to Aeneid 4', *Acta Classica*, 26 (1983), 83–94.

17 See Hornsby, *Patterns of Action*, p. 94, and Cairns, *Virgil's Augustan Epic*, pp. 137–50. Cairns connects Dido's behavior specifically with Roman love elegy. Cf. the lover in Theocritus, ii (The *'Pharmaceutria'*, or 'The Spell'), who resorts to magic to return her own lover to her, and will kill him if the charm does not work.

18 W. H. Roscher, *Ausführliches Lexikon der griechischen und römischen Mythologie* (Leipzig: Teubner, 1886–90), vol. 1.2, columns 2594–95; G. S. Kirk, *The Nature of Greek Myths* (New York: Penguin, 1974), pp. 192–3.

19 Concerning these materials and magical rites, see Pease, *Aeneidos Liber Quartus*, pp. 420–9; and A.-M. Tupet, *La magie dans la poésie latine, I: Des Origines à la fin du règne d'Auguste* (Paris: Les Belles Lettres, 1976), pp. 249–50. G. Luck, *Arcana Mundi: Magic and the Occult in the Greek and Roman Worlds* (Baltimore and London: Johns Hopkins University Press, 1985), pp. 78–84, places *Aeneid* IV.450–705 as an example of black magic along with the passages from Horace and Seneca.

20 Tupet, *La magie dans la poésie latine*, pp. 232–66, especially 245–59. As I show, however, I differ somewhat from Tupet's assumption that, 'dans le chant IV, et

dans l'epopée virgilienne en général, tout est ménagé pour concourir à un effet de tragique grandiose' (p. 245).

21 Ibid., p. 258.

22 The smoke of the pyre is a complex image: the smoke blends into the image of the blue-black storm, and so is a symbol of her curse and ultimately of the coming of Hannibal. But that in turn signifies the Punic wars and burning of Carthage at Roman hands in 146 BC. See R. J. Edgeworth, 'The Death of Dido', *Classical Journal*, 72 (1976–7), 129–33. This complexity does not make the image less melodramatic: the smoke signifies both the negative force of chaos and the ultimate defeat of that chaos by the positive forces of fate and history.

23 There are strong connections with Medea, who destroyed what she loved after being deserted by the man she called husband. Reminiscences can be noted of both Euripides' character, who kills her enemies with pyrotechnic poison, and of the Medea in Apollonius Rhodius' *Argonautica*, who is a rather spooky priestess of the witch-goddess Hekate. See Pease, *Aeneidos Liber Quartus*, pp. 13–14; Monti, *The Dido Episode*, pp. 1–2, with sources collected in note 2; and Lyne, *Further Voices*, pp. 127–32. Also in this connection there may be some reference to Cleopatra, whom Augustus' propaganda accused of bewitching Antony with love potions (Plutarch, *Antony*, 60). Cf. Pease, *Aeneidos Liber Quartus*, pp. 24–8, and Cairns, *Virgil's Augustan Epic*, pp. 56–7.

24 Cf. Otis, *Virgil: A Study in Civilized Poetry*, pp. 91–4.

25 Cf. V. Buchheit, *Vergil über die Sendung Roms* (Heidelberg: Carl Winter, 1963), pp. 75–6.

26 Hardie, *Virgil's* Aeneid: *Cosmos and Imperium*, pp. 282–5, notes that hyperbolic language at the end of the book connects Dido's end both with the curse she put on herself at the beginning of the book (lines 24–9) should she violate her honor and chastity, and with the ultimate, melodramatic destruction of her own city and people (see note 22).

27 W. R. Johnson, *Darkness Visible*, pp. 66–75. He observes that *varius* 'is a favorite word with Vergil when he wishes to stress complexity and confusion' (p. 69). He cites parallels at IV.564; VIII.21; XII.486, 665, 914–15 (note 60, p. 165). See also IV.569.

28 The rainbow is a sign of *approaching* (not departing) storm in Vergil, *Georgics* 1.380–81, Tibullus 1.4.44, and Seneca, *Oedipus*, 315–20. Seneca, *Natural Questions*, 1.8.8, specifies that certain rainbows portend storm while others portend the opposite. Livy, 41.21.12, reports that a rainbow appeared in a clear sky in 175 BC during a plague. Later commentators compared Iris, the rainbow, and *Eris*, strife, and suggested Iris brought discord and Mercury concord. (See Pease, *Aeneidos Liber Quartus*, on line 694, p. 530.)

29 M. C. J. Putnam, *The Poetry of the Aeneid* (Cambridge, MA: Harvard University Press 1965), p. 212. At the opening of Book IX, she again stirs up trouble with Turnus while Aeneas is visiting Evander.

30 For example, they both appeal to Jupiter (*Aen.* IV.590 / *Her.* VI. 152), ask that the Aeneas/Medea be outcasts (*Aen.* IV.616 / *Her.* VI.158, 162), that they be separated from their children (*Aen.* IV.616 / *Her.* VI.156), that they not be allowed to enjoy what they have gained (*Aen.* IV.619 / *Her.* VI.157), and their offspring be haunted by violence (*Aen.* IV.617–18, 628–9 / *Her.* VI.160). These passages seem to be part of a group of poetic curses. H. Jacobson,

Ovid's Heroides (Princeton University Press, 1974), p. 103, note 21, connects the passage from *Heroides* VI with similar passages from Euripides, Accius, and Catullus.

31 They were not necessarily taking the tactic from Ovid, of course. The Renaissance had already seen that inclusion of the sorcery could have a negative effect on the portrayal of Dido's character. (See B. J. Bono, *Literary Transvaluation: From Vergilian Epic to Shakespearean Tragicomedy*, Berkeley: University of California Press, 1984, ch. 3.) Tate's decision to separate the sorcery from the figure of Dido in the opera is more striking because in *Brutus of Alba* the Dido figure *had* asked the witch Ragusa for a storm to keep Aeneas in Carthage (act v). She is prevented from real complicity with the witch by the powers of hell, who recall Ragusa to them.

32 R. Savage, 'Producing *Dido and Aeneas*', in Price, *Dido*, pp. 264–5.

33 There is no need to see their lack of specific motive as a dramatic flaw to be explained somehow. (See e.g. Price, '*Dido and Aeneas* in Context', pp. 8–9.) Simple malice as a witch's motive for evil was perfectly intelligible to a seventeenth-century audience. See Savage, 'Producing *Dido and Aeneas*', p. 265, and compare the witch Ragusa in *Brutus of Alba*: 'By contract, son, I hate all humane kind, / But envy most the prosperous and great; / Thou art devoted to the Queen's destruction, / And so am I ...' (act III). Interestingly, this is at variance with what happened in the English courts of law, where very specific reasons were given for the malice of the accused witches. See A. Macfarlane, *Witchcraft in Tudor and Stuart England: A regional and comparative study* (London: Routledge and Kegan Paul, 1970), pp. 173–4.

34 Kerman, *Opera as Drama*, p. 47.

35 Craven, 'Nahum Tate's Third *Dido and Aeneas*', p. 69, suggests that the step had already been taken in *Brutus of Alba*, with similar motives, i.e. to provide spectacle.

36 Price, '*Dido and Aeneas* in Context', pp. 31–2.

37 Harris, *Henry Purcell's* Dido and Aeneas, pp. 73–4.

38 It has been suggested that the opera is a political allegory, with Aeneas and Dido representing the newly crowned William and Mary, and the witches the Catholic threat to the Protestant crown. (See Price, '*Dido and Aeneas* in Context', pp. 6–12.) Harris, *Henry Purcell's* Dido and Aeneas, pp. 17–33, has argued convincingly against such an interpretation. But even if one accepts the allegorical reading, the melodramatic aspect remains a simplistic interpretation of contemporary events.

39 Moore, *Purcell and the Restoration Theatre*, ch. 2, esp. pp. 47–50, 57–9; Kerman, *Opera as Drama*, pp. 43–7; Harris, *Henry Purcell's* Dido and Aeneas, pp. 107–12, 116–19.

40 Cf. Price's 'neurotic queen' in '*Dido and Aeneas* in Context', p. 6.

41 *Opera as Drama*, p. 46.

42 I would like to thank J. P. Aiken, H. D. Cameron, V. Castellani, R. A. Hornsby, D. F. Jackson, and A. F. Nagel for comments that have aided in the writing of this paper.

Guilbert de Pixérécourt: the people's conscience

J. PAUL MARCOUX

Guilbert de Pixérécourt, the father of melodrama, probably lived too long. After having enjoyed almost unprecedented popularity for thirty years, he was unfortunate enough to witness his own slow, painful artistic demise. It is difficult to imagine a sadder state for a playwright: to be the toast of Paris one day and a has-been the next. But even that was typical of Pixérécourt's colorful life, a life that was as melodramatic as the plays which made him famous.

Above all, he was a product of his time. He was a Frenchman living through the most turbulent times in the history of his country. He witnessed the political extremes of an age characterized by almost daily changes in everything from eating habits to methods of execution. At the height of his popularity he could barely leave the theatre without being mobbed by his admirers, who angrily jostled each other to get a glimpse of 'le grand Pixérécourt', 'le Corneille des boulevards'. Three decades later, he would retire to a small house in Nancy, far from Paris; sad, disillusioned, nearly blind, in constant pain and deteriorating health. Perhaps worst of all, he knew that even his most popular plays had become objects of ridicule and derision from an audience no longer attuned to his once universally accepted philosophy of theatrical entertainment. It is the object of this article to examine some aspects of this philosophy, particularly from the point of view of French popular morality during the early nineteenth century.

René-Charles Guilbert de Pixérécourt was born in Nancy on 25 January 1773. His family, an old and respectable one boasting several distinguished lawyers and theologians, had been granted the privileges of nobility in 1712 by Duke Leopold. There were also strong family ties with King Stanislas of Poland, who had established a well-known private preparatory school and college in Nancy, both of which young Guilbert attended. Even before his school years he seemed destined for unhappiness. Recalling his early life, Pixérécourt speaks of a 'wicked nurse' who nearly cost him his life and of his gratitude to a 'good peasant woman', who cared for him in his grandparents' home on the banks of the Moselle.

Of this lady he says: 'my benefactress, your name [Jeanne Debiége] is inscribed in letters of gold on marble as well as in my memory. As long as I live, I shall remember that it was you alone who brought about my miraculous resurrection. Your tender and vigilant care, the life-giving water of the Moselle and the rustic life style gave me a new and vigorous existence. To my great regret I was taken back to Nancy when I was four. From this moment all my happiness ended.'[1] Indeed, the horror stories he narrates in his memoirs do not leave much doubt regarding his misery. His father, a former army officer and a strict disciplinarian, is said to have had 'the soul of a feudal lord'. He was unyielding and apparantly devoid of compassion. At one point he made arrangements to send his ten-year-old son to a local reform school which also housed the insane. The boy's offense had been to shoot spit balls at one of his teachers, an offense for which he had already been punished at school by being forced to kneel on a stone threshold for hours. Guilbert ran away from home and even contemplated suicide rather than face the harshness of the *maison de force* to which he had been committed. It was through the intercession of his spiritual advisor and friend, a Father Munier, that the terrified boy was allowed to spend his school vacation with his grandparents in the country, far from his father's wrath.

The following year he was again away from Nancy and had to return to school alone and on foot because his father was on a fox hunt. In his writing he complains bitterly of the serious hardships (including a near-drowning) which he endured on the twenty-mile trip to Nancy from his father's country estate near Charmes. 'After fifty years, the memory [of fording a river, at dusk, with his clothes tied in a bundle on his head] still makes me shudder. Can you imagine this poor child of eleven, alone in this frightening situation? I could have perished a thousand times; only a miracle saved me.'[2]

His main consolation during these hard times seems to have been his unshakable faith in God, a faith which would sustain him throughout his life and which would be clearly reflected in his plays. He was also able to take some solace in his academic success. He was a good student and was the frequent recipient of book prizes for excellence. This started a life-long passion for collecting books. Pixérécourt's *ex libris* reads: 'A book is a constant friend.'[3] Over the years he amassed an impressive library. Unfortunately, he was eventually forced to sell his books to help settle legal claims brought against him late in life.

Despite an interest in art (he displayed considerable skill in drawing) and literature, he decided to study law upon completion of his early schooling. He had completed two years when the Revolution broke out. His father was dispossessed of his estates and the young Pixérécourt was forced to flee to Germany where he joined a community of French expatriates at a forest convent near the Moselle, the same river which had nurtured him in his infancy. It was here that he found love; probably the only true love of his life. Her name was Clotilde. She was eighteen and the orphan niece of the Mother Abbess. According to one researcher, she was also 'rich, well educated, laconic, and an accomplished young person'.[4] Guilbert fell head over heels in love with *la belle Clotilde*. She taught him German; he taught her French and drawing. They went for walks and exchanged chaste signs of their mutual devotion. Alas, the young man had to report for military service and was away for six months. When he returned to his forest sanctuary, he found to his horror that the Abbess had already died and that his beloved Clotilde was near death from tuberculosis. She died in his arms a few hours after his return. In his old age he declared: 'Clotilde's death was an enormous disaster for me. She was my future, my life, my whole existence, all my happiness. Her pure soul contained all that was in my own heart. Alas! I lost her! Never to return! Fifty years have not erased my sorrow.'[5]

Deciding to return to France, young Pixérécourt carefully made his way across the border. At one point he reports having to hide in a water-filled ditch in order to avoid the soldiers, who were everywhere.[6] He finally arrived in Paris in 1793, a hunted man, since he had illegally left the country four years earlier, albeit at his father's insistence. Calling himself simply 'Citoyen Guilbert', he shared an attic room with a friend and eeked out a bare existence. It was at this time that he wrote and sold his first dramatic adaptations of popular novels, and, although the plays were not produced, he was encouraged to consider playwriting as a career.

Yet another dramatic political event was to postpone the prospect. That same year, the newly formed Convention decreed universal conscription for unmarried men between the ages of eighteen and twenty-five. Pixérécourt had now to return to Nancy to join the army of the Republic. He was placed in a cavalry regiment but allowed to remain in Nancy. Representing the Convention was a man named Marat-Mauger. Willie G. Hartog, Pixérécourt's major biographer, describes him as an inhuman monster who went about the countryside violating young virgins. It seems that one of Marat-Mauger's victims was a friend of Pixérécourt's family. Shocked and insensed, young Guilbert was 'twenty times tempted to blow out his [Marat-Mauger] brains [but] ... chose a form of vengeance not less dangerous, but far less effective'.[7] He wrote a one-act play/vaudeville satirizing the hated man. *Marat-Mauger or the Jacobin On a Mission* was accepted by the local theatre company but not approved by the authorities, who promptly ordered his arrest. Luckily, Pixérécourt had had the foresight to secure a military leave and he remembers escaping to Paris through a grill at the rear of the house as the gendarmes were entering his front yard. Surely an event worthy of one of his melodramas!

Paris was in the full throes of *la terreur*, but Pixérécourt managed to work as a clerk in the war department for a while. He was discovered shortly after the Convention had ordered all ex-noblemen out of Paris and was denounced to Robespierre. Again his life was in danger; but an appeal to the Public Safety Committee through his friend, Lazare Carnot, got him off the hook. He left the security of the civil service at the formation of the Directoire because, 'The tiring life of a bureaucrat had affected my health; I had just gotten married and was beginning to write for the theatre.'[8]

Very little is known of Pixérécourt's marriage. His wife, Marie-Jeanne-Françoise Quinette de la Hogue was evidently from a good family. They were married in 1795. Of his early married life, Pixérécourt complains: 'During the first three years of my premature marriage I was completely miserable; all my hopes had vanished. I had neither property, nor position; no money, not even bread! ... and I had to support a wife and an infant still in [her] cradle.' Since his only child, Anne-Françoise Guilbert, was born in 1799, it appears that Pixérécourt's dates were off a bit. In any case, that complaint seems to be the only mention of his marriage in all of his writing. Hartog suggests that considering the significant details he gives us about his platonic dalliance with Clotilde, it would seem that 'his marriage was not a happy one, or at least that his wife did not play an important part in his life'.[9] In fact, she was not to play an important part even after his death in 1844. His will ordered that his monument in the cemetery at Préville near Nancy be a single piece of stone, large and heavy enough to ensure that, 'it could not be moved in order to one day place Madame de Pixérécourt next to him'.[10] Perhaps recalling the art lessons he had given to Clotilde, Pixérécourt took a job painting designs on ladies' fans, but continued to write. Toward the very end of the eighteenth century, his plays began to sell and he finally saw them produced in *les théâtres des boulevards*, the popular theatres of the day. He would eventually log 30,000 performances in Paris and the provinces of nearly 100 plays and would profoundly influence the course of French popular theatre, and consequently that of English and American melodrama.

If we are to understand Pixérécourt's role as a leading popular entertainer of the day, we must examine the development of French melodrama as a distinct dramatic genre. Since the late 1600s, the notorious boulevard du Temple area in the Saint-Martin quarter of Paris had been the city's fair grounds. Make-shift booths had housed jugglers, rope-dancers, magicians, puppeteers, clowns, animal acts and freak shows. Pantomimes using live actors instead of puppets were later added to the available entertainments and these proved to be the most popular of all, especially when music was used to sharpen the emotional impact of the moment.

These entertainments soon outgrew their settings and the booths eventually became permanent theatres. Since there were no government subsidies for these newly arrived establishments, they depended entirely on pleasing their patrons, and please them they did. As crude and unschooled as the amusements might have been, they soon began to compete successfully with the 'high-class' legitimate theatres. The oppressive and elaborate regulations governing theatre in France were, in part, a political result of this competition. Enterprising managers of the newer theatres had to walk a fine line when offering new pieces. To survive they had to please the crowds, but they could not offend the government-protected and often jealous major theatres. Censorship and legalistic interpretations of a growing list of criteria had become almost self-defeating when the Revolution virtually wiped out the entire system. Despite the resulting chaos followed by Napoleon's re-establishment of many of the same regulations, the boulevards remained active and very popular well into the nineteenth century.

Of course, there were other factors which affected the development of *le mélodrame*. Paul Ginsty, in a detailed study of the genre, summarizes the literary influences: 'Melodrama, this popular tragedy ... did not come into being full blown. It is the wayward son of sentimental drama ... it was taught by Beaumarchais. The seeds [of melodrama] are in Mercier's concepts ... its formula [can be traced] to Sedaine ... and to the German playwrights.'[11] Each of these influences represents a reaction to the neoclassical tradition which had held French culture in a tight grip for much of the early eighteenth century. The Enlightenment produced drama which was largely imitative of classical models, displaying a lofty simplicity, a high respect for an antiquarian setting and an emphasis on tradition. Racine (1639–99) had set the pattern in tragedy and the Académie Français upheld the philosophical precepts which governed the work of his immediate successors. Unfortunately, they never achieved Racine's grandeur nor his literary force and are long forgotten. Corneille's imitators in the tragicomic genre pale in comparison to the author of *Le Cid* as does the *comédie larmoyante* (tearful comedy) of the period, when compared to the brilliant satirical character studies of Molière.

The call for reform heard in the mid-eighteenth century is exemplified in the work of Voltaire (1694–1778), who was well aware of a growing demand for a more useful intellectualism but hesitant to kick over the traces of tradition. He never actually called for a revolution in French drama, but he did influence a less rigid application of the old criteria and introduced a number of significant developments in dramaturgy and staging techniques. He also saw and utilized the potential of drama as a didactic medium, a highly effective tool in his pursuit of social, religious and political reform. He laid the groundwork for Denis Diderot, whose dramatic theory extended beyond neoclassical models. Diderot wanted to develop a serious drama whose major aim would be to instruct and enlighten the middle class. Although his work remained largely theoretical, it was further developed by Sedaine and Mercier in the 1760s and 70s and implemented by August von Kotzebue (1761–1819), the popular German author of 'domestic tragedy'. He in turn strongly influenced Pixérécourt's dramaturgy.

Opposed to the didactic concept of drama, Jean-Jacques Rousseau, the other major theoretician of the period, was advocating a return to a 'natural' way of life. In fact, the idea of using the spoken word against a musical background, or more precisely alternating the two, in a performance piece, as distinct from combining them as in opera, seems to have originated with Rousseau, who thought French too harsh a language to be sung. He devised a kind of musical hop-scotch for his libretto to *Pygmalion*, a *scène lyrique* which opened in Paris in 1775. Within a short time, dialogue was not only alternating with musical passages but being spoken over the music, which provided emotional support. Thus, a new form developed, quite distinct from opera in its traditional sense. The term *mélodrame* gradually came to be used to describe the new 'natural' plays.

The latter half of the century produced Pierre-Augustin de Beaumarchais whose Figaro plays symbolize the inexorable movement toward revolution. The principal character in *Le Barbier de Seville* and *Le Marriage de Figaro* is a common barber who is far more clever than his master. Despite the fact that the plays are full of intrigue and deception and tend to ignore most of the traditional precepts of playwriting, they were universally admired, except by the waning aristocracy, who considered them dangerous and even seditious.

It seems clear that the literary influences which helped to produce *le mélodrame* soon merged with the political forces which would erupt in a bloody call for *liberté, egalité, fraternité*. The decline of classical French theatre was as much a political phenomenon as it was a literary development. At the close of the eighteenth century Racine and Corneille were still being played in the major theatres but had become elitist, and were attracting a very small portion of Parisian society. The vast majority represented 'a publc eager for thrills, a mob which had passed through the violence of revolution'.[12] The socio-political climate as well as the declining health of traditional theatre foretold the triumph of Romanticism in France. As the century drew to a close, the time was ripe for an upgrading of popular theatre; a theatre which would once more hold a 'mirror up to nature', a theatre that would restore man's faith in man and perhaps even man's faith in God while providing the pleasures of *le boulevard du crime* as the popular theatre district came to be known.

Like any dramatic genre, melodrama came to reflect a particular view of the human experience. Compared to tragedy, which according to at least one critic, 'implies a working of destiny, whether imposed from without or defined by inner nature',[13] melodrama is unadulterated, or 'monopathic' to use another term. Melodramatic man is whole and undivided. Since he is not concerned with destiny, he seeks extreme solutions to extreme adversity. In melodrama there can be no half-measures, no mitigating circumstances and no uncertainty. A single impulse is the only possible way to deal with a given stimulus. Danger begets courage in the hero; cowardice in the villain. Comingling is unthinkable. The protagonist in a melodrama deals only with external and controlable forces; he remains totally unconcerned with self-doubt or fate and he rarely hesitates except in an act of self-preservation. On the other hand, the tragic hero is characteristically as much at war with himself as with his enemies. He rails against fate while cursing his own weakness. He struggles to discover himself; not merely to preserve his life or his virtue. The tragic world is full of agonizing choice; the world of melodrama pursues relatively simple conflicts to extreme conclusions. James L. Smith put it like this: 'In melodrama we win or lose; in tragedy we lose in the winning like Oedipus Rex or Macbeth, or win in the losing like Hamlet or Antony and Cleopatra.'[14] A dramatic genre which views life as a battle between undivided man and external forces which is resolved by utilizing an extreme and often predictable solution might well seem ingenuous and pedestrian, even trivial; but in fact, it is closer to basic reality than the tragic vision of the human condition, as cathartic as that vision might be. Indeed, we are more likely to see our everyday experiences in melodramatic terms rather than as mini-tragedies. It is far easier to blame others than to wonder about our own shortcomings. To doubt ourselves requires less emphasis on the vindictiveness or pettiness of our neighbors. We can take comfort in our causes until they force us into self-examination. We are usually content to remain on the side lines, admiring our leaders or castigating them but rarely willing to exchange places with them. Even if we are certain that we are far better able to wage the battle than the principals, in the final analysis we often are content to *witness* rather than to *participate* in its conclusion, provided it is not a draw. Battles must be won or lost, not merely peter out. How else could we experience triumph or defeat and still remain unscathed? 'In short,' suggests Smith 'melodrama is the dramatic form which expresses the reality of the human condition as we all experience it most of the time.'[15]

Eric Bentley goes even further: 'The melodramatic vision is in one sense simply normal. It corresponds to an important aspect of reality. It is the spontaneous, uninhibited way of seeing things ... the dramatic sense is the melodramatic sense, as one can see from the play-acting of any child. Melodrama is not eccentric or decadent ... it is drama in its elemental form; it is the quintessence of drama.'[16] He argues convincingly that melodramatic vision corresponds to the magical world of the child and of the adult dream world, worlds in which magnified feelings are the norm and excess need not be defended. Peter Brooks later re-stated this quintessential nature of melodrama: 'The force of melodrama derives from the very origins of theatricality, of self-dramatization; in the infantile dream world ...'[17] However, this does not mean that melodrama is childish; rather, it is devoid of psychology. It is simple but not necessarily simplistic. In France at least, it became more a drama of signs than a drama of motives. The distinction is still viable and evidenced in contemporary melodrama.

If we accept the aesthetics of melodrama as an expression of a quotidian view of life, take into account the literary history of the genre, especially in France, and place the mix in the political maelstrom of a post-revolutionary era, we need but add a master playwright to complete a theatrical process which will flower for nearly a century. That master will add his own special ingredients, including a high standard of ethical behavior, and will nurture his creation with honest devotion. Pixérécourt was convinced that his purpose in life went far beyond amusing an unruly mob. In his own words: 'I launched myself on a thorny career in the theatre with religious [conviction], with ideas of Providence [and] with moral sentiments.'[18] His good friend, Charles Nodier, an important critic of the day, praised Pixérécourt's dramaturgy, his spectacular staging and his realistic style but above all he was impressed by the playwright's profound sense of morality and decency which he saw expressed in all of his work. In the introduction to Pixérécourt's collected works he says: 'I have seen them [the plays] in the absence of organized worship, take the place of the silent pulpit in providing serious and profitable lessons for the souls of his audiences, and always in a charming form ... Since the people had only the theatre through which to revive their religious and social education, melodrama provided a means of applying the fundamental principles of any civilization, [including] its providential aspects.'[19]

Setting Nodier's sententiousness aside, his basic observation remains true for philosophical as well as for historical reasons. It is certainly no accident that French melodrama as a dramatic genre was a product of revolution. Its traits are clearly those of a form hurtling toward democracy. Especially notable is that morality is no longer imposed from above but is now seen as a kind of grass-roots imperative. Peter Brooks speaks of the French Revolution and its aftermath as 'the moment that symbolically and really marks the final liquidation of the traditional Sacred and its representative institutions, namely Church and Monarch ... melodrama comes into being in a world where the traditional imperatives of truth and ethics have been thrown violently into question yet, [at a time] when the promulgation of truth and ethics, their instauration as a way of life, is of immediate, daily political concern.'[20] The Revolution can be viewed as the climax of a process of desacralization begun at the Renaissance and gaining momentum during the Enlightenment; a process which destroyed the power of traditional sacred myth and the power of its rituals, especially tragedy and epic poetry. What was to replace the old Sacred would be a democratic movement eventually to be called Romanticism. Myth-making now became everyone's prerogative. Good and evil became measures of individual behavior within a new social order. Morality now had more to do with a recognition of the diabolical forces which inhabit our world and our inner selves than with the acceptance of the need for communal purgation. Since these forces appear to abide in nature, we must look to nature for moral guidance. Melodrama in the hands of Pixérécourt and his contemporaries became, in a very real sense, 'natural religion' and what has been called 'an intensified primary, and exemplary version of what the most ambitious art, since the beginnings of Romanticism, has been about'.[21]

Consider the compelling image of Pixérécourt, still in his thirties, strolling on the boulevard du Temple,

> wrapped in the velvet of his cloak and decorated with his Legion of Honor cross ... silently followed at a distance by men, children, young girls and old people [who] with joined hands, exclaim passionately, 'Look, it is he! ... the great judge who reads the hearts of the perverted and punishes all crime' ... his head held high, with bright eyes and thoughtful brow he slowly passes amidst the murmurs of praise, admiration and curses.[22]

It is not difficult to appreciate this image in the light of melodrama as we have been examining it. If traditional worship had been de-mythified and its representatives rendered mute, there was now an urgent need for a new high priest who could teach the Word anew. He would need a voice that spoke the language of a people struggling to make sense of the chaos they themselves had produced. He would need to be absolute and non-compromising in the application of a people's morality. He would acknowledge God while constantly reaffirming the inherent goodness of human nature.

In fact, the basic structure of Pixérécourt's melodrama is dependent on the idea of reaffirmation. His plays begin with a presentation of virtue followed by the discovery of an obstacle or the threat of one which places that virtue in imminent and terrible danger. For most of the play the obstacle seems insurmountable for a host of reasons, often a variation of silence such as muteness, passivity, or a vow; but virtue (personified in the heroine) resists and is finally vindicated in a public trial during which the lies are revealed and the truth emerges. In Brooks's terms

> the play ends with public recognition of where virtue and evil reside, and the eradication of one as the reward of the other. The reward is ancillary to the

2 Pixérécourt's *Cœlina or the Child of Mystery*. Boston College production

recognition just as the threat to virtue is basically the refusal to allow its
claim, to recognize its nature ... [there is] a reforming of the old society of
innocence, which has now driven out the threat to its existence and reaffirmed
its values ... [there is no] reconciliation to a sacred order larger than man.
The expulsion of evil entails no sacrifice, and there is no communal partaking
of the sacred body. There is rather a confirmation and restoration.[23]

Thus the playwright, as the new redeemer, comforts and reassures. We
have glimpsed the darker side of man but the light of innocence again
burns as brightly as ever and we are safe as long as we remain in its glow.
If this appears irrational and wildly sentimental to a modern audience it
may be that we have failed to grasp the power of a truly elemental theatre,
perhaps the last one able to exist before we become transfixed with definitions of reality.

Frederick Brown speaks eloquently of such power:

in the melodramatic beyond, appearance always belies reality: the dead may
spring to life, and protagonists, whether heroes or villains, avail themselves of
a thousand masks. Lured by some 'mystery', that is some forbidden fruit
irresistible to the heart in him, what departure from rhyme and reason would
the average spectator not gladly oblige? For the privilege of committing
incest, burning houses, eating human flesh, exerting superhuman strength,

3 *Cœlina*. Boston College production

seeing in the dark, finding treasure troves, and then emerging from his debauch in an odor of sanctity, would he hesitate to lay his mind in forfeit? He inclined rather – and who does not once sleep descends? – to the wisdom of the Fathers: Credo quia absurdum (I believe because it is absurd).[24]

As we have seen, Pixérécourt's success with melodrama was due to several factors. No one can deny the historical/political forces which catapulted him to fame; nor is it possible to dismiss the philosophical, theoretical and literary influences which are an essential part of his dramaturgy. The fact that he was commercially successful[25] need not imply that he was merely giving the people what they wanted. Indeed, it appears that he sincerely believed he was giving them what they needed. His very strict upbringing, his traditional education, his early friendships with members of the clergy and his staunch belief in God's providence all contributed to his moral development. He seems to have had more than his share of bad luck, but he was able to rise above it and to concentrate on what he saw as the evangelical aspects of his calling. In his own words: '[Melodrama] offers to that segment of society most in need of good models, acts of heroism, bravery and fidelity. Thus, we show [them] how to become better [people] by demonstrating the noble aspects of the public record . . . Melodrama will always be a means of instruction for the people because it is an accessible genre.'[26]

According to some sources there was a reduction in crime in Paris during Pixérécourt's triumphal years. Paul Ginisty suggests that for the first time since the early Empire, the police had a deterent stronger than the threat of punishment; that it was 'the memory of beautiful sentiments faultlessly distributed at the Gaîté or at the Ambigu which inspired prudent reflection'.[27] It is difficult to assess and to verify the results of that prudent reflection but it does seem certain that while Pixérécourt's audience wanted to be amused they took their theatre seriously. Hartog surmises that had Pixérécourt ever produced a melodrama in which virtue did not triumph magnificently, there would have been a veritable uproar in the theatre. As naive as that may seem to us today, there is little doubt that the audience seated in the Ambigu-Comique in the early evening of 2 September 1800 fully expected poor Cœlina, cast out of her uncle's house through the unspeakable villainy of Truguelin, to be rewarded for her virtue. And who except the most perverted could identify with the villain or his robot-like henchman? They laughed with the simple hearted peasants; they cried for the horribly mutilated Francisque; they stamped and clapped in the fun-filled finale. It appears that they also thought about the wages of sin. Had they been granted the ability to move ahead in time they would have nodded in silent homage to the playwright lying by himself under his heavy stone. His epitaph reads *Vir Probus* (An upright man).

NOTES

1 René-Charles Guilbert de Pixérécourt, *Théâtre choisi*, 4 vols. (Geneva: Slatkine Reprints, 1971; original edition, Paris: 1841–3), vol. I, p. xvii. Translations of this and other French texts are mine.

2 *Théâtre choisi*, vol. I, p. xxvi.

3 The bookplate is reproduced in André Virely, *René-Charles Guilbert de Pixérécourt, 1773–1844* (Paris: Edouard Rahir, 1909). Virely was Pixérécourt's great-grandson.

4 Edmond Estève, *Etude de littérature préromantique* (Paris: Librarie ancienne, 1923), pp. 142–3.

5 *Théâtre choisi*, vol. II, p. xviii.

6 *Théâtre choisi*, vol. II, p. xv.

7 *Guilbert de Pixerécourt, sa vie, son mélodrame, sa technique et son influence* (Paris: Librarie ancienne, 1913), p. 24.

8 *Théâtre choisi*, vol. II, p. xxviii.

9 *Pixérécourt*, p. 27.

10 Estève, *Littérature préromantique*, p. 166.

11 *Le Mélodrame* (Paris: Louis-Michaud, 1910), pp. 11–13.

12 Hartog, *Pixérécourt*, p. 28.

13 Robert B. Heilman, *Tragedy and Melodrama: Versions of Experience* (Seattle: University of Washington Press, 1968), p. 4.

14 *Melodrama (The Cultural Idiom no. 28)* (London: Methuen, 1973), p. 10.

15 Ibid., p. 11.

16 *The Life of the Drama* (New York: Atheneum, 1974), p. 216.

17 *The Melodramatic Imagination: Balzac, Henry James, Melodrama and the Mode of Excess* (New Haven: Yale University Press, 1976), p. 34.

18 *Théâtre choisi*, vol. IV, p. 493.

19 *Théâtre choisi*, vol. I, p. 111.

20 *Melodramatic Imagination*, p. 15.

21 Ibid., p. 22.

22 Hartog, *Pixerécourt*, p. 35.

23 *Melodramatic Imagination*, p. 32.

24 *Theater and Revolution: the Culture of the French Stage* (New York: Vintage, 1980).

25 Hartog says that at the height of his fame, Pixérécourt was earning 25,000 francs (about 30,000 current dollars) annually from his plays. This was far more than his contemporaries. In addition, he enjoyed a substantial income from theatre management and civil service posts. He seems to have amassed a considerable fortune, but in 1835 a catastrophic fire at the Gaîté, which he had managed for ten years, almost wiped him out. The disaster was a major cause of his decision to return to the country a short time later.

26 Quoted in Hartog (p. 212), from an article by Pixérécourt which appeared in 1832.

27 *Le Mélodrame*, p. 20.

Pixérécourt and the French melodrama debate: instructing boulevard theatre audiences

GABRIELLE HYSLOP

The *Traité du mélodrame*, published in 1817, defined the nineteenth century as the age of 'le triomphe de la chimie et du Mélodrame' (the triumph of chemistry and Melodrama).[1] During the period following the French Revolution, melodrama radically affected both theatre itself and the way the theatre was critically evaluated. The term melodrama was first used to describe plays written for the popular theatres in 1798, and by the early 1800s melodramas were regularly reviewed in such reputable newspapers as *Le Courrier des spectacles* and *Le Journal des débats*. From the very beginning of its history, melodrama was always controversial, deplored by some as morally, politically and artistically subversive and welcomed by others as a source of much needed dramatic reform. The lively debate about melodrama which took place in the press is important because it throws new light on the French theatre at a crucial stage in its development. In this paper I shall examine documents including pamphlets, introductions and prefaces to editions of plays, and newspaper articles in which the controversy over melodrama was aired publicly. My aim is to establish what were the intentions and expectations of those who created and defended this popular genre, what were the dangers its opponents feared, and what were the critical approaches adopted by the people who wrote about this provocative new form of theatre. Both those who praised and those who attacked melodramas focussed on two main issues: (a) its moral and socio-political influence on audiences and (b) its influence on dramatic theory and performance practice. I shall concentrate here on those features of the French melodrama debate which related to the instruction of the public. While this will involve a certain amount of discussion about the artistic nature of melodrama, the debate concerning melodrama's influence on the writing and staging of plays must be dealt with elsewhere. I am not discussing melodrama's actual influence on audiences or on art, but rather the selective arguments presented by playwrights and critics as part of a public debate which often contained a hidden agenda. Within this debate, as in the recent debate about soap operas and blockbuster movies, what is not discussed often reveals the preoccupations and prejudices of the participants as clearly as the discussion itself. Melodrama emerged in post-revolutionary France as a phenomenon which challenged and disrupted people's ideas about the nature of theatre and its function as a form of social control. The debate reveals how commentators sought to come to terms with this disturbing and highly successful new form of popular entertainment.

All theatre takes place within a specific socio-political and cultural context and this context helps to shape the way plays are written, performed and interpreted by audiences. Melodrama was an urban phenomenon, produced in large theatres which could seat enough customers to finance the big budgets necessary to pay for the complicated machinery, many stage hands and large casts of actors, choristers and musicians on which the genre depended. In France the emergence of melodrama coincided with the end of the 1789 Revolution, a very different historical context from that of the Industrial Revolution which accompanied its emergence in England. The theatrical conditions within which early melodrama took place in Paris were also very different from those existing in London. By the turn of the nineteenth century growing numbers of Parisian spectators frequented the theatres in or near the boulevard du Temple where the popular as opposed to establishment drama was presented. The playwrights and critics who were associated with melodrama in post-revolutionary France were mainly educated members of the newly empowered bourgeoisie. Many of them believed that the Boulevard theatres offered one of the few opportunities available at the time for the ruling class to educate the subordinate classes. The active political role which had been played by the common people during the Revolution had alarmed many of the bourgeoisie and they were eager to instruct the boulevard public in those values which they believed were necessary to establish and maintain a new form of stable society. The relationship between those who create theatrical performances and those who pay to see them is always highly complex, and it would be incorrect to imagine that boulevard audiences passively absorbed the lessons which playwrights claimed to be presenting. Popular theatre in nineteenth-century Paris was big business and in order to survive commercially theatres had to satisfy as well as create the particular demands of their public. Playwrights and theatre workers also had to conform to the demands of the government, which changed frequently during melodrama's early years. In 1799 the Directory was replaced by the Consulat which was superseded by the Empire in 1804. In 1815 Napoleon was removed from office and the Bourbon monarchy was restored, only to be ousted by the July Revolution of 1830 which brought Louis Philippe into power. Each of these major political changes was accompanied by public discussion and often by new laws altering the regulation of theatres and plays. Although

censorship and other more subtle restraints prevented boulevard manage-
ments from presenting overtly provocative political material throughout
this turbulent period, changes in government influenced both the
repertoire of the popular houses and the critical responses to that
repertoire.

In analysing the debate about melodrama as instruction I shall focus
my attention upon writings by René-Charles Guilbert de Pixérécourt, who
has been widely referred to as the father of melodrama. More than any
other single playwright he was responsible for establishing not only the
basic conventions of melodrama but also its popularity among spectators
drawn from all sections of society. Pixérécourt began writing plays in 1793
and by the time he retired from public life more than forty years later, he
had written 120 plays, sixty-three of which were melodramas. His works
were successful because apart from his skill as a dramatist, he was also
actively involved in the theatrical developments of his time. He achieved a
high standard of production for his melodramas by directing and stage
managing them himself and introducing a notoriously demanding
approach to rehearsals.[2] Besides writing and producing plays, Pixérécourt
managed the Gaîté and Opéra-Comique theatres and helped to set up a
system of performance rights. He was a staunch advocate of the socio-
political as well as artistic value of melodrama and was a major con-
tributor to the great theatrical debate.

Pixérécourt produced a report (1795) and three articles (1818, 1832 and
1843) in which he argued consistently that the theatre should entertain
and instruct the public. His report, which appears to have been written for
the Ministry of Police in response to the Directory government's concern
about the theatre's influence on public opinion, addressed the general
issue of the theatre's didactic purpose:

> la morale a besoin de points de ralliement, où elle force l'homme à venir
> entendre ses leçons. Les théâtres y sont pour ainsi dire l'analyse, l'extrait des
> vertus, ou politiques ou individuelles, que chaque citoyen doit professer.

> (morality needs rallying points, where men are drawn to come and hear its
> lessons. The theatres are there so to speak to present the distillation, the
> essence of the virtues, either political or personal, which every citizen must
> profess.)[3]

This document argued that the theatre was a particularly important
source of instruction for audiences drawn from the common people. Pixérécourt stated that the establishment theatres such as the Théâtre
Français and the Opéra provided performances which were inappropriate
as instruction or entertainment for audiences who were 'sans éducation',
and that the repertoire available for the subordinate classes in the secondary theatres during the *ancien régime* was deplorable:

Si des grands théâtres nous passons à ceux que fréquentait le peuple, à ceux
que les dédains du gouvernement semblaient lui délaisser par une insultante
pitié pour sa misère, quel cloaque de saletés! quelle boue d'impures inepties!
et sans espoir jamais que la morale publique pût s'en dégager ...

(If we pass on from the major theatres to those frequented by the common
people, those theatres which the government's disdain seemed to abandon to
the people through an insulting pity for their extreme poverty, what a cess-
pool of filth! what foul, muddy stupidities! and never with any hope that
public morality might emerge from them ...)[4]

Pixérécourt's report contains no references to melodrama itself because
the term was not yet used to designate plays, but his later publications
vigorously defended the new genre precisely because it provided a high
quality of theatrical entertainment which was not only accessible to the
common people but also, most importantly, offered them instruction
which he claimed was morally and politically sound.

Apart from writing four pieces about the theatre, Pixérécourt edited a
four-volume *Théâtre choisi* (1841–3), which included twenty-three of his
most important melodramas, together with newspaper reviews of the
plays selected and commentaries on each of them written especially for
this edition by his admiring friends and colleagues. All of these publications reveal how Pixérécourt sought to protect his own reputation by
extolling the virtues of the genre with which he was identified. The arguments he used to convince critics that his particular type of melodrama
was politically and morally respectable provide valuable insights into the
ways that he believed his plays were understood by the public. Pixérécourt's audiences did not necessarily interpret his melodramas in the ways
he intended, but his theories help to explain certain optional readings that
were available to his contemporaries.

Besides Pixérécourt's own contributions to the great theatrical debate,
numerous other pamphlets and newspaper articles which were published
in France during the first forty years of the nineteenth century either
attacked or defended melodrama on moral and aesthetic grounds. In
putting forward their arguments for and against melodrama, early
nineteenth-century commentators were conscious of the fact that they
were taking part in a debate that had a long and well-established tradition
in France. Ever since the sixteenth century, French intellectuals and
artists had been writing about the theatre, its purpose, influence, form,
content and the criteria which should be used to evaluate it. Molière and
Corneille in the seventeenth century and Diderot and Mercier in the
eighteenth century were among those playwrights who defended their
work by appealing to classical precedent, in particular the theories of
Aristotle and Horace, which stated that the dual function of theatre was to
entertain and instruct. By placing melodrama within this larger neoclassi-

cal debate, Pixérécourt and his supporters hoped to establish the respect-ability of a genre which certain critics, such as the conservative writer Alexandre Ricord,[5] regarded as an alarming source of decadence in the French theatre.

Although these appeals to neoclassical authorities were part of a bid for respectability, they were nevertheless based on a genuine committment to the idea that theatre should teach as well as give pleasure. French writers examining theories about art over the previous two centuries had con-stantly addressed the question of the artist's didactic purpose, but this matter was taken especially seriously during Pixérécourt's career which began as the 1789 Revolution ended. The common people had begun to participate directly in public affairs during the Revolution, resorting to violence in the streets in order to fight for better living conditions and demanding direct participation in government. Pixérécourt was a member of the ruling class who regarded this active political role of the common people as highly dangerous and believed that the theatre provided one of the few opportunities for discouraging such behaviour and maintaining law and order. His views were shared by many of his contemporaries. A typical defence of melodrama's stabilising socio-political effect was made in 1839 by the conservative writer, de Pongerville:

> L'influence du mélodrame fut incontestable, et c'est par ses résultats qu'il faut l'apprécier. L'auteur faisait goûter à son public des préceptes d'ordre et de justice ...
> Les services que l'auteur rendait à la morale publique étaient surtout précieux dans ces temps où tout enseignement avait cessé. Le peuple, encore ému des tourmentes révolutionnaires, étonné des changements qui l'en-touraient, avait peine à se reconnaître lui-même ... Le théâtre devint son école. Là se développaient les leçons les plus profitables. Le crime lui apparaissait toujours odieux, et toujours puni; la bonne foi triomphait, l'inno-cence était protégée par une invincible main: enfin, on ne lui montrait pas le monde comme il est, mais bien comme il devrait être.

> (Melodrama's influence was incontestable, and it should be appreciated according to its results. The author made the public enjoy precepts of order and justice ...
> The services which the author rendered to public morality were especially precious at that time when all education had ceased. The common people, still moved by revolutionary torments, astonished by the changes which surrounded them, barely recognised themselves ... The theatre became their school. The most valuable lessons were unfolded there. Crime always appeared odious, and was always punished; sincerity triumphed, innocence was protected by an invincible hand: finally, people were not shown the world as it is, but rather as it should be.)[6]

It is clear from this passage, and from many others which developed similar arguments,[7] that one of the main defences of melodrama was that it provided a much needed form of social control for the potentially dangerous subordinate classes at a crucial stage in French political history.

All participants in the melodrama debate emphasized its socio-political function, but writers who were opposed to the genre put forward the argument that, far from being politically useful as de Pongerville and Nodier maintained, melodrama's pedagogical effects were socially harmful. Ricord's attack, for example, began by condemning melodrama's deletarious influence on audiences as well as on art: 'Le mélodrame est le genre de spectacle le plus pernicieux pour l'art dramatique, pour l'art théâtral et pour le peuple.' (Melodrama is the most pernicious form of theatre in terms of its effect on dramatic art, theatrical art and the common people.)[8] Enemies of melodrama believed that it was responsible for undermining the social hierarchy upon which stability and happiness depended, whereas those who supported it claimed that melodrama reinforced the common people's respect for authority.

Significantly, none of Pixérécourt's contemporaries defended melodrama on the democratic grounds that it encouraged spectators to challenge or even question the hierarchical structure of a society which consisted of different groups with different rights, duties and privileges. It is certainly possible that individual spectators found within the plays themselves representations of class conflict in which oppressed members of the subordinate classes triumphantly overthrew their ruling-class tormentors. For example, in Pixérécourt's *Rosa* (1800), a virtuous fisherman's actions result in the death of the lustful landlord who had abducted his wife and child. For some spectators, *Rosa* may have celebrated a rejection of vicious feudalism in which the landlord exploited his vassals. For others however, the play may have confirmed their faith in a moral system where virtue triumphs over vice. This second reading could have reinforced conservative rather than democratic values by showing that the stable social order which existed at the beginning of the play was purged of its flaws and therefore restored to its 'normal' state of peace and happiness. Spectators may have regarded the villain as either the representative of a hated class, identified with a system of oppression which deserved to be obliterated, or on the other hand he may have been seen as simply a corrupt individual, an aberration from the norm in an otherwise just world order. We cannot know today which of these or any other optional readings the spectators chose because no direct evidence concerning their responses exist. Apart from the material produced by playwrights, critics and their colleagues and friends, no writings survive concerning the interpretations of the plays by the bulk of the boulevard public. What the melodrama debate reveals is that there are no simple answers to the question of how spectators understood the plays and that we need to exercise great care when analysing the political functions of Pixérécourt's works.

Twentieth-century critics have found within melodrama the confirmation of various political positions. Peter Brooks considers that early French melodrama was democratic in content as well as in style:

> in both its audience and its profound subject, it is essentially democratic. It represents a democratization of morality and its signs.
>
> There are other elements as well that define the form's democracy. Villains are remarkably often tyrants and oppressors, those that have power and use it to hurt. Whereas the victims, the innocent and virtuous, most often belong to a democratic universe: whatever their specific class origin, they believe in merit rather than privilege, and in the fraternity of the good. Among the repressions broken through by melodramatic rhetoric is that of class domination, suggesting that a poor persecuted girl can confront her powerful oppressor with the truth about their moral conditions. If the social structure of melodramas often appears inherently feudal – landed gentry or bourgeoisie and their faithful yeomanry – it is also remarkably egalitarian, and anyone who insists upon feudal privileges is bound to be a villain.[9]

Thomas Elsaesser, on the other hand, regards post-revolutionary melodrama as a coercive tool of the newly empowered ruling class:

> Now, with the bourgeoisie triumphant, this form of drama lost its subversive charge and functioned more as a means of consolidating an as yet weak and incoherent ideological position.[10]

This comment, part of Elsaesser's introductory remarks in an article primarily devoted to Hollywood melodrama, appears to reflect a Marxist, perhaps Gramscian approach to the role of popular culture, rather than any specific research into post-revolutionary melodrama. The impressive research carried out by Michèle Root-Bernstein into boulevard theatre before and during the Revolution demonstrates convincingly that even before the triumph of the bourgeoisie, the commercial popular drama was not deliberately subversive although at times it was read subversively by spectators.[11] More work remains to be done on the politics of early melodrama, but the radically different interpretations of the class nature of the genre presented by Brooks, Elsaesser and Root-Bernstein indicate the need for further historical and theoretical research before such a study can produce worthwhile findings.

One of my major objections to the political analysis of melodrama offered by both Brooks and Elsaesser (this criticism does not apply to Root-Bernstein who writes about pre-melodramatic genres) is that they write as if all melodramatists and even all the plays operated in the same way. Moreover, these critics do not take into account the widely varying political positions which were taken up by different members of the boulevard audience. It would be sociologically as well as theatrically naïve to imagine that all spectators reacted alike to any single performance, much less to a whole genre in all its many manifestations over an extended period of social change. What the melodrama debate reveals is that among the ruling-class *critics* at least the response to melodrama was politically conservative. It was embraced by its supporters because it was believed to educate the public, particularly the common people, in bourgeois values. Its opponents feared that it fostered dissatisfaction among the subordinate classes and threatened to undermine the patriarchal family and hence society itself. Just how democratic early French melodrama was is clearly open to question.

Pixérécourt's stated purpose in 'inventing a new theatre' was to satisfy a sense of moral duty: 'C'est avec des idées religieuses et providentielles; c'est avec des sentiments moraux que je me suis lancé dans la carrière épineuse du théâtre.' (It was as a result of religious and providential ideas; it was as a result of moral sentiments that I threw myself into the thorny career of the theatre.)[12] Despite his didactic intentions, however, the newspaper reviews of Pixérécourt's works paid far more attention to recounting the plot and assessing the production of his melodramas than they did to analysing the performances as vehicles of instruction. Of the half a dozen or so reviews which appeared when Pixérécourt's first major success, *Cœlina*, opened in 1800, only one referred to the morality of the play: 'le spectateur attentif forme des vœux pour le triomphe de l'innocence et la punition du crime' (the attentive spectator comes to desire the triumph of innocence and the punishment of crime).[13] This passing reference to the moral outcome of the play hardly raised a major issue, poetic justice being a familiar component of both the contemporary highbrow theatre that was still dominated by the conventions of neoclassicism and of the more popular forms of entertainment found in the boulevard theatres. *Le Pèlerin blanc* (*The White Pilgrim*) (1801) was declared by at least two critics to be 'moral', even 'vraiment moral',[14] but generally the newspapers at the beginning of Pixérécourt's career paid little attention to melodrama and commented barely at all on its didactic function. The most interesting and powerful critic to write about melodrama early in the nineteenth century was Geoffroy, the critic for the prestigious *Journal des Débats*. In his review of *La Femme à deux maris* (1802), he concluded by saying blandly that, 'la première loi du code dramatique moderne ... est de réformer les mœurs et d'inspirer la vertu' (the first law of the modern dramatic code ... is to reform morality and inspire virtuous behaviour),[15] but he usually preferred to discuss the influence of melodrama on dramatic and theatrical art rather than the educative effects it had on spectators' behaviour. The debate over the politics and morality of melodrama began in earnest after the Restoration of the Bourbons.

The marked increase in the number of publications concerning melodrama that appeared after 1815 was primarily the result of the campaign for and subsequent change in government regulations concerning theatre licences and play censorship. A battle between the 'grands' and the 'petits' theatres in Paris had been going on for centuries because the minor theatres constantly threatened to undermine the profits and privileges of the establishment houses, particularly the Théâtre Français and the Opéra. In 1802 Geoffroy had warned that, 'Le boulevard semble être aujourd'hui la grande sphère d'activité de notre poésie dramatique.' (These days the boulevard seems to be the major sphere of activity of our poetic drama.)[16] The popularity of the secondary theatres with well-to-do spectators who were expected to patronize the establishment theatres continued to grow throughout the Empire period and those people eager to protect the dwindling supremacy of the establishment theatres and their repertoires began more and more loudly to express their hostility towards melodrama, which they regarded as a major threat. When the new Bourbon government was installed these defenders of the establishment sought to have even more stringent laws introduced than those restricting the secondary theatres under Napoléon. In 1807 he had limited the number of minor theatres to only four, the Gaîté and the Ambigu-Comique where melodramas were performed, plus the Variétés and the Vaudeville. The repertoire of these theatres was prescribed and all other minor theatres were forced to close.[17] After 1815, despite the conservative establishment's attempts to curb the boulevard theatres and limit the growing popularity of melodrama, pressure from liberal quarters resulted in an increase in the number of minor theatres and an expansion of their repertoire. Melodrama continued to flourish at the Gaîté and the Ambigu, and also at the Porte Saint-Martin which was increasingly identified with the new romantic melodrama. The case presented by the theatrical establishment to protect its financial welfare and prestige against inroads being made by its boulevard rivals was frequently couched in moral terms. The hidden agenda was that melodrama was depriving the Théâtre Français and the Opéra of both artistic supremacy and box office takings. People seeking to protect the profits of the major theatres disguised their self-interested fears by appealing to more respectable arguments.

Pixérécourt himself provided clear evidence that the upsurge in publications debating the advantages and disadvantages of melodrama during the Restoration was the result of the growing popularity of the boulevard theatres and their repertoire, which in turn prompted government moves to investigate theatrical activity. He explained that his pamphlet, ironically titled *Guerre au mélodrame!* (*War on melodrama!*), was prompted in 1818 by a Commission associated with the Académie Française and the Académie des Beaux-arts, set up in order to present to the Minister of the

Interior, 'un rapport sur les moyens de rendre à l'art dramatique et théâtral tout l'éclat dont il est susceptible' (a report on the ways to restore to dramatic and theatrical art all the brilliance of which it is capable).[18] Pixérécourt's defence of melodrama on moral and political grounds encapsulates the arguments used by his side of the debate at that time:

> Je vous ai prouvé, que *sous le rapport des mœurs*, non seulement il est très supérieur à l'ancien répertoire des théâtres secondaires, qui ne serait plus supporté aujourd'hui, mais il exerce une influence utile, puisque l'éternelle morale qu'on y recueille est la récompense des bonnes actions, et la punition des mauvaises; qu'enfin *sous le point de vue politique*, il mérite la bienveillance et la protection du gouvernement, car il concourt d'une manière efficace à l'instruction du peuple.

> (I have proved to you that, *from the point of view of moral behaviour*, not only is it far superior to the former repertoire of the minor theatres, which no one would put up with any more today, but it exercises a useful influence, since the eternal moral learnt from it is the reward for good deeds, and the punishment of bad ones; that moreover *from the political point of view*, it deserves the government's good-will and protection, for it contributes in an efficient manner to the people's education.)[19]

In this document Pixérécourt was bidding for government as well as public support at a time when legislative changes were being planned which were to have a profound effect on the Parisian theatres and hence on the future of melodrama. His case was therefore expressed in terms which associated him with a politically moderate position. From the time of his first theatrical success in 1797, he adopted this careful approach to whatever government was in power.

The opponents of melodrama, however, believed its content was shocking and protested against its iniquitous moral and socio-political influence. Ricord's *Quelques réflexions sur l'art théâtral ... (Some thoughts on theatrical art ...)*, published in the same year as *Guerre au mélodrame!*, is worth quoting at some length because it presents the major socio-political arguments put forward by Pixérécourt's opponents:

> Si l'on ne peut l'exclure [le mélodrame] du théâtre, il est indispensable de ne pas en faire l'apanage d'auteur (à quelques exceptions près), qui, sans expérience de la scène, sans instruction, ignorant même les premiers principes de la langue qu'ils ont la prétention d'écrire, n'offrent dans leurs monstrueuses productions que des tableaux d'assassinats, de trahisons, propres à altérer le respect que l'on doit aux plus grands personnages de la terre, et à déconsidérer aux yeux de la multitude, la classe de laquelle elle attend l'exemple de l'obéissance envers l'autorité, et celui des vertus domestiques et sociales. Pourquoi ne pas supprimer de ces pièces qui semblent toutes avoir été fondues dans le même moule, ces sentences philosophiquement triviales, et qui ne sont bonnes qu'à entretenir cet esprit de vertige qui avait naguère égaré des hommes qui doivent leur temps, leurs travaux, leurs sueurs à leurs familles, au point de leur faire quitter leurs ateliers, abandonner leurs

magasins pour s'entretenir à leur manière, de littérature, de politique, et même de législation. Ah! que le théâtre ne soit plus, pour cette classe intéressante de la société, un double mal, par la perte de son temps et par celle de ses mœurs.

(If it [melodrama] cannot be excluded from the theatre, it is indispensable that authors not be paid homage to (apart from a few exceptions), since they have no experience of the stage, no education, are ignorant even of the first principles of the language in which they have the pretention to write, offer in their monstrous productions nothing but pictures of assassinations and betrayals which serve to undermine the respect due to the important people on earth, and to lessen in the eyes of the multitude, the standing of the class which they expect to act as an example to them of both obedience towards authority and of domestic and social virtue. Why not cut out from these plays which all seem to have been formed in the same mould, those trivial philosophic sayings, which do nothing more than maintain that sense of bewilderment which formerly led astray men who owe their time, their labour, their sweat to their families, so that they were encouraged to leave their workshops, to abandon their shops in order to discuss in their fashion literature, politics and even legislation. Ah! if only the theatre were no longer, for this worthy social class, doubly harmful, wasting their time and undermining their moral behaviour.)[20]

This passage displays the paternalistic attitude towards the needs and taste of boulevard spectators frequently found in commentaries about melodrama's didacticism. Pixérécourt and his allies regarded the values they espoused as universal truths but they shared with their opponents, such as Ricord, a belief that the common people's lack of both formal education and intellectual taste necessitated a form of instruction which was different from that which tragedy provided for the ruling class.

Pixérécourt and the defenders of his plays spent considerable energy elaborating upon the techniques of instruction that were employed by melodramatists, amongst which the most important were concerned with the treatment of *character*, the exploitation of the *emotions* and the style of the *dialogue*. The debate concerning each of these central issues deserves detailed attention as it helps to illuminate our understanding of the approaches to this form of theatre which were adopted by contemporaries.

The relationship between melodrama characters and the audience was a complex one. One of the reasons why melodrama was thought to be a successful educational tool was because the social status of its characters was similar to that of its spectators and these characters were therefore considered likely to have a more direct appeal than the heroic figures of tragedy. In Pixérécourt's report he claimed that eighteenth-century audiences were not given the opportunity to empathize with either the tragic protagonists or their confidants because these characters' experiences were too far removed from the real life of the common people or even of courtiers.[21] He developed this point in *Le Mélodrame* when he argued that one of the great advantages of his plays, for both underprivileged and well-to-do spectators, was that they presented characters and situations with which the public could relate:

> nous éprouvions que nos larmes peuvent couler avec douceur pour d'autres malheurs que ceux d'Oreste et d'Andromache; nous sentions que plus l'action ressemble aux scènes ordinaires de la vie, plus les personnages sont rapprochés de notre condition, plus l'illusion est complète, l'intérêt puissant, et l'instruction frappante.

> (we discovered that our tears can flow gently for other sufferings than those of Orestes or Andromache; we felt that the more the action resembled that of everyday life, the more the characters shared our social condition, the more the illuson was complete, the emotional involvement intense, and the teaching effective.)[22]

We should not deduce from this passage that Pixérécourt's melodramas presented scenes closely resembling the everyday life of his spectators. He was certainly not proposing a realistic approach to characterization along the lines of Zola and Antoine, but he did claim to have created characters who were credible.

Pixérécourt argued that melodrama's virtuous characters operated as models which he hoped his spectators would imitate. His characters were often idealized constructs, celebrations of heroes and heroines from France's past. When justifying his creation of characters drawn from French history rather than fiction, Pixérécourt defended the educational value of his historical and nationalistic subject matter as follows:

> Hé quoi! vous que j'ai vu si chaud partisan des idées libérales, vous ne voulez pas que l'on offre à la classe de la nation qui en a lu plus besoin, de beaux modèles, des actes d'hérösme, des traits de bravoure et de fidélité? vous ne voulez pas qu'on l'instruise à devenir meilleure, en lui montrant, même dans ses plaisirs, de nobles exemples puisés dans nos annales?

> (What! you whom I have known as such a staunch partisan of liberal ideas, don't you want to offer to that class of this nation which has the greatest need of them, admirable models of behaviour, heroic acts, instances of courage and loyalty? don't you wish to teach them to improve, by showing them, even amidst their entertainment, noble examples drawn from our history?)[23]

The anonymous essay of 1825 supported Pixérécourt's view that melodrama should present spectators with heroes from their heritage to admire and emulate.[24] Arnault, who was critical of some of the fictional sources used as the basis for melodramas such as the popular Bibliothèque bleue, fairy tales and 'qui, pis est, des romans nouveaux' (worst of all, contemporary novels), declared that characters drawn from French history were far more uplifting than fairytale figures such as Tom Thumb or Bluebeard.[25]

Pixérécourt's characters were not as far removed from his spectators as those drawn from Greek sources who appeared in neoclassical tragedy, but the exotic and historical settings which predominate in his plays, less than ten per cent of which were set in nineteenth-century urban France, meant that the external reality of Pixérécourt's characters was almost as alien to his spectators as was the external reality of tragic characters. His statement that spectators could relate to his characters appears to be contradicted by the foreign and historical nature of those characters. When we consider the emotional situations in which these characters found themselves, however, we can see that they were familiar to the audience and were in no way exotic or fantastic. Rather than sympathizing with melodrama characters because of their specific social identity, therefore, spectators from all social strata were encouraged to empathize with the virtuous characters' familiar *emotional* situations. De Pongerville believed that the common people were particularly susceptible to this technique of empathetic persuasion, because he claimed that they were, 'naturellement imitateur, facilement entraîné par l'exemple' (natural imitators, easily led by example). According to this commentator, spectators left the theatre with an aversion towards 'la bassesse et l'iniquité' (baseness and iniquity) as profound as their 'sentiment de respect pour les actions généreuses' (feelings of respect for selfless actions).[26] It was principally through their feelings that melodrama spectators were believed to relate to the characters and hence to learn from their vicarious experiences.

Pixérécourt was proud of the entertaining and instructive use he made of emotion in his plays. The woman who participates in the conversation which is presented in *Le Mélodrame* declared, 'Faites-nous pleurer, messieurs, vous serez toujours certains de réussir.' (Make us cry, gentlemen, you will always be sure of success.)[27] This privileging of the power of emotion as an educative technique was regarded as one of the main differences between tragedy and melodrama. The debate highlighted the emotional appeal of melodrama compared to the more intellectual response demanded by tragedy. Alfred de Musset fixed forever the association between melodrama and tears, particularly as shed by women, when he wrote, 'Vive le mélodrame où Margot a pleuré' (Long live melodrama where Margot wept) and Boilly's painting *L'effet du mélodrame* also celebrated this link between melodrama and its overwhelmingly emotional effect, particularly on female spectators. Pixérécourt's audiences like melodrama audiences ever since, enjoyed having a good cry, but for early French writers of this genre, tears and the exhibition of emotion in general were more than just a source of pleasure. Product of the eighteenth-century age of sensibility as he certainly was, Pixérécourt regarded people's ability to express their true feelings as evidence of their virtue. The criticism of actors which is contained in his Report indicates how morally significant Pixérécourt considered people's emotional expression to be in everyday life. He condemned male and female actors because they were, 'obligés chaque jour de feindre tous les sentiments, et par conséquent blasés sur le crime comme sur la vertu' (obliged every day to disguise all their feelings, and as a result become insensitive to crime as well as to virtue).[28] In the theatre, the emotional states of the characters, made utterly explicit through the dialogue and the externalized acting style, were intended to reveal their moral identity and to reinforce the moral teachings of the plays. A typical example of Pixérécourt's use of emotional signals to identify and celebrate virtue occurs during the recognition scene between the passionate heroine and the disguised hero in *L'Homme à trois visages* (*The Man with Three Faces*) (1801). Rosemonde expresses herself 'avec beaucoup d'émotion et d'amertume' and 'avec la plus profonde sensibilité' (with much emotion and bitterness [and] with deepest feeling) and Vivaldi is forced to reveal his true identity as her long absent husband because he is overwhelmed by pity and love: 'Je ne puis résister à ses larmes ... Mon secret m'échappe malgré moi.' (I cannot resist her tears ... My secret escapes in spite of my efforts.) (II, 6) Villains in Pixérécourt's melodramas typically displayed emotions intended to warn spectators of the disastrous consequences of wicked behaviour for the villains themselves. Whether they appeared consumed with hatred and an implacable desire for revenge like Orsano in *L'Homme à trois visages* or wracked with terror and remorse like Truguelin in act III of *Cœlina*, villains delivered the unmistakable lesson that the sufferings caused by evil were no less painful for those who initiated those sufferings than they were for their victims.

It would be misleading to oversimplify the complex use of emotions in Pixérécourt's works and the audience's response to their appeal. What the debate reveals is a widespread belief among the critics that moral identity was both reflected and reinforced through emotional expression and that this applied as much to spectators as it did to fictional characters. Melodrama's inheritance from eighteenth-century notions of sensibility is clearly apparent in the view that audiences could be morally improved as a result of the feelings they allowed themselves to experience during a melodrama. Charles Nodier referred to this process in his introduction to Pixérécourt's *Théâtre choisi* when he explained the salutary effect of melodramatic emotion on spectators:

> la représentation de ces ouvrages vraiment classiques, dans l'acception élémentaire du mot, dans celle qui se rapporte aux influences morales de l'art, n'inspirait que des idées de justice et d'humanité, ne faisait naître que des émulations vertueuses, n'éveillait que de tendres et généreuses sympathies, et qu'on en sortait rarement sans se trouver meilleur.
>
> (the performance of these truly classical works, in the basic meaning of the

word which relates to the moral influence of art, inspired only ideas of justice and humanity, engendered only virtuous emulation, aroused only tender and generous feelings, and people rarely left such performances without being improved.)[29]

Nodier even went as far as claiming that the beneficial effects of melodrama's appeal to the emotions was responsible for a decline in the crime rate:

> en aucun temps, la classe qui la [cette puissante action de la comédie populaire] subissait immédiatement n'a été plus régulière dans ses mœurs, jamais les crimes n'ont été plus rares . . .
> . . . Dirai-je encore une fois que le crime n'a jamais été plus rare, surtout dans les classes inférieures? C'est que les classes inférieurs allaient chercher alors au spectacle des émotions qui étaient toujours sans dangers, qui étaient souvent salutaires . . .

> (at no other time has the class which submitted directly to the powerful action of popular drama been better behaved morally, never has crime been more rare . . .
> . . . May I say again that crime has never been more rare, especially among the lower classes? At that time the lower classes sought in the theatre emotions which were never dangerous, which were often salutory . . .)[30]

Particularly after the Restoration, crime was considered to be a major problem in French cities, and Nodier's use of this defence of melodrama was directed towards his readers' well-known fear of and interest in the rising crime rate.

A couple of years before the publication of the *Théâtre choisi*, the conservative writer Auger also acknowledged the emotional power of melodrama and recognized that this was central to its success with the common people. Unlike Nodier, he argued that the exploitation of excessive emotions in the theatre could produce socially harmful effects:

> c'est principalement sur le peuple que le théâtre agit et peut agir avec toute sa puissance: les facultés neuves de l'artisan sont facilement excitées; il saisit tout avec passion; il veut des impressions, il en demande au mélodrame, et, loin de profiter de cette disposition favorable et de répondre à cette confiance, on l'enivre, on l'empoisonne; on spécule sur sa bonne volonté à s'instruire.

> (it is mainly on the common people that the theatre acts and can act with all its power: the raw nerves of the artisan are easily stimulated; he grasps everything passionately; he wants to be impressed, he demands all this of melodrama, and, far from profiting from this favourable disposition and responding to this trust, melodrama intoxicates him, poisons him; the people's willingness to be instructed is taken advantage of.)[31]

Auger declared that melodramatists of the late 1830s used the theatre to inculcate dangerous political ideas in the spectator: 'il rêve un monde qu'il ne peut atteindre, et qui d'ailleurs n'existe pas' (he dreams of a world he can never attain, and which moreover doesn't exist).[32] Auger's paternalistic attitude towards the subordinate classes appears to have reflected a bourgeois fear of popular uprisings which was increasingly evident in the period leading up to the 1848 Revolution.

Pixérécourt had expressed a form of anxiety similar to Auger's more than forty years earlier, making a direct connection between audiences' emotional responses provoked within the theatre and their behaviour in the street. In his Report he commented on the ease with which different factions manipulated the theatrical public's emotions, and consequently their beliefs and behaviour, during the period of the Terror and the Convention.[33] His later discussions about the emotional impact of melodrama mentioned only its positive aspects. In 1832 he even asserted that emotionally and morally melodrama was more powerful and benefic-ial than tragedy:

> je préfère le mélodrame à la tragédie: j'y trouve plus de vérité, plus d'intérêt, plus d'entente de la scène, et surtout plus de naturel. Il me touche, m'émeut, m'attendrit; ce qu'il me retrace rentre dans les habitudes de la vie ordinaire, tandis que les grandes infortunes vraies ou supposées de ces héros montés sur des échasses et parlant un langage emphatique me laissent au moins indifférente.

> (I prefer melodrama to tragedy; I find it more truthful, more appealing, more theatrically skilful, and above all more natural. It touches me, stirs me, moves me; what it enacts for me becomes part of my behaviour in everyday life, whereas the great misfortunes true or otherwise of those heroes up on their stilts and speaking a bombastic language leave me at best indifferent.)[34]

Neither critics nor playwrights appear to have considered the possibility that spectators, swayed by melodrama's strong emotional appeal, applauded particular political or moral attitudes during a performance without necessarily incorporating these attitudes into their everyday life outside the theatre.

Although Pixérécourt was critical of the 'bombastic language' of tra-gedy, in his own plays he exploited a heightened style of writing as a means of externalizing the characters' emotional states and appealing to the spectators' feelings. One of the main criticisms levelled at melodrama was that its style was overblown, but a study of the debate reveals that there was a wide range of opinion concerning this matter. Pixérécourt shared Arnault's view that, 'l'emphase ridicule du style' (a ridiculously pompous style)[35] can exist in bad melodramas as well as bad tragedies, but he also argued that his own melodramas were free from these stylistic faults. He claimed that his writing had, 'un style naturel ... un style convenable', 'un style simple et vrai' (a natural style ... an appropriate style, a simple and truthful style).[36] Auger, like Pixérécourt, argued that, 'un langage pur sans prétention' (a pure and unpretentious style)[37] was necessary in order for drama to have an impact on the common people, but he was critical of early melodrama, including Pixérécourt's, stating with full elitist conviction that, 'Sans doute le style était ridicule, mais le peuple n'est pas un juge littéraire ... et il comprend bien ce qu'on veut lui dire.' (Undoubtedly the style was ridiculous, but the people have no literary judgement ... and accept anything you want to tell them.)[38]

Nodier, hardly less patronizing towards the boulevard public than Auger, agreed that popular theatre required dialogue that could be understood by everyone. Unlike his friend Pixérécourt, however, Nodier claimed that melodrama's style was neither simple nor natural. On the contrary, he pointed out that such an approach would not have satisfied the common people, particularly in the period just after the 1789 Revolution:

> On se tromperait beaucoup si on croyait le peuple fort susceptible de s'émouvoir aux beautés simples et naturelles du style. Il ne l'est point et ne l'a peut-être jamais été. A l'époque dont je parle, il aurait regardé ces mots du cœur dont nous faisons tant d'estime, comme un outrage indirect à son intelligence; il aurait réclamé ce qu'il regardait, lui, comme de l'éloquence et de la poésie, la phrase redondante et parée, la phrase gonflée d'épithètes et de figures.

> (It would be a great mistake to think that the people are truly susceptible to being moved by simple and natural felicities of style. They are certainly not and they probably never have been. At the time of which I am speaking, they would have regarded those heartfelt expressions which we value so highly as an indirect insult to their intelligence; they would have called for what they regarded as eloquence and poetry, in other words archaic and decorated sentences, sentences stuffed with epithets and figures of speech.)[39]

According to Nodier the people's appropriation of 'l'élocution emphatique' (pompous delivery) was the result of 'la période oratoire' (the period of oratory) which they experienced during the Revolution. Because of their strong diet of impassioned rhetoric, the only style the melodrama public appreciated was, 'une phraséologie creuse, mais sonore, dont le retentissement était devenu une habitude et un besoin' (a phraseology that was hollow but sonorous, with a reverberation that had become a habit and a necessity).[40] The *Traité du mélodrame*, although adopting a far less serious tone than Nodier's, confirmed his view that melodrama audiences demanded a heightened form of dialogue. The authors provided caricatured examples of moral sayings expressed in the embellished style typical of the genre: 'L'oreiller du remords est rembourré d'épines', 'La noirceur du crime ne peut être effacé que par le savon du repentir', 'La femme est une fleur intermédiaire entre le lys et la rose' and 'Le sentiment est la soupape de l'âme' (The pillow of remorse is stuffed with thorns, The foulness of crime can only be washed clean by the soap of repentance, Woman is a flower halfway between the lily and the rose, and Feelings are the safety-valve of the soul).[41] These parodies of the inflated style and clichéd platitudes contained in melodrama aphorisms did not discourage playwrights from continuing to make use of this explicit form of verbal teaching.

An examination of Pixérécourt's melodramas reveals that in fact they contain a variety of modes of speech, including the simple and natural as well as the heightened and rhetorical. The dialogue established differences between character types and depicted alterations in their emotional states. Pixérécourt's complex style remained consistent throughout his long career, despite the fact that other writers such as Ducange adopted an increasingly realistic and uniform style. *Latude*, which was Pixérécourt's last great melodrama, was greeted with enthusiasm by critics and audiences alike when it opened in 1834. As well as sections of dialogue written in the style of simple conversation, this classical melodrama contains poetic aphorisms typical of the early plays, such as, 'Ainsi va le monde! la fortune jette les lots ... ramasse qui peut' (That's the way of the world! chance throws the dice ... gather them up who can) (1, 2). This mixture of styles resulted in dialogue that was intelligible to all members of the audience, and at the same time satisfied their need for something more than the mundane. It was precisely this combination of the familiar and the exotic, the everyday and the strange, which made Pixérécourt popular with audiences drawn from all sections of society.

Much of the debate concerning the moral and socio-political teachings of melodrama ignored the presence in the auditorium of the well-to-do, and centred instead upon the needs of the common people as they were perceived by the ruling-class playwrights and critics. Pixérécourt is alleged to have said, 'J'écris pour ceux qui ne savent pas lire' (I write for people who can't read) and it is certainly true that he aimed to instruct and entertain 'le peuple'. This does not mean, however, that melodrama audiences consisted of the poverty-stricken, illiterate inhabitants of the poorer districts of Paris or the major provincial cities. Theatres were required by law to give free performances on public holidays such as 14 July and 15 August, and on these occasions the audiences appear to have included large, unruly crowds of people who could not normally afford to attend but who nevertheless enjoyed what was offered. The very poor were neither alienated nor totally excluded from the boulevard theatres, but as McCormick explains, they simply did not have the money to pay for tickets:

> Even the 50 or 60 centimes for the paradis of the Gaîté or Ambigu in the first half of the century would have been a heavy demand on any family in which the father earned only 2 francs a day, an average labourer's wage.[42]

Although the family income may have been higher than two francs a day because many women earned money by working inside or outside the home,[43] McCormick's comments remain valid. When we consider the cost of seats elsewhere in the house it is clear that tickets were not only beyond the reach of the very poor but that many spectators must have been relatively well-to-do. Thomasseau includes the following reference to boulevard ticket prices in about 1805: 'M. Bobêche était tout enthousiasmé de ce qu'il ne lui en coûtait que six francs pour voir six actes entre sept personnes qu'ils étaient.' (Mr Bobêche was absolutely delighted because it only cost him six francs for seven people to see six acts.)[44] Bobêche purchased tickets for three adults and four children, the equivalent of five full-price tickets. This means that an adult's seat at that time cost 1.20 francs, a sum equal to more than half one day's wage for an average labourer. In order to understand who actually constituted melodrama's public, we need to establish what Pixérécourt and his contemporaries meant by 'le peuple'.

As a social category, 'le peuple' was a loosely defined group which included people who were comfortably off and had received more than a basic education as well as those who were poor and illiterate. Pixérécourt's own writings, besides referring to melodrama audiences as the common people, used more specific terms on two occasions, describing his spectators as, 'l'artisan, le commis, le marchand' (the artisan, the shopkeeper, the salesperson) and later, 'le boutiquier, l'artisan, l'ouvrier' (the shopkeeper, the artisan, the worker).[45] Artisans encompassed a major social group within 'le peuple'. The range of property owned and education received by different members of this group was considerable as artisans included master craftsmen who owned their own shops, journeymen who were qualified craftsmen receiving day wages by working for a master, and apprentices who were learning a trade. That Pixérécourt's audiences included members of the common people who were able to read and to pay for copies of his plays is evident from the following comment:

> Le mélodrame a épuré le langage du peuple qui, après l'avoir vu jouer, le loue, moyennant deux sous, et le lit jusqu'à ce qu'il le sache par cœur.
>
> (Melodrama has purified the language of the common people who, after seeing it performed, borrow it for two pennies, and read it until they know it by heart.)[46]

Although the apprentices and servants who sat in the gods may have been illiterate and poor, a considerable number of Pixérécourt's spectators had learnt how to read, could afford to pay the library lending fee or even to buy outright the published editions of the plays which were on sale, and had time to read them more than once. The widely held view that early melodrama was patronized mainly by members of the most depressed groups in society is not supported by the evidence.

From very early in the nineteenth century, as the debate reveals, melodrama audiences included growing numbers of wealthy, ruling-class people. In 1804 the review in the *Gazette de France* of Pixérécourt's *Tékéli* began by stating, 'Il commence à devenir de mode de fréquenter les spectacles des boulevards' (It is beginning to become fashionable to frequent the boulevard theatres).[47] A few years later Geoffroy confirmed that this was the case when he commented that 'L'affluence des spectateurs au boulevard est une chose simple et naturelle ... On ne va point aux pièces du boulevard parce que j'en parle; mais j'en parle parce qu'on y va' (The crowds of spectators at the boulevard is a simple, natural thing ... People don't go to see boulevard plays because I talk about them; but I talk about them because people go to them).[48] Geoffroy was clearly referring to well-to-do spectators who also read his highbrow column. Pixérécourt himself was proud of the fact that his plays had attracted 'un grand nombre de spectateurs' away from the establishment theatres:

> [Le mélodrame] n'est donc pas si mauvais, puisqu'une partie de la bonne compagnie est venue le chercher là, et je crois, soit dit entre nous, que son plus grand tort est d'avoir su plaire.

> ([Melodrama] then is not so bad, because part of high society has sought it out, and I believe, between ourselves, that its greatest fault is that it is so entertaining.)[49]

By the time he wrote *Le Mélodrame*, his defence of his plays was even more strongly associated with their success among audiences extending beyond the common people. One of the speakers in the dialogue which Pixérécourt presented in this pamphlet was 'une dame jeune et belle qui cultive les arts avec succès' (a beautiful young woman who successfully cultivates the arts) and she argued passionately on Pixérécourt's behalf that melodrama deserved respect because of its popularity among ruling-class spectators:

> il me semble que vous avez été trop modeste en faisant au peuple les honneurs exclusifs de ce genre. La bonne société l'aime aussi et le recherche avec empressement.

> (it seems to me that you have been too modest in claiming that the common people are the only ones to benefit from this genre. High society loves it too and flocks to it with enthusiasm.)[50]

It is important to define the class composition and cultural expectations of Pixérécourt's public if we are to understand who he was really writing for and how he expected his plays to be received. The debate reveals that melodrama's popularity with all sections of society was regarded by its defenders as a strength and by its opponents as a threat.

As I noted earlier, we know very little about the ways Pixérécourt's public interpreted his melodramas. A well-to-do member of the audience may well have demanded the confirmation of a reality quite different from that sought by a less privileged spectator. Pixérécourt's audiences included different social groups with a broad range of desires and fears and a variety of social and theatrical experience, all of which helped to determine the readings arrived at by each spectator. Recent studies of audience responses to television soap operas have shown how immensely complex and subjective is the spectator's interpretation of drama in performance.[51] The debate constantly referred to a variety of ways that Pixérécourt's audiences read his plays in the theatre or on the page. Playwrights and critics continually acknowledged the need to protect the more vulnerable members of the boulevard public from potentially harmful dramatic entertainment. The most vulnerable spectators were considered to be those with the least social, economic and educational status, but the social group which Pixérécourt regarded as needing the most careful moral protection was the entire female population.

In *Guerre au mélodrame!* he was particularly keen to point out that male heads of households could take their young wives and daughters to see his plays without worrying about them being offended. He was proud of the fact that the nature of the entertainment and instruction he provided, as well as its relatively modest cost, meant that his plays were suitable as family entertainment. Pixérécourt referred to the need to protect women from the pernicious influence of those plays which he regarded as 'graveleux' (smutty):

> Un père sage, un mari prudent doit éviter avec soin tout ce qui peut éveiller l'imagination ou donner trop d'activité aux sens, et je soutiens qu'il ne peut aujourd'hui conduire sa fille ou sa jeune épouse au spectacle, sans avoir vu d'avance les pièces que l'on y représente.

> (A wise father, a prudent husband should carefully avoid anything which might stir up the imagination or overstimulate the senses, and I maintain that he cannot take his daughter or young wife to the theatre today, without first having seen the plays being performed.)[52]

According to Pixérécourt, the only theatrical entertainment suitable for a modest young woman at this time was to be found in the melodrama theatres: 'car c'est là seulement qu'elle pouvait ... trouver la morale unie à l'intérêt, à des idées nationales, et au plaisir des yeux' (for it is only there that she can ... find morality combined with appeal, patriotism and visual pleasure).[53] Little work has been done on the response of female spectators to nineteenth-century French melodrama. Just as it would have been possible for spectators to read *Rosa* as either an attack on feudalism or a defence of the social status quo, so it may have been possible for a female spectator to interpret that heroine's situation as either a vindication of her own feminine vulnerability or as a confirmation of her own courage and power. Pixérécourt's theoretical works prove that he was a staunch believer in patriarchy and was particularly concerned about the theatre's influence on 'the weaker sex'. When he wrote his 'Dernières réflexions' he argued that, 'les mères de famille ont déserté les spectacles où les jeunes filles ne pouvaient plus se présenter sans scandale et sans danger' (mothers with children have deserted the theatre where young women can no longer be seen without risk of scandal and danger).[54] This state of affairs, according to Pixérécourt, was caused by romantic plays, a new form of melodrama with which he in no way wished to be associated.

Pixérécourt and his supporters believed that all melodrama was didactic, but they did not defend the teaching transmitted through all types of melodrama. In his two theoretical works published after the triumph of *Hernani* on the stage of the Comédie Française in 1830, Pixérécourt condemned 'romantic melodrama' as stridently as Ricord had condemned his own plays some years before. Both *Le Mélodrame* and 'Dernières réflexions' made a clear distinction between his own 'mélodrame classique' and the more recent 'genre romantique'.[55] Pixérécourt's attack on the romantics was mounted primarily on moral grounds: 'On a battu toutes les routes du vice et du crime, épuisé toutes les ressources de l'absurde et de l'inconnu, toutes les combinaisons ridicules et atroces.' (They have marked out the highways of vice and crime, exhausted all the resources of the absurd and the unknown, all combinations of the ridiculous and the atrocious.)[56] In 1832 Pixérécourt expected that this new school led by wild young men would not last long but in fact it continued to flourish throughout the rest of his life. In 'Dernières réflexions' he contrasted the morality of his own output with what he considered to be the shocking material presented by the romantics:

> Jadis on choisissait seulement ce qui était bon; mais dans les drames modernes, on ne trouve que des crimes monstrueux qui révoltent la morale et la pudeur. Toujours et partout l'adultère, le viol, l'inceste, le parricide, la prostitution, les vices les plus éhontés, plus sales, plus dégoûtants l'un que l'autre.

> (Formerly people chose only that which was good; but in these modern dramas we find nothing but monstrous crimes which revolt our sense of morality and modesty. Always and everywhere there is adultery, rape, incest, parricide, prostitution, each vice more shameless, filthy and disgusting than the next.)[57]

Pixérécourt vehemently dissociated himself from these 'pièces romantiques, c'est-à-dire, mauvaises, dangereuses, immorales, dépourvues d'intérêt et de vérité' (romantic plays, that is to say, bad, dangerous, immoral, devoid of any appeal or truth), and he declared emphatically that, 'Ce n'est donc pas moi qui ai établi le genre romantique.' (It's certainly not I who invented the romantic genre.)[58] This statement resulted partly from his criticism of the aesthetics of romanticism but reflected primarily his objections to its moral teachings.

Throughout his career Pixérécourt's own writings revealed that he believed melodrama was a force for good in French society. From 1795 until 1843 all his theoretical works showed that he was firmly committed to theatre which offered moral and political teaching accessible to the common people. That the didactic function of melodrama was taken very seriously by his contemporaries, whether they attacked or defended the plays, is clear from an examination of the great debate which took place in post-revolutionary France. What needs to be carried out now is a detailed analysis of individual plays within their specific socio-political and theatrical contexts, in the light of the issues raised during the melodrama debate. Only then can we begin to establish the full impact of this controversial genre on the new society which emerged in France at the end of the eighteenth century.

NOTES

1 A!A!A! [Abel Hugo, Armand Malitourne and Jean Ader], *Traité du mélodrame* (Paris: Delaunay, 1817), p. 2. All translations are my own.

2 See Oscar Brockett, 'Pixérécourt and Unified Production', *Educational Theater Journal*, 9: 3 (1960), 181–7.

3 Pixérécourt's Report, *Observations sur l'état où se trouvaient les théâtres avant la Révolution, sur l'effet qu'elle a produit sur eux, sur l'influence que la tyrannie de Robespierre a eue sur les spectacles, et nécessairement de [sic] l'influence qu'ils ont à leur tour exercée sur le peuple, enfin sur leur situation actuelle*, is reproduced as an appendix in Edmond Estève, *Etudes de Littérature préromantique* (Paris: Champion, 1923), pp. 201–23.

4 Report, p. 207. Pixérécourt reiterated the same idea in his *Guerre au mélodrame!* (Paris, 1818), p. 19, when he compared what he regarded as the deplorable theatrical situation before the Revolution with the moral improvements which had taken place by the early Restoration: 'Il faudrait être bien morose ou bien mauvaise foi pour ne pas apprécier la différence qui existe entre le répertoire actuel des théâtres secondaires, et les pièces licencieuses que l'on y représentait dans ma jeunesse pour amuser les libertins qui s'y rendaient de tous les coins de la Capitale. Il y a, j'en conviens, beaucoup de Mélodrames insignifians, ennuyeux même, mais au moins ils sont sans danger pour les mœurs.' (You'd have to be really gloomy or else misguided not to appreciate the difference that exists between the present repertoire of the minor theatres, and the licentious plays that were presented there during my youth to amuse the libertines who gathered there, drawn from all corners of the capital. There are, I concede, many insignificant, even boring, Melodramas, but at least they do not endanger moral behaviour.)

5 Alexandre Ricord, *Quelques réflexions sur l'art théâtral* ... (Paris: Petit, 1818).

6 *Théâtre choisi*, vol. I, pp. 163–4.

7 See especially *Traité du mélodrame*; the anonymous 'Essai sur Le Mélodrame', *Chefs-d'œuvre des mélodrames* (Paris, 1825), vol. I, pp. i–vii; and Charles Nodier, 'Introduction', *Théâtre choisi*, vol. I, pp. i–xvi.

8 Ricord, *Réflexions*, p. 13.

9 Peter Brooks, *The Melodramatic Imagination* (New Haven: Yale University Press, 1976), p. 44.

10 Thomas Elsaesser, 'Tales of Sound and Fury. Observations on the Family Melodrama', *Monogram* (1973), pp. 2–15.

11 See Michèle Root-Bernstein, *Boulevard Theater and Revolution in Eighteenth-Century Paris* (New York: UMI Research Press, 1984), especially part II, 'The Dramatic Idiom and Literature of the Boulevard Stage', pp. 79–133.

12 Pixérécourt, 'Dernières réflexions de l'auteur sur Le Mélodrame', *Théâtre choisi*, vol. IV, p. 493.

13 *Théâtre choisi*, vol. I, p. 10.

14 *Théâtre choisi*, vol. I, pp. 79–80.

15 Julien Louis Geoffroy, *Cours de littérature dramatique* (Paris: Blanchard, 1825), vol. VI, p. 94.

16 Ibid., p. 88.

17 Maurice Albert, *Les Théâtres des boulevards (1789–1848)* (Paris, 1902), 220–35. The Porte Saint-Martin, which posed the greatest threat to the establishment theatres because of its elaborate facilities and sophisticated repertoire, reopened in 1809 only to be closed again in 1812. As a result of Napoleon's 1807 decree the other boulevard theatres, so-called because they were situated along or near the boulevard du Temple, were converted into cafés, rooms for balls and banquets or circuses.

18 *Guerre au mélodrame!*, p. 3.

19 Ibid., p. 33. Pixérécourt's italics.

20 Ricord, *Réflexions*, p. 14.

21 *Observations*, pp. 205–6.

22 Pixérécourt, *Le Mélodrame* (Paris, 1832), pp. 341–2.

23 *Guerre au mélodrame!*, pp. 17–18. Similar ideas are expressed in *Le Mélodrame*, p. 342. Among Pixérécourt's best-known characters drawn from French history are those found in *Charles-le-Téméraire* (1814) and *Latude* (1834).

24 'Essai sur Le Mélodrame', p. ii.

25 Antoine Vincent Arnault, 'Du mélodrame', *Œuvres Critiques philosophiques et littéraires* (Paris, 1827), vol. VII, pp. 349–50.

26 *Théâtre choisi*, vol. I, p. 164.

27 *Le Mélodrame*, p. 347.

28 *Observations*, p. 215.

29 Nodier, 'Introduction', p. iii.

30 Ibid., pp. iii, v–vi.

31 Hippolyte Nicolas Just Auger, *Physiologie du théâtre* (Paris: Firmin Didot, 1839), vol. II, p. 66.

32 Ibid., p. 65.

33 *Observations*, p. 214.

34 *Le Mélodrame*, pp. 345–6.

35 Arnault, 'Du mélodrame', p. 347.

36 *Guerre au mélodrame!*, pp. 9 and 22 and 'Dernières réflexions . . .', p. 493.

37 Auger, *Physiologie du théâtre*, p. 102.

38 Ibid., pp. 56–7.

39 Nodier, 'Introduction', pp. ix–x.

40 Ibid., p. xi.

41 *Traité du mélodrame*, pp. 33–4. See also the chapter on style, pp. 56–65.

42 John McCormick, *Melodrama Theatres of the French Boulevard* (New York: Chadwyck-Healey, 1982), p. 22.

43 See Joan W. Scott and Louise A. Tilly, 'Women's Work and the Family in Nineteenth-century Europe', in *The Family in History*, ed. Charles E. Rosenberg (Philadelphia: University of Pennsylvania Press, 1975), pp. 145–78.

44 *Les Aventures plaisantes de Bobêche*, quoted in Jean-Marie Thomasseau, 'Le Mélodrame sur les scènes parisiennes de Coelina (1800) à L'Auberge des Adrets (1823)' (thesis, University of Aix en Provence, 1973), p. 469.

45 *Guerre au mélodrame!*, p. 18 and *Le Mélodrame*, p. 343.

46 *Le Mélodrame*, p. 340.

47 *Théâtre choisi*, vol. I, p. 436.

48 Geoffroy, *Littérature dramatique*, pp. 62–3.

49 *Guerre au mélodrame!*, pp. 20–1.

50 *Le Mélodrame*, p. 345. In the 1820s the royal family visited the boulevard theatres, increasing further the resentment of the 'grands théâtres'. See Albert, *Théâtres des boulevards*, pp. 281–2.

51 See for example Ien Ang, *Watching Dallas. Soap opera and the melodramatic imagination* (London: Methuen, 1985).

52 *Guerre au mélodrame!*, p. 23.

53 Ibid., p. 24.

54 'Dernières réflexions', p. 498.

55 *Le Mélodrame*, p. 342 and 'Dernières réflexions', p. 499.

56 *Le Mélodrame*, p. 351.

57 'Dernières réflexions', pp. 497–8.

58 Ibid., pp. 498–9.

Pixérécourt's early melodramas and the political inducements of neoplatonism*

BRUCE A. MCCONACHIE

Critics and historians have noted the religious function of nineteenth-century melodramatic theatre. Commenting on performances of the plays Guilbert de Pixérécourt during the Napoleonic period before the widespread re-establishment of Catholicism in France, romantic critic Charles Nodier stated, 'I have seen them, in the absence of religious worship, take the place of the silent pulpit.' Recent scholarship on Pixérécourt, whose melodramatic formulas established the conventions and dominated the popularity of the genre in the West for the first third of the century, has examined his plays' conservative political ideology, their legitimation of patriarchal gender roles, and their formal similarity to the dynamics of the Terror during the French Revolution.[1] Surprisingly, scholars have yet to investigate the implicit theology of Pixérécourt's early melodramas, despite the relevance of the plays' religious orientation to their ideology. As the following discussion will demonstrate, Pixérécourt's melodramas during the Napoleonic period propagated an uneasy fusion of traditional Christian faith and popularized neoplatonism which wrapped traditional notions of social hierarchy in a mantle of mysticism. The religious orientation of his plays pushed beyond conservatism, however, to induce in his spectators a thoroughgoing rejection of the modern world and the enlightenment precepts of materialism, rationality, and individual freedom on which modernity is based.

During his prodigious theatrical career from 1800 to 1834 as a playwright, director, and manager, Pixérécourt put together over a hundred and twenty plays, the majority of them melodramas. Of these, *Cælina, or The Child of Mystery* (1800), *The Man With Three Faces* (1801), and *The Dog of Montargis, or The Forest of Bondy* (1814) are representative of Pixérécourt's Napoleonic plays, displaying minor variations within fairly consistent conventions. *Cælina*, accepted by most theatre historians as the progenitor of nineteenth-century melodrama, tells the story of a young girl's quest to wed her beau and save her true father from villainous

---

* A draft of this paper was read at the *Themes in Drama* International Conference held at the University of California, Riverside, in February 1990.

persecution. Pixérécourt based *The Man With Three Faces* on the German drama *Abelino* (1793) by Johann Zschokke. His reworking of the play – a romantic costume-piece replete with conspirators, outlaws, and disguises – into conformity with his own ideology reveals the extent to which his melodramatic vision departed from that of early romanticism. Pixérécourt termed *The Dog of Montargis* a 'melodrame historique' since his source for the story was popular history. It's actually closer to a murder mystery, focusing on a dog who 'identifies' his dead master's killer. These three plays are typical examples of Pixérécourt's early period of melodramatic writing.[2]

Pixérécourt stated that he wrote for 'people who cannot read'. Lower-class illiterates may have constituted a small part of his audience, but it was primarily the bourgeoisie who patronized the boulevard theatres specializing in melodrama. During the Revolution, many more working- and middle-class patrons had attended these playhouses than before 1789. After 1800, returning emigrés, the richer bourgeoisie, and increasing numbers of soldiers swelled the ranks of this theatre-going public – an audience which continued to flock to 'the boulevard of crime' even after the re-establishment of the Théâtre-Français as a subsidized state theatre by the Emperor in 1807. Recalled one actor of the period, 'The ladies of new France led the charge [to the Boulevard]. They'd rent a box for the season in our Théâtre-Français where they would come and spend an hour or two in order to flash their jewels; but on the outlying boulevards were the houses they preferred. There, for a nominal sum, they could get their thrice-weekly ration of catastrophe, fire, and carnage.' Even the Empress Josephine would sneak off to a house of melodrama while her husband was away, much to Napoleon's disgust. Apparently many spectators, whatever their political affiliations during the Revolution, enjoyed reliving the thrills and terrors of the past decade as long as they could come safely home to a stable polity at the end of their theatrical journey. According to Nodier, 'The entire people had just enacted in the streets and on the public squares the greatest drama of all time. Everyone had been an actor in this bloody play ... These spectators who smelled gunpowder and blood required emotions analogous to those from which they had been cut off by the re-establishment of order.'[3]

Pixérécourt supplied the emotional jolts his spectators sought, but avoided the subject of the Revolution. In part because of censorship restrictions, his plays side-step situations which involve mere political conflicts and resolutions to focus on actions which require transcendental intervention. As critic Peter Brooks notes, there's a 'cosmic ambition' at the heart of Pixérécourt's melodrama. But what is the theological nature of this ambition? Some theatre historians have identified nineteenth-century melodrama as an embodiment of Manichaeism, the middle-eastern religion in which good and evil cosmic forces fight as equals over the course of human history.[4]

Certainly evil carries great influence in the material world of Pixérécourt's plays, but these melodramas insist that God will eventually right all wrongs. The heroine's prayer in *The Man With Three Faces*, 'I offer thee thanks, oh Providence' (p. 228), echoes through *Cœlina* and *The Dog of Montagis* as well. In the latter play when a kindly innkeeper tells an innocent mute accused of murder that 'Heaven will not abandon you' (p. 286), the audience knows the Deity is listening. Sure enough, the dead hero's dog licks Eloi, the mute, but barks and snaps at the villain, leading the innkeeper to urge the judge to release Eloi. 'For lack of other proof, seize on that which Providence itself seems to offer', she pleads (p. 296). If the god of Pixérécourt's melodramatic universe is more energetic in righting man's affairs than traditional notions of the Christian deity would allow, villainous conspiracy has simply given Him more work to do. In *The Dog of Montargis*, His will is performed through man's best friend, ensuring that the saint of the play never becomes a martyr. The action of Pixérécourt's plays is fundamentally providential; despite its seeming omnipotence at the start of these melodramas, Evil can never overpower Good. The Catholic Church declared Manichaeism heretical in the early Middle Ages and it remains so in the symbolic universe of Pixérécourt's plays.

Perhaps, then, Pixérécourt's melodramas reflect popularized notions of medieval Christianity. These three shows do bear a certain resemblance to medieval cycle plays; both types of drama occur in a timeless present, for instance. Pixérécourt's notion of time is Augustinian: like the 'moment' of God's actions, time is both present and eternal in his melodramas. *The Dog of Montargis*, for example, is nominally set in the fifteenth century, but the beliefs and customs of its people are presented as universal, even though its settings and properties lend it the appearance of historical authenticity. History in *The Man With Three Faces* is reduced to fancy costumes and exotic deeds, the audience being expected to believe that the essentials of human existence and divine order will never change. Indeed, the rhythm of these plays is punctuated by moments of timeless tableaux, figural groupings which hint at a kind of eternity awaiting humble people of virtue and faith.[5]

Also like medieval cycle plays, Pixérécourt's melodramas embody the ascension from '*humilitas* to *sublimitas*', the trope Erich Auerbach identified as the primary motive of all Christian drama. The theatre of medieval Christianity, asserts Auerbach, 'opens its arms invitingly to receive the simple and untutored and to lead them from the concrete, the everyday, to the hidden and the true'. Consequently, 'there is no basis for a separation of the sublime from the low and everyday, for they are indissolubly linked in Christ's very life and suffering'. This ascension is best witnessed in the near epiphany of one of Pixérécourt's saints, Francisque Humbert, a mute, impoverished man at the beginning of *Cœlina*. Like Christ, Francisque suffers persecution to save the humble – in this case his daughter, Cœlina, and the family of his brother, Dufour, neither of whom knows of his relation to them at the start of the play. Francisque's 'expressive eyes' and 'profound grief' signal his transcendant selflessness and his saintly vulnerability. The mute must wander with his daughter and suffer in patience until the end of the play, when his *sublimitas* is recognized by all. The implicit prayer of Pixérécourt urges God to allow all His good characters to ascend to sublimity and remain there, fixed for eternity in the final tableau.[6]

No doubt many in Pixérécourt's audience would have recognized a kind of sainthood in Francisque and would have identified with actions leading humble characters from the concrete specifics of their lives to the sublimity of God's design. But Pixérécourt's embrace of Christianity is incomplete; he implicitly rejects any notion of original sin. His melodramas affirm that all good characters, not only saintly mutes, can achieve pure Christian morality if only they try hard enough. 'Our religion bids one love his neighbor as himself and we must obey our religion' (p. 243), announces the heroine in *The Dog of Montargis*, innocently assuming that such *agape* is truly possible. Given Pixérécourt's unambiguous segregation of purity from villainy, the herone's injunction is dramatically believable. Like utopian revolutionaries, Pixérécourt assumed the inherent perfectibility of man, a perfection violently at odds with traditional Christian belief.

Pixérécourt's commitment to the notion of man's inherent goodness within a world designed and directed by Providence suggests that his melodramas also embody many of the popularized beliefs of neoplatonism. Neoplatonism began in the third century BC in the philosophy of Plotinus and provided its later adherents with a conservative spiritual retreat from the moral disorder of the Roman Empire. Since then, its tenets and values have exerted wide influence on Christian doctrine and popular belief. Several early Christian theologians, including Origin, Augustine, and Boethius, incorporated aspects of neoplatonic thinking into Church dogma. Neoplatonism flourished in underground medieval sects and emerged during the Reformation in the theology of the Pietists in Germany and the Inner Light Puritans in England. At the same time, neoplatonic belief helped to shape the lore of alchemy, the superstitions of witchcraft, and the oral tradition of fairy tales. From the late eighteenth through the mid nineteenth centuries, Romantics such as Schiller, Coleridge, and Emerson consciously borrowed from neoplatonic doctrine to articulate their responses to political and economic revolutions. Pixérécourt's unknowing use of popular neoplatonism to shape the form and content of his melodramas provided yet another instance of neoplatonism's ability to induce images of stability and succor for audiences racked by moral crisis and rapid historical change.[7]

Central to neoplatonist belief, from Plotinus onward, is the notion that cosmic reality is circular, that all things emanate from a primal unity, achieve separation and differentiation, and then reconverge into 'the One', their initial point of departure. In Plotinus' cosmology, this circular pattern proceeds through three stages – spirit-intelligence, soul, and matter – before returning, via the same route, to 'the One'. According to Proclus, the influential fifth-century thinker who attempted to systemize the ideas of Plotinus:

> All that proceeds from any principle and reverts upon it has a cyclic activity. For if it reverts upon that principle whence it proceeds, it links its end to its beginning, and the movement is one continuous originating from the unmoved and to the unmoved again returning. Thus all things proceed in a circuit, from their causes to their causes again.

'To Real Being we go back, all that we have and are; to that we return as from that we came', states Plotinus. Sometimes Plotinus imagines the circular journey as a quest for a lost home in which a wandering daughter, temporarily swayed by mortal desire, leaves her father. 'But one day coming to hate her shame she puts away the evil of the earth, once more seeks the father and finds her peace' (v, i, i), Plotinus concludes.[8]

Neoplatonic circularity shapes the symbolic action of Pixérécourt's melodramas. In performance, his pilgrim characters progress through four stages: 1) separation from the oneness of relationship with loved ones; 2) quest to regain this unity; 3) revelation of transcendental truth; and 4) return to the oneness of familial bliss. The initial happy hierarchy of familial relationships is much the same in *Cœlina* and *The Dog of Montargis*. In both, a father-figure presides over his innocent children in an extended family maintained by comic underlings and servants. Pixérécourt celebrates the patriarchal family; he assumes that its traditional structures of authority are both God-given and natural. The initial vision of harmony and love is presented somewhat differently in *The Man With Three Faces*. Since the oneness of relationship involving the hero Vivaldi, his father, his wife, and their servants has already been shattered by a conspiracy of nobles against the Doge of Venice, the hero can only recall it longingly and vow to re-establish this lost paradise.

The sundering of blissful oneness by villainy is the first significant action in these plays. 'Oh God! Do not let me be separated from all that is dear to me' (p. 108), says Cœlina in an aside that foreshadows the trauma of the play's point of attack. Moments later, Truguelin's attempt to shoot

Francisque and Cœlina's rescuing scream break the Edenic unity of the household. A similar trauma is repeated in act II which leads to the banishment of Cœlina and her father, and the further dissolution of the Dufour household. Son Stephany rebels against his father, and servant Tiennette willfully disobeys her master. In *The Dog of Montargis*, villainy strikes when one archer, Macaire, kills another in a company of archers visiting a country inn and circumstantial evidence points to Eloi, the mute porter of the inn, as the murderer. As in *Cœlina*, the separation of innocence from the oneness of a happy hierarchy of relationships with loved ones initiates the essential action of the melodrama.

Identifying and eliminating villainy mark the quest to return to oneness, the second stage of these plots. The hero of *The Man With Three Faces*, Vivaldi, must seize more power than his villainous opponent to reconstitute his family and his state. Early in the play, Vivaldi tells a confidant: 'Count Orsano, the implacable enemy of my entire family, that monster who denounced my father eight years ago, is at the head of a formidable conspiracy which holds to nothing less than to dispatch the Doge and strike down with him thirty senators who are the most respected for their abilities and their virtues' (p. 163). To counter Orsano's evil plotting, Vivaldi hatches a conspiracy of virtue even more secretive and convoluted: disguised as Edgar, Vivaldi will win the confidence of the Doge and gain control of the Venetian army; donning a second mask and costume, that of Abelino, a bandit, Vivaldi will infiltrate the conspiracy and place himself at the head of the revolt; and when he has achieved absolute power in the palace and among the conspirators, Vivaldi will 'rescue the state ... avenge [his] father ... regain [his] honor and a wife from whom [he] was separated before having had the happiness of possessing her' (p. 166). The villain's goals mirror the hero's: to gain total power in the state, to continue his persecution of Vivaldi's family and, of course, to possess the hero's secret wife who spurns him. Virtue must assume many of the characteristics of vice to ensure a happy ending in *The Man With Three Faces*. To possess his wife, Vivaldi must initially spurn her as a means of preserving his secret; to regain his family's honor, he must, as Edgar and Abelino, denounce it; and to save the state, he must control it. Only the watertight compartments of morality built in to Pixérécourt's Neoplatonic universe rescue *The Man With Three Faces* from sinking into moral chaos.

Lacking a super-hero to restore peace and morality, the good characters of *Cœlina* and *The Dog of Montargis* struggle primarily to identify the cause of their distress, a task made all the more difficult by the victim's speechlessness. Francisque knows that greed drove Truguelin to rip out his tongue and to attempt to force his daughter Cœlina to wed his son, but the mute lacks the evidence to prove his case. Eloi has accepted a packet of valuables and a purse of gold from the murdered man but cannot demonstrate his promise to deliver them to the archer's mother. At the end of the second act, Eloi's arrest separates him from the innkeeper's household and all he can do is assert his innocence through pantomime:

> Eloi could, perhaps, accuse a Providence which allows him to be condemned for a crime he did not commit; but he respects the will of heaven and awaits his fate with resignation. Without kneeling, he clasps his hands and raises his eyes heavenward with noble assurance. He seems to soar up to the bosom of the Deity. All the onlookers dissolve in tears.   (p. 288)

The turning point of all three plots links the revelation of providential design to a conventionally Aristotelian scene of recognition and reversal. Macaire reveals his own villainy (with the help of Providence) when he makes a false move and the murdered man's dog barks at him. In *Cœlina*, Truguelin gives himself away by attempting again to kill Francisque; only this time, peasants and archers see him shoot at the mute. Pixérécourt takes full advantage of the conventions of disguise to crown the climax of *The Man With Three Faces*. Dressed as Abelino the bandit, Vivaldi 'captures' the Doge and his court in their palace and seems ready to carry out his *coup d'état*:

> Vivaldi. Soldiers! Arrest ...
> (*He appears to intend this order for the Doge, when suddenly, changing his stance and demeanor, he quickly adds as he indicates the conspirators:*)
> All these brigands!
> (*He throws off his hat, cloak and beard, and appears as Vivaldi in the courtly attire it is assumed he wore before his exile.*)
>
>   (p. 232)

In all three plays, the climactic scene of recognition and reversal reveals the cosmic justice of the action. *Cœlina*, for instance, uses a song to underline its lesson:

> The moral, friends should be quite clear,
> That all our crimes will be revealed
> And all our sins will reappear,
>   Just when we thought them well concealed.
> Be both honest and forthright
> Make others' joys your own delight;
>   Then merrily you'll dance
>   The rigadoon,
> Zig, zag, doon, doon;
> Good deeds do wonders to advance
> The tempo of our little tune.
>
>   (p. 156)

Providence, in other words, has been watching and shaping events all along. The play may be taken as a kind of microcosm of God's macrocosmic plan for rejecting evil and returning goodness to its previously utopian condition.

The final tableau circles each plot back to a purified depiction of the oneness of hierarchial loving relationships which began the play. Francisque has replaced Dufour, for example, as the beneficent patriarch in Cœlina's family portrait and a loyal senator steps in for Vivaldi's father, present at least in the hero's memory of past bliss. Patriarchial authority centers each of the tableaux. Two patriarchs, in fact, dominate the final picture in *The Dog of Montargis*: Eloi kneels at the feet of the judge and the peasants 'kneel as one' (p. 306) before the captain of the archers. Although both men were certain of the mute's guilt only moments before, Providence revealed the truth and changed their minds. Pixérécourt's final tableaux translate mundane authority into images of transcendental justice. Even the corrupt Doge of Venice becomes a benevolent patriarch by the final picture, apparently united through love and obligation to his children-subjects. Intellectual historian Wylie Sypher notes the tendency of nineteenth-century writers like Dickens, Marx, and Ibsen to insist on static finality in their systems, novels, and plays: 'The limit of the nineteenth-century imagination is the final expressive tableau, a stasis, a consummate act.' Melodrama in particular, states Sypher, 'cannot admit exceptions, for they would immediately involve the action too deeply within the context of actuality and trammel the gesture. The types must behave with a decorum of extremes; the resolution must be vividly sche-matic.'[9] Unlike the conclusions of many plays, then, Pixérécourt's final tableaux do not encourage their audience to project a continuing life for his characters after the curtain has fallen. Having attained perfection, Vivaldi, Eloi, Cœlina, and even the Doge do not live happily ever after, but freeze in position, eternal exemplars of the goodness of Providence. In neoplatonic terms, the final tableau presents a material symbol which approximates the spiritual life of 'the One'.

Within the overall circle of Pixérécourt's dramatic action smaller circles occur, epicycles whirling within the larger cycles of this Ptolemaic-like system. Truguelin and Macaire, for instance, are driven to return to the scenes of their earlier crimes. Each of the three acts of these plays also tends to recycle a similar dramatic form, beginning in materialism and ending in the transcendent foiling of villainy. Act III of *The Man With Three Faces*, to cite one of several possible examples, starts with a scene of comic bickering between the villain and a cowardly conspirator, moves to a scene centering on worldly power, focuses next on several episodes involv-ing love and the possibility of transcendence, and climaxes with Vivaldi's apotheosis. Pixérécourt structures most of his acts this way, gradually ascending from mundane problems up an idealistic ladder toward spiritual possibilities, and topping the action by providential revelation. Then he repeats this optimistic, transcending journey in the next act, climbing even higher.

Even smaller units of action, the epicycles of 'the One', tend to work the same way. Act I, scene ii of *Cœlina* begins with some expository dialogue between Stephany and the heroine concerning Truguelin's arrival, moves into a lightly comic interchange about love and marriage, and ends with Cœlina's memory of her dying mother's warning about the villainy of the Truguelins. 'To Real Being, we go back', states Plotinus, an injunction that seems to have been whispered in Cœlina's ear in this scene. As historian of Greco-Roman philosophy F. E. Peters notes, the thrust of neoplatonic spirituality is inward and upward 'toward progressively simpler and more authentic levels of being, back past action, thought, sensation and even intuition to that point of unity that is the One ... '[10] No doubt Pixérécourt's formula contains too much action and sensation (and too little discursive thought) to satisfy critical standards of Neoplatonic art, but its plot imitates the imminant and teleological thrust of Neoplatonism.

Intuition, central to neoplatonic transcendence, plays a major role in the implicit theology of Pixérécourt's melodrama. Plotinus taught that men might purge materiality from their souls by unifying and simplifying their thoughts, thus causing their ascent to the level of spirit-intelligence or even to 'the One' itself. He described the supra-rational insight gained from joining with the goodness of 'the One' as 'ecstasy', also 'simplicity' and 'self-surrender'.[11] Where spiritual insight and ascent come only after long study and contemplation in Neoplatonism, however, melodrama radically popularizes the intuitive process, rejecting rational preparation and opening up possibilities of transcendence to any good person who obeys the promptings of his or her heart. When pressed to swear they are telling the truth, the virtuous people of Pixérécourt's plays echo, in a variety of ways, Cœlina's vow: 'I swear by my heart, and by God above who knows if ever I have stooped to dissemble' (p. 120). Dissembling villains lacking intuitive perception, on the other hand, often grease their wickedness with the oil of reason. Orsano, for instance, hides his true motives from the conspirators, arguing reasonably that their *coup d'état* is for the good of Venice.

Among the three plays, the best example of the superiority of intuitive knowledge over rational intelligence is *The Dog of Montargis*. Despite the fact that the plot is an early variant of the murder mystery – a type of action that conventionally involves the ratiocination of 'who done it' – human intuition in tune with a dog's natural instincts solves the crime. The 'detectives', a judge and a captain in this case, stubbornly fix on the reasonable evidence of appearances – Eloi's possession of the hero's gold – ignoring the innkeeper's higher intuitive evidence of honor, religion, and love. 'This man is not guilty; it's impossible', she says.

> I admit all appearances are against him, but the appearances lead you astray. All this hides a foul mystery which you will uncover later; but what I can affirm, what I state without fear, what I dare stake my life upon, is that Eloi is not capable of being a murderer. One doesn't repress in an instant all the seeds of honor, all the principles of religion instilled in a fine spirit . . . Would I love him still, would he dare look me in the face, would I press him to my breast if he were a murderer? Oh! No, no, my heart would reject him; I would be the first to demand of you his punishment . . . Courage, my child, courage; Heaven will not abandon you. (*She runs out.*)   (p. 286)

But another bit of seeming evidence is discovered – Eloi's spade covered with dirt – and the judge is adamant. God's purposes are soon revealed, however, in the near epiphany of Eloi at the end of act II, disproving the evidence of the senses and enfolding intuitive virtue within the transcendental power of 'the One'.

Although the democratization of intuition in these plays has the potential of undermining the social hierarchy, Pixérécourt makes it clear that the promptings of the heart do not finally contravene one's social duty. Heart-felt belief may conflict with the social hierarchy during the course of the action, but the two are joined together by the final tableau. The melodramatic version of rendering unto Caesar what is Caesar's is best exemplified in *The Man With Three Faces*. One scene between the Doge and Vivaldi-disguised-as-Abelino includes the following dialogue:

> *Vivaldi.* Do you think a brigand such as I am beneath a Doge? It is not the purple that makes men great, and perhaps beneath this coarse exterior there is a heart more tender and a spirit more generous than your own.
> *The Doge.* How dare you compare yourself to me!
> *Vivaldi.* Have you never abused your power to subscribe to an injustice or to persecute an innocent!
> *The Doge.* What does it matter to you?
> *Vivaldi.* You have done so . . .
>
> (p. 204)

Of course since the hero isn't really a bandit, the audience never learns whether a brigand might be morally above a Doge. Further, Vivaldi has mounted an elaborate counter-conspiracy to maintain the Doge on his throne. Indeed, the saintly hero hands Venice back to the formerly corrupt monarch at the end of the play. Pixérécourt patches the crumbling edifice of worldly power with the glue of duty and the law and hopes his audience won't look too closely when he places the halo of intuitive grace over its not-so-kingly head.

Other aspects of the theology according to Pixérécourt, apparently anomalous when contrasted to traditional Christian belief, are congruent with the thrust of neoplatonic thinking. Nature in neoplatonic cosmology, as in that of the Stoics, is explicitly linked to man's deeds through cosmic sympathy. Since the universe is essentially a single moral organism in Plotinus' conception, a human activity such as a heroine's prayer or villain's curse will lead to a sympathetic reaction in another part of the cosmic body. At Orsano's entrance into a grotto of the palace gardens, for instance, a flash of lightning momentarily arrests the villain's violation of sacred ground. Cosmic sympathy also explains why dogs bark at their master's murderer and why villains suffer so much for their crimes – why, in short, Pixérécourt's God responds empathetically to everything that happens in these plays. A good character's intuitive sympathy, then, not only connects him or her to the goodness of others, it puts him in touch with cosmic goodness; it tunes him into the true harmony of the spheres.

In neoplatonic doctrine, cosmic sympathy results from divine emanation. 'The One' overflows in its fullness, emanating through spirit-intelligence and soul until it reaches matter, which includes material man. This doctrine, as popularized by Pixérécourt, provides an explanation for the sentimental flow of tears between loved ones. 'Do not grieve, dear father', says Cœlina to Francisque as they pause in their act III wanderings, 'Cœlina, close to you, will find her happiness in daily expressing her affection for you and in lavishing upon you the most earnest care' (p. 147). Love will out in these melodramas. Like the overflowing goodness of 'the One', love bursts all restraint, overcomes all obstacles to assert its primacy. Sometimes the affect of this melodramatic emanation is intentionally comic rather than pathetic. In a long scene in which Vivaldi is trying to hide his identity from his wife, the hero can barely contain his true feelings, which explode in asides of 'Delicious moment' and 'Oh happiness', alternating with others of restraint like 'Foolhardy man' (p. 197). Finally: 'I cannot resist her tears. My secret escapes me in spite of myself. (*Aloud with the tenderest of expressions*). Dear Rosemonde! Recognize that husband in Edgar [Vivaldi's disguise at the moment]' (p. 195). The episode ends in tears of joy and a silent embrace held for the tableau. Other good characters, too, are given important scenes in which social propriety or their own welfare mandates emotional restraint. But in each instance, love overwhelms them and they 'speak their hearts'.

Love emanates from 'the One' in neoplatonism but, paradoxically, 'the One' is unmoved and passive in the process. Similarly in Pixérécourt's formula, mutes like Francisque and Eloi overflow with love, inspiring it in others, but remain essentially passive in confrontations with villainy or misguided authority. These saintly characters are partial embodiments of a popularized 'One', both emanating love and drawing love to themselves. Their effect on the action of their plays is not unlike that of the mythical Philosopher's Stone in alchemy which reputedly had the power to speed up the return of all matter to its origin, transforming, in the process, base metals to their primordial perfection as gold.[12] Eloi and Francisque act as similar catalysts, bringing out the goodness in other characters and speeding the return of the initial utopian vision when the multiplicity of matter shall melt down into the simplicity of pure spirit in the final tableau.

Some base substances, it was thought, would be burned away completely in the alchemical reaction, vanishing as villains do in the purification process that constitutes the action of the play. Evil has no essential existence in neoplatonic thinking. Rather, it is the simple absence of good in ephemeral matter, a polar separation from 'the One' resulting when a man's soul becomes turned in upon itself. Plotinus foresees a point when some souls

> become partial and self-centered; in a weary desire of standing apart they find their way, each to a place of its very own. This state long-maintained, the Soul is a deserter from the All: its differentiation has severed it; its vision is no longer set in the intellectual; it is a partial thing, isolated, weakened, full of care, intent upon the fragment, severed from the whole ... (IV, viii, 4)

Consequently, when 'the One' gathers itself unto itself, the tarnish of evil is simply shuffled off, polished away.

Melodramatic villainy is close indeed to Neoplatonic evil. All of Pixérécourt's monsters are mired in materialism: Truguelin in greed, Orsano in lust for power, and Macaire in jealousy of worldly success. Instead of emanating goodness, each is turned in upon himself, staked to a futile mulling-over of past sins and imagined wrongs. 'Hardly two hours have passed since I defiled myself with murder', moans Macaire, 'and already I have felt all the torments of hell' (p. 275). Though nominally related to other villains in their conspiracy against virtue, each monster is fundamentally alone and seeks self-sufficiency, not interdependent relationship. Truguelin, for instance, tries to force his son to marry Cœlina and even ruins his sister's marriage to Francisque to advance his selfish ends. Family ties of trust and love stand in the way of villainous purposes. Not only are these wicked men outside the circle of family love, they are usually excluded from the larger circle of organic society as well – monsters socially as well as morally. Just as 'witches' bore revealing marks of their 'otherness' in the Reformation era, so these villains often reveal their separation from upright society through physical abnormalities. Thus the entire village will vouch for Eloi's hearty innocence, but Macaire's sin 'seeks a place of its very own' to hide its trembling fright.

Villainous conspiracy, seemingly omnipotent at the point of attack, is gradually burned away in the transforming crucible of dramatic action until it vanishes by play's end. In effect, the villains are driven even further into separation and confounding multiplicity, their selfish individualism ultimately proving the cause of their own downfall. Had Truguelin not attempted to shoot Francisque, for instance, his initial crime against the saintly figure might never have been revealed. Although Vivaldi's heroism is the main cause of Orsano's demise, the senator's conspiracy, overextended and too complex to remain a secret, is already beginning to topple in on itself when the hero delivers the *coup de grace*. Truguelin and Macaire, deserted by their accomplices, shunned by polite society, and terrified by their fate, are more alone than Orsano near the end of their careers. Truguelin blurts out a prayer, but then stops himself in an agony of remorse: 'Halt miserable man! Do not outrage Heaven! Consolation for you! This grace is reserved for innocence alone. You will never enjoy it. Tears, the scaffold: here is the fate which awaits you and from which you cannot escape' (p. 140). In their final scene, each villain is typically alone, center stage, with the law moving in on either side, a striking visual contrast to the 'oneness' of relationship among the good characters in the final tableau.

Pixérécourt's popular fusion of neoplatonism and traditional Christian belief places his melodramas among the many novels, essays, and musical compositions of the early 1800s that historian Louis Bergeron terms the 'anti-rationalist reaction' in France. The anti-rationalists blamed the excesses of the 1790s on the individualism, empiricism, and materialism of the Enlightenment. 'It is to the vanity of knowledge that we owe almost all our misfortunes', claimed Chateaubriand, the leading illuminist of the movement. In his widely read *Genius of Christianity*, Chateaubriand promoted emotional mysticism to salve current distress, a balm touted by other French writers in the first decades of the nineteenth century. In *Suzette's Diary*, for instance, Fievée exalted the lost morality of the *ancien régime* while Mme Cottin praised the nobility and holiness of medieval royal love in her *Mathilde*. At the same time, several French composers turned from writing revolutionary songs to composing liturgical hymns, masses, and requiems, drawing their musical aesthetics from the religious past. In his influential *Essay on the Generative Principle of Political Constitutions* and *On the Pope*, Joseph de Maistre used providentialist doctrine to argue for the restoration of the monarchy and an eventual return to papal political authority. While de Maistre and a few other anti-rationalists urged that France return to a lost golden age of Catholic faith, most followed Chateaubriand in praising Napoleon as a 'man of Providence who has saved us from the abyss'.[13]

Though less explicit theologically and politically than the works of most anti-rationalists, Pixérécourt's plays implicitly reject Enlightenment rationalism and embrace traditional notions of mysticism and authority. His good characters would have no use for Diderot's *Encyclopedia*, for instance. Not by scientific investigation nor even by reading is wisdom attained in the world of his plays. Rather, Pixérécourt induces his audience to believe that humility, good deeds, and 'natural' intuition are sufficient. Nor is human psychology and social behavior the result of cause and effect relations among material phenomena, as the French physiocrats understood. Instead, Providence plans individual action, moving discrete, microcosmic events toward the macrocosm of His design. Likewise, faith in material and moral progress toward an enlightened future is foolish and immoral; the happiest, truest future lies in circling back to the oneness of the past. Only villains use reason to explain their actions, confuse material advancement with morality, and seek the illusion of individual freedom. The path of the Enlightenment is not the way of 'the One'.

Regarding the political implications of Pixérécourt's popularized neoplatonism, his melodramas continued the logic of moral extremism rampant during the Terror, but redirected the chiliastic thrust of the Revolution, the desire of its leaders to establish a rational heaven on earth, toward obedience to patriarchal authority. Theatre historian Fredrick Brown's assertion that Pixérécourt's melodramas 'ritualized the Terror' is only half right. Brown correctly argues that the world view of these plays, like the ideology of Robespierre, 'allowed of no profane middle ground between virtue and evil' and 'pictured innocence hard put by enemies whose deviousness and implacability constituted a kind of brute nature transcending the merely human'.[14]

But Pixérécourt firmly rejected the aims of the Terror. As historian Crane Brinton notes:

> Robespierre wanted a France where there should be neither rich nor poor, where men should not gamble, or get drunk, or commit adultery, cheat or rob, or kill – where, in short, there would be neither petty nor grand vices – a France ruled by upright and intelligent men elected by the universal suffrage of the people, men wholly without greed or love of office, and delightedly stepping down at yearly intervals to give place to their successors, a France at peace with herself and the world.[15]

Not only were Pixérécourt's melodramas more tolerant of small vices; more important, his plays idealized monarchy and the stable, hierarchical relations of pre-Revolutionary France. The rational and democratic political procedures envisioned by Robespierre conflicted directly with the power of patriarchy embodied and celebrated in Pixérécourt's final tableaux. In so far as Napoleon reconstituted traditional social relations, these plays helped to legitimate his rule. But Pixérécourt's melodramas probably did little for the Emperor in his roles as the rationalizer of France, the scourge of European monarchy, and the leveller of papal authority. Although Vivaldi has much in common with Napoleon, the super-hero handed Venice back to its hereditary ruler.

Perhaps Pixérécourt did help his audiences to passively accept the wrenching consequences of the Empire as a part of providential design. More likely, though, his plays made them yearn nostalgically for a return to the 'oneness' of monarchy and mysticism. In rejecting the rationalism and materialism of the Enlightenment, Pixérécourt's melodramas turned their back on significant aspects of the modern world. As historian Arthur M. Wilson notes, 'the *philosophes* were striving for almost every condition now considered an essential ingredient of modernization'.[16] In the West, Enlightenment values fostered the spread of literacy, the rationalization of social institutions, and the incursions of market capitalism into traditional social practices. Pixérécourt's plays induced their spectators to reject these changes. In accord with their popularized neoplatonic orientation, these melodramas situated their Parisian audiences in the reactionary politics of nostalgia.

NOTES

1 Nodier quoted in Peter Brooks, *The Melodramatic Imagination: Balzac, Henry James, Melodrama and the Mode of Excess* (New Haven: Yale University Press, 1976), p. 43. For recent scholarship on Pixérécourt's melodramas, see Fredrick Brown, *Theatre and Revolution: the Culture of the French Stage* (New York: Viking Press, 1980), pp. 83–105; Gabrielle Hyslop, 'Deviant and Dangerous Behavior: Women in Melodrama', *Journal of Popular Culture*, 19 (Winter 1985), 65–77; Hyslop, 'Researching the Acting of French Melodrama, 1800–1830', *Nineteenth-Century Theatre*, 15(1987), 85–114; Julia Przybos, 'La Conscience populaire et le mélodrame en France dans la première moitié du dixneuvième siecle', *French Review*, 57 (February 1984), 300–8; Przybos, *The Melodramatic Enterprise* (Paris: Corti, 1987); Jean-Marie Thomasseau, *Le Mélodrame sur les Scenes Parisiennes de Cælina (1800) a l'Auberge des Adrets (1823)* (Lille: Service de Reproduction des theses, 1976).

2 On the number and type of Pixérécourt's plays, see the introduction to his *Théâtre choisi* (Nancy: Raybois et Cie, 1841), vol. I, pp. xliv–lxxxviii; Willie G. Hartog, 'Guilbert de Pixérécourt: the Father of the Melodrama', *Fortnightly Review*, 108 (1920), 130–4; and Alexander Lacey, *Pixerecourt and the French Romantic Drama* (University of Toronto Press, 1928). Lacey differentiates between Pixérécourt's early and later melodramas, detecting the influence of Byronic romanticism on his post-1815 plays (p. 68). William H. Akins, Jr, in his 'Three Melodramas by Guilbert de Pixérécourt' (Diss., University of Denver, 1971), provides fine translations (as well as useful introductions) to each of the three plays. Because act and scene designation often varied widely from one edition to another in the publishing of popular melodramas, I shall cite subsequent quoted material from all plays with a page number from the Akins's translation. Pixérécourt recorded 1,476 performances of *Cælina*, 1,022

performances of *The Man With Three Faces*, and 1,158 of *The Dog of Montargis* during his lifetime (he died in 1844).

3 Quotations in Brown, *Theatre and Revolution*, pp. 95, 97–8, 88. Regarding the audience for Napoleonic melodrama, I wish to thank Marie-Pierre Le Hir for sending her paper, 'Early Nineteenth-Century French Melodrama: a Landmark in the History of Popular Culture?' to me after presenting it at the *Themes in Drama* conference on 'Melodrama' at the University of California, Riverside in February 1990. Le Hir shows that the audience for Pixérécourt's early plays was primarily bourgeois.

4 Brooks, *Melodramatic Imagination*, p. 54. For critics who discern Manichaeism at the heart of melodrama, see Theodore W. Hatlin, *Orientation to the Theatre* (New York: Appleton, 1962), pp. 86–98; Lacey, *Pixerecourt*, pp. 10–11; and James S. Smith, *Melodrama, The Critical Idiom*, no. 28 (London: Methuen, 1973). Robert Corrigan's discussion of melodrama as 'the drama of disaster' essentially defines a Manichaean viewpoint for the form, although Corrigan does not use the term to describe it ('Melodrama and the Common Man' in *The Forms of Drama*, ed. Robert W. Corrigan and Glenn Loney (Boston: Houghton Mifflin, 1972), pp. 187–96).

5 I am using Martin Meisel's definition of tableau: 'Figural groupings symbolizing relationships and states of feeling and incorporating bodily attitudes that [are] themselves expressive and symbolic', stated in 'Speaking Pictures', in *Melodrama*, ed. Daniel Gerould (New York: New York Literary Forum, 1980), p. 57. Cultural historian David Grimsted notes the ideality of tableaux in American melodramas of the same period (most of which were based on Pixérécourt's popular formulas): '[The Tableau] was less a conscious imagining of what society might or should become than an ideal that was considered a kind of reality, experience not withstanding' (*Melodrama Unveiled: American Theater and Culture, 1800–1850* (University of Chicago Press, 1968), p. 230).

6 Eric Auerbach, *Mimesis: The Representation of Reality in Western Life*, trans. Willard Trask (1953: rpt Garden City, New York; Doubleday, 1957), pp. 135, 138. Francisque's piety, perseverance, and humility are similar to the qualities of St Bernard of Clairvaux, the gentle, twelfth-century spokesman for popular piety. 'Therefore, dearly beloved, persevere in the discipline which you have taken upon you, so that by humility you may ascend to sublimity, for this is the way and there is no other. Who walks otherwise falls rather than rises, for it is humility alone which exalts, humility alone which leads to life', preached St Bernard (Auerbach, pp. 132–3).

7 For discussions on the origins and history of Neoplatonism, see M. H. Abrams, *Natural Supernaturalism: Tradition and Revolution in Romantic Literature* (New York: W. W. Norton, 1971), pp. 146–63; Philip Merlan, 'Neoplatonism', *The Encyclopedia of Philosophy* (1967; rpt New York: Macmillan, 1972), vol. v, pp. 473–6; Merlan, 'Plotinus', *The Encyclopedia of Philosophy*, vol. vi, pp. 351–9; F. E. Peters, *The Harvest of Hellenism: a History of the Near East from Alexander the Great to the Triumph of Christianity* (New York: Simon and Schuster, 1970), pp. 588–93; Philippus V. Pistorius, *Plotinus and Neoplatonism: An Introductory Study* (Cambridge: Bowes and Bowes, 1952); and R. T. Wallis, *Neoplatonism* (London: Duckworth, 1972).

8 Proclus, *The Elements of Theology*, ed. and trans. E. R. Dodds (Oxford University Press, 1933), Prop. 33; Plotinus, *The Six Enneads*, trans. Stephen MacKenna and B. S. Page (University of Chicago Press, 1952), ii, ix, 1.

9 Wylie Sypher, 'Aesthetic of Revolution: the Marxist Melodrama', *The Kenyon Review*, 10 (Summer 1948), 435, 436.

10 Peters, *Harvest of Hellenism*, p. 590.

11 Quoted in Merlan, 'Plotinus', p. 355.

12 F. Sherwood Taylor, *The Alchemists* (New York: Collier, 1962), pp. 12–21, 117–80.

13 Chateaubriand quoted in Bergeron's *France Under Napoleon*, trans. R. R. Palmer (Princeton University Press, 1981), pp. 199, 198. Regarding melodrama's attitude toward inherited wealth, Przybos notes, 'Et tout comme dans la formule de Chateaubriand, c'est l'hérédité qui enfante la légitimité' ('Conscience populaire', p. 302).

14 Brown, *Theatre and Revolution*, p. 89.

15 Crane Brinton, *The Anatomy of Revolution*, rev. ed. (New York: Vintage, 1965), p. 116.

16 Wilson, 'The *Philosophes* in the Light of Present Day Theories of Modernization', in *Comparative Modernization: A Reader*, ed. Cyril E. Black (New York: Free Press, 1976), p. 118. Regarding the Enlightenment and the process of modernization, see also Robert Anchor, *The Enlightenment Tradition* (Berkeley and Los Angeles: University of California Press, 1979); David Apter, *The Politics of Modernization* (University of Chicago Press, 1965); and Karl Polanyi, *The Great Transformation* (1944; rpt; Boston: Beacon, 1957).

From comedy to melodrama: the transposition of a Polish theme

HALINA FILIPOWICZ

The greatest success in the history of American melodrama, Harriet Beecher Stowe's *Uncle Tom's Cabin*, 'unmasked', in Daniel Gerould's apt observation, 'a super melodramatic villain' who ruthlessly destroyed the integrity of the Christian family:

> What all the most pernicious villains of nineteenth-century melodrama could accomplish only on a small personal scale in the way of assaults on virgins and mothers, the legal institution of slavery in the United States perpetrated every day against an entire race.[1]

At the same time in what had once been Poland, the super melodramatic villain was the legal institution of the partitions, while the assaulted victim was the Polish people. In the late eighteenth century, Poland was forced to yield to the political ambitions and military might of Russia, Prussia, and Austria. Until the end of World War I, it existed not as a geographic and political entity, but as a stateless nation and a community of shared tradition. The Poles repeatedly rose in rebellion against the foreign rule. From 1794 until 1863, no generation escaped a patriotic call to arms. The major insurrections in the nineteenth century were those of 1830–1 and 1863–4, known as the November and the January Uprisings.[2] Like the other Polish uprisings, they failed to restore national sovereignty and ended in executions, exile, and emigration. But they have become important markers in the cultural heritage of a people who were disinherited of their statehood for over a century. As one historian has pointed out, without the countless conspiracies and numerous uprisings the Poles would certainly have emerged from the long and testing period of foreign rule a very different people.[3]

One might expect that the uprisings would have left a rich legacy of melodrama anchored to the Polish struggle for independence. After all, by the mid nineteenth century the popularity of melodrama was sweeping both sides of the Atlantic Ocean, and the topic of Poland as victim and the invaders as villain was well suited to melodramatic formulae and functions. The plot of melodrama is propelled by the machinations of the villain, but by the final scene moral justice prevails. Melodrama is thus inherently optimistic in its belief in a sudden reversal of fortune, which restores the ethical equilibrium: the villain will be exposed and punished, the virtuous will be rewarded.

Audiences in the New World responded enthusiastically to melodrama, which perfectly fitted 'the rough and ready ethos of nineteenth-century Americans'.[4] Melodrama, in fact, has dominated the American theatre and media since it was imported from Europe in the late eighteenth century.[5] The ethos of nineteenth-century Poles, on the other hand, was shaped by the situation of foreign occupation and geographical non-existence. Defeat in an uneven struggle for a just cause was regarded as a moral victory because even a doomed uprising kept the idea of an independent Poland alive. Every failed insurrection thus became a living symbol of national martyrdom. No topos has been as deeply encoded in the Polish cultural mythology as that of *ofiara* (sacrifice as well as sacrificial victim). With the topos of *ofiara* defining its sense of national destiny, and with the ancient Roman concept of *vae victis!* (woe to the defeated) transformed into *gloria victis!* (glory to the defeated), could Poland develop a native tradition of melodrama?[6] This is a question that must be left hanging, at least for the purposes of this article. But an investigation of melodramatic representations of the Polish conspiracies and uprisings fits within the scope of a preliminary study.

In the United States, the Polish Revolution of 1830–1 reverberated in Silas S. Steele's *The Brazen Drum; or, The Yankee in Poland. A National Drama* (1846). In Poland, it inspired the canonical works of the dramatic repertory: Part Three of Adam Mickiewicz's *Forefathers' Eve* (*Dziady*, 1832), Juliusz Słowacki's *Kordian* (1834), Stanisław Wyspiański's *November Night* (*Noc Listopadowa*, 1904). To trace the melodramatic formulae and functions, however, one must turn to texts which have been slighted or ignored by the canon.[7] These plays make no pretense at intellectual complexity. They delight in aesthetic embarrassments such as cliché-ridden plots and character stereotypes. At the same time, they depend on 'a covert symbolic and mythical code'[8] or a sign-system which draws on traditional topoi, while capturing the spirit of the times.[9] Thus, aside from the dead-end pronouncement that these plays lack artistic merit, there is also a possibility that, in their own way, they assume the civic responsibility which has characterized the Polish theatre since Jan Kochanowski's Renaissance drama, *The Dismissal of the Grecian Envoys* (*Odprawa posłów greckich*, 1578).

The first set of plays is concerned with the November Uprising.[10] All of them were written – and a few were staged – while the uprising was still being fought. In fact, two of the playwrights (Stanisław Bratkowski and Zygmunt Edwin Gordaszewski) were soldiers in the insurrectionary army.

These plays are: Bratkowski's *The Warsaw Student* (*Akademik warszawski*) which opened on 1 January 1831 in Warsaw; Józefat Krzaczkowski's *An Invalid, or, Valor Rewarded* (*Inwalid czyli Męstwo nagrodzone*); Paweł Felicjan Miłkowski's *The Twenty-Ninth of November* (*Dzień dwudziesty dziewiąty listopada*) which premièred in Cracow on the fortieth anniversary of the Constitution of 3 May 1791; Wanda Szopowicz's *The Entry of the Polish Army to Volhynia* (*Wejście wojsk polskich na Wołyń*);[11] Augustyn Zdżarski's *The Cracow Student, or Sacrifice for the Homeland* (*Akademik krakowski, czyli Ofiara dla Ojczyzny*); the anonymous *The Spy and the Poet: the Rivals* (*Szpieg i poeta: Rywale*) and Gordaszewski's *Muscovites Put to Flight* (*Popłoch Moskali*). The last-mentioned was given an amateur performance on 24 January 1831 at Warsaw's Narodowy Theatre as a benefit for the insurrection.

I have juxtaposed these works with two plays written after the failure of the January Uprising: Leopold Starzeński's *The Star of Siberia* (*Gwiazda Syberii*) and Gabriela Zapolska's *The Other One* (*Tamten*). The former premièred on 1 November 1868 in Lvov, the latter, under the pseudonym of Józef Maskoff, on 22 March 1898 in Cracow. Of dozens of late nineteenth-century Polish plays on the national insurrections and conspiracies, I have chosen these two for a very banal yet not insignificant reason: *The Star of Siberia* and *The Other One* were among the most popular dramas of post-1863 Poland. At the turn of the century, *The Other One* was considered 'the best patriotic play since *The Star of Siberia* and was ranked above *The Wedding* [*Wesele*]', Wyspiański's masterpiece of 1901.[12] Zapolska, actress as well as dramatist, learned the tricks of the melodramatic trade during her stay in Paris, but the conflict and characterization in *The Other One* owe much to *The Star of Siberia*. In fact, she played Olga, or the Star of Siberia, in an 1882 production of Starzeński's play. *The Other One* is one of the most spectacular successes in the history of the Polish stage. By 1914, it reached almost 500 performances in the Austrian- and German-occupied parts of Poland. Abroad the response was no less impassioned. In Berlin, where *The Other One* opened in 1916 as *Die Warschauer Zitadelle*, it was performed 380 times.[13] The play was also adapted for the screen in Poland (in 1921) and Germany (in 1917 and 1937).

The nine plays[14] begin with a melodramatic situation: innocent Poland suffers at the hands of ruthless invaders who have violated divine and human law. The conspiracies and uprisings usually function as catalysts rather than as a mere backdrop for the dramatic action; they determine the course of events even when they are a foreign body inserted into the dramatic structure. In the plays of 1831, evil is purged and virtue vindicated when the insurrectionists take control of Warsaw from the Russians. These plays, we will remember, were written for a moment, out of the moment. They bespeak an emphasis on the here and now, on the collective experience of author and audience in actual historical encounters.[15]

They are essentially optimistic, hence it is not surprising that they take the form of *komedioopera*, or light comedy interspersed with song and dance.[16] Miłkowski assigns to his work the subtitle of 'a historical-dramatic sketch' ('rys historyczno-dramatyczny'), possibly to emphasize its topical character, but the play hardly differs from the *komedioopera*.

The circumstances thirty years later were quite different. The national mourning of the early 1860s kept Polish patriots away from the theatre. Then the collapse of the most bloody, hopeless, and prolonged of the Polish uprisings brought the nation to the brink of catastrophe, and the Russian partition subsequently lost its limited autonomy. When a repertory of plays about Polish conspirators and insurrectionists emerged, it was to be found only in the Austrian partition, where censorship was less severe. Starzeński's *Star of Siberia*, which premièred barely four years after the January Uprising, anticipated the patriotic repertory that began to flourish in Cracow and Lvov in the 1880s. Like *The Other One*, it seems to fall under the category of melodrama more readily than the vaudevilles of 1831. In fact, Starzeński's play, which uses incidental music, ostensibly follows the old-fashioned musical melodrama. But both *The Star of Siberia* and *The Other One* complicate the clear-cut moral categories of melodrama in ways which, one might speculate, should have been unacceptable to Polish audiences. A few spectators of *The Other One* indeed registered their uneasiness,[17] yet the immense popularity of both plays indicates that most of the viewers welcomed the innovation.

At first sight the seven plays of 1831 are little more than light-hearted bagatelles. There was, however, a more serious purpose underlying each of them. They satisfied an intense desire for the symbolization of current political reality – the same desire which, on 29 November 1830, prompted the Warsaw insurrectionists to stop at the Society of Friends of Learning (Towarzystwo Przyjaciół Nauk) and remove from its museum collection two flags which had belonged to General Henryk Dąbrowski. Under these national emblems of freedom they continued their march through the night-time city.[18]

The action of these plays coincides with the outbreak of the uprising; it usually begins just days after the evening of 29 November, when the Cadet Corps in Warsaw took to the streets and stormed the Arsenal. The plot is always very simple: young lovers put aside their private interest, when shackled Poland calls for self-sacrificing champions of liberty. The plays are thus grounded in the traditional Polish concept of active citizenship, which equated patriotism and freedom: to love and serve the homeland is to offer oneself to the cause of freedom regardless of indivdual aspirations. Only Walery of *The Spy and the Poet* has to be reminded that his first and foremost responsibility is to liberate Poland rather than stay at home with

Zosia. But then, it is the only play in which the uprising is not integral and integrating, but superimposed and detachable.

Except for Miłkowski's play, the action takes place outside Warsaw, in villages and manors. The countryside seems to provide a sense of security that the city lacks. Jonek, the student in Żdżarski's play, in fact has fled from Warsaw to his brother's estate to avoid arrest for political activities. But the villages and the manors are hardly protective enclaves drowsing smugly and peacefully. In Bratkowski's play, a judge has been stripped of his office because someone has denounced him to the Russian authorities as a Polish patriot. In Szopowicz's play, a militant squire is under house arrest, yet he finds a way to rally neighbors in support of the uprising. The countryside may appear a locus of sylvan innocence, but granaries, barns, and cellars are veritable arsenals. The deceptiveness of external appearances is also conveyed by costuming: Jonek wears a military uniform underneath his peasant disguise. When the news of the uprising arrives, the characters bring guns, swords, and pikes out of hiding. For the contemporary audiences, both the proliferation of arms and the display of Polish uniforms on stage were emblems of national pride, which offered a feast for the eyes. Concomitantly, the spectacular representation of the entire nation in arms made a powerful appeal to the patriotic feelings of the audiences at a time when only popular support for the uprising could match the overwhelming numbers of the enemy.

Although the Polish Revolution began in the capital, it is the countryside which is seen as a stronghold of moral and patriotic values, indeed, a home to tradition and the spirit. In Żdżarski's play, the land-owner is named Rzetelnicki, or Mr Reputable, in Bratkowski's – Zacniewska, or Mrs Decent. In *Muscovites Put to Flight*, the estate is owned by Staropolski, or Mr Old Polish, and it is managed by Godnicki, or Mr Worthy. In the same play, an old veteran, Odważnicki (Mr Courage), praises the rural world of clear and constant values. The dramatists thus seem to play on the nostalgia of their audiences while exploiting the conservative characteristics associated with the countryside. The provincial setting, however, does more than underscore the old opposition between town and country. Szopowicz's play, set in Volhynia which is not an ethnically Polish province, stresses the solidarity of the eastern borderlands with Poland in the struggle against the Russian occupation. Żdżarski and Bratkowski situate their plays in the countryside near Cracow, in the vicinity of Racławice, the site of Tadeusz Kościuszko's victorious battle against the Russians on 4 April 1794. The symbolic significance of Racławice is so powerful that even the plays set elsewhere reverberate with its echoings and with references to Kościuszko's peasant scythe-men whose brave charge during the battle has guaranteed their place in the Polish cultural pantheon.

The playwrights do not look for hidden analogies, but show a continuity of the insurrectionary tradition which has resisted foreign repressions. In one play after another, the characters – be they peasants, servants, or squires – proudly introduce themselves as participants or as descendants of participants in the battle of Racławice. The scythes and swords they carry are no ordinary weapons, but rather sacrosanct emblems of the glorious past. Sons have inherited them from fathers who fought under the leadership of Kościuszko. The November Uprising is thus seen as the new Racławice. As one character exuberantly proclaims, 'The times of Kościuszko are coming back!' (*AK*, p. 26). When the characters join the uprising, they revive the past through a magic gesture of repetition.[19]

Crucial to the plays is a vision of a united nation free of internal discord. We see a hierarchical but harmonious social order in which everyone is happy with his or her station in life. In Żdżarski's play, Basia, the bailiff's daughter, loves Jonek, the squire's brother. According to the premises of the play, however, she accepts the fact that her husband will be a man of her own class. Like the other peasants in the play, the bailiff speaks against transgressions of class boundaries. 'I like my modest situation', he says, and a similar declaration could have been made by the other peasants or servants in all these dramas (*AK*, p. 3). Szopowicz's comedy echoes the Enlightenment's principle of the equality of all people when in the opening scene the squire resolves to liberate his serfs in accordance with the Constitution of 3 May 1791. 'From now on', he announces, 'in time of peace as well as war, we will all be equal' (*WWP*, p. 2). In the other plays, the firmly defined world of social relations is always accepted as a guarantee of stability and prosperity. At the end of Żdżarski's play, the squire, in order to celebrate the outbreak of the uprising, wants to free the peasants from servitude, but they refuse. He has taken such good care of them, they argue, that they want to remain under his paternal wing.

It may be that the higher good – Poland's independence – motivates the authors; their vision of national concord and harmony undoubtedly has a didactic purpose. At the same time, the playwrights, consciously or not, draw on the ideological legacy of the Gentry Republic of the pre-partition era. An integral part of that legacy was

> a peculiar view of nationhood – a view which saw the nation as an extended family, a moral community, sharing the same essential values and, therefore, possessing a unitary will, capable, in principle, of approaching the ideal of unanimity and solving all its problems by conscious decision-making, with fullest participation of all its members.[20]

In the old Polish Republic, the nation was identified with the gentry. The plays of 1831 move away from the earlier concept of the gentry as collective sovereign to the idea of the sovereignty of the entire nation. To a Russian policeman in Szopowicz's play Żelisław is just a servant, but the squire's daughter promptly corrects this agent of Russian oppression: 'Don't servants have the right to defend their honor?' (*WWP*, p. 13). The characters in this and other plays always consider themselves children of one mother, Poland. 'All of us are Poles', proudly declares a farm hand who rebukes the gentry for believing that honor, valor, and deep attachment to Poland are their exclusive values (*I*, p. 13). The plays promulgate a traditional social order, but their ideological content is not unequivocally conservative.

The uprising, although called a revolution, is perceived not as a destructive force that will inevitably lead to chaos and anarchy, but as a redemptive measure that will bring back a lost golden age. 'The history of the world has never seen a revolution more noble than ours', proclaims the student of Bratkowski's play (*AW*, p. 16). The plays open on a world turned upside down, in which laws and constitutional rights are not respected, churches serve as prisons, traitors hold government offices, and patriots are persecuted. By the end of each play, the Polish Revolution reestablishes, rather than violates, the moral order. The oppressors and the traitors have received their due, and those who have suffered at their hands witness the restoration of a just universe through the intervention of Providence. The sign of its working is the liberation of Warsaw by several scores of students and cadets who have acted purely and selflessly and thus represent the antithesis of a Machiavellian ethic. But what Jerry Palmer said of French classical drama applies to these plays as well: 'Providence ... can only operate in a world where someone is prepared to make an exceptional effort; to be good is not enough.'[21]

The plays move from the illegitimate present to a reclaimed Polish past which is to be the future. The present is seen as 'an iron peace', or a new order imposed by force (*I*, p. 24). The past is remembered as an age of national grandeur by the characters who combine the *ubi sunt* topos with that of the golden age (cf. *AW*, p. 11; *I*, p. 12; *PM*, p. 13). They fondly remember the institutions of the Gentry Republic and would like the 'old tribunals' restored (*I*, p. 21; cf. also *WWP*, pp. 1–2). They yearn for the Edenic innocence of old Poland. Yet on occasion they explain the reality of the foreign occupation as God's punishment for ancestors' sins (cf. *I*, p. 25; *PM*, p. 24). It is not unusual for them to lament the 'dire discord [*czarna niezgoda*]' and the 'anarchy [*bezrząd*]' in pre-partition Poland, while hoping for a restoration of the glorious past (*I*, p. 25). Such inconsistencies might be interpreted as flaws in the playwrights' craft, were it not for the fact that these discrepancies reveal a frame of mind not limited to the characters in the plays. The situation of foreign oppression, argues the historian Janusz Tazbir, reversed the negative aspects of gentry mentality: conservatism changed into a determination to preserve national tradition and identity, and obstreperous opposition to royal power became active resistance to the foreign invader.[22] The characters' yearning for the golden age, moreover, is not mere nostalgia. In the words of a young insurrectionist, 'It's time to become the Poles of old, ... it's time to revive the bygone moments of our glory' (*DDDL*, p. 30). If the present seems uncertain, one might conclude, the past appears as the most reliable source of clear-cut norms. But the issue is more complex. To turn to the past is to validate the legality of the claims to Poland's independence. What seems to us a conservative strategy was, paradoxically, a revolutionary one – especially from the point of view of the partitioning powers.

Bratkowski's and Żdżarski's plays are unusual in that they have no malevolent characters. The foreign oppression is a violation of human and divine law, but its agents are conspicuously missing from the uplifting reality of both dramas. In the other works, melodramatic villain-traitors appear, only to be put to flight by the entry of the noble and joyous insurrectionists. The villains' service to the invaders of Poland is predicated on their own alien identity which lacks the Poles' code of honor and love of freedom. A traitor 'may have a Polish name, but not a Polish soul' (*SIP*, p. 15). This is true of Starościc in *The Invalid*, who is about to marry Rozyna, the daughter of Staropolski. Disharmony is signalled through costume: we know that something is wrong when the squire wears the traditional dress of the Polish gentry, whereas Starościc favors a more contemporary, worldly fashion devoid of specific Polish markings. That Starościc is a foreign agent is confirmed by a letter which the squire receives just in time to cancel the marriage. Another renegade and spy is a Jewish scribe in *Muscovites Put to Flight*, who has changed his name to the Polish-sounding Mośkowski. The spies in *The Entry of the Polish Army to Volhynia* and *The Spy and the Poet* are foreigners: Petrow is Russian, Krauter is German. Dołkiewicz in Miłkowski's play is Polish, but he makes no pretense about his profession, and his name inescapably evokes a Polish idiom, *kopać pod kimś dołki* (to ensnare someone).

Free from fatality and dark forebodings, the plays undoubtedly indulge in an idealization of reality, but history in the making offered the dramatists much assistance. The Poles, always described in the plays as valiant, virtuous, and high-minded, had just liberated Warsaw from the rule of 'the vile Russians'. The playwrights spare no evidence of Russian barbarities in Poland. Miłkowski interpolates a vivid description of the bestiality of the Russian troops in the fall of 1794 when they stormed Praga, a suburb of Warsaw, and put the civilian population to the sword.[23] As Żdżarski's play points out, the Russians' most severe transgression is the exclusion of Poles from the community of 'God's creations', whereby the invaders feel justified to treat the Poles as sub-human (*AK*, p. 26). Bratkowski's play is unique in that Jan, the student, cautions the overly zealous bailiff: 'We'll fight only those Russians who would try to take away our freedom; those who support us are our brothers' (*AW*, p. 35).

Most of the plays end in a celebratory scene which is usually motivated by the marriage of the young lovers before the man goes off to war. The basic aim of these plays, then, is to dramatize a deadly threat to or the sickness of the contemporary way of life (both identified with the foreign rule) and the final triumphant recovery in the symbolic harmony of wedding, banquet, and dance. When the men join the uprising, it is always either to win or to perish, in keeping with the classical lesson of civic virtue. 'If you lose, do not return to hear our curses', says Laura to Wacław in *Muscovites Put to Flight*, paraphrasing *vae victis!* (*PM*, p. 34). Each play articulates in some form the Horatian maxim, 'Dulce et decorum est pro patria mori'. The Latin original appears verbatim as the final line in *The Invalid* (*I*, p. 41), the Polish translation is quoted in *The Warsaw Student* (*AW*, p. 14), and there are differently worded formulations of this sentiment in the other works.

The plays of 1831, written while the defeat of the November Uprising was still months away, give a melodramatic – and thus optimistic – reading of reality. A sense of injustice is apparent, but hope is not deferred. Having expelled the enemy from the capital and driven out the spies, the patriots take destiny in their hands as they prepare to clear the provinces of the invaders.

While the authors of the seven plays of the November Uprising take Polish–Russian antagonism for granted, Starzeński in *The Star of Siberia* and Zapolska in *The Other One* emerge as authors who can lend imaginative sympathy to rival characters if not points of view. Zapolska takes a step further by introducing psychological complexities into her play that erode the polarity of victim and villain.

Starzeński's play is set in 1854. The protagonist, Kazimierz, is a political prisoner in a Siberian fortress. He is about to marry Olga, daughter of Tatrow, the commander of the fortress, who is a rare instance of the good Russian in Polish drama. 'I won't do anything against my conscience just to get a kind word from the governor or another medal', declares Tatrow within the first five minutes of the play (*GS*, p. 7). Indeed, the elaborate intrigue of the play depends on Tatrow's willful decision to disregard the governor's order years ago in sparing the life of Kazimierz's father.

Tatrow and his daughter may be humane Russians, but to marry a national enemy would be a betrayal of Polish loyalties. Kazimierz finds himself in a particularly difficult position because he is involved in a conspiracy among Polish prisoners who plan an escape from Russian captivity. The accommodating playwright comes to Kazimierz's rescue and removes Olga from his path not once, but twice. Early on, she is compelled to marry a Russian villain; in the final scene, she throws herself from a cliff into the sea. The curtain falls upon Kazimierz's waving a French flag as he sails away to liberty on a French ship along with the other Polish prisoners.

In western melodrama of the same period, a suicide or a prisoners' escape would have been no more than a spectacular, sensational device of which audiences were very fond. Here, the suicide and the escape are markers of a symbolic code. As we have seen in the earlier plays, central to this code is the topos of patriotic self-sacrifice. Those plays unquestioningly assumed that the good of the country always comes before private matters. Here, the code is violated before it can be restored. Not only does Kazimierz choose the confines of domesticity over loyalty to the fellow conspirators, but his engagement to the Russian woman cancels his allegiance to the national cause. Once he has placed himself outside the Polish patriotic community, he becomes vulnerable to blackmail by the villain who threatens to have his father killed.

Kazimierz's father fought in the November Uprising. Unlike the Kościuszko Insurrection in the earlier plays, however, the uprising is hardly an inspiration for the present. To look back is to detract from the present course of action, from the business at hand, which is the escape from the fortress. Kazimierz gives in to the blackmailer and betrays the other prisoners in order to save his father. The betrayal, of course, is a logical consequence of Kazimierz's entanglement in private relations. When later in the play he desperately seeks to warn the prisoners about a trap set by the villain, they do not trust him. To convince the Poles that Kazimierz is again on their side, that is, to restore his patriotic bond with the fellow conspirators, Olga takes her own life. He rushes to save her, but his colleagues hold him back. His life, they say, belongs to Poland. To put it differently, Olga dies to redeem Kazimierz as a good patriot.

By the final scene, then, the play restores the code which requires that patriotic commitment take precedence over personal attachments. But it should give us pause that Kazimierz's return to the national cause is prompted by the self-sacrifice of a Russian woman and by the foreign intervention represented by the French ship. While in the plays of 1831 the Poles took national destiny in their own hands, here the optimistic outcome depends on outside factors. But perhaps the play owed its popularity precisely to the utopian vision whereby Russia repents its sins against Poland, the West comes to the Poles' aid, and the country emerges triumphant from captivity.

The protagonist of *The Other One* is also named Kazimierz. The action is set in Warsaw of the 1880s among young conspirators who, in their own way, carry on the insurrectionary tradition; indeed, the father of one of them fought in the 1863 uprising. After a year spent in the Warsaw citadel, Kazimierz is no longer an ardent, idealistic patriot, or 'the other one', but rather a sober, law-abiding citizen. Zapolska denies the audience any privileged insights into his conversion by carefully avoiding what Julia Przyboś called 'one of the essential strategies of the melodrama', that is, an 'enormous disproportion between the information accessible to the characters and that which the audience receives'.[24] There is no exposition to give background details. There are no telling names or costumes. Until the police launches an investigation of Kazimierz and his colleagues (act III), we as spectators are not privy to any information denied the characters on stage. The play's subtitle, 'a contemporary drama', might well be 'a realistic drama'.

Kazimierz, we gradually find out, has been released from the citadel because he gave his word of honor to Kornilov, the head of the police, that he would not engage in anti-Russian activities again. While Starzeński's Tatrow was a good Russian but a flat character, Zapolska boldly portrays a Russian police officer as a complex human being – for the first time in Polish drama. Even the critics, who took *The Other One* to task for its falsification of the clandestine activities in the Russian partition, were willing to concede that the Russians in the play command more respect, indeed admiration, than the Poles.[25] Actors and audiences particularly appreciated the role of Kornilov. As Karol Irzykowski observed,

> Kornilov is like a sphinx ... He seems in love with Kazimierz; he risks his own life to save Kazimierz's honor as a loyal subject. Is he a conscientious official who takes his duties seriously? There is no telling.[26]

In her presentation of the Polish characters, Zapolska juxtaposes the established code of patriotic melodrama with a popular plot about the moral fall of a protagonist who subsequently rises above his transgression. Nothing elicited so much admiration in audiences as the sinner reformed through the efforts of a dedicated woman. In Zapolska's version of the plot, Kazimierz is engaged to a virginal woman conspirator while he enjoys the sexual ministrations of a flirtatious waitress. Such a plot in a patriotic play subverted a sacrosanct Polish tradition whereby, in Irzykowski's apt phrase, 'Political martyrdom liked the company of asceticism.'[27] It might well be that Zapolska's strategy, which situated the play outside cultural propriety, accounted for the play's immense popularity.

For all his incisiveness, Irzykowski indulged in a facile explanation when he applauded Zapolska's rejection of the stale patriotic convention. Anna, the woman conspirator, he argued, is 'frigid and has no effect on Kazimierz sexually, therefore he must turn for earthly love to a real woman'.[28] But Zapolska's subversion of the ideal of sublime and chaste patriotism does not stop at making Kazimierz's sexual appetites the pivot of the intrigue that leads to his fiancée's deportation to Siberia. When initially he cannot accept Anna as a human being in her own right, his reasons go beyond what Irzykowski diagnosed as Anna's frigidity. 'I'm tired of the boundless intelligence of my fiancée', Kazimierz says of Anna early in the play (*T*, p. 15). He finds the waitress appealing precisely because she does not think. Anna is hardly a traditional feminine ideal – a subordinate, nurturing figure. Throughout the play, she is strong-minded, steadfast, and dedicated to the national cause. She retains her presence of mind during an arrest, refuses to submit to authority, and resists all tricks and deceptions during a police interrogation. In western melodrama, a woman's salvation is assured by the will of a man. Here, Kazimierz's salvation is assured by Anna's will. By the play's end, he is ready to join her in Siberian exile in order to win back his identity as 'the other one' and thus to secure her pardon and acceptance.

The artistic value of the nine plays is minimal. They are second- or third-order works which provided a serviceable vehicle for popular patriotism but are now mostly forgotten. However, when we uncover the acts of symbolization and the underlying codes which organize and give meaning to these texts, we begin to realize that they develop an aesthetic which embodied and, in turn, shaped the Poles' perceptions of national identity and history. The plays are thus not merely a Polish variation of a popular genre. They fill a ready-made form to bursting point with a Polish content and axiology, with obvious national emblems and covert symbolic codes.

Unlike melodrama in the West, these plays did not develop in 'an ethical vacuum in the public sphere',[29] but in a political situation which made a system of moral values and patriotic imperatives increasingly strict. The men and women of these plays live in a world controlled by foreign invaders. They are all subject to the illegitimate foreign rule which depends on forced submission.

The Star of Siberia conforms to what Ann E. Kaplan identified as a male type of melodrama,[30] but the other plays subvert a number of assumptions about the genre itself. Set in the domestic realm, they are in fact about the public realm. That is to say, the domestic realm is the only one in which the characters can fully exercise their public commitment – by engaging in uncensored education, collecting arms, planning another uprising. This is a patriarchal society, to be sure, but with important modifications. All of the characters identify with mother (Poland), and loyalty to the maternal order requires disobedience to the invaders. It is no coincidence that Jadwiga in Wanda Szopowicz's play has promised her dying mother to resist the enemy. Szopowicz does not fail to impress the significance of the pledge upon her audience: first, we learn about the pledge from Jadwiga herself, then the Russian police officer finds a written record of the oath and reads it aloud.

The Polish women in the plays are not excluded from the public realm and assigned to its periphery. As Maria Janion observed in a study of the literary legacy of the January Uprising, '*The civic patriotic emancipation shaped a new concept of the feminine.*'[31] Szopowicz's Jadwiga and Zapolska's Anna clearly represent this new concept, as does, for example, the woman insurrectionist in Antoni Stefan Ździebłowski's *The Heroine of the 1863 Uprising* (*Bohaterka z Powstania 1863 roku*, 1893). (*The Star of Siberia*, which needs only a Russian woman as a sacrificial victim, is quite unusual in the context of the countless plays about the Polish conspiracies and uprisings, which depict female strength, endurance, and leadership.) Unlike their western counterparts, the women in these plays are in fact 'arbiters of good and evil in the public sphere'.[32] 'You owe your life to Poland', says mother to son in *Muscovites Put to Flight*. 'Purge Poland of invaders because I don't want to bear slaves any more' (*PM*, p. 46).

The plays vary in their theatricalization of political reality and draw different sustenance from the melodramatic genre. But, to paraphrase Dobrochna Ratajczak, for the men as well as the women of these plays the space is Poland, and the time is history.[33]

NOTES

1 Daniel C. Gerould, 'The Americanization of Melodrama', in *American Melodrama*, ed. Gerould (New York: Performing Arts Journal Publications, 1983), p. 15.

2 The November Uprising has also been called the Polish Revolution.

3 See Emanuel Mateusz Rostworowski, *Popioły i korzenie: Szkice historyczne i rodzinne* (Cracow, 1985).

4 Gerould, 'Americanization', p. 8.

5 See, for example, Oscar G. Brockett, *The Theatre: An Introduction* (New York: Holt, Rinehart and Winston, 1979), p. 198; Gerould, 'Americanization', p. 8; Ann E. Kaplan, 'Theories of Melodrama: A Feminist Perspective', *Women and Performance: A Journal of Feminist Theory*, 1 (Spring/Summer 1983), 40.

6 It is not unusual for a Polish critic to claim that Poland has not had its own melodramatic repertory. See, for instance, Małgorzata Szpakowska, 'Melodramat czyli potrzeba serca', *Dialog*, 34 (January 1989), 110.

7 For a pioneering study of the noncanonical texts, see Dobrochna Ratajczak, 'Komedioopera polityczna powstania listopadowego', in *Warszawa teatralna*, ed. Lidia Kuchtówna (Warsaw, 1990).

8 Ibid., p. 7.

9 I owe my definition of topos to Ernst Robert Curtius, *European Literature and the Latin Middle Ages*, trans. Willard R. Trask (New York: Pantheon Books, 1953), and to Stefan Morawski, 'The Basic Functions of Quotation', in *Sign, Language, Culture*, ed. C. H. Van Schoonevelt (Hague: Mouton, 1970), pp. 690–705. I

understand topos not as a motif imposed on an artistic structure, but as the organizing principle of such a structure, indeed 'the scaffolding of the new whole' (Morawski, p. 698).

10 This set includes all the extant texts which I have been able to trace, except Ludwik Adam Dmuszewski's *The Rising of the Nation* (*Powstanie narodu*) which is a monologue rather than a play proper. It was performed, with music by Józef Elsner and set design by Józef Hilary Głowacki, as a curtain raiser at the Narodowy Theatre in Warsaw on 1 January 1831.

11 *The Entry of the Polish Army into Volhynia*, in which the defeat of the Russians in 1830 allows the Polish heroine to rebuff the advances of a Russian policeman, might be a version of the now lost *A Broken Engagement, or the Uprising* (*Przerwane zaręczyny, czyli Powstanie*) which opened on 6 April 1831 at the Rozmaitości Theatre in Warsaw.

12 Karol Irzykowski, 'Sprawozdanie teatralne: *Tamten*', *Robotnik*, 34 (3 September 1928), 2. *The Star of Siberia* and *The Other One* were also frequently performed by Polish-language theatre groups in the United States (see Emil Orzechowski, *Teatr polonijny w Stanach Zjednoczonych* (Wrocław, 1989)).

13 For much of the production history of *The Other One*, I am indebted to Irzykowski, 'Sprawozdanie teatralne', and Zbigniew Raszewski, 'Zapolska – pisarka teatralna', in Gabriela Zapolska, *Dramaty*, ed. Anna Raszewska, vol. II (Wrocław, 1961), pp. xx–xxx, lxxiii.

14 References to the plays will be identified by an abbreviation of the title followed by page numbers. In this key to the abbreviations, whenever appropriate, information given in brackets refers to the first publication:

AK: Augustyn Żdżarski, *Akademik krakowski, czyli Ofiara za Ojczyznę* (Poznań 1897) [Płock 1831].

AW: Stanisław Bratkowski [published anonymously], *Akademik warszawski* (Warsaw c1831).

DDDL: Paweł Felicjan Miłkowski, *Dzień dwudziesty dziewiąty listopada* (Warsaw 1831).

GS: Leopold Starzeński, *Gwiazda Syberii* (Chicago 1910) [Lvov 1881].

I: Józefat Krzaczkowski, *Inwalid czyli Męstwo nagrodzone* (manuscript no. 3892, Czartoryski Library in Cracow).

PM: Zygmunt Edwin Gordaszewski, *Popłoch Moskali* (published anonymously, Warsaw 1831).

SIP: Anonymous, *Szpieg i poeta: Rywale* (Warsaw 1831).

T: Gabriela Zapolska, *Tamten*, in *Dramaty*, ed. Anna Raszewska, vol. II (Wrocław 1961) [Cracow 1899].

WWP: Wanda Szopowicz, *Wejście wojsk polskich na Wołyń* (manuscript no. 5674, Library of Jagiellonian University in Cracow).

15 During the November Uprising, performances at the two theatres in Warsaw, the Narodowy and the Rozmaitości, served as a platform for political opinions as well as a popular festival. They were an occasion for spontaneous demonstrations of collective patriotic sentiments, in which actors and audiences joined in dancing and singing together (see Henryk Eile, *Teatr warszawski w dobie powstań* (Warsaw, 1937), pp. 43–137). The history of the

Warsaw stage during the uprising contests Jean Duvignaud's argument that during revolutions theatre as an institution becomes superfluous (see his *Le Théâtre, et après* (Tournai, 1971), pp. 53–9, 114–16; and *Les Ombres collectives: Sociologie du théâtre* (Paris, 1973), pp. 383–417). Writing about the dramas of the French Revolution, Duvignaud argued that they 'sought to express liberty but represented it in lifeless figures and in a dead frame, a type of *ghetto* with no relation to existence' (*Les Ombres collectives*, p. 401; emphasis in original).

16 The Polish *komedioopera* is related to *vaudeville* in its original French meaning. See Phyllis Hartnoll (ed.), *The Oxford Companion to the Theatre* (Oxford University Press, 1983), p. 859.

17 See especially T. Z. Królewiak, 'Z powodu sztuki Maskoffa *Tamten* (O ile wiernie są skreślone w tej sztuce stosunki polskie w zaborze rosyjskim)', *Promień*, 1 (1 March 1899), 43–5; T. Z. Królewiak, 'Z powodu sztuki Maskoffa *Tamten* (Dokończenie)', *Promień*, 1 (1 April 1899), 65–7; and an anonymous review in two parts, '*Matka-Polka*', *Głos Narodu*, 7 (31 August 1899), 5–6, and *Głos Narodu*, 7 (1 September 1899), 5.

18 See especially Ryszard Przybylski, 'Symbolika powstania listopadowego', in Jerzy Skrowronek and Maria Żmigrodzka (eds.), *Powstanie listopadowe 1830–1831: Geneza–uwarunkowania–bilans–porównania* (Wrocław, 1983), pp. 341–64.

19 Ratajczak, 'Komedioopera polityczna'. The symbolism of the Kościuszko Insurrection is still very strong. During a visit to Cracow in October 1980, Lech Wałęsa pledged to uphold the cause of Solidarity. For his speech, he chose what he called a 'noble eighteenth-century context': he spoke in exactly the same spot of Cracow's Market Square where Kościuszko, on 24 March 1794, had sworn a solemn oath to free Poland (Lech Wałęsa, *A Way of Hope*, trans. by various hands (New York: H. Holt & Co., 1987), p. 172). Moreover, the re-emergence of Solidarity in 1989 was viewed as the bloodless Racławice. On Whitsunday (14 May 1989), three weeks before the first semi-free election in postwar Poland, Wałęsa rode in a horse-drawn carriage across the fields of Racławice. Dressed in national costume, like Kościuszko before him, he carried an upright scythe, the weapon of Kościuszko's peasant soldiers. He was surrounded by horse-mounted peasants in the garb of Kościuszko's troops. His speech underscored the importance of national unity on the eve of the election (cf. 'Wałęsa pod Racławicami', *Gazeta Wyborcza*, 1 (16 May 1989), 1).

20 Andrzej Walicki, *The Three Traditions in Polish Patriotism and Their Contemporary Relevance* (Bloomington: Polish Studies Centre, 1988), p. 13.

21 Jerry Palmer, 'Merit and Destiny: Ideology and Narrative in French Classicism', in *1642: Literature and Power in the Seventeenth Century*, ed. Francis Barker et al. (Colchester: University of Essex Press, 1981), p. 123.

22 Janusz Tazbir, *Kultura szlachecka w Polsce* (Warsaw, 1978), pp. 71–2.

23 From Warsaw, Colonel William Gardner thus reported to the British Secretary of State about the storming of Praga: 'the most horrid and unnecessary barbarities – Houses burnt, women massacred, infants at the breast pierced with the pikes of cosaques and universal plunder' (cited in Norman Davies, *God's Playground: A History of Poland*, vol. 1 (New York: Columbia University Press, 1982), p. 544).

24 Julia Przyboś, *L'Enterprise mélodramatique* (Paris: Corti, 1987), p. 125.
25 Królewiak, 'Z powodu sztuki Maskoffa *Tamten* (Dokończenie)', p. 65.
26 Irzykowski, 'Sprawozdanie teatralne', p. 2.
27 Ibid.
28 Ibid.
29 Kaplan, 'Theories of Melodrama', p. 41.
30 Ibid., pp. 43–4.
31 Maria Janion, 'Szalona', *Twórczość*, 44 (October 1988), 73; emphasis in original. The January Uprising, in fact, has been regarded as a women's uprising because of their central role in organizing it (see, for example, Maria Bruchnalska, *Ciche bohaterki: Udział kobiet w powstaniu styczniowym [materiały]* (Miejsce Piastowe, 1933)).
32 Kaplan, 'Theories of Melodrama', p. 43.
33 Cf. Ratajczak, 'Komedioopera polityczna'.

La Dame aux Camélias: the myth revised

SUSAN PAINTER

In every generation star performers and their admirers have found *La Dame aux Camélias* fascinating. The greatest popular success of the nineteenth-century European stage has retained its magnetism, finding perennial life in the presentation of sex, disease and death. Dumas's romantic and sentimental melodrama together with its derivatives have been continually in production for the very reason that the playwright indicated in his preface: 'It is no longer a play, it is a legend.' And the legend has been consumed in all of the possible forms. The 1848 novel and the theatre text of 1852 have been followed by numerous film versions, and the original play is regularly re-made for television in expensive productions with star actors. *La Traviata* is always in the Opera House repertoire and among the balletic versions are Frederick Ashton's *Marguerite and Armand* and John Neumeier's *The Lady of the Camellias*. Meyerhold directed it; Brecht adapted it; Bernhardt performed Marguerite over three thousand times, and even old age and the amputation of one leg could not deter her; D. H. Lawrence in 1908 was overwhelmingly moved by the play; there was insatiable demand throughout the world for Duse's sensitive, psychological rendition of the heroine; in 1936 Garbo's vivacious fragility won Hitler's heart and he insisted on a wide distribution in Germany of the Hollywood melodrama despite the 'racial impurity' of its director, George Cukor.[1]

There has been an acceptance in our culture of the myth of Marguerite Gautier, an absorption of its ideology, its hypocrisy, and its analysis of male–female relationships. The myth was constructed by a man who had an obsessional fear of female independence, whose hatred for women was repetitiously and proudly expounded in the long-winded prefaces to his plays. There have been many adaptations by men[2] but this paper will consider two revisionist versions by women. Pam Gems's *Camille* for the Royal Shakespeare Company in 1984 offers us an implacable feminist view of Armand as a cruel, selfish aggressor. Nancy Sweet's *Camille* for the Edinburgh Fringe in 1987 depicts a Sartrean eternal limbo in which she portrays the actual historical people being forced to act and re-enact the

4 Sarah Bernhardt, 1882

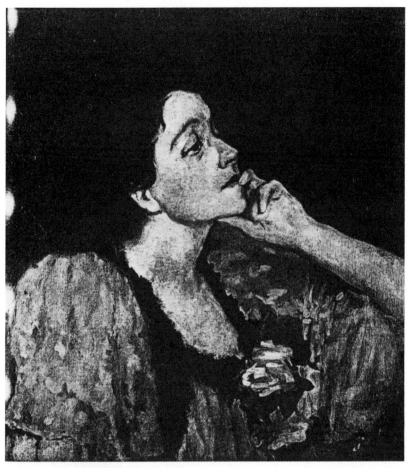

5 Detail of E. Gordigiani's portrait of Eleonora Duse, 1896

story that Dumas imposed on them in the process of turning experience into propaganda.

My intention is first of all to analyse the astonishing success of the original play. Why did it please so much? What was Dumas's attitude to women? Was he writing theatre useful to society (as he claimed he was doing) or was he offering his own neurotic attitudes for public approval? Dumas was a self-righteous moralizing misogynist. His virulent attacks on women accompany his exploitation of an affair with a prostitute in a version calculated to justify his own behaviour by presenting Armand as a romanticized surrogate.

In this theatrical auto-hagiography Dumas tactically aimed to make a fortune at the box office through tear-jerking manipulation. Of the

6 Greta Garbo as Camille, 1936

notorious nineteenth-century stage deaths, that of Marguerite Gautier is the most famous.[3] A skilled handling of the scene buys plentiful tears: the female revisionist texts emphasize for us that it is not ethical for women to present this death uncritically for the satisfaction of voyeuristic spectators. Dumas's play version followed helter-skelter on the success of his novel of the same title: the ending is crucially different in the play, happier, more sentimental, calculatedly manipulative of the audience's emotions. The ambivalent life experience was simplified into suitable stage material for Dumas's purposes, and the genre he chose was that of melodrama, a genre that deals in strong antitheses and ethical absolutism.[4]

The story of the play is easily recounted. Marguerite Gautier, the most sought after, beautiful, fashionable courtesan in all Paris (despite her peasant origins), entertains the nobility in grand style. Armand Duval, from a rich bourgeois family, falls madly in love with Marguerite. He persuades her to stop trading sex for money, and to have a grand passionate affair with him. Armand and Marguerite go off to the country in the hope of curing Marguerite's cough with the healing fresh air away from the emotionally empty city environment. Their country idyll is cut short by the arrival of Armand's father, who persuades Marguerite not only that she is endangering her son's reputation, but also that her association with Armand is threatening to ruin Armand's sister's marriage because the fiancé's family disapprove of Armand's behaviour. Marguerite agrees to leave and makes the realization for herself that, as a fallen woman, she does not deserve a place in society; she writes a deceiving letter to Armand to the effect that she is involved with another man. Armand returns to Paris to humiliate Marguerite at a ball: he showers her with banknotes, crying, 'I call upon you all to witness that I owe this woman nothing!'[5] In act 5, six months later, there is a reconciliation between the lovers. Armand's father has written to tell him the truth, and Armand returns to Marguerite to forgive her. But it is too late: Marguerite dies of tuberculosis, and her friend points the moral: 'Much will be forgiven you, for you loved much' (p. 164).

Dumas was consciously writing a manipulative play. The central figure is a sympathetic whore, a whore with a heart of gold. Dumas's attitude is that this woman makes a big sacrifice so she is partially redeemed, but that, because of her trade, she is still a threat to family, virtue, religion, and the whole thrust of bourgeois morality. She must be made to submit to society's laws, so she is killed off. In this respect, the audience is made to feel very gratified, smug, and assured in their own middle-class moral convictions: whores must be punished and the sex industry must be condemned. What Dumas has put together is a congratulatory piece with tabloid press ingredients; the audience delight in salacious interest in

7 'Much will be forgiven, for you loved much.'

illicit sex; moral satisfaction in seeing social superiors behave badly; puni-
tive vindictiveness in seeing a whore die; sentimental indulgence over an
illness and death presented in a sanitized and glamorous way; final
affirmation of the values of marriage, religion, the family, prompt payment of taxes, the right of the older generation to dictate to its offspring
the correct way to behave, and the perpetuation of male authoritarianism.

At the very centre of the play's structure lies the entrance of Duval *père*.
The assumption is confident: it is that the audience are committed to all
that Duval embodies. He speaks for the perpetuation of male
authoritarianism and in so doing he is not evil; he is not a villain. He
merely puts the voice of bourgeois morality. Duval is a father, a representative of the establishment, head of the family, connected to the heart of
the capitalist mode of social organization in his profession as tax collector.
The father earns his money by taking part of people's earnings to plough
back into the social organization, to keep it going. He tells his son what is
right, and his son will become a father to tell other sons what is right, to
perpetuate an entire way of looking at the world. His confrontation with
Marguerite is unequal from the start. From Dumas's point of view she is a
woman, therefore she is inferior. She is a 'woman with a past' so she must
be expelled from society. She is a non-conformist deviant. But from a
feminist viewpoint the very worst characteristic of Marguerite is that she
yields so readily to the social argument. She agrees to be a victim; instead
of telling the father that he is talking nonsense, instead of standing up for

her rights as an independent being, she agrees with him. She acknowledges, on behalf of Dumas, on behalf of her society, that 'the woman, once she has fallen, can never rise again' (p. 141). In Dumas's version of the myth she accepts that her death is a necessary punishment: 'believe me, God sees more clearly than we do' (p. 163) she assures Armand on her deathbed.

Marguerite is clearly exploited on several levels. Whereas Marx and Engels would say that as a member of capitalist society she has to prostitute herself to make money, however alienated she may be from her occupation, radical feminists would say that as a woman she is dominated by the male terms on which she is allowed to act. The parameters of her existence are closely dictated by men. She is not even allowed the freedom to do what she wants with her own body; her body is another male commodity, and has value only in that respect. And when she breaks out of this mould, the punishment is death. As a character in a play she is the object of the audience's salacious interest. As a character created by the male playwright Dumas she is made to voice his own prejudices; ironically she becomes Dumas's own raisonneur. She is a victim of Dumas's exploitation, of Dumas's repressive morality.

And, most reprehensibly of all, Dumas has exploited the actual woman on whom he based the character of Marguerite. This reactionary moralist had had a short-lived affair with Marie Duplessis, the famed courtesan whom the demi-monde revered as arbiter of taste and fashion. Through the play's strict condemnation, Dumas has found his revenge: he has used bourgeois morality against the fictional Marguerite to deny his guilt over the historical Marie.

The novel *La Dame aux Camélias* was published in 1848, the year that Marx and Engels wrote *The Communist Manifesto*. When they pointed out, in what was to be understood as an outrageous comment, that

> Our bourgeois, not content with having the wives and daughters of their proletarians at their disposal, not to speak of common prostitutes, take the greatest pleasure in seducing each other's wives[6]

they could have taken Dumas's private life as a clear example. Whereas Marx and Engels use the prostitute throughout their work as metaphor of the proletarian victims of capitalist exploitation, Dumas projected in his plays and prefaces all his own victimizing hypocrisy.[7] He whitewashed his own adultery in plays and prefaces that condemn adultery. He fathered a child by a mistress while he was married but he inveighed against illegitimacy. He castigated prostitution in delirious outbursts of manic condemnation but his short affair with the most famous courtesan of the period was distorted by him into a sentimental plot that made and still makes his entire reputation throughout the world.

Dumas's prefaces are full of virulent attacks against women. He first used the writing of prefaces as therapy following a period of breakdown and psychological crisis; he was actually encouraged to formulate his attitudes to his plays by George Sand's doctor.[8] In 1867 he set about it. He decided to say that he wanted to inaugurate what he called 'le théâtre utile',[9] a theatre of moral use to society. He wavered in the prefaces between, on the one hand, offering bourgeois maxims about how to get through the day, and, on the other, revealing his obsessional paranoia about prostitution, adultery and illegitimacy. In the general introduction to his plays Dumas is at his most priggish about how to lead an ordered existence:

> Walk two hours every day, sleep seven hours every night; go to bed, always alone, as soon as you feel like sleeping; get up as soon as you wake up; work as soon as you have got up. Eat only when you are hungry, drink only when you are thirsty, and always slowly. Talk only when it is necessary and say only part of what you think ... Esteem money neither more nor less than it should be valued: it is a good servant and a bad master ... Strive to be uncomplicated, to be useful, to stay free; and wait, before denying God, until someone has proved conclusively that He does not exist.[10]

This Polonius-like list of platitudes conjures up the decorum and regularity of the middle-class 'respectable', God-fearing, Christian morality-adhering man that Dumas wanted to be. In actuality, he had no systematic religious faith, his private life was anarchic, and he would have welcomed the certainty of a religion to live by. He spent his entire life reacting against the excesses of his father whose abandonment of him as a child blighted his experience of the world. His father had not married his mother and, in his childhood, he was subjected to taunts of 'bastard' from his schoolmates. Although the father did, after the early years, lavish every kind of care and money on his son, there were still moments when Dumas *fils* strongly felt an impulsive desire to kill his father.[11] As a result, the father in *La Dame aux Camélias* was given all the moral attributes that Dumas would have appreciated from his own father. In the following quotation we hear the father's principles and they are comparable with Dumas's little list of maxims to the reader. Duval *père* talks to Marguerite:

> You have known Armand for three months and you love him, but are you so sure that this love will last for ever? He will take the best years of your life and then what will happen? Either he will leave you or he will act honourably and marry you. This marriage, which will not have chastity for its foundaton, nor religion for its support, could lead to nothing but disaster. What career would remain open to him? What will be left to you both when you are old? Who can promise you that he will not be less dazzled when time casts the first shadow over your beauty? That the passing of your youth will not also mean the passing of his illusion? Cannot you see what your old age will be, doubly deserted, doubly desolate? What memories will you leave behind you? What

good will you ever have accomplished? You and my son have two very different roads to follow; chance has brought them together for a moment. You have been happy for three months; keep the memory of it always in your heart. Let it strengthen you; it is all you have the right to ask of it. One day you will be proud of what you have done, and all your life you will respect yourself for it. It is as a man of the world that I am speaking to you, it is as a father that I am pleading with you. Come, Marguerite, prove to me that you really love my son, and take courage. (p. 140)

The emphasis here on self-sacrifice and on Christian morality reveals one side of Dumas, the acceptable public face. Here Dumas allows the voice of respectability to subdue the force of female sexuality, to curb the embodiment of the anti-social passion that society must expel. It is a calm utterance in the voice of a character. The later prefaces, in Dumas's own voice, get hysterical on the same issue, and reflect a typical nineteenth-century male double standard. Dumas firmly believed that no man is capable of complete fidelity,[12] and he himself had frequent extra-marital liaisons. But women, unfaithful in marriage, are killed off in his later plays, and he tries to persuade us in the prefaces that this is the only possible course of action.

In the preface to *L'Ami des femmes* Dumas refers to the 'Woman-Animal', the emancipated woman akin to the prostitute who doesn't want any longer to be wife or companion, who wants to be an adversary of the man. She destroys the family, she wants pleasure, she is convinced that she is man's equal in intelligence and strength, she wears culottes; she is, however, nothing at all separated from man because her function and destiny are determined:

The Woman is a circumscribed, passive, instrumental, available being, one in perpetual expectation. She is the sole unfinished being that God permitted Man to take back and finish ... God made Man with his own hands, then he made woman as a part of Man ... Her liberation would be her death. The brain of the woman is a vessel and her stomach a mould. Neither takes a form until Man puts something there ... She is purely passive and instrumental ... He holds her in submission. Man is the instrument of God, Woman is the instrument of Man. [After marriage] our cause is common, we have nothing to fear of life's hazards ... We are that which is most powerful, most pure, most sacred, we are the family.[13]

Here, Dumas sees woman as the biblical Eve, and he extols the social institutions of family and marriage as natural. Roland Barthes defines the essential function of myth as 'the naturalisation of the concept';[14] the socially constructed myth that woman is unfinished until man comes along, that woman is passive, an instrument, and that her prime purpose is to reproduce the species, is repeated in the most explicit terms by Dumas, and he extols this myth as natural; the woman choosing not to wear skirts, who wants emancipation from the oppression of male control, is an unnatural animal. This viewpoint reaches an ugly pitch of hysteria in the preface to *La Femme de Claude*.

Continuing his study of woman, Dumas creates a vision of 'La Bête', the Beast who metaphorically represents the adulteress, the prostitute and the independent woman. The Beast is responsible for the moral degeneration of society; through her, honour, fortunes, the family and marriage are destroyed; through her, illegitimacy and abortion continue. Indeed, France lost the Franco-Prussian war because of this monster; right-thinking citizens must exterminate the Beast and its anarchical powers. Dumas's hyperbolic description of the Beast is extraordinary:

> I saw an enormous bubbling produce itself in the crucible; and out came a colossal Beast which had seven heads and ten horns, and on those horns ten crowns ... This Beast was similar to a leopard, its feet were like a bear's feet, its jaws like the jaws of a lion, and the dragon gave it its power. And this beast was clothed in purple and scarlet, it was trimmed in gold, with precious stones and pearls, it held in its milk-white hands a gold vase full of the abominations and impurities of Babylon, of Sodom and of Lesbos ... And the seven heads of the Beast surpassed the most high mountains ... Its seven mouths, always open and smiling, were red like the embers of a fire; its fourteen unblinking eyes were green like the waters of the Ocean ... And above each of the ten diadems above the ten horns, in the middle of all sorts of words of blasphemy, flamed this word, larger than all the others: PROSTITUTION. Now, this Beast was no other than a new incarnation of woman, deciding to make a revolution in her turn ... I thought that the theatre would serve me to denounce her publicly, since it is the case that she has modified, perverted, contaminated love ...[15]

This hatred of women was concentrated – both for Dumas and great numbers of people in his audiences throughout the western world – on Marguerite Gautier. The theatre allowed him to denounce and take revenge on the historical courtesan through the character of Marguerite, whose punishment is the vindictively judgmental weapon of the self-righteous moralist. Dumas cites the homiletic episode of The Woman Taken in Adultery, and then applies an Old Testament attitude of remorseless castigation.

This section of the preface makes reference to Dumas's 1872 pamphlet *L'Homme-Femme* which stresses the offensive and harmful nature of women, and urges ways in which women's influence can be squashed.[16] Dumas provoked a fierce response from both men and women with his ideas here because he strongly argues the moral entitlement of husbands to kill wives who commit adultery. He urges that the husband is justified in acting as the avenger of heaven and that the adulterous woman is purely animal. The pamphlet ends on the exclamatory words 'kill her!' In the preface to *La Femme de Claude* Dumas defends these ideas to a certain

M. Cuvillier-Fleury who had been particularly harsh on him. This is the defence:

> It is said that he [Jesus] pardoned the adulterous woman, which is absolutely false. He pardoned her not at all; he made an error in his argument against the Pharisees, above all. He said to them: 'Who amongst you is without sin? If there is one, let him throw the first stone.' Happily for that woman, all the men were more or less guilty; so she wasn't stoned, and Jesus said to her, 'Go on your way, and in future sin no more.' ...
>
> If one of the Pharisees, the husband, for example, had been without sin, and had come out of the crowd saying 'Master, I am without sin' Jesus would have been forced to say to him, 'Strike her.'
>
> So, Monsieur, you see how one can be wrongfully blamed, the 'Kill her!' which ends my pamphlet *L'Homme-Femme*, which scandalized so many people and which you forbade me to say, is only the paraphrase of the word of Christ to those who brought to him the adulterous woman.[17]

This deliberate misinterpretation of the parable supports his own prejudice. It proves that Dumas is so fundamentally gripped by the need to be judgmental that he can ignore the lynchpin of Christ's teaching: that everyone is a sinner. And in the play *La Femme de Claude* itself we find a severely judgmental treatment of the plot. Claude the husband brutally kills Césarine his adulterous wife and is congratulated for doing so. He has killed a representative of the insatiable Beast who undermines society.

The subject now deserves widening out. The manic attack against women and the perpetuation of the Eve myth which sees woman as temptress, whore, and destroyer of society, are dangerous because they are so acceptable, particularly in Britain in the late 1980s where we have a backlash against all extra-marital expressions of sexuality. In Thatcher's Britain the central government passed legislature to force local government to be repressive with regard to attitudes to sexual education. The Dumas frame of mind, the judgmental paranoia, goes along with this pattern of attitudes in Britain. Just as audiences in the mid nineteenth century were openly receptive to confident congratulatory moralizing, just as Marguerite is made to speak on behalf of the playwright, saying that of course it is right that she should die in agony, just as female sexuality is condemned in the Dumas play and the devil is not given her due, so, in a recent Hollywood melodrama, *Fatal Attraction*, Dumas's ingredients are recycled.[18] In the mid nineteenth century audiences were sent home to their bourgeois marriages as the very best thing after all; in the late 1980s of the twentieth century we are served with an identical argument. *Fatal Attraction* involves a rich good-looking family with a nice little child; the husband is a lawyer, with all the chic glamour of attractiveness, money, parties, possessions, an office and a secretary. He and his pretty wife are never seen in sexual activity. She is a Madonna figure, pure and virginal, the child seemingly a product of Immaculate Conception.

The husband meets La Bête in the shape of an alluring, extremely beautiful and available independent woman, a whore (because this is how she is judged), who gets him into the sink, the elevator, and eventually into her bed, for sex, when the wife is away for the weekend. The Beast does not leave poor husband alone after this encounter, and becomes a liability, slitting her wrists, declaring that she is pregnant, demanding attention, visiting and spying on the husband's house, kidnapping the child and boiling the child's pet rabbit. The wife gets hurt in a car crash, finds out all about the affair, but eventually stands by the husband and heroically shoots the mistress dead when the Beast fails to drown in the bath. The final image is of child, wife and husband reunited, the inviolable family. It is clear that the Beast in *Fatal Attraction* embodies the threat of AIDS and that is one reason why the film was such an enormous success: the villain who can pass on an incurable virus must be punished. The woman carries all the punishment, however. Poor husband who fancied a bit on the side and got more trouble than he bargained for, is let off with a little guilt. He is allowed a reconciliation that endures, he receives forgiveness from the doting faithful wife; and he is received back into the society he deviated from. He has learnt his lesson.

Unsurprisingly, feminist reactions to the film have been very strong: why should woman carry the punishment for sexual gratification; why should woman be labelled as villain, the mythic Eve temptress figure? And although the mistress is allowed a small argument on behalf of her actions, to protest against adulterous men who leave 'the other woman' pregnant, and to convey her longing to be part of a family, this argument is immediately discredited because she is mad, in the most female way, being depressive. Her lack of independence and her longing to be part of the family unit press another kind of satisfaction from the audience: single women do not like being single. And the audience also get thrills and spills: the boiled rabbit is a high point of sensationalism as is the helter-skelter ride when it seems that the kidnapped child will be killed; salacious gratification is a primary aim throughout; sentimentality is wallowed in when there is danger to the wife in a car crash; final moral satisfaction is the reward when the audience can judge and punish the Beast. The film is an ugly piece of propaganda that loathes women and reassures the audience, including the women who have embraced the system.

Dumas's play was the first world-wide success in the process of dramatizing a frame of mind that is always with us. The Madonna/Whore myth is repeated in *Fatal Attraction* and has a similar popular drawing power. Dumas had demonstrated an extremely effective way for modern drama to formulate the myth. The judgmental frame of mind accompanies a whole pattern of attitudes: the prejudices of sexism and racism; the eagerness to revive judicious murder; hatred of homosexuality

– all the prejudices of Thatcher's Britain are in the mould of the Dumas frame of mind. And moralism is used by extremists as a justification for prejudices such as these. Dumas claimed to be 'un chrétien du dehors',[19] one who adhered to Christian moralism without engaging with the metaphysics. In practice this meant that he could direct his venom against women in his prefaces, plays and pamphlets, misinterpret the Gospels, and wish the Jews out of France[20] – it is worth bearing in mind that Hitler found *Camille* to his taste.

Very recently, two feminist playwrights have attempted to deconstruct Dumas's misogynist view of the world. In 1984 Pam Gems critically re-examined the Camille myth, introducing a son for Marguerite, and looking in a tough-minded way at the aggressive social organization that caused Marguerite to turn to the streets of Paris.[21] In 1987 Nancy Sweet revised the material in terms of Dumas's exploitation of the historical Marie Duplessis.[22]

Like Dumas, Gems offers us a myth drama. Her characters are representative of man and woman existing in a male-dominated social structure: we are not interested in their individual male–female relationship. Armand is raised to aristocratic status and, with a father who is a marquis, he is significantly further removed in class terms from his prostitute mistress. He is so far removed from her that he cannot understand the thought processes that Marguerite has out of necessity adopted. Their reconciliation is placed before the deathbed scene but it is short-lived; when Marguerite, with an eye to practicality, suggests going to work one last time with the Russian prince to buy them a dowry, Armand, in a fit of cruel jealousy, throws money in her face and rejects her for the final time. He still will not understand the way the social structure has forced her to sell her body as a commodity in order to make a profit from the transaction; above all he will not understand how this transaction is separate from her love for him, how the act is pragmatic, how it is not a betrayal.

It is Prudence who makes a crucial point to Armand: 'Has it never occurred to you that some of us might prefer the life – given the alternatives?' (p. 152) We must ask what alternatives there are for Marguerite: poverty is one, or the laundry where her mother worked, 'Arms swollen with soda from washing stains from other people's linen' (p. 158). Prostitution is available to Marguerite in several forms: the life of a courtesan allows her access to a high-class world; the sad truth is that it is an occupation equally as exploitative as others available to her but it is better paid. Ironically, society has been organized in such a way that Marguerite is a victim whichever way she turns; her love cannot survive because she is condemned for her profession. And falling in love is a risk to her livelihood.

Gems vigorously propounds the thesis that society has been organized by men so that women are victims; that it is a Darwinian struggle between men and women to survive and that men have the upper hand. Men have destroyed Marguerite's life. In act I, scene 6, set in the bedroom, site of sex and profit, after she has allowed Armand to stay with her for the first time, she explains her past. She accuses Armand:

> I know the way you live! Hot-house grapes, lofts full of apples, figs with the bloom on them ... stables, libraries, a fire in your room. I used to clean the grates with my mother ... 5 o'clock in the morning on tiptoe while you snored. I saw them! The rugs, the pictures, the furniture ... chandeliers ... music rooms, ballrooms ... all a hundred metres from where we lived on potatoes and turnips, and slept, the seven of us together, in a coach-house loft.
>
> (p. 106)

Marguerite continues by detailing her relationships with men: at thirteen she became a housemaid on a big estate; at fifteen the marquis took her to bed; at sixteen she had a son and was dismissed because of it. But she found the answer to survival when her cousin had sex with her and gave her a gold coin. This is her revelation:

> And there it was. I knew. All of a sudden. How to do it. How to go through the magic door. How to be warm, how to be comfortable ... eat fine food, wear fine clothes, read fine books, listen to fine music. I had the key. A golden key. After all ... what had I got to lose? Innocence? That had gone before I was five. Look at me. I was a pretty child – do you know what that means? It means when your uncle sits you on his lap and gives you sweets he puts his thumb in you. It was worse after my father died. I had no protector – no one to break their jaws ... and, there are the cakes ... the apples ... the money pressed into your hand, if you promise not to tell. My mother sent me for some vegetables one day. It was Sunday, the church bells were ringing. My uncle was in one of the hot-houses, pruning the peaches. He said I looked flushed – I was hot, I'd been running. And then he said, 'Come over here' ... and sat on some sacks. So I sat down. And he said, 'Well, my little maid, are you ready for me yet?' God, you should have seen the mess. I put up a terrible fight, had the whole tree down on him, but he took me anyway. He made me get a bucket of water after – to clean up the blood in case the dogs came sniffing.
>
> (pp. 107–8)

Here, in Marguerite's confession, Gems not only condemns the social organization that deprives the working class, she also vehemently shatters the myth of 'happy families' that Dumas had been so keen to defend. As their natural right, uncles put their thumbs in their pretty nieces' vaginas, then rob them of their virginity through rape. Men fancy their female cousins and pay them for sex. The men violate the women over and over again. The argument about the male domination of the family is extended and strengthened by Gems's most effective political twist to the original plot. Marguerite tells Armand early on that the father of her child is a marquis. We are invited to judge Armand 'like father, like son', for, in the big confrontation scene, the revelation is made that the marquis is Armand's father.

Several of the press reviewers called this a melodramatic coincidence.[23] They were missing the point. The man who, in the stage directions, is namelessly labelled 'The Father' mouths establishment sentiments such as these:

> Permanence, continuity, the preservation of the line – they're of the utmost value. What else is there? What else stands against chaos and dissolution?
>
> (p. 121)

Following on from this statement of values comes the towering and frightening rage that the father turns on Armand when his son discusses his respect for Marguerite:

> Respect? Respect?! For a whore?! You dare to talk of love ... you dare to talk of friendship – with a whore? You dare to come to me, talk of marriage? Introduce a harlot? Into my family? Are you seriously suggesting ... that you want ... as your life's companion ... before God and the Church ... as the mother of your children ... my heirs ... a woman who has felt the private parts of every man in Paris? ... Good God, boy, what does it matter? One woman's slot or another?   (pp. 122–3)

That the language and hatred for women shown here are meant to be typical of all aristocratic fathers is made explicitly by Prudence, and Sophie drives home the general point:

> *Prudence.* I know these aristocrats. They're cold. Finished off in the cradle. He's like his father. Ruthless ... No man's constant, Marguerite. It isn't in their nature.
> *Sophie.* Why ruin yourself for a man?
>
> (p. 128)

When the father confronts Marguerite he tries to bribe her to leave Armand. She refuses money; she stands up for herself as the original Marguerite in Dumas was not allowed to do:

> You think because I'm a woman you can come here and bully and threaten? You think I'm nothing? Something to be pulled out of the way, like a piece of wood on the road? We don't need you. You pollute the air you breathe, the ground you walk on. You have no control, no influence over us. So take your foul breath and your rotting teeth and your stinking ass out of my house! Get out!   (p. 133)

The violence of her verbal attack is matched when she seizes a knife to defend herself. But when Marguerite's son comes running on, her courage deflates. The father gives the son, gives *his* son, a gold coin, and his argument is as good as won. Without the father's support, the boy's future is bleak, he will have no schooling to speak of and he might become a labourer if he is lucky. But the father offers him the family name, and an education. He threatens Marguerite that, if she does not leave, he will get a magistrate's order that she is an unfit mother. Marguerite chooses for the child and not for herself. She gives away the creature she most loves to the man she most hates and she is promised by the father that she will see the child again 'when he is a man' (p. 136).

Gems's feminist argument has been neatly put. The son has to be educated by men to survive; he will perpetuate the male-dominated social structure that his father represents; all the cruelty, tyranny and aggression will repeat itself in the next generation. A new myth, antithetical to Dumas's misogyny, is clearly spelt out: fathers steal sons and turn them into 'real men'. Throughout Marguerite's life she has been destroyed by men, and the final sacrifice is wrought here, when she once more becomes submissive for the advantage of her son. Where is she in all of this? She is a victim, suffering on behalf of the male order of things. Gems is standing Dumas's version of the myth on its head and, in her rewriting, it is the men who are villainous.

Marguerite's relationship with Armand now presents a certain incestuous complexity in Gems's argument. It is clear throughout that Armand is hateful. He has made Sophie pregnant and left her. He has had a homosexual fling with Bela and left him, despite Bela's attempt at suicide. If Armand doesn't get exactly what he wants he is selfish, aggressive and cruel. Why therefore does Marguerite feel so much for Armand? The subtextual answer seems to be that she feels so much because Armand is the half brother of her son. Marguerite's affection for Armand is for a surrogate son; she mixes maternal and sexual affection.

And if in the Gems version heterosexual relationships are wholeheartedly condemned as hateful, male homosexual relationships fare little better. To the extent that there is any kind of tenderness possible it is between women. It is made obvious that Sophie and Marguerite could form an affectionate and loving alliance, but homosexual men are shown to be – in a different kind of way from heterosexual men – hateful to women. Bela has tender feelings towards Armand but he has the vices of the heterosexual men in a snider way; he guffaws at Sophie because he has stolen Armand from her and she is upset. The one man in the play who is seen in a positive light is Gaston: for the very reason that he has no child and no wife and no sexual relationship.

Gems has written a version of *La Dame aux Camélias* where Dumas's female Beast has been replaced by a male devil. Marguerite tells Armand 'You have a black heart. You're a monster' (p. 102). To the father she cries 'You devil. You're a devil' (p. 135). Gems has used the material to portray a world where women love children to the point of self-destruction and where men are monsters who steal sons and educate them to hate women. It is a treatment of the myth as one-sided as Dumas's own: in Dumas what is wrong with male–female relationships is the emancipated woman, the Beast; in Gems what is wrong with male–female relationships is the Monstrous Men.

Nancy Sweet's version does not strive to be one-sided. Her *Camille* was researched and written simultaneously with a five-week rehearsal process under the direction of Catherine Carnie, and there is a further pooling of gender collaboration with the female designer and female music composer. The conditions of performance were those of Poor Theatre, in direct contrast with Pam Gems's RSC transfer to the West End and the expensive sets and costumes that could be afforded in that situation. For the London audience of Nancy Sweet's version, at the Old Red Lion pub in Islington, there was a sense of authenticity because of the tiny space, the exciting theatricality that was built up through collaborative female effort, and the way in which the Second Empire wealth was caught by simple means such as the magenta and gold design and the tableaux based on the visual arts of the period.

The intention of the play is to bring into the audience's perception the historical woman whose life Dumas ruthlessly exploited. Set in an eternal hell of re-enactment, the tyrannical Dumas is a character within the play. He directs his mother, his friends, and his mistress – here known as Alphonsine – in a perpetual play about Marguerite and Armand. He is shown to be fascinated by women's suffering and death, never more so than when he sadistically shines a torch into the dead Marguerite's face. He quotes pompously from his prefaces when he gives director's notes; he gets furious at his mistress's provocative additions to his script, not even allowing her to douche herself when, in the role of Marguerite, she has had sex with a client. Dumas at all points tries to control the performance, distorting real life into romantic art with the manipulative ease of a dictator.

The constant subversive distancing effects that are built into this political dream play draw a dialectical thought process from the audience. The awareness that these are actors playing roles; the way the story is told at the very beginning to avoid suspense: these common devices are for once very effective. Then, swiftly following each other come opposing opinions concerning women's responses to male pressure. First there is the voice of Dumas's mother who unthinkingly swallows her son's repressive attitudes:

> *Catherine Lebaye.* His [Dumas's] father'd sit at his desk 'composing his thoughts', not a sou coming in. It's not that I minded, he was higher class than me: but what he did have he spent on going to the theatre and such. The baby needed feeding, more clothes to wash, I was tired. He up and left. Wish it was like that for us. Just up and leave it all, everything. I couldn't

8 John Waddington, Annabelle Apsion and Logan Murray in a publicity still for
Nancy Sweet's *Camille*

leave the baby. What's done is done I say. You can't change them, it's how
God made them isn't it? My son's always writing about it in his books . . .
'man is God's instrument, Woman is Man's . . .' Isn't he clever putting it
like that. I'd never have thought of it.

(p. 32)

The key point here is that Dumas's mother accepts that, because of the class and gender differences between herself and her son's father, he should have a more privileged life than herself, that it is his right. She thinks in terms of eternal truths that cannot be changed, and knows that woman's role is to submit to male domination; but then an opposing voice is heard. Prudence jolts the audience into thought about change. She addresses the issue of what is available as work, and the implication is that the social organization dictates not only how women choose to run their lives, but also how all workers, male and female, can survive:

> Before I did this job I ran errands for a milliner, shit pay and shit hours. No-one gave you any respect. You had to lick the customers' arses to get any sort of measly tip. Well I thought when I saw the tarts from the cafés come into our shop to buy their fancy hats and kid gloves, if life is either a case of sucking cocks or licking arses, I might as well do both. Pay's better.   (p. 77)

In the father confrontation scene another type of distancing effect allows the audience to judge the argument. The actors in Dumas's rehearsal process play the game 'We the Jury', taking sides as the persuasion of the father urges them to concede to or deny his point of view. We judge as the actors judge, and there is only one person still on Marguerite's side at the end. This character, the Newcomer, is of central importance as the force for change in the play. He is a window for the audience's eyes, urging the women to change the situation, questioning why the *Camille* play has to be re-enacted without altering the story. He is an instigator, a metaphor for political action and political ideas. He does not embody the old male values; perhaps he is a representative of the New Man, soft, objective, and open to sensitive discussion of the women's plight. But he needs others to realize that they have to take control of their destiny, he cannot in a vacuum lead a rebellion, and, like everyone else, he acts out his role to the climax. At the end the Newcomer cannot breathe, he gets panicky, he rebels, he refuses to learn his lines: he compels Alphonsine: 'Destroy and create ... Take a brick, smash the window' (p. 90).

Alphonsine acts on this at last. She rips up a sheet of Dumas's script; she sees it is easy to destroy, she is happy. She destroys the set, a rush of air comes in; she and the Newcomer can breathe. But at the very end 'she gets depressed, doubtful, and starts trying to tidy up' (p. 91). The ambiguity of this final action throws the question open to the audience. Is it better to be safe, controlled, exploited, your script provided, your destiny dictated? Or is it better to destroy, let the air in? The audience must find a solution to the problem that the play leaves them with: how do we create after we destroy? How do we build the new society? Nancy Sweet has found an open-ended form that manages to question the male myth without replacing it by an equally intransigent female myth, a dialectical form that analyses the politics of gender.

It is clear that Dumas's *La Dame aux Camélias* in 1852 is the first major example of a mixed genre important in modern theatre: the modern myth play. This genre purports to be a theatre of moral and social ideas but in actuality it is also a theatre of the autobiographical, emotional life of the playwright. Dumas's own hatred of women is at the basis of *La Dame aux Camélias*. And when Pam Gems alters the myth she melodramatizes her own psychological torment in her hatred for male oppression and emphasis on maternity as a life-long process of fulfilment. When Nancy Sweet alters the myth to offer an open-ended, dialectical form, she shifts the revisionist approach into a more persuasive genre. Her play creates a synthesis from the thesis of Dumas and the antithesis of Pam Gems. Nancy Sweet has shown Marguerite in a critical light: we must, in this version, criticize Dumas's character Marguerite through the representation of Dumas's mistress Alphonsine who plays the part critically. At the end of the play, when Alphonsine takes steps to change her situation, to take control of her destiny, when she refuses to play the part of Marguerite as Dumas wants her to be perceived, she is being revolutionary. On behalf of the playwright, she is offering us a new direction in the uses of melodrama. On behalf of women, she refuses to play the woman written by a man who hated women.

NOTES

1 Alexandre Dumas *fils*, 'A propos de *La Dame aux Camélias*', *Théâtre complet*, vol. 1 (Paris: Calman Levy, 1893), p. 28: 'ce n'est plus une pièce, c'est une légende'.

Neumeier's film version of his ballet was released simultaneously in Hamburg and Stuttgart in November 1987. It stars Marcia Haydée as Marguerite and Ivan Liska as Armand.

The Lady of the Camellias was presented at the Meyerhold Theatre on 19 March 1934 with Zinaida Raikh as Marguerite. See Edward Braun, *The Theatre of Meyerhold* (London: Methuen, 1979), pp. 251–5.

See Klaus Völker: *Brecht: A Biography* (London: Marion Boyars, 1979), pp. 107–8.

There are many accounts of Bernhardt's Marguerite. See Gerda Taranow, *Sarah Bernhardt: The Art Within the Legend* (Princeton University Press, 1972), for an especially detailed account of the choreography of the death scene with particular reference to the 1912 film version.

See John Stokes, Michael R. Booth and Susan Bassnett, *Bernhardt, Terry, Duse: the Actress In Her Time* (Cambridge University Press, 1988), pp. 54–5.

Duse's Marguerite is fully documented. Of especial interest are the accounts of the debut in Paris at the Théâtre de la Renaissance where Duse courageously and successfully rivalled Bernhardt's performance of the role at Bernhardt's theatre with Bernhardt in the audience; see, for example, Giovanni Pontiero, *Eleanora Duse: In Life and Art* (Frankfurt am Main: Verlag Peter Lang, 1986), pp. 148–50.

See Raymond Durgnat and John Kobal, *Greta Garbo* (London: Studio Vista, 1965), p. 23.

For an analysis of *La Dame aux Camélias* as myth see Roland Barthes, '*The Lady of the Camellias*', *Mythologies* (London: Granada, 1973), pp. 103–5.

2 See for example Tennessee Williams, *Camino Real* (1953) and Terence Rattigan, *Variation on a Theme* (1958).

3 See Taranow, *Bernhardt*. For an analysis of the most protracted death scene in all Garbo's films see Charles Affron, *Star Acting: Gish, Garbo, Davies* (New York: E. P. Dutton, 1977), pp. 199–205.

4 See Dumas's account in 'A propos de *La Dame aux Camélias*'. For the censorship reports see A. Dumas *fils*, *Théâtre complet*, vol. VII (Paris: Calmann Levy, 1892), pp. 415–21.

For analysis of the evolution of the endings from novel to play to opera versions of the myth see Tadeusz Kowzan 'Le Mythe de la Dame aux Camélias: du mélodrame au mélodramatisme', *Revue des Sciences Humaines*, 41: 162 (1976).

5 *Camille* in Stephen S. Stanton (ed.), '*Camille*' and Other PLays (Mermaid Drama-book, New York: Hill and Wang, 1957), p. 155.

6 Karl Marx and Friedrich Engels, *The Communist Manifesto* (Harmondsworth: Penguin, 1967), p. 101.

7 A useful account is to be found in F. A. Taylor, *The Theatre of Alexandre Dumas, fils* (Oxford University Press, 1937).

8 Ibid., p. 22.

9 Preface to *Le Fils Naturel* in A. Dumas *fils*, *Théâtre complet*, vol. III (Paris: Calmann Lévy, 1893), p. 30.

10 See 'Au Lecteur', in A. Dumas *fils*, *Théâtre complet*, vol. I, p. 4 for the passage in the original. Translation by Susan Painter.

11 See Taylor, *Theatre of Dumas*, p. 20.

12 See Taylor, *Theatre of Dumas*, p. 52.

13 See Preface to *L'Ami des Femmes*, in A. Dumas *fils*, *Théâtre complet*, vol. IV (Paris: Calmann Lévy, 1893), pp. 45–8 for the passage in the original. Translation by Susan Painter.

14 Roland Barthes, 'Myth today', *Mythologies*, p. 131.

15 See Preface to *La Femme de Claude*, in A. Dumas *fils*, *Théâtre complet*, vol. V (Paris: Calmann Lévy, 1925), pp. 196–9 for the passage in the original. Translation by Susan Painter.

16 A. Dumas *fils*, *L'Homme-Femme* (Paris: Michel Lévy, 1873).

17 See Preface to *La Femme de Claude*, pp. 217–18.

18 *Fatal Attraction*, dir. Adrian Lyne, starring Michael Douglas, Glenn Close and Anne Archer, released in Britain by Paramount on 15 January 1988.

19 Taylor, *Theatre of Dumas*, p. 83.

20 See Preface to *La Femme de Claude*.

21 Pam Gems, *Camille* in *Three Plays* (Harmondsworth: Penguin, 1985).

22 Nancy Sweet, *Camille* (unpublished). All subsequent quotations refer to the script provided by the author. First performed in 1987 at the Richard Demarco Gallery Theatre, Edinburgh, and subsequently at The Old Red Lion Theatre, London.

23 See *London Theatre Record*, 9–22 April and 23 October–5 November 1985.

Exhuming *Lady Audley*: period melodrama for the 1990s*

JOEL H. KAPLAN

The Adelphi Screamers is a Canadian-based production company formed in 1988 to bring to Victorian and Edwardian plays in performance some of the fruits of recent stage scholarship.[1] Our name – an allusion to the screaming farces and melodramas of the old Adelphi Theatre – is, in fact, a convenient umbrella for a series of independent Equity Co-operative ventures. What ties this work together is a common commitment to archival research as a necessary tool for understanding nineteenth-century sensibilities and reclaiming for our own age earlier modes of gestural performance. We are aware, of course, of the pitfalls of authenticity. Any attempt to replicate a night at a Victorian theatre is compromised at the outset by the impossibility of providing authentically Victorian spectators. The social and aesthetic gaps that divide us from the pastimes of our forbears are further widened by distinctions between, say, the expectations of a mid-century audience at the up-market Olympic Theatre and one at the largely working-class Britannia or Royal Victoria. With such reservations in mind, however, we believe that it is possible to catch something of the power and energy of nineteenth-century popular drama if playtexts are taken seriously and presented with a full knowledge of the stages for which they were written. In this paper I would like to suggest some of the ways in which this can be done, drawing examples from the Adelphi Screamers' 1989 production of Colin Hazlewood's 1863 adaptation of *Lady Audley's Secret*.[2] My focus will be upon both the sources available to would-be producers of melodrama – period music, acting manuals, early films, and contemporary parodies – and the manner in which such material may be used to create an appropriate production style.

A word of caution at the outset. Much recent writing about melodrama has been both formal and taxonomic, plotting fashions in playmaking against a grid of recurring actions and character types. A producer, especially one intending to build a repertoire of Victorian works, needs to

---

* A draft of this paper was read at the *Themes in Drama* International Conference held at the University of California, Riverside, in February 1990.

begin at the other end, fixing upon the textures and topicalities of particular plays. He must, at any rate, be clear in his own mind as to why, apart from the exigencies of casting and venue, he chooses one piece above another. In the case of Hazlewood's two-act *Lady Audley*, what intrigued us was the manner in which a popular work of fiction had been reshaped for the stage by a competent if routine theatre professional. At first glance, Mary Elizabeth Braddon's 'sensation' novel, published in serial form in 1861–2, seems an odd choice for melodramatic representation.[3] Its tale of a young woman who plots to murder her husband when he arrives to challenge a bigamous second marriage sounds promising enough, as does the detective work by which Robert Audley seeks to reveal the identity and guilt of his uncle's new wife. Yet Braddon is less interested in moral combat than in the complexity of characters built, for the most part, upon generic antitypes. Lady Audley, as feminist critics have been quick to point out, is no simple adventuress. Her secret (in Braddon's novel) refers not to her attempted murder of husband George Talboys, nor her concealed marriage, but the emotional frigidity and societally triggered bouts of madness she fears she may have inherited from her mother. Not only do her blue eyes, blonde curls, and china-doll complexion constitute a raid upon the physiognomy of the stage heroine, her eventual confinement in a continental madhouse (to spare the Audley family the embarrassment of a public trial) is designed to raise unpleasant questions about the nature of happy endings. Robert Audley, in turn, makes an unconventional hero, reluctant to avenge either his friend's death or uncle's honour. An idler by temperament, he is, in his own words, an unmanly man buffeted about by a world of strong-willed women. The same rattling of expectations appears in Braddon's secondary figures. Phoebe, Lady Audley's sentimental maid, turns out to be a crafty extortionist, while step-daughter Alicia, the ingénue of the piece, is unbecomingly sullen and petty. Indeed, the only characters who strike what we might call ready-made theatrical poses are George Talboys, who falls into a dead faint on hearing rumours of his wife's death, and Harcourt, his father, an affected prig who refuses to believe 'that circumstances [ever] mitigate the blackness of wrong or weaken the force of right' (p. 119).

Clearly Hazlewood had his work cut out for him. An extended stint at the East End's Britannia Saloon – billed on its broadsides as 'the people's theatre' – stood him in good stead. Through the 1850s Hazlewood had experimented with the stagecraft of the 'realization', building popular entertainments out of such unlikely stuff as Abraham Solomon's Academy painting *Waiting for the Verdict* (C.L. January 1859) and Henry O'Neill's *Return of the Wanderer* (*Jessy Vere* Brit. February 1856).[4] During the following decade he would transform James Greenwood's muckraking journalism into *The Casual Ward* (February 1866), a nasty but effective piece that placed upon the Britannia stage the miseries of an English workhouse.[5] In reshaping *Lady Audley* for the equally plebeian Royal Victoria – a theatre alternatively known as 'the Blood Tub' – Hazlewood began by sorting Braddon's characters into opposing camps of good and bad hearts. *His* Lady Audley, still porcelain in appearance, hides a dagger in her bodice; her treachery is manifest early in the play when we *see* her push husband George down a well at Audley Court. (Braddon keeps us guessing until her heroine is sympathetically established.) Robert Audley, recast as avenging angel, becomes both manly and sanctimonious, offering comfort to a muted Alicia, while pursuing his wicked step-aunt. He is, he tells us, bound to his task, as a galley slave to his oar. Even Phoebe has her cunning shifted to the drunken Luke Marks, a more predictable comic villain. Structurally, Braddon's action is reworked as a series of dialogues – most of Hazlewood's own devising – in which female vice and male virtue openly confront one another. Towards the close of act I George Talboys and Lady Audley (who never appear together in the novel) indulge in an extended bout of mutual recriminations. In the second act, after two attempts on his life, Robert wrestles Lady Audley's dagger to the ground on the line: 'And thus I rob the serpent of its sting!' (p. 265). What sympathy remains for his murderess, after an interpolated mad scene and on-stage death, Hazlewood gathers in a concluding *tableau* of grief.

Yet for all this there is a curious leakage between novel and play. Whether Braddon's text proved in the end intractable, or Hazlewood used it with uncharacteristic subtlety, the figures of the drama trail through the work clouds of their former selves. Often the result is unwittingly comic: George and Lady Audley, for example, quibbling in act I about who deserted whom. At its best, however, in Lady Audley's act II soliloquies or final mad scene, the effect can be genuinely unsettling. It is a quality, at any rate, we sought to capture in our production, playing the piece ramrod straight and as 'period' as possible. Our most reluctant compromise was with set. We had initially designed a system of grooves and shutters to reproduce Hazlewood's five locales and six shifts of scenery. Our first venue, however, assigned by the Vancouver Fringe Festival, had a floor-level stage and no proscenium. Not only did this defeat plans for a practicable trap, it meant restricting scenery to a mock well, a painted backcloth ('*The Lime Tree Walk; [Audley] Hall ... seen in the distance*', p. 237) and two reversible wings, used for the split interior of Luke's Inn at Mt Stanning (II, iii). It also meant that the look of our play would depend largely upon our use of costume. Here we had greater success, drawing heavily upon contemporary photographs, paintings, fashion plates, and caricatures to evoke an age of ditto suits, sack coats, and hoop skirts. Our intention was to push the already exaggerated fashions of the early 1860s to theatrical extremes, creating a world as historically anchored as Brad-

Lady Audley's Secret

Phœbe   Lady Audley   Alicia

9 Costumes by M. Gottler

don's but melodramatically oversized. The violent purples, magentas, and
acid greens of the period, made possible by the recent discovery of aniline
dyes, as well as the outsized hoops and baggy coats that gave the decade
its peculiar silhouette, were also used to register social and moral positions. Lady Audley's sham innocence was conveyed in act I by a straw hat
and cotton dress, her brazen ambition by a second gown of turquoise
taffeta with black lace flounces and four-foot circular hoop. Step-daughter
Alicia, to the manner born, had three costume changes, including a dinner
dress of mauve satin with a hoop of the more fashionable ovoid shape.
Similar distinctions were drawn among the men. Luke, the only one of
Hazlewood's figures described in Lacy's acting edition, got his '*flowered
waistcoat . . . cord breeches and gaiters*' (p. 237). The remainder of his costume
was pieced together from hints in Braddon and the frontispiece to Cumberland's text of Buckstone's *Luke the Labourer*. Robert, in act I, was the
novel's phlegmatic fop, with burgundy bow tie and checked trousers. For
act II we metamorphosed him into Hazlewood's avenger, his noble mono-

10 Robert Audley. Costume by B. Jurenka

11 Robert Audley, act II

mania suggested by a mourning suit and crepe hat band. George Talboys's wooden machismo (in play and book) was further stiffened by
making him a military man. In Braddon, when he leaves England, he
labours for three years in the Ballarat gold fields. Hazlewood sends him to
India in an unspecified (probably commercial) capacity. We returned him

larger-than-life in the boots, helmet, and cream-coloured Khakis of the Madras Sappers and 1st Punjab Volunteer Rifle Corps.[6]

In constructing what we felt to be an appropriate performance style, we turned first to the theatre music of the period. As the most essential of melodrama's 'mediating discourses' music seemed to us indispensable as a carrier of emotion and organizer of moral experience. Indeed, it was music that – quite literally – defined melodrama, in an age in which most theatres had in-house orchestras, and many companies a full-time *chef d'orchestre*.[7] For a surprising number of plays holograph scores still survive. David Mayer, of the University of Manchester, has compiled a useful finding list of piano and orchestral parts for some two dozen works by Boucicault, Sims, Fitzball, Jerrold, Walker and Pocock.[8] In an appendix to Mayer's *Henry Irving and 'The Bells'* (Manchester University Press, 1980), Nigel Gardner supplements this with piano transcriptions of Etienne Singla's 1869 music for *Le Juif polonais* (used by Irving in his production) and what is to date the only detailed discussion of an individual melodramatic score (pp. 108–31). For plays for which no music survives, or for which original music was never written – *Lady Audley* fell into this category – producers have the option of drawing upon the stock *melos* of Alfred Edward Cooper (1840–1901). Music Master at a number of theatres in the southeast of England during the 1860s and 70s, Cooper, sometime after 1857, composed a book of melodic cells, no more than a few bars each, designed to accommodate the character types and situations of popular drama. Helpfully labelled *furiosos, agits* or *agitatos, misteriosos* and the like, the fifty-three themes and *segues* that comprise Cooper's folio were intended to satisfy hard-nosed managers unwilling or unable to commission individual scores. Twentieth-century producers will find in the collection signature pieces for heroes, heroines, villains, and comic couples, as well as generic music for scenes of struggle, sentiment, and bustling farce. All are scored for a moderately sized pit orchestra: five violins, two second violins, cello, bass, two clarinets (the second doubling with flute), and – for the more martial of the airs – a pair of cornets. For groups still able to rouse such resources, instrumental parts may be had on hire from Samuel French Ltd. For those, like the Screamers, whose 'pit' consists of piano and pianist, Cooper's music is more readily accessible in the piano reductions of Matthew Scott, reproduced together with additional *melos* by Cooper's contemporaries, Michael Connelly and Pierre Joseph Varney, in Mayer's invaluable *Four Bars of 'Agit'* (London: French, 1983).

In assembling a score for *Lady Audley* we began with some dozen of Cooper's themes, using them initially as entrance and exit cues. A *misterioso* in G minor (Cooper 45a), described by Scott as 'good music for a villain', was used to 'bring on' Luke Marks, and later identified with his blackmailing activities:

Ex. 1

The opening bars of a *presto* in the same key (Cooper 22) became the first of a number of themes assigned to Lady Audley, here meant to evoke her madness (see example 2). To Cooper's *melos* we added another dozen of our own composed in a sympathetic style by Screamers' Music Master, Randall Plitt. A brisk three-bar hunting motif was created for Alicia, a sentimental waltz for Phoebe, and a second theme for Lady Audley, related to Cooper 22, but associated more specifically with her ambition (see example 3). The brevity of both Cooper's *melos* and our own allowed us to use each elastically, altering tempi, dynamics, and key signatures to augment stage action. At its simplest this meant minor third trills for the burning of Luke's inn, ascending chromatic chords for George's recognition of his wife's portrait, and repeated octaves (G1, G2) played over Alicia's theme for the tolling of Sir Michael's funeral bell. For more complex passages, Lady Audley's soliloquies and her confrontations with George and Robert, *melos* were thematically developed, resulting in quasi-operatic episodes used to sustain heightened gesture and emotive posturing. At scene closes music was nearly continuous, and through-scored for the end of both acts. The apparent murder of George and disposal of his body at the end of act I was accompanied by a *forte* playing of Lady Audley's ambition motif, interrupted by a fragmented version of her mad-theme. The '*tableau of sympathy*' Hazlewood insists upon for his act II

2

Presto

Ex. 3

conclusion was supported by a reprise of both themes, alternating with a *melo* of the domestic–pathetic type (Cooper 8). At our initial venue, Vancouver's Heritage Hall, the play was introduced by a prelude of 'scurry' music largely based upon Cooper 21 and an *agitato* (A3) from Connelly's score for Sims's *Lights o' London* (1881). For our transfer to the Vancouver East Cultural Centre for a brief commercial run this was expanded into a three-part overture in the French style (slow/fast/slow), in which *melos* associated with George, Robert, and Lady Audley fought one another in anticipation of the play's central action. Throughout we attempted to use music to map both the moral and emotional relationships of Hazlewood's world, encouraging spectators, in the words of Charles Reade, Hazlewood's playwright contemporary, to '[see] with the ear as well as the eye' (quoted in *Four Bars*, p. 2).

The introduction of music at an early point in the rehearsal process – shortly after the first read-through – helped a number of our actors overcome their Method training. Indeed, Cooper's *melos*, particularly his character signatures, proved ready cues for a set of spontaneous postures that looked remarkably like the formal attitudes encountered in Victorian theatre engravings and studio photographs. To fine-tune the process we used a number of nineteenth-century acting manuals, from Leman Rede's *The Road to the Stage; or, the Performer's Preceptor* (London: Smith, 1827) to Gustave Garcia's *The Actor's Art: A Practical Treatise on Stage Declamation, Public Speaking, and Deportment* (London: Simpkin, 1888) and Hugh Campbell's *Voice, Speech and Gesture: A Practical Handbook to the Elocutionary Art* (London: Deacon, 2nd edn 1895). The advantage of such handbooks lies in their compulsive labelling of stances, gestures, and facial expressions, offering modern readers a systematic guide to the semiotics of melodramatic performance. We learn from them, for example, that malice is expressed by setting the jaw, clenching both fists, and bending the elbows in a straining manner (Rede, pp. 82–3), noble assertion by raising the hands above the waist, while keeping the fingers close together, and palms well exposed (Garcia, p. 62). By mid century such volumes had become storehouses of theatrical iconography, supplementing verbal accounts with innumerable drawings of gross and fine stage movement. Campbell uses fifteen figures alone to lay bare the mysteries of eye rolling and eyebrow elevation (pp. 148–50). The chief drawback to these volumes is the *naïveté* of their compilers. Neither Campbell nor Garcia was himself an actor or had a professional's knowledge of the stage. The former was a medical man interested in the physiology of performance, the latter a Professor of Declamation and Singing at the Royal Academy of Music. Their advice, moreover, is directed to amateurs more concerned with elocutionary self-improvement than careers in the theatre. It is, at any rate, difficult to imagine serious students much helped by Garcia's advice not to knock things over while making an entrance (p. 24), or Campbell's remedies for stage stuttering (pp. 33–4). To build uncritically upon such work is to invite the same kind of skepticism that met scholarly attempts, four decades ago, to reduce Elizabethan acting to the rhetorical handbooks of *that* period.[9]

There is, however, a fortunate exception. Campbell's unit on 'Gesture' (pp. 103–69) was not written by Campbell himself but by Henry Neville, an experienced player of melodramatic leads through the 1860s and 70s. A professional from the age of four, Neville was best known for his portrayal of Bob Brierly, the Lancashire Lad of Tom Taylor's *The Ticket-of-Leave Man*, a role he created at the Olympic Theatre on 27 May 1863, two days after the opening of Hazlewood's *Lady Audley*. In later years Neville both managed the Olympic and, together with his brother Fred Gartside, founded one of England's first Schools of Dramatic Art.[10] In his contribution to Campbell's book, Neville displays, as one might expect, a lively sense of stage action as dynamic process. Attitudes, for example, are not only poses struck for their iconic value, but parts of a dramatic continuum – positions, in Neville's words, one adopts at the end of a walk or stage stride (p. 112). When discussed, they are accordingly grouped in sets or

12 Position of body, feet and lower limbs (Campbell, figs. 7, 8 and 9)

13 Campbell, figs 10, 11, 12

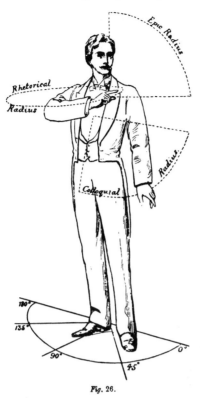

Fig. 26.

14 The stroke and time of gesture (Campbell, fig. 26)

pairs, accompanied by illustrations resembling modern strip cartoons.
Sequences used by Neville to trace the path from nobility to assertion
(figures 7–8) and alarm to anger (figures 10–11) were fed directly into our
gesture bank. Upon the former we built Robert's return to Audley Court
and subsequent accusation of Lady Audley ('Madam, this is *your* likeness',
p. 254), upon the latter George's discovery of his wife's infidelity ('What is
this? *Her* face? ... Woe to the traitress', p. 244). We attempted, in the
process, to maintain Neville's distinction between what he calls colloquial,
rhetorical, and epic movements. The first, he explains, are those everyday
actions successfully rendered by the forearm sweeping beneath the
shoulder. Phoebe and, for the most part, Alicia were restricted to such
gestures. Rhetorical, or moral, positions were signalled, as Neville suggests, by raising the forearm to shoulder height and pointing an
accusatory finger. Robert was, in this sense, our most obliging rhetorician.
Neville's epic radius – arms raised to the head (madness) or above it
(denunciation) – was more sparingly used, chiefly by George and Lady

Audley. We found, however, a particularly telling application at the close of act II, where Phoebe, realizing for the first time the treachery of her mistress, shot her arm bolt upright to condemn her (p. 264). The action, supported by a major chord, drew surprising strength from the fact that this had hitherto been for Phoebe forbidden territory.[11]

In recovering Neville's method we found a useful control in material from the US Library of Congress Paper Print Collection, taking advantage of recent work by Kemp Niver, P. G. Loughney and (once again) David Mayer.[12] The archive, the significance of which is only now being appreciated by stage historians, consists of the remnants of some 5,000 opaque nitrate strips deposited for copyright purposes between 1895 and 1912. There, together with much non-theatrical footage, scholars will find fixed-camera records of Victorian and Edwardian actors on sophisticated period stages. Through the good offices of Mayer and Joseph Donohue we were able to screen a number of items from the collection on a specially prepared videotape. Of particular use was *The Drunkard's Reformation* (FLA 5347 394 feet), a 1909 melodrama in which a dipsomaniac father is cured by taking his daughter to see a temperance play. Much of the piece takes place in a theatre in which an American adaptation of Charles Reade's *Drink* (Princess's 1879) is being presented. The deliberately archaic style selected by the film maker for his 'mousetrap' play – Mayer believes that the acting of the drunkard Coupeau looks back to Charles Warner's original performance – allowed us to see stage postures in the context of stage action, suggesting ways in which our characters might be moved from one stance to another. In addition, both inner and outer plays supplied rare footage of group movement and ensemble blocking, points upon which the individually aimed actors' manuals are understandably silent. Also of help was D. W. Griffith's 1908 adaptation of Sims's 1878 ballad *Ostler Joe* (FLA 5622 329 feet). Here the director's 'realization' of elements from two familiar paintings, Augustus Egg's *Past and Present* (1858) and Luke Fildes's *The Doctor* (1891), offered insights into the dynamics of the *tableau*, showing how emblematic moments might be held or prolonged without halting dramatic action. Together with material from a 1903 *Uncle Tom's Cabin* (FLA 5913 507 feet), Griffith's 'realizations' helped us plan Hazlewood's final '*tableau of sympathy*', in which pathos for the dead Lady Audley is evoked by pictorial as well as musical means.[13]

One final, if obvious, source remains to be considered. In 1889 Jerome K. Jerome issued in book form fourteen satiric character studies he had previously published in *The Playgoer*. Illustrated by Bernard Partridge, *Stage-land: [The] Curious Habits and Customs of its Inhabitants* (London: Chatto, 1889) became the period's best-known lampoon of melodramatic conventions. Both Jerome and Partridge had acted professionally, and Jerome, by 1889, had had four of his plays produced in West End theatres.

Their joint gallery of melodramatic types presents, accordingly, a witty but informed guide to the expectations of late-Victorian playgoers. We used the work in two ways. Initially, we ransacked it for accidental details of character and costume. We found, for example, that manly heroes were invariably called George, and wore patent leather boots on the unlikeliest occasions (pp. 1, 6–8). The twin observations persuaded us to keep George Talboys, for all his Punjab service, in theatrically spotless footgear. Partridge's four-block engraving of a dying villainess (p. 37), likewise, helped in choreographing the collapse of our hoop-skirted Lady Audley. The tone of the volume, however, suggested a second and more far-reaching application. Both Jerome and Partridge were sophisticated playgoers with misgivings about the value of popular art. Yet in *Stage-land* each displays a genuine respect for – and readiness to react to – the affective force of his subject. Indeed, Jerome in his autobiography regrets that *Stage-land* may have hastened the departure of the stock types he and Partridge had burlesqued.[14] Jerome's own plays, to be sure, continued to display touching faith in the 'curious habits' of *Stage-land* – something his critics never let him forget. Partridge, who had used himself and Gertrude Kingston as models for *Stage-land's* Hero and Adventuress, was, while preparing his sketches, appearing with Kingston in identical roles in Jerome's *Woodbarrow Farm* (Comedy, 1889).[15] Five years later, as Bernard Gould, he would draw upon the same set of heroic turns to create the schizophrenic Sergius in the first performances of Shaw's *Arms and the Man* (Avenue, 1894).[16] To us, Jerome and Partridge seemed ideal as a 'target audience' for melodrama in our own day. And it was to their mix of skepticism and visceral response that we decided to pitch our production. Our initial task, we agreed, was to create spectators literate in the aural and visual signs of the genre. To this end, audience members, while directly addressed in soliloquies and asides, were never recognized as twentieth-century individuals superior to either the material or form. We went out of our way to avoid knowing winks, nods, or 'Hiss the Villain' placards that might plead for patronizing tolerance. We were not always successful in dampening unwanted laughter. Yet we tried to distinguish between mannered details at which Jerome and Partridge might have smiled – Robert's self-righteousness was a particular problem – and the broader emotive effects reclaimed from Cooper, Neville, and the Paper Print Collection. What surprised us, in the end, was how much audiences were prepared to accept on these terms, and how willing critics seemed to be to see melodrama, historically mounted, as experimental theatre. We were particularly gratified by the response of Vancouver's alternate press, which, viewing *Lady Audley* as what it called 'truly radical theatre', found that reviving 'grand gestures and ringing tones' did not preclude 'playing for truth'. 'Our laughs', one critic concluded, '[were] of affectionate recog-

15 Alicia (S. Stowell) discusses her suspicions with Robert Audley (S. Thorne)

nition, instead of the embarrassed snickers of an audience at the usual
send-up renditions of melodrama' (*Georgia Straight* 15 Sept. 1989, p. 21).[17]
Our own verdict, more briefly put, is best summed up by recasting a line
George Talboys speaks at the end of act 1 to the 'defunct' Lady Audley: for
a play supposedly dead and buried, it looked remarkably well.

NOTES

1 I am greatly indebted to Mara Gottler, Tracy Holmes, David Lemon, David
  Mayer, and Randall Plitt for assistance in the preparation of this paper.
2 Vancouver Fringe Festival (Heritage Hall), 8–14 Sept.; Vancouver East
  Cultural Centre, 1–2 Oct. Stage direction: M. Millerchip*, Music direction: R.
  Plitt, Set: K. Bright, Costumes: M. Gottler, B. Jurenka. Cast: Phoebe: B.
  Cormack, Lady Audley: T. Holmes*, Alicia: S. Stowell, Sir Michael Audley: A.
  Holland*, Luke: S. Jenner*, George Talboys: J. Smith, Robert Audley: S.
  Thorne*. (*Participated with the permission of Canadian Actors' Equity
  Association.)
3 *Lady Audley's Secret* was first serialized in *Robin Goodfellow* (July–Sept. 1861), a

humour magazine published by Braddon's lover. After the magazine failed in 1861, the novel was continued in the *Sixpenny Magazine* (Jan.–Dec. 1862). The immediate and immense popularity of the work is reflected in the nine book-form 'editions' published by Tinsley in 1862. Three months before Hazlewood's adaptation appeared at the Royal Victoria, George Roberts staged his own version at the St James's (28 Feb. 1863). In this paper references to Braddon's novel are to the 1887 edition reprinted with an introduction by Norman Donaldson (New York: Dover, 1974); references to Hazlewood's play are to *Lacy's Acting Edition* reprinted in *Nineteenth Century Plays*, ed. George Rowell (Oxford University Press, 1953).

4 Martin Meisel, *Realizations: Narrative, Pictorial, and Theatrical Arts in Nineteenth-Century England* (Princeton University Press, 1983), pp. 294–7, 121n.

5 Jim Davis, 'A Night in the Workhouse, or the Poor Laws as Sensation Drama', *Essays in Theatre*, 7:2 (May 1989), 111–26.

6 In Braddon George Talboys was originally a dragoon, and much is made of his military carriage. His appearances in the novel itself, however, are entirely in mufti.

7 In smaller provincial theatres the orchestra was often replaced by a piano or harmonium. See David Mayer and Matthew Scott, *Four Bars of 'Agit': Incidental Music for Victorian and Edwardian Melodrama* (London: French, 1983), pp. 1–6.

8 Ibid., p. 8. The catalogue will no doubt grow as scholars begin to search actively for such material. Last year, while working at the Garrick Club, I quite accidentally stumbled across a twelve-part orchestral score for Pinero's *Profligate*.

9 See, for example, Bertram Joseph's *Elizabethan Acting* (London: Oxford University Press, 1951). Many of the volume's initial claims were more cautiously restated in a 1964 revision.

10 Erskine Reid and Herbert Compton (eds.), *The Dramatic Peerage: Personal Notes and Professional Sketches of the Actors and Actresses of the London Stage* (London: Raithby, 1892). 'In melodramatic comedy,' the entry continues, 'Mr. Henry Neville is second to none, and as the heroic stage lover is perhaps the finest the stage has ever seen' (pp. 161–2).

11 We permitted Luke and Sir Michael to breach the pattern for comic ends, creating for each a style we dubbed 'mock-epic radius'. This was used for Sir Michael's dismissal of Robert, and Luke's multiple stage deaths.

12 Kemp Niver, *Early Motion Pictures: The Paper Print Collection in the Library of Congress* (Washington, DC: Library of Congress, 1985); P. G. Loughney, 'The Library of Congress Paper Print Collection: The Evolution of a Preservation Strategy', in *Preserving America's Performing Arts*, ed. Barbara Cohen-Stratyner and Brigitte Kueppers (New York: Theatre Library Association, 1985), pp. 96–7; David Mayer, 'The Victorian Stage on Film: a Description and a Selected List of Holdings in the Library of Congress Paper Print Collection', *Nineteenth Century Theatre*, 16:2 (1985), 111–22.

13 We were also guided by Meisel's consideration of Hazlewood's first act closing tableau for his stage version of *Aurora Floyd*, another popular Braddon novel of the early 1860s (p. 45).

14 Jerome K. Jerome, *My Life and Times* (London: Harper, 1926): 'They were well known characters. All now are gone. If Partridge and myself helped to hasten their end, I am sorry. They were better – more human, more understandable – than many of the new puppets that have taken their place', p.84. Joseph Connolly, Jerome's most recent biographer, finds the stand 'strange and inconsistent' (*Jerome K. Jerome: A Critical Biography* (London: Orbis, 1982), p. 46). It seems to me, to use Jerome's own words, human and understandable.

15 Ruth Marie Faurot, *Jerome K. Jerome* (New York: Twayne, 1974), pp. 101–2. See also Jerome, p. 84 and Connolly, p. 49. Partridge, of course, also illustrated melodramas for London's non-parodic press. Only the thinnest of lines separates the burlesque types of *Stage-land* from their 'straight' counterparts in Partridge's drawings for plays like Jones and Barrett's *Hoodman Blind* (1885) or *The Lord Harry* (1886).

16 Aubrey Beardsley's *Pall Mall Budget* cartoon 'Mr. Bernard Gould [Sergius] and Miss Florence Farr [Louka]' (26 April 1894) pays clever tribute to Partridge, recreating the actor-illustrator (but not Farr) in a broad rehandling of his *Stage-land* style.

17 The reviewer was Canadian playwright John Lazarus, who has incorporated elements of melodrama into some of his own recent work. See also: *[Vancouver] Province*: 14:8 and 10:9; *Vancouver Sun* 16:9; *Ubyssey*: 22:9; *CBC (radio)* 11:9; *CHQM* 15:9; *CBC (television)* 12:9.

Henry Irving, the 'Dr Freud' of melodrama*

DENIS SALTER

While Henry Irving's Lyceum Theatre effectively functioned as England's unofficial national theatre in the 1890s, Shaw appointed himself as the unofficial spokesman for the new generation of progressive dramatists who sometimes complained bitterly about Irving's preoccupation with 'the old Barry Sullivan repertory of mutilated Shakespear and Bulwer Lytton, to which he actually added The Iron Chest of the obsolete Colman. From the public point of view,' Shaw concluded, 'he never looked back: from my point of view he never looked forward.'[1] Regrettably, these complaints, however justified in their own time, have obscured an important paradox which is central, I shall argue here, to our understanding of Irving's artistic achievement. Although much of his repertoire indeed came from the early part of the century, and although he tended to think of himself as artistic heir to, among others, Edmund Kean and Fechter,[2] he was nevertheless a leading figure in the contemporary fascination with the psychological analysis of character.[3] In the novel, he has been likened to Dickens, George Eliot, and Balzac; in poetry, to Tennyson; in music, to Stanford and Wagner; and in painting, to Salvator Rosa, Fuseli, Doré, and Daumier.[4] Irving once foolishly declared that '"Ibsen, in my opinion, has not had any permanent effect upon the theatre"',[5] but Shaw thought that Irving's genius for an intense kind of modern psychological realism would make him ideal as Bishop Nikolas in The Pretenders, Halvard Solness in The Master Builder, and John Gabriel Borkman, or indeed as a Shavian character like Napoleon in The Man of Destiny.[6]

The emblematic suggestiveness of Irving's mask-like face reminded Craig of Chaplin and provided support for Craig's controversial theory of the Übermarionette. Craig also thought that Irving's consummate skill in unleashing deeply experienced emotions and in casting an almost uncanny spell over his audiences was somewhat similar to the early experiments in hypnosis conducted by Dr Mesmer.[7] An unwitting early Freudian,[8] Irving dedicated much of his acting career to the reanimation

* A draft of this paper was read at the *Themes in Drama* International Conference held at the University of California, Riverside, in February 1990.

of the melodramatic formula, by investigating its Gothic-derived themes of repressed desire, nameless dread, and liberated fantasy; and by acting out – in vivid, sometimes hallucinatory detail – its obsession with the type-character of the fated man who struggles with the daemons buried within his unconscious while yearning for a kind of absolute state-of-being in which he will stand redeemed, as though forever.[9]

Alan Hughes, in his study of Irving's Shakespearian productions, has described the actor's sensibility as being essentially Manichaean.[10] As a young boy growing up in his birthplace of Somerset and then later on in Cornwall, Irving's imagination was in part nourished by the Bible, *Don Quixote*, Washington Irving's *Sketch Book*, and a collection of old ballads. His family's Methodism, particularly the ardent kind practised by the aunt who virtually raised him, gave him an unshakeable sense of right versus wrong – of salvation, on the one hand, and damnation, on the other – which remained with him even after he had decided to become an actor.[11] His first real theatregoing experience was of Samuel Phelps as Hamlet at Sadler's Wells: it struck him with all the force of a revelation;[12] the theatre became, in fact, a kind of second religion to Irving, a sacred responsibility to which he quite literally sacrificed both body and soul right up to the time of his death from exhaustion in 1905.[13] More than one contemporary observer compared the Lyceum audience to a devoted congregation attendant at a special rite with Irving officiating as its high priest, controlling – but also controlled by – its ineffable mysteries.[14] Many of his productions were symbolic variations of an essential scenic design: as in medieval iconography, the stage itself was meant to represent an idealized human community, while beneath it was the eerie effulgence of Hell, and above it, the golden radiance of Heaven. In the bewitching atmosphere created by the gaslight, Lyceum audiences willingly relinquished their individuality and surrendered themselves to the actor's spell.

These productions took on a mythic importance which enhanced the somewhat complex role which Irving came to play in English society. The first actor to be knighted, Irving never lost his bohemian affect; as Peter Thomson has perceptively argued, there was something peculiar about Irving's search for respectability, for official legitimation, as though it were intended to mask 'a unique and dangerous access to the secreted self'.[15] Like melodrama, both Irving's life and art were based on the unwavering principle that the world *must* rid itself of all forms of Evil, no matter the personal cost. At the same time, to escape the whims of Fortune, and to triumph over his status as a mere rogue and vagabond – Max Beerbohm wittily dubbed him 'the Knight from Nowhere'[16] – he exercised absolute control over the cultivation of his knightly persona both on and off the stage. Like Bernhardt, with whom he was often compared,[17] Irving's Manichaeism allowed his audiences the perverse pleasure of reconciling themselves to his double guise as a kind of 'Sacred Monster'. During an actual performance, the monstrous or profane side of human nature could be indulged and purged; but during the final curtain speech he gradually became 'Sir Henry' again and the sacred side of things – with all its confident assumptions about proper social conduct in proper English society – could be asserted without the worry of even vestigial ambivalence. A 'Lyceum' in the original sense of the word, his theatre's moral lessons were thus rendered irresistible and soothed an age which needed to view itself idealistically. 'The theatre must always be an indirect mechanism of teaching', Irving once explained. 'Its work must be in the main transcendental: for mere realism is insufficient to stimulate the imagination or to rouse the sensibilities or the emotions.'[18]

In creating the Lyceum repertoire, Irving was guided not just by sound business sense but also by his predilection for those plays which could be written or adapted to suit the configurations of his melodramatic imagination. *Vanderdecken* (1878) by W. G. Wills and Percy Fitzgerald is an early example of what came to be known as a typical Lyceum dramatic situation. Like Wagner in *The Flying Dutchman*, Wills and Fitzgerald were indebted to Heine's version of the legend for the notion that the hero will achieve his eagerly sought redemption through the constancy of love and the intervention of the feminine ideal.[19] Irving chose to play Vanderdecken as part human, part spirit, a remote lugubrious character bearing the burden of a crime, of nothing less than cosmic import, for which the audience was of course persuaded to forgive him. After Thekla, the woman who eventually saves him from his eternal wanderings, had recited the ballad of Vanderdecken, there was a roar of thunder and a flash of lightning, and then the audience could see – approaching slowly from afar – 'the blood-red sails of Vanderdecken's phantom ship'.[20] To add suspense and mystery to his characterization, his actual arrival was delayed until the next scene at a fishing quay beside a Norwegian fiord; Stoker has left us with a vivid impression of how Irving created an appropriately uncanny atmosphere here:

> Sea and sky were blue with the cold steely blue of the North. The sun was bright and across the water the rugged mountain-line stood out boldly. Deep under the shelving beach, which led down to the water, was a Norwegian fishing boat whose small brown foresail swung in the wind. There was no appearance anywhere of a man or anything else alive. But suddenly there stood a mariner in old-time dress of picturesque cut and faded colour of brown and peacock blue with a touch of red. On his head was a sable cap. He stood there, silent, still and fixed, more like a vision made solid than a living man, realising well the description of the phantom sailor of whom Thekla had

told in the ballad spoken in the first act ... It was marvellous that any living man should show such eyes. They really seemed to shine like cinders of glowing red from out the marble face. The effect was instantaneous ...[21]

The curtain then slowly fell on this striking picture of unearthly strangeness, isolation, and plaintive yearning for human compassion.

Near the end, Vanderdecken engaged in what some critics disparaged as a Surrey-side combat with the young sailor, Olaf, his rival for Thekla's love. After much struggle, the powerful Olaf threw Vanderdecken down from a precipitous cliff into the sea from which he had first come; but shortly thereafter, the waves cast Vanderdecken alone onto the shore. He then spirited Thekla away to the phantom ship – the final evocative tableau showed the two of them on deck, sailing away into the hazy distance as Vanderdecken portentously gestured towards the 'promised land'.[22] An exotic setting, a story of mythic implications, the interpenetration of the human and the divine,[23] and a sensuous appeal to a refined sense of beauty: these and similar themes and conventions can be found in all Irving's important productions, especially *Faust* (1885) and *Becket* (1893). Indeed, in many ways, Irving at the Lyceum was engaged in a spiritual and artistic experiment not unlike the one which preoccupied Wagner at Bayreuth.[24]

Irving's Vanderdecken, as a significant variation of the type-character of the fated man, was transfigured not just by a woman but also by the intensity of his own suffering. For this character-type, death – real or imagined – always brought with it a kind of perverse ecstasy, the theatrical equivalent of the romantic agony. In his psychological masterpiece, *The Bells* (1871), Irving decided to make it clear to the audience from the outset that the leading character, Mathias, is indeed a guilty murderer; however, some of the traditional critics, hoping for a murder mystery, wanted him to withhold this information as long as possible, perhaps right up until Mathias's death at the very end of the play.[25] Irving's decision was in fact an artistic revolution: by breaking down the barrier normally created by the proscenium arch, he allowed the audience to feel as though it were entering directly and completely into Mathias's inner life: 'The "Bells" is not a three hours' excitement', declared the critic Frederick Wedmore, 'but a psychological study'.[26] No common murderer from a blood-and-thunder melodrama, Irving's Mathias had clearly been forced to commit the crime for the sake of his impoverished family, a sacrifice of his noble character which made him into the kind of hero with whom a Victorian audience was readily prepared to identify. During the third act, Mathias dreams of a courtroom where he is on trial for his crime: here, with sometimes unbearable intensity,[27] Irving re-enacted under the spell of a mesmerist the murder of the Polish Jew which had taken place some fifteen years earlier. Mathias's final death, before his mystified family and

16 Irving as Vanderdecken

friends, was therefore not brought about by the mere force of the law but by his own hypersensitive *conscience* as he imagined himself being hanged by the neck as payment for his crime.[28] The production succeeded, then, as an effective reconciliation of old-fashioned notions of poetic justice and modern theories of psychological analysis. An extraordinairly popular

17 Irving as Mephistopheles in *Faust*. Courtesy of the Theatre Museum

catharsis of both public and private forms of guilt, it was a mainstay of Irving's repertoire for over thirty years, and was performed over 800 times. Shaw, despite his reservations about Irving's antiquated repertoire, praised Irving's performance, among other things, for its 'finished execution',[29] and Peter Thomson has recently called it 'as profound a study of the human conscience as *Lord Jim*'.[30]

Many of Irving's melodramatic roles were in fact elaborate variations on the Mathias theme. By instinct, Irving tended to internalize his personal preoccupation with the ancient principle of fate, so that the so-called villainous hero was revealed, like Mathias, as divided against himself, fixated on a terrible crime committed in the past, and projecting a redeemed (but, alas, often unattainable) life for himself in the future. Irving's Eugene Aram (1873), after a long soul-stirring monologue in which he confessed how he had been tempted, against his will, to commit murder, died slowly in the soothing arms of his true love, Ruth, in a country graveyard beside a large black cross and beneath the branches of a dark fate-tree as it was gradually illuminated by the red-glow of sunrise.[31] His Sir Edward Mortimer in Colman's *The Iron Chest* (1879) – the play on which Shaw heaped contempt – died from terror and remorse over the sudden discovery of his crime, and although his dying was realistically detailed, it had what the *Morning Post* (29 September 1879) called 'a touch of poetic grace' which saved him from complete ignominy. His Robespierre (1899), written specially for him by Sardou, was eventually sacrificed to the bloody revolution which he himself had helped to create, but not before he had achieved a sentimental reconciliation not only with his former mistress but also with his illegitimate son, neither of whom shared his revolutionary ideals.[32] Similarly, his Robert Landry in *The Dead Heart* (1889), killed, in an act of justifiable revenge, the man who had arranged for his imprisonment in the Bastille, and then saved himself from the despair of a 'dead heart' by saving the son of his former mistress from death on the guillotine. Characteristically, the penultimate scene showed Landry in the first light of dawn at the base of 'the scaffold on which the guillotine is erected, by the side of the skeleton limbs of the tree of Liberty – a horribly weird and suggestive' picture; the final tableau portrayed him as a living testament to the redemptive power of love, a 'splendidly picturesque figure ... standing by the guillotine, black and terrible against the morning sky, with the howling mob around him, his arms pointing towards the distraught woman for whose sake he has thrown away his life – the crown of a career of suffering and self-sacrifice'.[33] In all these performances, Irving's audiences were willing to accept any number of historical and psychological improbabilities as long as the conventional melodramatic pattern – the expiation of guilt followed by a kind of secularized apotheosis or revolution of the spirit – was faithfully and powerfully rendered.

When we review Irving's entire Lyceum repertoire, we find that this essential pattern was repeated, although sometimes psychological issues were dramatized through externalized character conflicts rather than interiorized dilemmas. Irving's gallery of evil characters – Mephistopheles in *Faust* (1885), Louis XI (1878), and Synorix in Tennyson's *The Cup* (1881), for example – were all morally and physically misshapen characters, made tolerable to Lyceum audiences only because they were so unequivocally defeated at the end. *Faust* concluded with a golden tableau in which Margaret, the paragon of goodness, constancy, and love, was seen about to ascend to Heaven, while Mephistopheles and Faust, wrapped in a shroud of fire and smoke, were seen descending into the depths of Hell to the accompaniment of thunder and lightning.[34] The final act of *Louis XI*, a medieval-inspired *danse macabre*, consisted of a detailed rendering of the King's gradual death, and although his physical suffering evoked some sympathy together with revulsion, there was general relief combined with a sense of renewal ('The king is dead! / Long live the king!')[35] as he took his last gasping breath.[36]

Faust and *Louis XI* presented relatively uncomplicated moral lessons, but *The Cup*, by accident or design, was a more problematic treatment of Irving's moral preoccupations. It reached an oddly satisfying conclusion when the lecherous Synorix (Irving) died slowly after drinking from a poisoned cup offered to him by Camma (Ellen Terry), the victim of his illicit desires. While Synorix, like Louis XI, writhed through the agonies of death, the Lyceum audience could also reflect on Camma, dressed in a shimmering diaphanous robe of gold and green, an embodiment of ideal (Victorian, despite the ancient setting) loveliness who had managed, against all odds, to resist defilement.[37] An elaborate art-for-art's-sake ritual mostly invented by Irving in spite of its professed concern for verifiable historical details,[38] the production was an intensely sensuous (indeed, almost sensual) experience – an early form of environmental theatre complete with the smell of burning incense wafting into the Lyceum auditorium.[39] It proved enormously popular with Grosvenor Gallery types who could relish its flirtation with decadent desires, enhanced by the subtext of Irving and Terry's rumoured love affair, while pretending to be immune to its conventional moral outcome: 'the aesthetes, in their heart of hearts, are worshipping these divinities of society, Ellen Terry and Henry Irving', Henry Labouchère commented in his review for *Truth* (13 January 1881); 'Never before were the favourites placed in so gorgeous a frame.' This was a classic instance of the kind of moral double standard which the Lyceum in fact promoted.[40] Concluding images of thwarted evil, however seductive, were always accompanied in Irving's productions by counterbalancing images of transcendent goodness. Its status as a kind of national theatre meant that the Lyceum could not afford to do otherwise.

Villainy, however, was only one side of the Janus-head: Irving also made a specialty of martyred saints who struggled not so much with the

18 Irving as Louis XI. Caricature by Harry Furniss. Courtesy of the Museum of London

dark side of their own natures but also with the instruments of darkness in a fallen world – corrupt kings, robbers, political malcontents, unrepentant sinners, even wayward children. His Charles I (1872) was a thoroughly domesticated uxorious king, too preoccupied with his wife, children, and garden to trouble himself very much about mere politics. As he was going off to the scaffold, he turned back, adopted a suitably dignified attitude, and then said his last word – 'Remember' – in such a gentle mournful voice that audiences were close to tears.[41] Ellen Terry insists that this was no mere trick of pose, make-up, and delivery, but an emotional change which had taken place deep within Irving's imagination: 'However often I played that scene with him, I knew that when he first came on he was not aware of my presence nor of any *earthly* presence: he seemed to be already in heaven.'[42] Irving's greatest triumph in this line of parts was in Tennyson's *Becket* (1893) which Irving himself had extensively adapted into the form of a medieval passion play marking the stages of the Archbishop's spiritual growth. Early on, Irving's Becket is a pleasure-seeking companion to King Henry II; once appointed Archbishop, however, he is a spiritual leader in conflict with the usurping authority of the crown; at the end, he reaches a state of transcendent grace when, after being murdered by the King's Men, he seems to rise up, in a sublime apotheosis, into the arms of his Lord.[43] Similarly, his Dante (1903), also tailor-made for him by Sardou, was a noble, austere figure combining paternal tenderness and sacerdotal resolve in such a way as to be not just a mortal character but an eternal symbol of the human soul in search of spiritual liberation,[44] and climaxed as Dante saved his illegitimate child from the hands of a wicked Cardinal.[45] Irving was embarrassed by both the contrived text and the special effects needed to tart it up in production – ' "They can take it away and burn it. Do they think I'm a damned showman?" ' he is said to have screamed during rehearsals[46] – but the play's moral pattern was not so different from the kind of thing Irving had started doing so successfully over thirty years earlier in *Charles I*. By 1903, however, even the actor's most loyal admirers could not work up much enthusiasm for this sort of dramatic situation, and they urged him in no uncertain terms not to be so stubbornly out-of-date.[47]

The best of these mature performances would not have been possible if as a young actor Irving had not experienced an unusually gruelling apprenticeship touring the provinces where he mastered the technical skills needed for success in various types of melodrama. In Edinburgh alone, in a period of two and a half years from February 1857 until September 1859, he played at least 400 different parts, that is, a new character almost every two days – a unique record in the annals of stage history.[48] Melodrama of course depends on a highly developed visual language of gesture, pose, and facial expression, what is aptly known as

19 Irving as Sardou's Robespierre. Drawing by Bernard Partridge. Courtesy of the Metropolitan Toronto Library Board

the 'silent speaking of the passions', and Irving's body – tall, lean, and angular – was an ideal instrument for this kind of traditional performance style. He could create any number of striking attitudes, each picturing a dominant or cardinal emotion. His 'long and delicately shaped hands'[49] could inscribe elaborate dance-like patterns of significance in the air – 'With them he could *speak*' Stoker has explained[50] – and his restless, sometimes grotesque stage walk, combined with a tendency to stamp the feet and bob the head in moments of intense passion, gave him a strangely fascinating quality, hampering him as a dashing lover (Claude Melnotte in Bulwer-Lytton's *The Lady of Lyons*, 1879)[51] but assisting him brilliantly as a metaphysical villain (Mephistopheles in *Faust*, 1885).[52] His face, with its large domed forehead, deep-set penetrating eyes, and overhanging shaggy eyebrows – which George Sampson also thought 'almost capable of speech'[53] – together with high gaunt cheekbones and thin mobile lips, seemed infinitely adaptable. Shaw is rumoured to have quipped that Irving had no face, meaning that he had as many different faces, or character-masks to use Craig's vocabulary, as he wished to project.[54] Indeed, it was Irving's practice to show a character's changing emotions through elaborately varied facial expressions before actually speaking his lines, a trick of technique which he liked to pass on to younger actors.[55] In part, he relied so much on the 'vocabulary of passions' alive within every muscle of his face because his voice, although it improved with experience, was never really strong or flexible,[56] and also because in this way both sound and picture were synchronized, enhancing each other as they reached the audience in a relatively large theatre like the Lyceum.[57]

Above all, in physical gifts, temperament, and training, Irving was a singularly 'picturesque' actor: this is the critical term which contemporary observers used most often to sum up the distinctive qualities of his art.[58] It can be a somewhat imprecise word but it tends to mean heightened (or idealized), vivid (or graphic), mysterious, surprising, memorable (or striking) and, of course, pictorial (as in a picture or painting).[59] Although the picturesque bears some similarities to the cognate styles of realism and naturalism, it is in fact a third, quite distinct, theatrical style which Irving, in particular, did so much to refine. A detailed analysis of the picturesque cannot be undertaken here, but some aspects of it should be briefly examined to indicate how it served Irving when presenting melodrama.

The picturesque style of performance suited melodrama, for like that genre, the picturesque, by its very nature, mediated between an idealized representation of life, on the one hand, and a realistic representation, on the other. Macready, for example, successfully used the picturesque mode for the psychological development of an historical character like Cardinal Richelieu: commonplace details and grandiose effects could be more easily

DUBOSC   LESURQUES

20 Irving as Dubosc and Lesurques in *The Lyons Mail*. Charcoal sketch by
Bransby Williams. Courtesy of the estate of Eric Jones-Evans

accommodated here than in his Shakespearian roles.[60] In Irving's time, as in Macready's, Shakespearian characters were expected to be heroic, a stylistic ideal at odds with the idiosyncrasies (or mannerisms as they were sometimes called) of Irving's picturesque style of performance. He was more readily accepted in contemporary character parts, as Shakespearian villains (Iago and Richard III, but not Othello and Macbeth) where heroism was not thought so desireable, or as the highly coloured villains and heroes of melodrama, where the picturesque, as a stylistic compromise, was thought entirely suitable, especially by traditional critics like Dutton Cook and Joseph Knight.[61] Whereas realism and naturalism (low mimetic) were best used for the microscopic examination of contemporary social issues, the picturesque (middle mimetic, as it were) was best used for a kind of painterly evocation of the once-upon-a-time, where extraordinary emotions and archetypal myths were placed directly at centre stage. Not surprisingly, Irving's most picturesque productions, such as *Louis XI*, *Faust*, and of course *Becket*, tended to be set in medieval Europe: in this seemingly real, but mostly symbolical milieu, the intensity and elaborateness of his Gothic sensibility could be vividly expressed.[62]

For Irving, the picturesque was more than a theatrical style, it was also a way of experiencing life. When he went on working holidays to the continent, for example, he was always searching for picturesque effects which could be transferred to the Lyceum stage; and when he first visited Niagara Falls, he was entranced by its picturesque beauty and sublime effects.[63] Moreover, he seems to have accepted without question melodramatic characters, both on stage and off, whose simple black and white vision of the world was not so different from his own. In performance, their attitudinizing and exaggerations were toned down and made to seem entirely natural, psychologically compelling, and worth all the attention (despite Shaw) which he had chosen to lavish on them. Critics on both sides of the Atlantic marvelled at his emotional intensity, obsession with character-detail, and almost mystical level of concentration, combined with a protean genius for literally getting inside his parts,[64] whether they were elaborately individualized, like the rascal Digby Grant in Albery's *Two Roses* (1881) or broadly drawn, like Edgar of Ravenswood in Herman Merivale's *Ravenswood* (1890), an adaptation of Scott's *The Bride of Lammermoor*.[65] Irving used to insist that ' "every part" ', whichever the kind of play, ' "should be a character" ', based on lifelike details but heightened for proper stage effect.[66] In practice, this meant that all the parts in his repertoire warranted some kind of picturesque treatment, no matter the somewhat conventional expectations of his critics. Despite his success at probing character-analysis, Irving was sometimes said to be incapable of impersonation; eventually his performances were subsumed to his increasing importance as a public figure.[67] The paradox of being both character

21 The duel in the forest of Fontainebleau. Courtesy of the McLennan Library,
McGill University

and actor, at once, contributed to Irving's lifelong preoccupation with the
figure of the double. In Reade's adaptation of *The Lyons Mail* (1877), for
example, he played both the brutal ruffian Dubosc and the gentle hero
Lesurques, two men so uncannily similar in appearance – but so different
in character – that Lesurques is mistakenly, and almost tragically,
arrested for a murder committed by his villainous double.[68] Similarly, in
Boucicault's adaptation of *The Corsican Brothers* (1880) he played the two
brothers of the play's title, Fabien and Louis Dei Franchi. Irving's
audiences of course knew from their programmes that he was cast as both
Corsican brothers, and so, at one level, they could appreciate it as a tour
de force of acting; at another level, however, they recognized that the
brothers were, in a sense, the physical manifestations of a *single* personality. In London, the *Era* (26 September 1880) thought that their
relationship ('Weird, mysterious') was 'almost mythical' in effect; and in
Boston, the *Evening Transcript* (14 October 1895) thought that the
sympathetic bond between them was a contemporary reworking of the
ancient Biblical theme, 'Am I my brother's keeper?'

The story, like *Vanderdecken*, is indeed full of archetypal elements emerging from the main theme – the primordial desire for revenge. Louis and
Fabien are both in love with a beautiful woman, Emilie de Lesparre;
Louis follows her from Corsica to Paris where he protects her from the
roué M. de Château Renaud; they fight a gentlemanly duel in the Forest

22 Irving as Fabien dei Franchi in Corsica and as Louis dei Franchi in Paris.
Courtesy of the McLennan Library, McGill University

of Fontainebleau but Château Renaud wins and Louis dies. The scene shifts back to Corsica where Fabien, finishing up a letter to Louis, suddenly has a vision of his dying brother, or, as the souvenir programme puts it, 'the living and the dead stand face to face'.[69] Fabien, dutiful to the last drop of his Corsican blood, then travels to France, in search of retribution, and through the kind of fateful coincidence which paradoxically both relieves and enhances anxiety, winds up fighting a duel with Château Renaud at the very time and place where his brother Louis had died. On this occasion, however, it is Château Renaud who must die, a victim of the inexorability of fate and of the kind of moral accountability on which melodrama always insists. As he does so, there appears a second vision of Louis – 'the dead and the living stand side by side' once again, the souvenir programme explains – as Louis speaks his final words, '"Mourn not, my brother, we shall meet again."'[70] Revenge has been achieved; evil (Château Renaud) has been vanquished (or perhaps just repressed for the time being?); a woman (Emilie de Lesparre), as a symbol of idealized values, has not only been saved from ignominy but has made two brothers whole in spirit if not in fact; and fate, although frightening, has been depicted as an ally of human destiny.

Through the hypnotic intensity of his acting, Irving made audiences feel as if they could almost see the invisible spiritual bond uniting the two brothers. His Fabien tended to be a melancholy personification of vengeance, the dangerous wild-blooded Corsican of popular stereotype, charming but also resolute in the expression of both love and hate. His Louis, in marked contrast, was graceful, courteous, refined, a more sentimentalized character whose beseeching looks as he died made audiences weep.[71] The mystic affinity between them was most impressive during the final duel between Château Renaud and Fabien in the Forest of Fontainebleau. As we would expect from Irving's concern for the picturesque rendering of melodrama, it was the highly physicalized atmosphere of the setting which brought out the play's spiritual significance and conveyed the ever-shifting character relationships. The ground, covered with heavy snow, stood out against the bleak leafless trees which were suitably 'gaunt and weird', illuminated by cold moonlight.[72] Fabien, like the trees, was a black figure, an instrument of implacable revenge, an emblem of Fate; his pale face, however, gave him a ghostly aura, an effect enhanced by the moonlight and the ominous silence of the forest. The snow stopped as he and Château Renaud fought their duel, and then it began to fall again, softly, intensifying both the mood of 'cold solitude' and the sense of relief once the clarity of revenge had in fact been achieved.[73] The pervasive impression throughout the scene – of civilized restraint, on the one hand, and primeval terror, on the other – remained with audiences for many years afterwards,[74] as did the classic evocation of *eros* and *thanatos* in the final tableau of the two brothers – separated yet strangely together, different yet strangely the same – as they looked yearningly towards each other in the wintry light of breaking dawn. 'We left the theatre in awe, in something of fear, in strange perturbation of spirit', explained the painter Graham Robertson. 'We had come to see a play called *The Corsican Brothers*, but we had actually seen the transfigured face of Henry Irving ...'[75]

Irving's career ended as it had begun, touring the provinces, basking in the applause of his ever-loyal fans, and remaining faithful, despite illness, to the creed of his art, to what Bridges-Adams has aptly described as his 'pilgrim's march' towards the ideal.[76] He died in Bradford on 13 October 1905 (a Friday the 13th, noted those who believed in fate) shortly after speaking Becket's last ennobling words, 'Into Thy hands, O Lord – into Thy hands!'[77] This became an essential part of the myth of Irving, as though he had managed, through a mystic concentration of will, to sublimate himself into the very kind of apotheosis which he had spent a lifetime perfecting on the Lyceum stage. There was some controversy about the decision to bury him in the Poet's Corner, Westminster Abbey – he was, after all, still something of a rogue and vagabond, a mere actor – but it was eventually quashed, and the nation mourned him in appropriate ceremonial splendour.[78] Like the many villains he had played, the monstrous side of his art was now laid to rest; the sacred avowal of life in the midst of death best sums up the melodramatic spirit which informed the kind of picturesque theatre in which both he and his audiences had done their revelling.

NOTES

1 'Preface' to *Ellen Terry and Bernard Shaw: A Correspondence*, ed. Christopher St John (New York: G. P. Putnam's Sons, 1931), p. xxi.

2 Edward Gordon Craig, *Henry Irving* (1930; rpt New York and London: Benjamin Blom, 1969), pp. 127 and 131–2; Henry Irving, 'Does Punch feel?', *The Era Almanack* (1881), pp. 97–8; and Henry Irving, *The Drama: Addresses* (1893; rpt New York and London: Benjamin Blom, 1969), pp. 120–38.

3 [William Archer and Robert W. Lowe], *The Fashionable Tragedian: A Criticism* (London: George Taylor, 1877), pp. 4 and 15–20, and William Wallace, 'Sir Henry Irving's Claims', *National Review*, 28 (September 1896), 83–5.

4 L. J. Claris, 'Henry Irving, Actor and Artist', *Theatre*, 3rd series 5 (1 March 1882), 157; Craig, *Henry Irving*, pp. 127–9 and 133–4; Kenneth DeLong and Denis Salter, 'C. V. Stanford's Incidental Music to Henry Irving's Production of Tennyson's *Becket*', *Theatre History Studies*, 3 (1983), [68]–86; Joseph Hatton, *Henry Irving's Impressions of America*, 2 vols., 2nd edn (London: Sampson Low, Marston, Searle, & Rivington, 1884), vol. II, p. 97; H. Chance Newton, *Cues and Curtain Calls* (London: John Lane/The Bodley Head, 1927), pp. 4 and 7–8; Edward R. Russell, 'Mr. Irving's Interpretations of Shakspeare', *Fortnightly Review*, NS 34 (1 October 1883), 468–9; Wallace, 'Sir Henry Irving's Claims', p. 76; *Chicago Tribune*, 25 January 1885; and *World* (London), 20 March 1878.

5 Quoted in *New York World*, 7 November 1893.

6 'Preface' to *Ellen Terry and Bernard Shaw: A Correspondence*, p. xx, *Our Theatres in the Nineties*, 3 vols. (London: Constable, 1932), vol. III, pp. 145–6, and *Pen Portraits and Reviews*, rev. edn (London: Constable, 1932), p. 168; see also Michael Holroyd, *Bernard Shaw*, vol. I: *1856–1898, The Search for Love* (London: Chatto & Windus, 1988), especially pp. 350–5.

7 *Henry Irving*, pp. 32 and 109–10, and [Craig], 'Henry Irving notes mss E.G.C.–', in the Bibliothèque Nationale [France] (R. 53.254), p. 10: 'Chaplin in the earlier pictures is inscrutable – because he understood so well what Irving understood even better, the prime importance of the mask: both allowed their mask to do the work for them.' Cf. Irène Eynat-Confino, *Beyond the Mask: Gordon Craig, Movement, and the Actor* (Carbondale and Edwardsville: Southern Illinois University Press, 1987), pp. 187–8. Shaw was also reminded of Chaplin: see 'Preface' to *Ellen Terry and Bernard Shaw: A Correspondence*, p. xx.

8 There is no evidence, however, to suggest that Irving was familiar with Freud; but his acting manager at the Lyceum and biographer, Bram Stoker, might have known a fair amount: see Nina Auerbach, *Woman and the Demon: The Life of a Victorian Myth* (Cambridge, MA and London: Harvard University Press,

1982), pp. 22–3. Freudian themes and conventions can be found not only in Stoker's *Dracula* but in Irving's production of *Faust* (1885) which had a significant influence (one which remains to be explored) on Stoker's novel. Throughout this article, I am thinking of Freudianism as a generalized metaphor for psychological investigation.

9 This character-type has been concisely analysed by G. R. Thompson, 'Introduction: Romanticism and the Gothic Tradition', in *The Gothic Imagination: Essays in Dark Romanticism*, ed. G. R. Thompson (Seattle: Washington State University Press, 1974), pp. 1–10; see also Peter Brooks, *The Melodramatic Imagination* (New Haven and London: Yale University Press, 1976), pp. 16–20.

10 *Henry Irving, Shakespearean* (Cambridge University Press, 1981), p. 243.

11 Laurence Irving, *Henry Irving: The Actor and His World* (1951; rpt New York: Macmillan, 1952), pp. 32–7, 46–7, and 62.

12 H. J. W. Dam, 'Sir Henry Irving', *Playgoer*, 1 (October 1901–March 1902), 69 and 71.

13 There is a good deal of evidence for the continuing influence which religious faith exerted over Irving's life and imagination: see Laurence Irving, *Henry Irving*, and *The Autobiography of Sir John Martin-Harvey* (London: Sampson Low, Marston & Co., n.d.), pp. 324–6.

14 See, for example, *New York Herald*, 21 September 1890, and Wallace, 'Sir Henry Irving's Claims', p. 76.

15 '"Weirdness that lifts and colours all": The Secret Self of Henry Irving', in *Shakespeare and the Victorian Stage*, ed. Richard Foulkes (Cambridge University Press, 1986), p. 99.

16 *Around Theatres*, 2 vols. (New York: Alfred A. Knopf, 1930), vol. II, p. 511.

17 Joseph Hatton, *Cigarette Papers* (London: Anthony Treherne, 1902), pp. 108–9.

18 'The Theatre in its Relation to the State', *Fortnightly Review*, NS 64 (1 July 1898), 91.

19 See [Dutton Cook] in *World* (London), 12 June 1878.

20 Clement Scott, *From 'The Bells' To 'King Arthur'* (London: John Macqueen, 1896), p. 136; see also *Pall Mall Budget* (London), 15 June 1878.

21 Bram Stoker, *Personal Reminiscences of Henry Irving*, 2 vols. (New York: The Macmillan Company; London: Macmillan & Co., Ltd., 1906), vol. I, pp. 55–6.

22 Unidentified newspaper cutting in the Theatre Museum (London); the other business is drawn from two London newspapers: *Daily Chronicle*, 10 June 1878 and *John Bull*, 15 June 1878.

23 Shaw praised this quality in particular: *Our Theatres in the Nineties*, vol. III, p. 145.

24 Wallace, 'Sir Henry Irving's Claims', p. 76 and Talcott Williams, 'Sir Henry Irving', *Atlantic Monthly*, 96 (December 1905), 830.

25 Scott, *From 'The Bells' to 'King Arthur'*, pp. 3–4 and *Morning Advertiser* (London), 28 November 1871.

26 'Restoration Comedy and Mr. Irving's Last Parts', *Gentleman's Magazine*, 244 (May 1878), 589.

27 [Joseph Knight] in *Athenaeum* (London), 2 December 1871, *Era* (London), 3 December 1871, and [John Oxenford] in *The Times*, 28 November 1871.

28 The production has been fully reconstructed in *Henry Irving and 'The Bells'*, ed. David Mayer (Manchester University Press, 1980).

29 *Pen Portraits and Reviews*, p. 163. See also his 'Preface' to *Ellen Terry and Bernard Shaw: A Correspondence*, p. xxii.

30 'The Secret Self of Henry Irving', p. 100.

31 This description is based on reviews in two Chicago newspapers (both 15 January 1885): *Daily Inter Ocean* and *Tribune*.

32 I am grateful to Robert Eddison for lending me Irving's marked study copy of *Robespierre* (privately printed).

33 *Pall Mall Gazette* (London), 30 September 1889.

34 Promptbook for *Faust*, p. 61 and opposite (at the University of Manchester); see also Michael R. Booth, *Victorian Spectacular Theatre 1850–1910* (Boston, London, and Henley: Routledge & Kegan Paul, 1981), p. 123.

35 [Casimir Delavigne], *Louis the Eleventh* [adapted by Dion Boucicault], p. 68 of marked study copy in the Ellen Terry Collection at Smallhythe Place. Quoted courtesy of the National Trust.

36 See Henry Arthur Jones, *The Shadow of Henry Irving* (1931; rpt New York: Benjamin Blom, 1969), p. 40 and Wedmore, 'Restoration Comedy', p. 596.

37 *Standard* (London), 4 January 1881.

38 The production is treated in some detail by Martin Meisel, *Realizations: Narrative, Pictorial, and Theatrical Arts in Nineteenth-Century England* (Princeton University Press), pp. 411–16.

39 *Era* (London), 8 January 1881, and promptbook for *The Cup*, pp. 40–1 (at the Tennyson Research Centre [Lincoln]).

40 Like Bernhardt, Ellen Terry was an acceptable symbol of displaced eroticism: see W. Graham Robertson, *Time Was* (London: Hamish Hamilton, 1931), pp. 107–28 and 139–61; for more recent treatments of this theme, see Nina Auerbach, *Ellen Terry: Player in Her Time* (New York and London: W. W. Norton, 1987) and John Stokes, Michael R. Booth, and Susan Bassnett, *Bernhardt, Terry, Duse: The Actress in her Time* (Cambridge University Press, 1988).

41 George Pleydell Bancroft, *Stage and Bar* (London: Faber and Faber, 1939), p. 59; *Chicago Tribune*, 23 January 1885; and *Daily Evening Bulletin* (San Francisco), 13 September 1893.

42 *Ellen Terry's Memoirs*, ed. Edith Craig and Christopher St John (1932; rpt New York: Benjamin Blom, 1969), p. 139.

43 See DeLong and Salter, 'C. V. Stanford's Incidental Music to Henry Irving's Production of Tennyson's *Becket*', pp. 71–2.

44 *Daily Telegraph* (London), 1 May 1903 and *Illustrated Sporting and Dramatic News* (London), 16 May 1903.

45 The plot is summarized in *Era* (London), 2 May 1903.

46 Quoted in Lena Ashwell, *Myself a Player* ([London]: Michael Joseph, 1936), p. 87.

47 A. B. Walkley, *Drama and Life* (London: Methuen, 1907): 'Could not some real poet have contrived a worthier scenic arrangement of the Dante legend which might still have exhibited Sir Henry Irving on every side of his remarkable personality?' (p. 165).

48 Austin Brereton, *The Life of Henry Irving*, 2 vols. in 1 (1908; rpt New York and

London: Benjamin Blom, 1969), vol. II, pp. 337–43 and 345; details confirmed by Laurence Irving, *Henry Irving*, pp. 91 and 685–94.

49 Richard Dickins, *Forty Years of Shakespeare on the English Stage* (n.p.: n.p., n.d.), p. 20.

50 *Personal Reminiscences of Henry Irving*, vol. II, p. 63.

51 *Bell's Weekly Messenger* (London), 28 April 1879.

52 Booth, *Victorian Spectacular Theatre*, pp. 125–6.

53 *Seven Essays* (Cambridge University Press, 1947), p. 161.

54 The quip is perhaps apocryphal but the sentiment is nevertheless true; details about Irving's physical technique are available in [Archer and Lowe], *The Fashionable Tragedian*; Craig, *Henry Irving*; William Archer, *Henry Irving: Actor and Manager* (London: Field & Tuer; Simpkin, Marshall; Hamilton, Adams, 1883); Henry A. Clapp, 'Henry Irving', *Atlantic Monthly*, 53 (March 1884), 413–22; and William Winter, *Henry Irving* (New York: George J. Coombes, 1885).

55 *The Drama: Addresses*, pp. 64–5.

56 His voice was often criticized; Shaw made some of the sharpest criticisms but also gave some of the most generous praise: *Collected Letters 1874–1897*, ed. Dan H. Laurence (London: Max Reinhardt, 1965), p. 650 and *London Music in 1888–89 As Heard By Corno Di Bassetto (Later Known as Bernard Shaw)* (London: Constable, 1937), pp. 253–5. See also Richard Bebb, 'The Voice of Henry Irving: an investigation,' *Recorded Sound*, no. 68 (October 1977), 727–32.

57 Irving increased the seating capacity of the Lyceum several times so that eventually there was enough room for about 2,000 people: see Bram Stoker, 'The Question of a National Theatre', *Nineteenth Century*, 63 (May 1908), 737.

58 See [Archer and Lowe], *The Fashionable Tragedian*, pp. 12–15; Clapp, 'Henry Irving', p. 418 ('the most entirely picturesque actor of our time'); and J. Ranken Towse, 'Henry Irving', *Century Magazine*, NS 27 (March 1884), [660]–9.

59 There is an extensive literature on the picturesque as it relates to art and literary history; see, for example, Walter John Hipple, *The Beautiful, the Sublime, and the Picturesque in Eighteenth-Century British Aesthetic Theory* (Carbondale, Ill.: Southern Illinois University Press, 1957) and Alexander M. Ross, *The Imprint of the Picturesque on Nineteenth-Century British Fiction* (Waterloo: Wilfrid Laurier University Press, 1986). But in theatre history studies, the subject still requires full-length analysis. Some useful remarks about the picturesque and related aesthetic issues in the nineteenth-century theatre can be found in Augustin Filon, *The English Stage* (London: John Milne and New York: Dodd, Mead, 1897); Helena Faucit, Lady Martin, *On Some of Shakespeare's Female Characters* (Edinburgh and London: William Blackwood and Sons, 1885), especially p. 371; and Henry James, *The Scenic Art*, ed. Allan Wade (1948; rpt New York: Hill and Wang, 1957). Peter Conrad, *The Victorian Treasure-House* (London: Collins, 1973) makes a number of wide-ranging arguments about the picturesque as a distinct aesthetic phenomenon.

60 See Denis Salter, 'A Picturesque Interpretation of History: William Charles Macready's *Richelieu*, 1839–1850', in *When They Weren't Doing Shakespeare*, ed. Judith L. Fisher and Stephen Watt (Athens and London: University of Georgia Press), pp. 39–63.

61 Cook, *Nights at the Play* (London: Chatto and Windus, 1883) and Knight, *Theatrical Notes* (1893; rpt New York: Benjamin Blom, 1971/2).

62 The Gothic character of Irving's imagination was often noted in his own time: see T. H. Hall Caine, *Richard III and Macbeth* (London: Simpkin, Marshall & Co., 1877), p. 15; Mrs Aria, *My Sentimental Self* (London: Chapman and Hall, 1922), p. 89; and Bertram Joseph, *The Tragic Actor* (London: Routledge & Kegan Paul, 1959), p. 367 and n. 4.

63 Joseph Hatton, 'An Actor's Holiday', *Art Journal* (1886), pp. 207–12 and [245]–8 and also Hatton's *Henry Irving's Impressions of America*, vol. II, 145–52. Niagara, then as now, has of course been a great gathering spot for those in search of frisson of the picturesque and similar aesthetic pleasures: see Elizabeth McKinsey, *Niagara Falls: Icon of the American Sublime* (Cambridge University Press, 1985).

64 Among the many sources describing these qualities in his art, see *The Autobiography of Sir John Martin-Harvey*, pp. 328–33.

65 Percy Fitzgerald, *Henry Irving* (London: Chapman and Hall, 1893), pp. 46–9 and 176–80 and Scott, *From 'The Bells' To 'King Arthur'*, pp. [316]–30.

66 Quoted in *New York Herald*, 22 October 1883.

67 See Beerbohm, *Around Theatres*, vol. II, p. 513.

68 *Morning Post* (London), 21 May 1877.

69 *The Corsican Brother: Story of the Play* (London and Belfast: Marcus Ward, n.d.), n.p.

70 Ibid.

71 The differences between the two performances are well described in Scott, *From 'The Bells' To 'King Arthur'*, pp. 177–90.

72 *Era* (London), 26 September 1880.

73 Ibid.

74 See M. Willson Disher, *Melodrama: Plots That Thrilled* (London: Rockliff, 1954), p. 148.

75 *We Saw Him Act: A Symposium on the Art of Sir Henry Irving*, ed. H. A. Saintsbury and Cecil Palmer (1939; rpt New York and London: Benjamin Blom, 1969), p. 189.

76 *A Bridges-Adams Letter Book*, ed. Robert Speaight (London: The Society for Theatre Research, 1971), p. 43.

77 Alfred Lord Tennyson, *Becket* ([London]: privately printed for stage use only, 1893), p. 70.

78 The circumstances surrounding his funeral are described in Laurence Irving, *Henry Irving*, pp. 671–3.

Strindberg's *Oväder*: melodrama pays a visit*

ROBERT F. GROSS

I

Plot summaries can be most deceptive. Take, for example, a summary of the action of August Strindberg's first Chamber Play, *Oväder*, variously translated as *Storm*, *Thunderstorm*, *Storm Clouds*, *Storm Weather*, and even *Stormy Weather*. An elderly divorced gentleman finds that the newly opened gambling club above his apartment is run by no other than his ex-wife and her new husband, a dissolute gigolo. This scoundrel not only abuses his spouse, but hopes to corrupt the old gentleman's eighteen-year-old daughter as well. The guilty ex-wife turns to her wronged ex-husband for help in saving their daughter, just in time to learn that the gigolo has left for the train station with not only the daughter in tow, but the daughter of the local confectioner as well. The gentleman overcomes his resentment, arranges for the defeat of the gigolo. Mother and daughter, delivered from the power of the unprincipled cad, set off 'till landet, i ett gott hem' (for a good home in the country) (p. 73),[1] and the gentleman's peace of mind is restored. Curtain.

A villain, who victimizes no less than three helpless women is finally defeated by the power of the patriarch; the forces of sexual license are defeated by bourgeois domestic values. Today we see these melodramatic elements as hackneyed; they were scarcely fresh when Strindberg wrote the play in 1906. The play's melodramatic pattern is sufficiently strong and predictable to lead more than one eminent critic astray by it. Written in the wake of the elderly Strindberg's unsuccessful marriage to the much younger Harriet Bosse, *Oväder* has been dismissed as a compensatory fantasy on the part of the playwright, in which he imagines his treacherous ex-wife humiliated and saved by himself. 'He wanted to settle the score', is about all Evert Sprinchorn has to say about the play in his admirable study, *Strindberg as Dramatist*.[2] 'The infantile nature of this revenge-fantasy is entirely characteristic of Strindberg', sniffs Maurice

* A draft of this paper was read at the *Themes in Drama* International Conference held at the University of California, Riverside, in February 1990.

Valency.[3] *Strindberg's Dramaturgy*, a recent collection of fine essays on Strindberg's plays, passes over the play without critical comment.[4]

Neglected by critics, it has found few champions on the stage; directors turning to the later works have been far more inclined to choose *The Ghost Sonata* or *A Dream Play*. In recent years, only Giorgio Strehler's much-acclaimed 1982 production has sparked any reconsideration of the play's merits.[5]

Not only the plot, but the atmosphere and imagery encourage a reading of the play as melodrama. The summer night, 'oldigt varm' (unbearably hot) (p. 8), which builds to a flash of heat lightning at the climax of the first scene, and rain at the climax of the second, only to clear with the defeat of the gigolo, is familiar scenic underscoring for melodrama. The genre is invoked in the opening moments of the play, as the Gentleman's brother, the Brother, looks up at the second-floor gambling club of the ex-wife, Gerda, with its red shades 'lysa' (glowing), and imagines it as the stage for a melodrama:

> De fyra röda gardinerna se ut som ridåer, bakom vilka man repeterar blodiga dramer ... så inbillar jag mig; där står en fenixpalm som järnris och kastar skugga på en gardin ...
>
> (Those four red shades look like theatre curtains behind which bloody dramas are being rehearsed ... that's what I imagine; there's a palm tree that casts a shadow like an iron funeral spray on one shade ...)   (p. 9)

The second-floor apartment becomes a proscenium stage within the proscenium, a melodramatic theatre of luridly glowing red shades, and sinister shadows, presaging death. But those shades never rise to reveal the melodramatic scene, which remains only in rehearsal. It *isn't* an iron funeral spray that we see projected on the shades, but the shadow of a palm tree. Even the Brother, as he invokes melodrama, admits that it is not an autonomously existing spectacle, but a heteronomous one: 'så inbillar jag mig' (that's what I imagine) (p. 9) he explains. Melodrama is a mental possibility here, rather than a social reality. *Oväder* invokes the plot elements, character types, imagery and *mise-en-scène* of melodrama, yet displaces these elements to the margins of the theatrical composition, and presents us with a decidedly non-melodramatic world in which the melodramatic imagination only functions fitfully, like flashes of heat lightning.

II

The melodramatic stage of *Oväder* is only one of three prosceniums within the larger proscenium stage. The set for the first and third scenes shows us the sidewalk outside a large, modern house in Stockholm. The house's facade has three openings: Gerda's second-story apartment, the Gentleman's dining room below, and the arch leading to the below-street-level courtyard and the Confectioner's kitchen. Only the first of these three spaces is defined through reference to melodrama. The other two are gentler spaces, characterized by their retreat from conflict and the world at large. The Confectioner's major activity takes place off stage; his wife, whose voice we hear, never appears on stage, and his relationship to his daughter remains ambiguous. He has no telephone; 'men ibland är det gott att slippa – meddelanden' (sometimes it's just as well to get awawy from – messages) (p. 61) he explains. His wife, he tells us, is going blind, but has decided not to have the operation that might help her 'Det är ingenting att se på, säger hon, och hon önskar sig ibland vara döv med' (There is nothing to look at, she says, and sometimes she wishes she'd go deaf, too) (p. 18). The Confectioner's detachment is so complete that his neighbors cannot decide whether he knows anything about his daughter Agnes's involvement with the gigolo or not. He and his wife are busily engaged in putting up preserves, an activity that both contributes to the seasonal atmosphere of the play, with late summer turning to autumn, and which relates to one of the major themes of the play, the preservation of the past in the form of memory. Preserves are tricky, we are reminded, they can mold and ferment. You must watch them 'på okynniga barn' (like mischevious children) (p. 60). The past is unstable and mischievous; it must be monitored. Some people use salicylate in preserves, but the Confectioner suspects it, describing it as 'nya knep' (a new trick) (p. 60). People differ in their methods of dealing with the past, and the Confectioner's methods resist innovation. He prefers to preserve with old-fashioned methods. The world of the Confectioner is that of withdrawal from the world at large.

The Gentleman, whose apartment is next to the Confectioner's entrance and beneath the gambling club, shares in the qualities of both, but prefers to stress his affinities with his neighbor. 'Jag har liksom levat hans liv och burit hans börda parallellt med min egen ... har ingen framfart' (In a way I've shared his life and his troubles have run parallel to my own ... he's got no drive) (p. 12). While the Confectioner spends his time in his kitchen, the Gentleman has spent the summer in his apartment, not going outside during the light summer nights in Stockholm. These nights frighten him; they are 'emot naturens ordning, nästan hemskt' (against the order of nature, almost eerie) (p. 11), and this evening, the first evening dark enough to require the services of the lamplighter, is the first night he is going out since the summer began. Like the Confectioner's wife, he is retreating from vision, but unlike her, he is motivated less by boredom than by anxiety. A natural occurrence, the summer night, seems unnatural to him, and only the replacement of natural light with the artificially created and controlled street light can make him feel at ease. He has spent the summer in his artificially created environment, involved in his own personal work of preservation. Since he separated from Gerda five years ago, he has not changed a single thing in his apartment: the picture of his wife and child remains in its place, surrounded by flowers; the thermometer that they quarreled over is still hidden in the place Gerda put it years ago. The apartment is a shrine to the past. The present, the Gentleman argues, does not exist to consciousness; consciousness is always consciousness of the past or the future, and he has chosen the past. His memories are not ghosts that haunt him, but are 'mina dikter på vissa verkligheter' (my poems made out of certain truths) (p. 39).

Poems made out of certain truths – things that really happened. This is an ambiguous formulation. It posits historical verity at the origin of the poem, but does not explain whether there is any of that verity left in the end result. Just as the Brother takes the red shades and transforms them into curtains for a melodrama, and the shadow of the palm into an iron funeral spray, so too the Gentleman's formulation of a sentimental idyll owes far more to heteronomy than history. His shrine to wife and child denies the fact that he left them years ago. The Gentleman controls the stage setting of a normal domestic life within the proscenium theatre of his apartment, despite the fact that it has no reality. He is not a fond father and devoted husband; he does not even know where his wife and child are. And his performance is less than convincing. This 'devoted husband' considers wives tyrants, and marriage enslavement. He panics at the thought of his wife and child returning to him. The Gentleman's poetry is a lie, erratically told, and only intermittently successful.

From the first, there are suggestions that the Gentleman's attempt to retreat into his tableau of domestic reminiscence has not succeeded in fulfilling his emotional needs. He has stayed indoors all summer, to avoid the light evenings, but the lack of exercise has made it hard for him to sleep. Later, we learn that the death of a bank clerk in the apartment above the Gentleman a few weeks before Gerda moved in has troubled him, as well as the problems of the Confectioner and his wife. He is so ill-at-ease with his solitude that he unsuccessfully seeks the company of the iceman and mailman. Far from the detached, untroubled old age that he repeatedly claims for himself, he is troubled, resentful, paranoid, anxious, and lonely.

This failure of human beings to detach themselves from worldly concerns is subtly echoed in the behavior of the Confectioner toward his wayward daughter, Agnes. Although none of the characters in the play can determine whether the father knows anything about her behavior, it is clear to the audience that he worries about her. He wonders if the Gentleman's young relative and housekeeper, Louise, gets restless in this quiet house they all live in. He asks her to confirm his belief that the Gentleman must, after all, be worried about his daughter, even though he is outwardly unconcerned. The preserves are to be watched like naughty children. Despite his claims of detachment, and his casual, seemingly empty exchanges with his daughter, he gravitates toward the troubling subject all the same. Denial is never totally successful as a defensive strategy.

In *Oväder*, the melodramatic stage exists in tension with stages that are set up to deny even the possibility of conflict. It is a social space, given to strange comings and goings in the night, music and entertainment. It is noisy, contrasting with the quietness of the rest of the building; live people are seen leaving that apartment, unlike the corpses that were seen leaving the nursing home, or the coffin of the bank clerk, which the Gentleman saw carried down the stairs. It is a theatrical world, inhabited by an ex-singer, a pianist, and a young woman who may become a ballerina. Its proprietor looks like 'operett, på gränsen av varieté' (operetta, on the verge of music hall) (p. 14). And yet this most theatrical of spaces is carefully placed in an upper corner of the set, where no scene is played, where the shades are usually drawn, and are opened in the final scene only to reveal an empty space.

Of the melodramatic chamber's three inhabitants, only Gerda is drawn with any detail as a character. Fischer, her husband, appears on stage but never speaks, and the daughter, Ann-Charlotte, is never even seen. Important scenes in the melodramatic plot, such as the quarrels between Fischer and Gerda, the attempted corruption of Ann-Charlotte, the romance with Agnes, and the defeat of Fischer at the railway station, are banished from the stage. Therefore, although the plot is impelled forward by the introduction of melodramatic characters and situations, those very elements are given as little presence on stage as possible. The protagonist does not even confront Fischer, the villain of the piece, but sends his brother on that errand, thus avoiding what would be the *scène à faire* in a well-made melodrama.

Not only is the obligatory confrontation between good and evil banished off stage and arranged through the agency of a secondary character, but the villain's plans comically miscarry on their own. When Agnes learns that her corrupter has not bought first-class train tickets, she throws the third-class tickets in his face and returns to her parents. The wages of sin, it seems, are disappointingly low, and Fischer's hold over any of the women suddenly vanishes. Melodrama dissipates into comedy at the play's climax. *Oväder* introduces melodrama to banish melodrama, infuses the play with melodramatic energy in order to defuse it. Melodrama in *Oväder* is both desired and feared, invoked and exorcised.

III

Why is melodrama desired in *Oväder*? First, because without melodrama, there is no play. The gambling club, with its red shades, its artistic inhabitants, its nocturnal activity, its suggestions of lurid passion, its shadows, which, like the shadows in Plato's Cave, offer no certain knowledge of the nature of thngs, embodies the theatrical. Without the theatrical, there is only retreat; the apathetic acquiescence into blindness, the retreat of the Gentleman into solitude, the lack of communication between the Confectioner and his daughter. The house has been dubbed 'det tysta huset' (the silent house) (pp. 8–9). The Confectioner observes 'Det synes snarare som om man gömde sig' (It almost looks like we're all hiding). Corpses are taken out of the house, and the Confectioner's chief activity, preservation, carries overtones of embalming. Without the gambling club, there is no action. It is its presence that challenges the Gentleman's detachment. No sooner does the Gentleman boast of the advantages of solitude than the red shades raise briefly, showing the bottom of a woman's skirt, and lower again. No sooner does he recommend ignorance of one's neighbors than Fischer enters, provoking speculation about him. The music that wafts down from the club reminds him of the music that used to be played in his house. The club repeatedly calls him back to the world, to life, to human interaction.

The nature of that interaction is based on the satisfactions that melodrama offers. As Robert Heilman has argued, melodrama is structured around the conflicts:

> undergone by characters who are presented as undivided or at least without divisions of such magnitude that they must be at the dramatic center.[6]

In the world of melodrama, characters assume simple and coherent identities. The Gentleman is the wronged husband, divorced and slandered by his wife, who nobly defends her and their child when they are threatened. This is the revenge fantasy, remarked upon by Sprinchorn and Valency, in which the wife is repentent Magdalene, Ann-Charlotte and Agnes are the innocent maidens in distress, and Fischer is the heartless Lothario. In this plot system, characters are given the satisfaction of a single, unambiguous version of events, and clear characterizations.

But the very simplifications that allow Gerda and the Gentleman to play their melodramatic confrontation scene are precisely those that make melodrama an inadequate description of reality. For Agnes is not a total innocent, but a young woman who refuses to travel third class. And the Gentleman is not the man who loves his erring wife and innocent daughter, but a man who enjoys his bachelor's life and is upset at the prospect of any imposition upon it. And even the flattest character in the play, Fischer, who is never allowed to voice a word in his own defense on stage, is given a chance to tell his version of things to the Brother off stage, and convinces his interlocutor 'han hade också sina sidor' (he has his side, too) (p. 70). Strindberg witholds this account from the audience, but the mere fact that such an account exists suddenly suggests an entirely different play, in which Fischer's actions, largely reported in *Oväder*, would take on another significance. The melodramatic account, though satisfying in its clarity and fixity, is always an oversimplification.

It is an oversimplification because it assumes that the psyche is whole and undivided in its attitude towards external objects. The relationship between the Gentleman and the Brother rejects that model. At the beginning of the play, it seems the two brothers are congenial, even close. Louise does not even know which is the elder, since they treat each other with such mutual deference that both could be the elder. Yet there is a more troubled side to their relationship. The Brother accuses Gerda of using him as an accomplice against the Gentleman, and he falls into that role again, when he tells Gerda about her ex-husband and later helps her gain access to his house. Near the end of the play, the Gentleman accuses his brother of treachery, and attributes two motivations to him. The first is a common melodramatic motif; the Brother, he insists, loved Gerda himself. The revelation of the second motivation is suppressed – the Brother cuts his brother off before we can hear the accusation. Like Fischer's version of his story, this suppressed second motive, of which we are given no information, save that it may exist, if only as an accusation, undermines the audience's assurance that it has enough information to understand the dramatic figures and their actions. Yet this burst of fraternal resentment is quickly submerged; only a few lines later, the Gentleman is begging his brother not to go upstairs and turn off the lights in the upper apartment, but to stay on the sidewalk with him. Perfect brothers or fraternal rivals? Castor and Pollux or Karl and Franz Moor? Strindberg is not asking the audience to resolve the relationship into one paradigm or the other, but to accept the fact that both exist at once.

Oversimplification of psychic life had always been an object of scorn for Strindberg. As early as 1886, in his first autobiographical volume, *Tjän- stekvinnans son*, he presented his young self as 'characterless',[7] a field of various forces and impulses without any fixed role to play. He contrasts this with the person who is commonly described as having 'character':

> he has only one posture from which to carry on the extremely complicated business of life, and has decided to hold one definite opinion on any given matter for the rest of his life. And in order not to be accused of 'lacking character', he never changes this opinion, however foolish or impossible it may be. It follows that a man of character must be just a very ordinary man, and one might say, a little stupid.   (p. 237)

Intelligence requires that one understand oneself not as a fixed essence, but as a multiplicity of impulses. This insight led to what he called the 'characterless characters' of *Fröken Julie* and *Erik XIV*, dramatic figures of radical instability.[8] In his post-Inferno plays, most notably *Ett drömspel* of 1902, he broke with all the rules of well-made dramaturgy to create dramatic universes of continual flux. It is not surprising, then, that Strindberg would view melodrama, with its necessary simplifications, as untrue.

And yet, as I observed earlier, *Oväder* relies on melodrama. Like the Gentleman's poetic memories, like the preserves with salicylate, it is a falsification, a 'trick', but a part of the process which changes life into artifact. That genre, so much a part of the popular theatre of Strindberg's day, is required even for this intimate chamber play for the art theatre movement. It cannot be suppressed; it will return, like the deserted wife, to lure a theatre of stasis and interiority, back into action. The play is structured around seasonal occurrences; the preparation of preserves for the winter, the lengthening nights, the coming of the first lamplighter of the season. The Gentleman's final proclamation of tranquility is no more certain than his first ones. Melodrama is always a return, the return of half-forgotten figures behind red shades, which returns with its half truths and fixities to upset the half truths and fixities that have formed in its absence. For the Strindberg of *Oväder*, as with all the Chamber Plays, with their blackmailers, adulterous wives, embezzlers, rival brothers, elves, vampires, and spectral presences, a theatre that is only melodramatic may be false, but a theatre totally without melodrama is unthinkable. The very title of this cycle, 'Chamber Plays', complete with opus numberings, and extensive use of music, both as a structural device and an actual presence, harks back to the very origins of melodrama as musical drama. But Strindberg both contains and supersedes melodramatic plots and conventions. In *Oväder*, melodrama must be invoked and banished, so it can return, and the theatre find life again. When the red shades are raised and the lurid room prove to be empty, the show is over.

NOTES

1 Quotations are from August Strindberg, *Oväder, Samlade skrifter*, vol. XLV (Stockholm: Albert Bonniers, 1921). Page numbers for all further citations from this source are indicated in parentheses. English translations of these passages are my own.

2 Evert Sprinchorn, *Strindberg as Dramatist* (New Haven: Yale University Press, 1982), p. 248.

3 Maurice Valency, *The Flower and the Castle: An Introduction to Modern Drama* (New York: Grosset & Dunlap, 1963), p. 347.

4 Göran Stöckenstrom (ed.), *Strindberg's Dramaturgy* (Minneapolis: University of Minnesota Press, 1988).

5 For a fine account of Strehler's production, see Arthur Holmberg, *Theatre Journal*, 35 (October 1983), 406–7.

6 Robert Heilman, *Tragedy and Melodrama: Versions of Experience* (Seattle: University of Washington Press, 1968), p. 86.

7 August Strindberg, *Son of a Servant. The Story of the Evolution of a Human Being 1849–1867*, trans. Evert Sprinchorn (Garden City, NY: Doubleday, 1966), p. 243.

8 See August Strindberg, *Pre-Inferno Plays*, trans. Walter Johnson (Seattle: University of Washington Press, 1970), pp. 76–7; *Öppna bref till intima teatern* (Stockholm: Björck & Börjesson, 1909), pp. 14–15.

'Man against man, brain against brain': the transformation of melodrama in science fiction*

GARY WESTFAHL

Of all modern forms of fiction and film, none seems more closely linked to melodrama than science fiction: Garff Wilson observes that 'The western, cops-and-robbers, and science fiction serials are all as melodramatic as any play of the nineteenth century';[1] and in describing modern descendants of melodrama, Frank Rahill mentions that 'Science fiction, in its more lunatic manifestations, and the monster theme formed a fruitful alliance (*King Kong, The Thing from Outer Space*, etc.), the scientific binge of our generation contributing to the size of their public'.[2] However, these commentators have failed to note that in adopting this theatrical form, science fiction reconstructed melodrama in a manner which complicated and undermined its traditional clarity; and in examining this transformation, we see both the inherent limitations, and the continuing power, of this dramatic genre.

The descent of modern science fiction from nineteenth-century American melodrama is unusually well documented (as shown by the chart below). First, when melodrama became a major American form in the nineteenth century, there simultaneously arose the genre of dime novels, crude adventures which were, as Michael Denning notes, 'clearly connected to popular melodramas'.[3] One prominent author of dime novels, Luis Senarens, created the subgenre of the 'invention story', where the plucky hero is typically a young inventor who, as the story opens, has just built a wonderful new device which then figures in the otherwise routine melodramatic action. One representative invention story is Senarens's *Jack Wright and His Electric Air Rocket, or, The Boy Exile of Siberia*, where the eponymous hero jumps in his newly constructed airplane and goes to Russia to rescue a young lad who has been kidnapped by an evil uncle trying to steal his inheritance. This adventure is obviously related to melodrama, since it includes a scene where the friend is tied to the railroad tracks, and Jack must fly his airplane and untie him before the train comes!

* A draft of this paper was read at the *Themes in Drama* International Conference held at the University of California, Riverside, in February 1990.

The descent of science fiction from melodrama

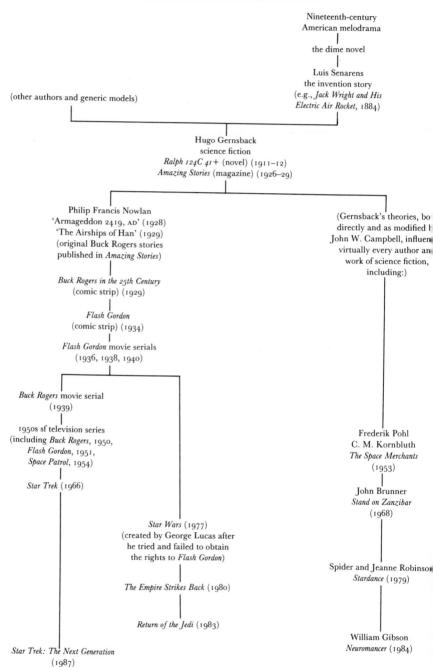

Nineteenth-century
American melodrama
|
the dime novel
|
Luis Senarens
the invention story
(e.g., *Jack Wright and His
Electric Air Rocket*, 1884)

(other authors and generic models)

Hugo Gernsback
science fiction
Ralph 124C 41+ (novel) (1911–12)
Amazing Stories (magazine) (1926–29)

Philip Francis Nowlan
'Armageddon 2419, AD' (1928)
'The Airships of Han' (1929)
(original Buck Rogers stories
published in *Amazing Stories*)

Buck Rogers in the 25th Century
(comic strip) (1929)

Flash Gordon
(comic strip) (1934)

Flash Gordon movie serials
(1936, 1938, 1940)

Buck Rogers movie serial
(1939)

1950s sf television series
(including *Buck Rogers*, 1950,
Flash Gordon, 1951,
Space Patrol, 1954)

Star Trek (1966)

(Gernsback's theories, bo
directly and as modified b
John W. Campbell, influen
virtually every author an
work of science fiction,
including:)

Frederik Pohl
C. M. Kornbluth
The Space Merchants
(1953)

John Brunner
Stand on Zanzibar
(1968)

Star Wars (1977)
(created by George Lucas after
he tried and failed to obtain
the rights to *Flash Gordon*)

The Empire Strikes Back (1980)

Return of the Jedi (1983)

Spider and Jeanne Robinso
Stardance (1979)

Star Trek: The Next Generation
(1987)

William Gibson
Neuromancer (1984)

The influence of Senarens can then be seen in the theories and writing of Hugo Gernsback, the man who created the term 'science fiction' and started the first American science fiction magazine: in the 1920s, he published two articles calling Senarens the 'American Jules Verne';[4] he defined science fiction as 'thrilling adventure';[5] and his novel *Ralph 124C 41+* is melodramatic both in its plot – a virtuous young scientist named Ralph must rescue his fiancée from a villain named Fernand who has kidnapped her – and in its dialogue:

> 'You coward,' [Alice] blazed, 'how dare you keep me here! Turn around and take me back at once – at once, do you hear?'
> Fernand, in the act of opening her door and going back to his laboratory, paused smilingly.
> 'My dear girl,' he said mockingly, 'ask of me anything and I will grant it – except that. You have a temper that delights me. Your smiles will be all the sweeter, later.' (p. 172)

Gernsback had a powerful impact both on written science fiction, as even his critics acknowledge,[6] and on filmed science fiction; for in 1928 and 1929, Gernsback published two stories by Philip Francis Nowlan, 'Armageddon 2419 AD' and 'The Airships of Han', which became the basis for the popular *Buck Rogers* comic strip. Its success led to the similar *Flash Gordon* comic strip and the *Flash Gordon* and *Buck Rogers* serials, which later served as the models for various television series of the 1950s – including *Buck Rogers*, *Flash Gordon*, and *Space Patrol*; and these in turn led to the superior, but equally melodramatic, *Star Trek* and *Star Trek: The Next Generation*. The *Flash Gordon* serials also helped to inspire George Lucas's 1977 *Star Wars* – a film which Lucas created only after he had first tried and failed to obtain the rights to *Flash Gordon*. We can thus attribute the continuing prominence of melodrama in written and filmed science fiction directly to Gernsback's influence.

However, while Gernsback took the form of melodrama from Senarens, he also embedded special purposes in his new genre which disturbed and distorted the melodramatic structure. First, Gernsback wanted science fiction to incorporate accurate scientific information, so that science fiction could be 'a means of educating the public to the meaning of science',[7] and second, he believed that stories should describe proposed new inventions in detail, in order to offer useful and stimulating ideas to scientists: 'The professional inventor or scientist ... gets the stimulus from the story and promptly responds with the material invention'.[8] In these ways, science fiction could inspire support for, and improve, science and scientific progress.[9] One problem is immediately clear: while melodrama, according to Peter Brooks, is dedicated to 'Emotions ... given a full acting-out ... a full emotional indulgence',[10] science fiction mandates unemotional accounts of scientific data and ideas far exceeding the traditional amount of exposition needed to explain the plot, thus compromising the characteristic tone of melodrama. But the structure is altered as well: for to make melodrama serve the ideology of science fiction, Gernsback had to make Ralph, the hero of his novel, resemble both a conventional hero and a conventional villain, thus threatening the integrity of the melodramatic form.

To explore Ralph's strange character, I propose a model of conflict in melodrama based on Robert Heilman's position that melodrama is 'a polemic form' in 'the realm of social action', that it works with 'whole rather than divided' characters,[11] and that particularly in its American form, characters are, in Garff Wilson's words, 'either completely good or completely bad'.[12] In this framework, I note three important and inter-related themes in the conflict between villain and hero.[13]

The first is *intellect versus emotion*: David Grimsted notes that August von Kotzebue, one influence on American melodrama, preached that 'impetuous feeling rather than reason or custom was the proper basis of conduct' and that melodramas usually had villains with 'intelligence' and heroes who 'seldom showed signs of great learning or rationality'.[14] The villain is usually older, more knowing, and better educated than the hero; he is described as cold and calculating; and he uses sophistry in making his case, perhaps with logic or the letter of the law on his side in foreclosing a mortgage.[15] In contrast, the hero is young, naive, and unschooled; he seems emotional, impulsive; and he opposes the villain based on simple morality, not complex reasoning – despite the law, people should not be thrown out of their homes.

A related theme is *indirect action versus direct action*. The villain, typically employing what Grimsted describes as 'diabolic subterfuge',[16] has henchmen do the dirty work so he is elsewhere, with a perfect alibi, when the crime is committed, or sets events in motion and leaves, tying the heroine to the railroad tracks or the hero to a log in a sawmill, so that machines, not the villain, will do the actual killing. However, the hero acts on his own without relying on other people or devices; the villain may be absent at the climax, but the hero is always there to save the day. And though the hero may occasionally indulge in his own scheming, this is justified as a needed response to the villain's machinations.

A third theme is *the elite versus the common man*; Michael Booth points out that 'Melodrama clearly reflects class hatreds. Villains tend to be noblemen, factory owners, squires; heroes peasants, able seamen, and workmen'.[17] Thus, the villain is typically a wealthy man, owning considerable property, and he may enjoy power over others, the open or covert support of law officers, or an official position; but the hero is poor, with no friends in high places, no official co-operation in opposing the villain, and no title or social status. Indeed, the hero may be seen as a rebel, an outcast, or even, as Booth says, a 'criminal-hero'.[18]

These villainous and heroic qualities illustrate Gernsback's dilemma in creating science fiction melodrama: for in celebrating the value of science, Gernsback was promoting intellect over emotion; in depicting new inventions to replace manual labor, he was advocating indirect action over direct action; and in supporting the scientific community, he was favoring the interests of an elite over those of the common man. Yet his chosen genre – melodrama – was a form that was *directly antithetical to all of these concerns*. His solution was to create a hero who alternately displayed all the attributes of both hero and villain, so that Ralph could be a traditional hero while also advancing Gernsback's untraditional agenda.

The contradictory qualities of Ralph's character emerge repeatedly. Ralph is 'one of the greatest living scientists' (p. 25) who once called love 'nothing but a perfumed animal instinct' (p. 140), but his love for Alice leads this intellect to scream at his servant, lose a tennis game because he cannot concentrate, and madly dash off to save Alice when she is in danger. He first rescues Alice with scientific indirect action: when Ralph learns an avalanche is about to destroy her faraway home, he tells her to set up an antenna, goes to his laboratory to create a storm of energy, and broadcasts heat to melt away the threatening snow. Yet when Fernand later kidnaps Alice and flies into space, Ralph eschews any complicated scientific scheme and simply gets in a spaceship to go after her. Finally, due to his vast intellect Ralph is 'one of the ten men on the whole planet earth' with 'the Plus sign after his name' (p. 25); because of that title, he enjoys generous financial support and personal access to the Planet Governor who controls the entire world. Yet to maintain Ralph's scientific productivity, the government forbids harmful activity and Ralph 'grew restive under the restraint' (p. 41), calling himself 'nothing but a prisoner' (p. 42). And when the Planet Governor expressly tells him not to pursue Fernand, Ralph defies the order and leaves anyway, effectively becoming an outcast and criminal.[19] In displaying conflicting impulses, Ralph might become a divided and, in Heilman's terms, tragic character, thus moving away from melodrama; this does not occur because Ralph, as Heilman says of Bosola in Webster's *The Duchess of Malfi*, 'is one thing at one moment and another thing at another moment; rarely . . . a human totality in which rival urgencies are operative at the same time'.[20] That is, in his alternating and contradictory modes, Ralph fails to become a character at all – a minor problem with a secondary figure like Bosola, but a crucial flaw in a melodramatic protagonist with whom audiences must identify.

Later creators of science fiction devised a solution to Gernsback's problem which I call the *counterhero*: the hero, stripped of scientific knowledge and abilities, reverts to his traditional character, while a new hero with villainous traits is created to be his companion. While this figure first begins to emerge in the scientific Dr Heur who becomes a key character in the *Buck Rogers* comic strip, the Flash Gordon serials set the pattern. Here, melodramatic conventions initially seem in place: Dale Arden is the lovely heroine, Ming the Merciless is the despicable villain, and Flash is the perfect hero – handsome, brave, and not too bright. But the troublesome figure of Dr Zharkov, his mentor and companion, does not fit in so well. Zharkov's Russian name, in the political climate of the times, suggests villainy, and the stories seem to cast doubt on his character, his loyalty, even his sanity. Yet Zharkov is indispensable: his spaceship takes Flash to the planet Mongo, and when a situation arises that cannot be handled by Flash's physical strength, Zharkov's scientific knowledge provides the answer. Thus, Zharkov and Flash embody the antithetical elements in Ralph's character: Zharkov cold and intellectual, willing to employ devious scientific methods, and, by virtue of his title, rather patrician; Flash passionate, inclined to direct action, and lacking in social position. Creating two separate heroes with opposed attributes removes an implausible single character like Ralph, apparently strengthening the melodrama; however, the counterhero, necessarily a divided character – essentially a villain supporting heroic causes – can, if examined, move the melodrama into tragedy. This does not happen in the Flash Gordon serials, as Zharkov is never the center of attention.

That problem does emerge, however, in the original *Star Trek* series, where we see another pairing of two heroes with different attributes: Spock cool and logical, skilled in indirect science, and from an aristocratic family on Vulcan; and Kirk emotional, direct in his actions, and of undistinguished parentage. Like Zharkov, Spock is a counterhero whose competence and character are questioned: 'The Galileo Seven' and 'The Tholian Web' suggest that due to his logical nature, Spock is not suited to command, and 'The Menagerie' and 'The *Enterprise* Incident' seem to catch him in the act of treason. Yet Spock's knowledge and abilities, also like Zharkov's, are essential in threatening situations. As a divided character, half human and half Vulcan, driven to both heroism and villainy, Spock can become, in Daniel Cohen's words, 'an almost tragic figure',[21] shifting the focus from external conflicts – melodrama – to internal conflicts – tragedy. Thus, for example, a sense of victory over the Romulans in 'The *Enterprise* Incident' is weakened and complicated by Spock's sympathy for the Romulans and regret over the tactics he used against them.[22]

At this point, one might argue that the device of the counterhero is really nothing new, since many nineteenth-century melodramas have second heroes – typically comical, energetic, and perhaps a bit brighter than the hero. However, there are significant differences between these figures and the counterheroes of science fiction. The second hero is, in keeping with the name, a secondary figure, presented as the hero's sidekick or assistant, and often absent from the stage. In contrast, the counterhero observes no hierarchy: Spock's position as second in command of the *Enterprise* gives him a large degree of authority and autonomy, and he is sometimes obliged to take actions which Kirk does not endorse; and since Zharkov built and commands the spaceship that takes Flash to Mongo, he can in some ways be considered Flash's commander. In addition, the counterhero is almost always at the center of activity, fighting alongside the hero, and in some cases the counterhero may even usurp the hero at the story's most crucial point – the climax – and perform the final rescue. In *Star Trek* episodes, for example, it is striking how often Kirk, the ostensible hero, is reduced to a helpless position in crisis situations, sitting in his captain's chair and barking out pointless orders while Spock, or the similar Mr Scott, is busy jury-rigging the device which will actually save the *Enterprise* from doom.

Space does not permit a full discussion of the many counterheroes found in science fiction. In film, the most familiar version is the older scientist who is also the heroine's father, and robots sometimes fill the role, like Robby the Robot in *Forbidden Planet*. More unusual variations are found in Hal Clement's *Needle*, where a friendly protoplasmic alien invades the young hero's body so that they can work together to track down an alien criminal; in the *Outer Limits* episode, 'Demon with a Glass Hand', where the hero has a mechanical hand which advises him as he battles mysterious foes; and in Gregory Benford's *Great Sky River* and *Tides of Light*, where the hero has several 'Aspects' – personalities of prominent dead people – implanted in his brain, with one of these, the Arthur Aspect, ready to regularly provide scientific information and explanations. One particularly interesting example is the computer HAL in the film and novel *2001: A Space Odyssey*, apparently a helpful companion to the astronauts but actually a tragically divided counterhero, driven insane by his conflicting instructions to cater to all the crew's needs – an heroic trait – and to withhold from them the true nature of their mission – a villainous trait. Despite his murderous acts in *2001*, he is explicitly rehabilitated, exonerated, and restored to heroic status in the book and film sequel, *2010: Odyssey Two*, and appears as a reborn companion to David Bowman and Heywood Floyd in the third *2001* book, *2061: Odyssey Three*.

The device of the counterhero need not damage the structure of melodrama because the undivided main hero may dominate the action, shifting attention away from the divided, potentially tragic double hero.

But the double hero can generate another complexity with more ruinous effects: as hero splits into heroic hero and villainous hero, the villain may split into villainous villain and heroic villain.

This pattern of a *countervillain* appears in Gernsback, where Ralph has two rivals for Alice's love: Fernand and a Martian, Llysanorh'.[23] Fernand is a conventional villain: aloof and uncaring, he wants Alice simply for the satisfaction of conquest; devious and indirect, he seizes Alice with an invisibility device and uses confederates to seize her again; wealthy and well connected, his schemes suggest high social status. Llysanorh' is completely different – 'a very decent chap', who is 'hopelessly infatuated' with her (p. 68). Alice 'could not deny the fact of his genuine ... fervent love' (p. 193), even after he kidnaps her; his abduction is an impulsive, individual action; and as a Martian, he is by definition a social outcast, legally forbidden to marry an Earth woman despite his deep love – thus, he is a victim of society and to Alice seems 'very pathetic' (p. 190). Though ultimately driven to kidnap and murder Alice, he resembles a melodramatic hero, and one wonders why Gernsback would complicate his narrative with this character; the novel's final chapters are particularly clumsy, as Ralph, having flown to Alice's rescue and confronted Fernand, finds that Llysanorh' has now kidnapped Alice from Fernand, which forces Ralph to effect a second rescue.

However, Llysanorh's presence is readily explained: since Ralph has the attributes of both hero and villain, a purely evil character like Fernand is not sufficient to serve as his foil; while Fernand can oppose Ralph when the scientist is emotional and daring, he cannot be his adversary when Ralph is intellectual and prudent. Thus, a second, more sympathetic villain is required as a counterpart to the sometimes unsympathetic hero.

We see the two villains functioning exactly this way in the novel. In response to Fernand's deviousness, Ralph acts directly and personally: after Fernand invisibly abducts Alice, Ralph rushes after her, finds where she is hidden, and frees her. When Fernand kidnaps Alice in his spaceship, Ralph flies into space, locates and overtakes Fernand, and confronts him with startling passion and violence, exclaiming 'If you and I ever meet again I will pound your miserable cowardly body into jelly!' (p. 169)

Ralph acts differently in response to Llysanorh's direct actions: learning that Llysanorh' has taken Alice from Fernand and is heading to Mars, Ralph calculates he will not have enough time to overtake Llysanorh's ship before he reaches Mars and arranges to forcibly marry Alice. He then resorts to a trick: in his spaceship laboratory he creates an artificial comet and sends it towards Mars. He reasons that Llysanorh', for the sake of his fellow Martians, will change his course to intercept and destroy the comet, thus giving Ralph time to catch his ship. Though the stratagem works, it seems unheroic to play upon an opponent's altruism; the scheme resembles the moment in a melodrama when the trapped villain grabs an innocent bystander and puts a gun to his head: surrender, or I will kill him. The difference is that Ralph is pointing a gun at the entire planet of Mars. And there is something cold about his reaction when Ralph finds Llysanorh' has killed both himself and Alice: while returning to Earth, he methodically drains Alice's blood and tries to invent a way to bring her back to life. While understandable, these actions are an oddly unemotional way to respond to the death of a loved one.

The pattern thus emerges: cold and devious Fernand opposes Ralph's passions, while emotional and direct Llysanorh' opposes Ralph's intelligence; hero and counterhero have spawned villain and countervillain. Therefore, when Ralph proclaims his 'fight is to be man against man, brain against brain' (p. 153), Gernsback, perhaps inadvertently, suggests the complexity of his narrative, with one difference: the fight is Ralph the man against Fernand the brain, and Ralph the brain against Llysanorh' the man.

The countervillain also appears in the alien races of *Star Trek*: Romulans and Klingons. Romulans are classic villains; like the Vulcans they resemble, Romulans are cold and unemotional; their characteristic weapon is a 'cloaking device' making their ships invisible, thus perfect for sneak attacks; and their manner is haughty and aristocratic.[24] In contrast, Klingons are emotional and violent; they prefer direct attack and personal combat; and their unkempt appearance, crude language, and bad table manners mark them as proletarians. Therefore, the Romulans fit the model of villainy, while the Klingons, though repulsive and violent, fit the model of heroism.

These countervillains serve to further blur the division between good and evil, compromise the clarity of the melodramatic conflict, and create the possibility of inappropriate alliances – that is, the villainous counterhero may be drawn to the villainous villain while the heroic hero may be drawn to the heroic countervillain. Several *Star Trek* episodes suggest such linkages. In 'Balance of Terror', Spock is suspected of secretly sympathizing with the Romulans; and in 'The Enterprise Incident', he apparently betrays his human friends and joins forces with the Romulans. Similarly, there are episodes which explicitly link Kirk and the Klingons: in 'The Trouble with Tribbles', Kirk enjoys a kind of camaraderie with a Klingon captain; in 'Errand of Mercy', Kirk and a Klingon become bizarre allies in arguing with aliens for their right to continue a war; and in 'Day of the Dove', Kirk and a Klingon commander unite against an alien invader and defeat the being by joining in derisive laughter.

The original series never carried these tendencies to their logical conclusions, and Spock has never joined the Romulans in villainy – some lines, it seems, cannot be crossed. Still, it should be noted that the traditionally evil Romulans continue to serve as villains in episodes like 'The Enemy' and 'The Defector' of the new series *Star Trek: The Next Generation*; and the Romulan character in *Star Trek V: The Final Frontier* remains unsympathetic. However, the Klingons have in fact become heroic: in the new series, the Klingons belong to the Federation, a Klingon serves on board the *Enterprise*, and Klingons are depicted as hot-headed but basically good characters. And in *Star Trek V*, a Klingon general becomes Kirk's ally, and even a violent Klingon captain trying to destroy the *Enterprise* is finally recast as an impetuous youth.

This virtual transformation of countervillain into hero can create awkwardness and further distort the conventions of melodrama, as clearly shown by the episode of *Star Trek: The Next Generation*, entitled 'A Matter of Honor'. Here, the Klingons again function as enemies, as their warship approaches the *Enterprise* and threatens its destruction; but to maintain their new image, the conflict is laboriously framed as a misunderstanding – the Klingons believe the *Enterprise* is responsible for an infestation attacking their vessel – and when matters are explained, they become friendly again. In addition, the Klingons are defeated not by space combat, but by an elaborate ruse, as Captain Picard's First Officer Ryker contrives to assume command of the Klingon vessel. Thus, just as the device of the counterhero can lead melodrama into tragedy, the device of the countervillain can lead melodrama into comedy: that is, we move from a pattern of fundamental conflict leading to victory in violent battle – the structure of melodrama – and reach a pattern of confusion leading to clarification and reconciliation by means of gentle trickery – the structure of comedy.

This tendency toward comedy also emerged earlier in episodes of the original *Star Trek* series involving Klingons. 'The Trouble with Tribbles' is frankly comic, and Kirk's only 'victory' over the Klingons is that he infests their ship with the alien pests called tribbles; Klingons and Kirk's crew interact peaceably under truce conditions in both 'The Trouble with Tribbles' and 'Day of the Dove', suggesting the compromising spirit of comedy; and 'Errand of Mercy' makes both Kirk and the Klingons seem ridiculous in their desire to carry on with a pointless war. Thus, even before the Klingons' official conversion to heroic status, we detect an urge to reconcile Klingons and Earthmen, a resolution typical of comedy, but antithetical to melodrama.

Again, one might observe that there are many second villains in earlier melodramas, usually serving as comic, sympathetic, and stupid assistants to the main villain; and again, the science fiction countervillains do not fit this pattern. To be specific, the countervillain is not a subordinate of the other villain, but an independent agent, and he is often as menacing, or more menacing, than the traditional villain. For example, Ralph can brush away the machinations of the villain Fernand, but his climactic struggle and triumph involve the countervillain Llysanorh'.

While not as common as the counterhero, countervillains can be found in other science fiction works. In the film *Forbidden Planet*, Dr Morbius has unconsciously spawned the completely malevolent Monster of the Id, which emerges as the ultimate threat; and although he often functions as an opponent to the film's heroes, Morbius himself is finally cast as a sympathetic, though tragically divided, character. In Spider and Jeanne Robinson's *Stardance*, the first villain in the final scenes is thoroughly callous, driven by his own desire for wealth and power, while the second, more sensitive villain is driven to act by a misguided concern for the future of the human race. And in the film *Superman II*, the major menaces are the implacably diabolic super-villains from Krypton, while Superman's traditional foe, Lex Luthor, emerges as an oddly likable and not particularly evil character.

Science fiction melodrama does not always grow complex and generically mixed, since writers can always ignore the potential problems and proceed in a conventional way, as in most comic books and cartoons. However, when a work of science fiction is created with care and intelligence, complications of this kind frequently emerge, as seen, for example, in George Lucas's three *Star Wars* films.

The opening of *Star Wars* presents a classic melodramatic trio: virtuous young hero Luke Skywalker, captured heroine Princess Leia, and heartless villain Darth Vader. Yet there must be another character, Ben Kenobi, to contribute the experience and knowledge Luke needs to fight the evil Empire. As a counterhero, Kenobi is prominent in the action: he obtains the needed spaceship, begins training Luke, and battles Darth Vader when he knows that Luke is not ready. Even after he dies, the story cannot do without him, for he returns as a ghost, helping Luke attack the Death Star. In the second film, *The Empire Strikes Back*, the dead Kenobi visits again, while a new character, Yoda, appears to replace him as the counterhero; but the sedentary Yoda is fundamentally unsuited to the role and is also killed.

In *Return of the Jedi*, the story line suddenly lurches in another effort to replace Kenobi. When Leia is revealed to be his sister, Luke can no longer romance her and so cannot serve as the main hero; Han Solo, previously serving as the secondary comic hero,[25] is structurally promoted to the protagonist's role, since he will now rescue and marry the Princess. Luke, assuming Kenobi's role of counterhero, dresses in black and becomes cold and withdrawn. As Luke takes on these unemotional, unsympathetic attributes, emerging as a divided and potentially tragic counterhero, the villain correspondingly becomes emotional and sympathetic; so the despicable Darth Vader, already revealed as Luke's father, emerges as a divided countervillain, a good man corrupted by the Dark Side and thus another tragic figure. And because an heroic countervillain cannot stand alone, a new main villain must be created – the Emperor, as evil and heartless as Darth Vader once seemed to be.

These transformations are artful, but the contrast between the glorious conclusion of *Star Wars* and the end of *Return of the Jedi* shows how much melodramatic clarity has been muddled to produce a hopelessly compromised happy ending. The final celebration in the third film is not a grand ceremony but a small gathering around a campfire, symbolizing a shift from attention to the public issue – defeating the Empire – to the private matter of Luke's personal tragedy. The audience's presumed joy over the coming marriage of Han and the Princess is alloyed by their disappointment that Luke has been denied that satisfaction, and he stands aloof from the merriment; the ghostly visits of Kenobi, Yoda and Darth Vader – a sort of tragic hero who found peace – do not mitigate the isolation of the tragic hero who has found no peace. Having reached this problematic conclusion, Lucas dropped plans for more *Star Wars* films and has recently worked in less troublesome genres like pure melodrama (the Indiana Jones films) and fantasy (*Howard the Duck* and *Willow*).

In written science fiction, we find many authors apparently determined to ignore melodrama and write in a different style; but melodrama still rises to the surface, as in the aforementioned *Stardance*. The Robinsons' novel begins as a sensitive, lyrical depiction of six dancers' efforts to create and perfect the art of zero-gravity dance; and the descriptions of their practice and performance seem far away from a sense of melodrama. But later, when the dancers become 'interpreters' on a diplomatic mission to aliens who communicate by movement, the climax is incongruous – and melodramatic – as not one but two of the diplomats pull out a gun, threaten to kill the dancers, and reveal a scheme to seize control of the ship. Now the dancers must use their skills to overpower the villains and thwart their schemes. Melodrama in science fiction, then, is like the beast-flesh in the creatures of Dr Moreau: invisible at first, it inexorably and inevitably emerges.

Three other examples of this phenomenon come to mind. First, Frederik Pohl and C. M. Kornbluth's *The Space Merchants* begins as a satirical depiction of a world driven mad by advertising, with the ultimate joke being that the hero's unprincipled advertising agency is persuading people to migrate to Venus, a planet that is a living hell; yet it ends with the hero rescuing his girlfriend from an evil rival and desperately attempting to escape to Venus – now recast as a desirable haven from a corrupt Earth. Second, John Brunner's *Stand on Zanzibar* is first structured like a futuristic version of John Dos Passos's *USA*, with a kaleidoscope of different scenes and characters, but ultimately comes to focus on the efforts of one reluctant hero to carry out a daring rescue of a defector from a totalitarian enemy nation. Finally, William Gibson's *Neuromancer* opens as a tribute to the hard-boiled detective story and the *film noir*, with a thoroughly amoral hero, but concludes with the protagonist's struggle to rescue his girlfriend from the clutches of evil villains – a classic melodramatic structure, though well concealed under Gibson's irony. In all three cases, a science fiction novel which initially seems based on a radically different generic model concludes with a situation right out of melodrama.

The importance of melodrama in science fiction is also shown – paradoxically – by the notably anemic genre of science fiction theatre: although science fiction derive from stage melodrama, Maxim Jakubowski and Peter Nicholls note that 'specifically stage-bound science fiction is rare ... a small number of unrelated plays'.[26] The reason is that unlike written and filmed science fiction, shaped by Gernsback's insistence on melodrama, science fiction theatre, unaffected by Gernsback and lacking a strong contemporary tradition of melodrama, attempts unsuccessfully to build on other genres: the symposium play – Richard Ganthony's *Message from Mars* (1912); satire – Karel Capek's *R.U.R.* (1921); comedy – Ray Bradbury's *The Day It Rained Forever* (1966); and farce – Spike Milligan and John Antrobus's *The Bed-Sitting Room* (1969). In the weakness of such plays, we observe the weakness of the genre of science fiction when it is separated from melodrama.[27]

In all these works the basic problem of melodrama in science fiction emerges: if science fiction writers begin with melodrama, their genre's concerns create complications and generic confusion; but if they try to escape from melodrama, they risk either being driven back to its structures or losing needed vitality. Simply put, science fiction cannot cope with melodrama – and it cannot avoid melodrama.

The relationship between melodrama and science fiction leads to two conclusions about melodrama in other genres. First, there are limits in the form's adaptability. Heilman argues that melodrama can be employed both by 'dissenters' and 'the order that is attacked'[28] – that is, by either side in a given dispute – suggesting the genre lacks ideology; similarly, Brooks calls melodrama 'a remarkably adaptable form'.[29] However, the example of science fiction suggests that through the very act of simplifying reality, melodrama in fact generates a populist ideology of simplicity – favoring simple emotions, simple actions, and simple people – which ill accords, for example, with the ideology of science fiction.[30] Thus, certain cases and causes cannot be effectively advanced by means of melodrama.

Second, there is true power in melodrama. Even though I have shown that melodrama is an inappropriate vehicle for the argument of science fiction, its creators have not abandoned, and cannot abandon, the form. As one of its contradictions, the elitist genre of science fiction has always sought, as Gernsback said, to 'influence the masses';[31] and the best way to do so is apparently melodrama. If science fiction is truly a predictive literature, then, one of its implicit predictions is that melodrama will continue to be a major literary force.

NOTES

1 Garff B. Wilson, *Three Hundred Years of American Drama and Theatre: From Ye Bare and Ye Cubb to Hair* (Englewood Cliffs, NJ: Prentice-Hall, Inc., 1973), p. 107.

2 Frank Rahill, *The World of Melodrama* (University Park: Pennsylvania State University Press, 1967), p. 301. Rahill is no doubt inadvertently combining the names of two films, *The Thing (from Another World)* and *It Came from Outer Space.*

3 Michael Denning, *Mechanic Accents: Dime Novels and Working-Class Culture in America* (New York: Verso, 1987), p. 24. Denning cites an 1879 reviewer describing some dime novels simply as melodramas 'narrativized for the story paper' (p. 24) and discusses authors like Albert Aiken and Bartley Campbell who wrote both melodramas and dime novels (p. 215). In addition, Daniel C. Gerould mentions that 'stories [for melodramas] could be appropriated from dime novels' ('The Americanization of Melodrama', in *American Melodrama*, ed. Gerould (New York: Performing Arts Publications, 1983), p. 9); and Rahill calls Wild West melodrama 'Plays of the Beadle dime novel school' (*World of Melodrama*, p. 237) and notes that 'The dime novel discovered [the cowpuncher] (circa 1885), and his numerous stage representations in the proletarian theatre stemmed from this source' (p. 238). In addition to these documented links, we repeatedly find in dime novels the sorts of virtuous heroes, imperiled heroines and dastardly villains featured in stage melodrama.

4 This was high praise indeed, by the way, since Gernsback had elsewhere called Verne his 'favorite author' (Introduction to 'Dr Ox's Experiment', *Amazing Stories*, 1 (August 1926), 421). The articles, 'The American Jules Verne', *Science and Invention* (1920) and 'An American Jules Verne', *Amazing Stories*, 3 (1928), were both unsigned but possibly written by Gernsback himself.

5 'Science Wonder Stories', *Science Wonder Stories*, 1 (June 1929), 5.

6 For example, Harlan Ellison declared that 'No one can sanely deny that Gernsback's *Amazing Stories* in 1926 was the most obvious ancestor of what today ... we call "speculative fiction"' ('Introduction: Thirty-Two Soothsayers', in *Dangerous Visions no. 1*, ed. Ellison (New York: Berkley Books, 1967, rpt 1969), p. 21). The ways in which Gernsback and his successors created and influenced the modern genre of science fiction are discussed in Gary Westfahl, 'On *The True History of Science Fiction*', *Foundation*, 47 (Winter 1990) and '"An Idea of Significant Import": Hugo Gernsback's Theory of Science Fiction', *Foundation*, 48 (Spring 1990).

7 'Science Fiction Week', *Science Wonder Stories*, 1 (May 1930), 1061.

8 '$300.00 Prize Contest – Wanted: A Symbol for Scientifiction', *Amazing Stories*, 3 (April 1928), 5.

9 Gernsback's theories are actually a bit more complex, since he saw science fiction as a way to reform and improve, and not simply support, the scientific community, as discussed in Gary Westfahl, '"A Tremendous New Force": How Science Fiction Proposes to Change the World', Paper presented at the Interdisciplinary Literature Conference on the Fantastic Imagination in New Critical Theories, College Station, Texas, 1990.

10 Peter Brooks, *The Melodramatic Imagination: Balzac, Henry James, Melodrama, and the Mode of Excess* (New Haven: Yale University Press, 1976), p. 41.

11 *Tragedy and Melodrama: Versions of Experience* (Seattle: University of Washington Press, 1968), pp. 97, 81.

12 *Three Hundred Years*, p. 101.

13 I will use the terms 'villain' and 'hero' throughout this discussion strictly for convenience, for properly speaking, the structure of melodrama requires three characters – an heroic figure, a villainous figure, and a figure whom the heroic figure must rescue from the villainous figure – and only tradition dictates that the heroic and villainous figures be male and the rescued figure be female. To note two variants, the invention stories of Senarens and other dime novels for young male readers often substitute a male friend for the heroine, and the 1989 film *Supergirl* involves a heroine's effort to rescue a handsome but helpless male from a villainess. If I pay little attention to the rescued figure – usually, the heroine – in this discussion, it is because she seems unaffected by the transformations of melodrama in science fiction; thus, throughout the complications involving the heroes and villains of the *Star Wars* films (discussed below), Princess Leia remains the same type of spunky heroine found in numerous nineteenth-century melodramas.

14 David Grimsted, *Melodrama Unveiled: American Theater and Culture 1800–1850* (University of Chicago Press, 1968), pp. 13, 177, 210. In addition, Rahill describes the archetypal melodramatic hero in Pixérécourt's *Cœlina* in this way: 'Somewhat stupid, he will often be outwitted by the clever villain in his long stage career, but not in a hundred years will he be worsted in a fair fight' (*World of Melodrama*, p. 31); and Michael Booth claims 'The basic hero is really rather stupid' (*English Melodrama*, London: Herbert Jenkins, p. 15) and quotes one stage villain who proclaims, 'Men of brains and cunning must rule the world' (ibid., 152). Of course, Grimsted also cites a play which describes a villain's 'dauntless passion' (*Melodrama Unveiled*, p. 215) and I do not wish to imply in this model that villains are completely without emotions while heroes are completely without reasoning ability. The distinction is more in the realm of *how one publicly justifies one's actions*: for example, the villain may provide logical reasons why an evil act should be done, but the hero will offer a visceral and emotional rejection of evil.

15 This exact attitude appears in an exchange from T. P. Taylor's *The Village Outcast* (1846), cited by Booth:

> *Muzzle.* What's the law to do with age? That's Nature's business. What's the law to do with infirmities? ... the law says this here wery [sic] building is to come down for improvements, consequently removal's the word.
>
> *Alice.* And tomorrow I'm to be driven from the roof which has so long

sheltered me – helpless and almost sinking into the grave – to die, perhaps in the fields.

Muzzle. That is the law, of which I am the executive.   (p. 63)

16 *Melodrama Unveiled*, p. 178.

17 *English Melodrama*, p. 62. Also, Heilman points out that 'royalty and nobility were the first villains' in American melodrama (*Tragedy and Melodrama*, p. 104), while, as Grimsted observes, melodrama 'took the lives of common people seriously and paid much respect to their superior purity and wisdom' (*Melodrama Unveiled*, p. 248); William Paul Steele observes that the villain 'is often of high rank' (*The Character of Melodrama: An Examination through Dion Boucicault's The Poor of New York*, with a foreword by James B. Bost, Orono, Maine: Maine University Press, 1968, p. 4); and Brooks says that in melodrama, 'Villains are remarkably often tyrants and oppressors, those that have power and use it to hurt. Whereas the victims, the innocent and virtuous, most often belong to a democratic universe' (*English Melodrama*, p. 44).

18 *English Melodrama*, p. 64.

19 One might protest that Ralph simply undergoes a character transformation and is related to other melodramatic characters who initially seem cold and uncaring but are converted to heroism by the love of a beautiful woman; but no such coherent pattern of change can be imposed on Gernsback's narrative. After every passionate outburst Ralph reverts to his cold, impersonal self; after taking direct action to rescue Alice from Fernand, he returns, as described below, to indirect action in rescuing her a second time; and after he returns from his forbidden mission to space, all is forgiven and he is restored to his elite position.

20 *Tragedy and Melodrama*, p. 293.

21 Daniel Cohen, *Strange and Amazing Facts about Star Trek* (New York: Pocket Books, 1986), p. 26.

22 Since Heilman discusses numerous instances of melodrama moving into the realm of tragedy, one might ask why this tendency is so noteworthy in science fiction. The answer is that in other genres, writers *have the option* of complicating and deepening the melodrama by introducing an element of tragedy, sometimes as a way to appeal to a more sophisticated audience; however, due to the unique critical tradition of science fiction, writers *are driven* into such complications, even while continuing to appeal to an unsophisticated audience.

23 Reflecting no doubt some novelty in Martian pronunciation, Gernsback spells the name with a final apostrophe; lacking a model in English for making such a name possessive, I have simply added an s: hence, Llysanorh', Llysanorh's.

24 Interestingly enough, Mark Lenard, the dignified actor who portrayed the first Romulan commander, was later called back to play Spock's father, a high-ranking Vulcan offical, further suggesting the relatedness of the Vulcans and Romulans.

25 As described by Booth, 'the comic man ... is a friend or manservant of the hero, and sometimes carries on the battle against villainy (though by comic means) in the absence or incapacity of his superior' (*English Melodrama*, p. 33). In the first two *Star Wars* films, Solo's constant wisecracks and blunders mark him as a comic hero, despite occasional earnestness; but when transformed into the

main hero in *Return of the Jedi*, he significantly begins to act in a more serious manner.

26 'Theatre', in *The Science Fiction Encyclopedia*, ed. Peter Nicholls (Garden City, NJ: Doubleday & Co., 1979), p. 600.

27 In his introduction to *Six Science Fiction Plays*, Roger Elwood maintains that the sheer scope of science fiction makes it incompatible with the stage: 'The two forms do not meld easily. It is difficult to translate the imaginative leaps characteristic of science fiction writing into the hard reality of dialogue between articulate characters. Writing a science fiction play is a bit like trying to picture infinity in a cigar box' (*Six Science Fiction Plays*, New York: Pocket Books, 1976, p. vii). But it is difficult to argue that science fiction is so uniquely and incredibly 'imaginative' that dramatization becomes impossible; certainly, any critic can cite scores of examples of plays that effectively present bold and vast ideas. I suggest instead that the problem is poor choice of genre: without the energizing framework of melodrama, science fiction tends either to become a stagnant airing of an author's ideas about man and society – as in Ganthony's, Capek's, and Milligan and Antrobus's plays – or to dissolve into inconsequential pleasantries, as in Ray Bradbury's plays. And if further proof is requested for the notion that the genre of science fiction theatre is indeed 'anemic', I note that in assembling his anthology, Elwood found only three actual *plays* and had to complete his collection with three television and film scripts.

28 *Tragedy and Melodrama*, pp. 96–7.

29 *Melodramatic Imagination*, p. 89.

30 Since Heilman sees melodrama and tragedy as complementary, all-encompassing dramatic forms, an interesting question emerges about science fiction: if the genre is not melodramatic, is it then tragic? A possible answer would go as follows: science fiction begins by accepting the melodramatic convention of simplified characters but rejects the convention of simplified events; reality is too complex, particularly in the light of scientific knowledge and progress. Since simple characters cannot be expected to cope with complex events, it becomes necessary for writers to create complex, divided characters – counter-heroes and countervillains – although they tend to avoid focusing on them. Thus, for all his potential fascination, Zharkov is largely ignored in the *Flash Gordon* serials; and as Daniel Cohen notes, Spock is most tragic in 'the early Star Trek episodes ... Later he is able to relax and become more comfortable with his dual nature' (*Strange and Amazing Facts*, p. 24) – which is another way of saying that later episodes move away from confronting his dilemma. The cycle is repeated in the *Star Trek* films, where the first two re-examine Spock's tragic plight while the last three forget about it. While shying away from tragic characters, science fiction does achieve a tragic sense in contemplating the situation of the entire human race: typically, writers conclude that the problems of humanity are fundamentally unsolvable but accept the possibility that a scientifically transformed human race, or some successor to humanity, might achieve satisfying solutions to human problems and a utopian existence. While this position might be seen as an evasion of tragedy – in asserting that only more advanced beings, not people themselves, might reach this heightened state – it can also be seen as a true expression of the ultimate meaning of

tragedy, that humanity might gain from its experience insights to be fruitfully passed on to its successors. Shorn of dramatic terminology, this argument is developed in "'The Gernsback Continuum'": William Gibson in the Context of Science Fiction', in *Fiction 2000: Cyberpunk and After*, ed. Tom Shippey and George Slusser (Athens, GA: University of Georgia Press, 1991).

31 'Editorially Speaking', *Amazing Stories*, 1 (September 1926), 483.

STORIES, PLAYS AND FILMS CITED

'Balance of Terror', *Star Trek*. New York: NBC, 15 December 1966

The Bed-Sitting Room. United Artists, 1969. Based on the play by Spike Milligan and John Antrobus

Benford, Gregory. *Great Sky River*. New York: Bantam Books, 1987
  Tides of Light. New York: Bantam Books, 1989

Bradbury, Ray. *The Day It Rained Forever: A Comedy in One Act*. New York: Samuel French, Inc., 1966

Brunner, John. *Stand on Zanzibar*. New York: Ballantine Books, 1969, 1968

Buck Rogers. [serial] Universal, 1939

Capek, Karel. *R.U.R.* Translated from the Czech by P. Selve and adapted for the English stage by Nigel Playfair. London: Oxford University Press, 1923. Originally published in 1921

Clarke, Arthur C. *2001: A Space Odyssey*. New York: Signet Books, 1968
  2061: Odyssey Three. New York: Ballantine Books, 1987
  2010: Odyssey Two. New York: Ballantine Books, 1982

Clement, Hal. *Needle*. New York: Avon Books, 1968, 1950

'Day of the Dove', *Star Trek*. New York: NBC, 1 November 1968

'The Defector', *Star Trek: The Next Generation*. Los Angeles: KCOP, 15 April 1990

'Demon with a Glass Hand', *The Outer Limits*. New York: ABC, 1 December 1964

Elwood, Roger, ed. *Six Science Fiction Plays*. New York: Pocket Books, 1976

The Empire Strikes Back. Lucasfilm/Fox, 1980

'The Enemy', *Star Trek: The Next Generation*. Los Angeles: KCOP, 18 November 1989

'The *Enterprise* Incident', *Star Trek*. New York: NBC, 27 September 1968

'Errand of Mercy', *Star Trek*. New York: NBC, 23 March 1967

Flash Gordon. [serial] Universal, 1936

Flash Gordon Conquers the Universe. [serial] Universal, 1940

Flash Gordon's Trip to Mars. [serial] Universal, 1938

Forbidden Planet. Metro–Goldwyn–Mayer, 1956

'The Galileo Seven', *Star Trek*. New York: NBC, 5 January 1967

Gernsback, Hugo. 'Editorially Speaking', *Amazing Stories*, 1 (September 1926), 483
  Introduction to 'Dr Ox's Experiment', *Amazing Stories*, 1 (August 1926), 421
  Ralph 14C 41+: A Romance of the Twenty-Sixth Century. New York: Frederick Fell, Inc., 1925, rpt 1950. Originally published in twelve installments in *Modern Electrics* in 1911 and 1912

'Science Fiction Week', *Science Wonder Stories*, 1 (May 1930), 1061

'Science Wonder Stories', *Science Wonder Stories*, 1 (June 1929), 5

'$300.00 Prize Contest – Wanted: A Symbol for Scientifiction', *Amazing Stories*, 3 (April 1928), 5

Gibson, William. *Neuromancer*. New York: Ace Books, 1986, 1984

Howard the Duck. Lucasfilm, 1986

It Came from Outer Space. Universal, 1953

King Kong. RKO, 1933

'A Matter of Honor', *Star Trek: The Next Generation*. Los Angeles: KCOP, 12 February 1989

'The Menagerie', *Star Trek*. New York: NBC, 17 January and 24 January 1966 [two episodes]

Message from Mars. UK Films, 1913. Based on the play by Richard Ganthony

Nowlan, Philip Francis. *Armageddon 2419 AD*. New York: Ace Books, 1962. Originally published in two parts in *Amazing Stories* in 1928 and 1929

Pohl, Frederik, and C. M. Kornbluth. *The Space Merchants*. [original title *Gravy Planet*] New York: Ballantine Books, 1953

Return of the Jedi. Lucasfilm/Fox, 1983

Robinson, Spider, and Jeanne Robinson. *Stardance*. New York: Dell Books, 1980, 1979. Based on the novella of the same name originally published in *Analog Science Fact/Science Fiction* in 1977

Senarens, Luis. [as by 'Noname'] *Jack Wright and His Electric Air Rocket, or, The Boy Exile of Siberia*. *The Boys' Star Library*, no. 341 (3 August 1884)

Star Trek V: The Final Frontier. Paramount, 1989

Star Wars. Lucasfilm/Fox, 1977

Supergirl, Warner Brothers, 1989

Superman II. Warner Brothers, 1980

The Thing (from Another World). Winchester Pictures/RKO, 1951

'The Tholian Web', *Star Trek*. New York: NBC, 15 November 1968

'The Trouble with Tribbles', *Star Trek*. New York: NBC, 29 December 1967

2001: A Space Odyssey. Metro–Goldwyn–Mayer, 1968

2010: Odyssey Two. Metro–Goldwyn–Mayer/United Artists, 1984

Willow. Lucasfilm, 1988

The face of fear*

JEFFREY D. MASON

From the moment that Tom saw him approaching, he felt an immediate and revolting horror at him, that increased as he came near. He was evidently, though short, of gigantic strength ... his large, coarse mouth was distended with tobacco, the juice of which, from time to time, he ejected from him with great decision and explosive force; his hands were immensely large, hairy, sunburned, freckled, and very dirty, and garnished with long nails, in a very foul condition.[1]

Thus Harriet Beecher Stowe relates Uncle Tom's first impressions of Simon Legree. He is more than an exemplary or even archetypal villain; his evil is so comprehensive, from his shocking malefactions to his revolting physical presence, that we may regard him as Stowe's worst nightmare come to life on the page, the fantastic incarnation of her terror and loathing, the result of her effort to forge a creature that would give a name and a presence to her apprehension, anxiety and anger. In Simon Legree, Stowe sees the face of fear, and it is such fear that forms the seed – the creative irritant – of all melodrama.

There are significant distinctions between the villain as a character type, evil as a perceived force, and fear as a generative impulse. The villain customarily serves as the agent or manifestation of evil, but some works we call melodramas employ villains who operate simply as antagonists, without an integral context of evil, while others include that evil without a clearly defined villain standing forth as its avatar. Fear is the only essential component of the three, for it is the emotion from which melodrama springs, inspiring first a conception of evil to rationalize the fear, and then a villain to mythologize that evil, giving it a form and a voice.[2]

Melodrama works on us in layers, each a bit more removed from our immediate experience but supporting the one before it. The most proximate includes those characteristics that form the familiar descriptive list that sometimes, fallaciously, serves as a definition of the genre: thrilling

* A draft of this paper was read at the *Themes in Drama* International Conference held at the University of California, Riverside, in February 1990.

incident and exciting alternation between disaster and recovery, uninhibited show of spectacle according to the potential of the medium, open
display of violence and catastrophe, exaggerated expression of emotion,
and the foregrounding of entertainment value at the expense of any subtle
meaning or complexity of narrative, all of which carry us away, willy-
nilly, with the piece. The next layer involves the leading characters, the
hero and heroine earning sympathy and identification, and the villain
provoking revulsion and hisses from what is usually assumed to be a mass
audience. The third layer is the struggle between virtue and evil as
irreconcilable, absolute opposites, and it is this layer that seems to function as the basis for the rest of the structure. Without this starkly polarized
and simplistic conflict, there is only feeble justification for the incident,
spectacle, violence, and wild emotionalism that constitute the matter and
the fascination of melodrama; that is, the nature of melodrama is a product and an expression of that essential conflict.

    In theorizing and understanding the workings of melodrama, we must
search for the fundamental layer, that which supports and produces the
others. Peter Brooks has said that

> melodrama typically not only employs virtue persecuted as a source of its
> dramaturgy, but also tends to become the dramaturgy of virtue misprized and
> eventually recognized. It is about virtue made visible and acknowledged, the
> drama of a recognition.[3]

In other words, melodrama is a means of revealing the nature of virtue.
Yet I contend that because melodrama is, ostensibly, the voice of the
virtuous world, then virtue itself is a putative transcendental signified, a
given. Each melodrama must satisfy its audience concerning the nature
not of virtue, but of evil, of that which places virtue in jeopardy, of that
which virtue fears. 'Good' is the world as it should be, stable, safe, and at
rest, while 'evil' sends the planet hurtling uncontrollably towards some
ineffable future. 'Good' is the state to which melodrama must inevitably
return, while 'evil' is the canker to cosmic action, the force that shatters
complacency and calls any order into question. 'Good' is the self, and
'evil' is the other – the stranger. I therefore gaze in a different direction
than Brooks, away from the contemplation of virtue and toward the
regard of evil, but always evil as virtue sees it and fears it. From virtue's
point of view, evil is the unsettler, the destroyer, the vandal, the
iconoclast, the unpredictable spirit of negation. Virtue knows that evil will
attack, but it never knows how, so it spins apprehensive fantasies. The
point of melodrama is to enact those fantasies for its sentimental audience,
to give evil a mask in order to replay its inevitable defeat and reassure the
virtuous that though their fears be valid, their optimism is justified.

    Melodrama assumes a set of values shared among the participants –

playwright, actors, spectators – who represent their culture, speak for it, and respond for it; I shall refer to them as the collective author of melodrama in general. The classic pattern begins with the definition of a condition that is presented as both ideal and normal. The action accelerates as some outside influence threatens that condition, and ends when evil is vanquished and the virtuous characters return to the condition they cherish and deserve. Insofar as melodrama articulates the shared values of the collective author, it becomes part of the myth-making apparatus of its culture, offering metaphorical and even allegorical action that conveys a world view.

Yet American melodrama, strangely, makes a myth that has little to do with our alleged preoccupation with individualism, freedom, and our sense of romantic mission. Instead, it projects what Richard Slotkin calls 'the trinity of values on which Anglo-American society is based – social progress, piety, and the family'.[4] It is largely domestic, by which I mean that no matter what the setting or the nature of the action, it is ultimately concerned with the family. For example, the antebellum temperance drama helped establish a model composed of the family as the foundation of prosperity and repository of value, the wife as loyal but helpless, the husband as the well-intentioned provider but wayward, unwilling agent of destruction whose fall and regeneration provide the requisite arc, and the home as the idealized expression of that most treasured abstraction, respectability.[5] Our consecration of home and family yet endures, and so does melodrama in its many guises, presenting a conservative, protective vision which may express the deeper feelings of our society and, more relevant to my topic, the deeper fears.

Stowe presents Legree as the most reprehensible example of the abuses that slavery fosters, but he expresses her nightmares at a more fundamental level – he is the absolute nemesis of the family. He separates Emmeline from her mother and he scorns the woman who shrinks away from Sambo and Quimbo on the grounds that she left her 'old man' in New Orleans. Such attachments mean nothing to Legree, but everything to Stowe. Legree is the polar opposite of the kind of man Stowe approves. He is unmarried, living in sin with a succession of slave women, he drinks, he beats his slaves brutally, and there is no place in his life for the word of God. His home was once the product of the care and refinement that Stowe cherishes, but now it is an anti-home, a perversion of the ideal, surely the product more of the author's imagination than her experience, a pit of coarseness, brutality and vulgar debauchery. The neat lawn has degenerated into a tangle of littered weeds, the windows are broken and neglected, and the dirty, damp rooms offer crude shelter not only to the master but also to his pack of dogs. He is the scourge of chastity, of charity, and of love. A family is an intimate gathering-together of people, and Legree is the spirit of their fear that some force may tear them apart – if they lose each other, then they lose their collective identity. When Legree approaches, families tremble.

He inspires fear from his first appearance at the slave auction. He manhandles and then purchases both Tom and the delicate, innocent, beautiful quadroon, Emmeline. His inspection violates them and transforms them into commodities; he forces open Tom's jaws to examine his teeth, and then fondles Emmeline's breasts in front of her anguished mother. He strips Tom of his belongings, his clothing, his hymnal, and most painfully of those keepsakes whose only value was their sentimental connection with Little Eva. He displays his hardened fist and assures the newcomers that his will, not theirs, will prevail. He assaults his slaves with words, blows, and his very presence.[6]

Fear takes away the self. Tom is a man as long as he dares to help his fellow slaves; to put handfuls of cotton into a sick woman's bag, or to read the Bible aloud. Legree threatens to turn Tom's concern away from others and into himself. If he submits to Legree and whips the other slaves, or even if he loses faith enough to fear his master, he loses his soul. Tom's victory is that he maintains his faith even though the other slaves on the Red River have ceased to believe that God even knows about their plantation.

While *Uncle Tom's Cabin*, like the temperance dramas, sought reform, Augustin Daly's *Under the Gaslight* (1867), perhaps the apotheosis of mid-century American melodrama, cuts loose from social issues but retains the machinery and essential, domestic concerns.[7] Laura bounces from home to home, and from family to family; the central question concerns where she truly belongs. By the end of the play, we learn that she began life in the privileged, upper-class Courtland family; was kidnapped by Byke and Old Judas (who left their own child in her cradle) and raised as a pickpocket; was, at the age of six, discovered but not recognized by her parents, who believed her to be an abused waif of the streets; and grew up to become engaged to a fashionable young man. She leaves polite society amid rumors of her true origins, fights the attempts of Byke and Old Judas to take her under their control, and finally comes to rest when Byke reveals the truth.

For Laura and all those who identify with her, Byke's is the face of fear, the fear that her comfortable home and family are not truly hers. He is a parody of sentimental fatherhood, telling Laura,

> Paternal feeling has been long smothered in my breast. Come to my arms, my child, my long-estranged child! ... Come, go with me; and cheer my old age. Aint I good, to take you back after all these years?[8]

While Legree was openly and physically cruel, Byke's threat is more insidious because he mocks respectability right up to his last exit, when he pretends to mourn for the just-deceased Old Judas. His performance is just smooth enough to evoke the tiny possibility that he is sincere, and the circumstances suggest that he might actually be Laura's father. He takes her to court in order to enforce his will on her and lend legitimacy to his scam. Byke and the story itself suggest that what seems to be stable might not be so, that no one can feel truly secure.

Daniel C. Gerould has asserted that

> the universe of melodrama is totally devoid of fatality and inevitability. Contingency rules; things can and will be otherwise. The individual can make of himself what he will.[9]

While Laura's experience would seem to bear out Gerould's postulate, his analysis is valid only *within* the structure of melodrama, taken from the perspective of the character herself. From *outside* of the structure, we can see that Laura's restoration to respectability and comfort is inevitable, that the play seeks to affirm a vision of reality that makes her continuing misery unthinkable. She may see herself as helpless, blown this way and that on the winds of circumstance, but we know that virtue must triumph and evil must fall if the moral order is to be affirmed. By its very nature and method, melodrama must satisfy its audience's expectations rather than present a confrontation with belief and value.[10]

We now perform Daly's play, and others of its era, as burlesques of what they once were, a practice which raises the question of whether the paradigm I am exploring survived beyond the mid nineteenth century. In the subsequent plays that we still rather generally label melodramas, the dramaturgy became milder as the thrills, the threats, the violence and the emotionalism subsided. The use of spectacle increased with the development of technical expertise, then faded as more and more plays were set in realistic interiors. Most important, the distinction between virtue and evil lost its relentless clarity, and the uncompromising moral conflict ceased to provide the essential foundation for the action. Neither playwrights nor spectators felt a need to define and sublimate cultural fear as overtly as during the previous generation.

Yet the model persists, not as much in the drama as in film, and appropriately so, since the cinema has claimed most of the audience that supported the popular, legitimate stage during the nineteenth century. One popular example is George Lucas's *Star Wars* (1977), a tale of a rebel alliance which seeks to free the galaxy from the dastardly empire, a film offering revisions of all the melodramatic components of yesteryear – the special effects of intergalactic battle, the suspenseful heroics of the leading rebels, the shamelessly named Luke Skywalker who joins the cause because the storm troopers have murdered his family, and, of course, that marvelous face of fear, the impassive Darth Vader, a high-tech Simon Legree whose black helmet, flowing robes, and casual brutality (not to mention the chilling soundtrack music that follows him wherever he goes) inspire even the most cocky rebel with dread.[11] In the two sequels, Lucas turned the story away from politics and back to the family, revealing that Darth Vader is actually Skywalker's father, a renegade family man drunk with power rather than demon rum, who finally repents before dying in his sorrowing son's arms.[12]

I find the strongest and most recent evidence of classic melodrama's vitality in Tim Burton's film, *Batman* (1989). The source of fear, reflecting late twentieth-century anxiety, is now the whole gestalt of life in the contemporary urban wilderness. Gotham City is a nightmare version of New York, a Babylon where criminals and corrupt officials rule, and beleaguered families hope in vain for a hero who will make the city safe for decent people.

Batman is their advocate. In real life, he is Bruce Wayne, a fabulously wealthy, mysterious, and reclusive young bachelor who, as a boy, watched, paralyzed, as a smiling hoodlum shot both of his parents to death, and subsequently developed his implacable alter ego in order to avenge them. His hooded, horned mask shows only unblinking eyes and an impassive mouth and chin, and wings enfold his body as he rises out of danger, apparently by magic but actually by using one of the many grappling cables he shoots out from under his wrists. The Batmobile races right out of the dreams of Jules Verne, with sectioned armor that opens and closes like the carapace of an insect. He is a classic American icon, an urban version of the lone horseman who seems to validate the romantic individualism of America but who dedicates himself to protecting the domestic ideal.

His adversary is mobster Jack Napier, whom Batman once caught in mid-crime and dropped into a vat of bubbling green chemicals, whence he returned to life with a clown-white skin and a permanent, grotesque grin – the Joker. He is completely amoral, a delightfully cruel psychotic who dresses like a bizarre harlequin in purple and green, donning a cliché painter's beret to deface canvases in the city museum. Wayne realizes that it was Napier who murdered his parents when he hears the trademark, mocking question with which the criminal needles his victims: 'Did you ever dance with the devil by the pale moonlight?' The two men have an additional matter to settle; the Joker has taken a liking to Vicki Vale, a hotshot, freelance photographer who is seeing Wayne because a compulsive fascination with bats has inspired her to search for his alter ego.

The Joker challenges Batman to a duel in the center of the city at midnight, and he rolls through the streets surrounded with clownish parade balloons, dancing to the music of Prince and scattering cash to the greedy populace. Batman strafes him from the Batplane, but the Joker pulls from his trousers a three-foot revolver, and he disables the craft, which crashes on the steps of Gotham Cathedral. The Joker grabs Vale, climbs to the top of the tower, and swings her into a demonic waltz – she does, it seems, dance with the devil by the pale moonlight. She is a melodramatic heroine for our time; barefoot, her blonde hair long, loose and enticingly disheveled, wearing only a simple white dress as she sags, exhausted, against the Joker's body. Batman arrives, having survived the crash, and apparently knocks the Joker over the edge of the precipice, but the villain reaches up from under the corner and pulls both Batman and Vale out into space.

The Joker capers on the roof, laughing wildly like a green-haired Quasimodo as he slams his feet into the crumbling stone cornice where his victims are hanging on by Batman's fingertips. His helicopter is about to lift him away when Batman shoots a cable out from his wrist and lashes the Joker's legs to one of the cathedral gargoyles, which breaks loose and pulls him to his death, several hundred feet below. The police gather around the still-grinning body and discover in his coat pocket a novelty gizmo that incessantly synthesizes a manic laugh. From start to finish, the film offers all the old familiar signs, codes and excesses, but not merely for effect; the whole structure serves a confident conception of good and evil as inherent and absolute.

The Joker's permanent grin captures everything that terrifies the decent, respectable people, everything that would take away not what they have but what they are. His expression can never be sincere; his is a human face forced into a mask, an indelible mockery of joy. When he first sees himself after his chemical accident, he laughs uncontrollably at the immense jest of his existence, that he, the emblem of evil, should walk the streets of Gotham like a perverse zany. As long as the Joker smiles, there can be neither true merriment nor true sorrow, for his unique inscrutability undercuts both ways and subverts the very gravity of fear.

The recurring physical metaphor is falling, falling from a Gotham skyscraper to one's death, or falling from the height of virtue into dark degeneracy. The decent people, the families, caught within the action, fear both the fallen and falling itself, not realizing that they are safe, that the collective author will protect their respectability, able to brook neither their destruction nor their corruption. Melodrama's generative fear derives partly from the collective author's uncertainty as to whether virtue is inherent or earned.[13] The collective author hopes that all of its constituents are deserving, so melodrama becomes a ritual of self-reassurance.[14]

As a contemplation of the nature of good and evil, melodrama must ultimately consider the question of priority. As they engage in their last battle, the Joker, referring to his rebirth out of the vat of chemicals, tells Batman, 'You made me', but Batman, alluding to the consequences of his parents' murder, assures him, 'You made me first.' He defines evil as that which forces good to stand forth, to give itself a name by acknowledging its fear and attempting to vanquish it. Uncle Tom and Laura each face fear and survive, not as heroes of tragic dimension, who grasp the moment and assume responsibility for their own destinies, but as helpless proxies for the collective author. Their careers validate the collective fear but also prove its ultimate impotence. The restoration of the moral order, with which melodrama must inevitably close, is also an affirmation of the self-knowlege that fear makes possible.

NOTES

1 Harriet Beecher Stowe, *Uncle Tom's Cabin* (1852; rpt New York: Airmont, 1967), p. 311. Although some might argue that a paper on melodrama should treat not Stowe's novel but George Aiken's dramatic adaptation, I have chosen to discuss the original for the following reasons: (1) I suspect that the novel is more widely read than the play, (2) although Aiken's play alters its source – and the transformation from novel to play provides an interesting topic by itself – those aspects which are relevant to this paper were, essentially, Stowe's creations, and (3) I wish to suggest that melodrama is not limited to the stage, or even to the stage of a certain era, but appears in many venues.

2 Eric Bentley wrote, 'Melodramatic vision is paranoid: we are being persecuted, and we hold that all things, living and dead, are combining to persecute us' (*The Life of the Drama*, 1964; rpt New York: Atheneum, 1966, p. 202).

3 Peter Brooks, *The Melodramatic Imagination* (New Haven: Yale University Press, 1976; rpt New York: Columbia University Press, 1984), p. 27.

4 Richard Slotkin, *Regeneration Through Violence: The Mythology of the American Frontier, 1600–1860* (Middletown, CT: Wesleyan University Press, 1973), p. 279.

5 Temperance drama was one of many forms of temperance writings to which I refer generically as the temperance narrative in my paper, 'Poison it with Rum; or, Validation and Delusion: Antebellum Temperance Drama as Cultural Method', delivered 10 November 1989 at the annual meeting of the Philological Association of the Pacific Coast in Claremont, California, and published in *Pacific Coast Philology*, 25 (1990).

6 Aiken builds Legree almost entirely of cruelty and violence, ameliorating most of Stowe's attempts to make his character more complex. Into one scene, he condenses several incidents from the novel: Legree promising to give Emmeline a pair of earrings and let her live like a lady, Legree commanding Tom to stop singing a hymn, Legree whipping Tom because he won't flog another slave, and Legree proclaiming himself owner not only of Tom's body but also of his soul.

7 Stylistically, *Under the Gaslight* prefigures realistic drama, especially in the conversational quality of the dialogue, but Daly's manipulation of the story falls squarely in the melodramatic tradition.

8 Augustin Daly, *Under the Gaslight* (1867), in *American Melodrama*, ed. Daniel C. Gerould (New York: Performing Arts Journal Publications, 1983), p. 156.

9 Daniel C. Gerould, 'The Americanization of Melodrama', in *American Melodrama*, p. 9.

10 As the play closes, the character who might be most inclined to view life as contingent is Pearl, the young woman who never doubted she was a Courtland until the very last moment, when she learns that she, not Laura, is the changeling.

11 Since Vader hides his face behind a mask with only faint, abstract resemblance to a human visage, a more apt, if awkward, phrase might be 'non-face of fear'.

12 One significant distinction between such films and mid-nineteenth-century stage melodramas is that spectacle has almost completely overpowered dialogue, so that the counterpart to the last century's inflated rhetoric is not the clipped speech of today's characters, but the exaggerated images that surround them.

13 This dichotomy offers an intriguing secular parallel to the old Protestant dilemma regarding salvation through predestination as opposed to good works.

14 Robert Bechtold Heilman says that 'melodrama is the realm of social action, public action, action within the world; tragedy is the realm of private action, action within the soul. Melodrama is concerned with making right prevail in the world and between persons, or with observing that it does not prevail; tragedy, with the problem of right in the self' (*Tragedy and Melodrama: Versions of Experience*, Seattle: University of Washington Press, 1968, p. 97).

The eroticism of evil: the vampire in nineteenth-century melodrama

ROXANA STUART

When we go to the theatre, we want to be delighted and instructed, certainly, but we want much more: to fall in love, to have the limits of our imagination stretched, vicariously to survive terrible ordeals and gain our heart's desire, to defy the hostile stars as we go down to death while triumphing over it. But one pleasure the theatre offers, better than any other art form, is to thrill us by scaring us out of our wits. Ever since Aeschylus' Furies caused people in the audience to die of fear and women to miscarry, this tradition has been part of theatre. Terror is one of the two essential elements of Aristotelian catharsis. As Eric Bentley notes, 'In the theatre, phenomena like ... Dracula are not eccentricities but prototypes ... There is no comparison ... between the potency of the novel and acted play. Physical presence on the stage makes an essential difference here. It is not in the quiet of libraries, bedrooms or kitchens that devotees of ... bloodsucking swoon. It is in the theatre.'[1]

The vampire perfectly embodies the revulsion and attraction to the erotic that lies at the heart of human experience, the simultaneous longing for – and terror of – being devoured. A vampire is a symbol that confronts us with much that is hidden from the conscious mind – attitudes toward sex and death that are less than rational – fearsome, shameful, and nightmarish. According to Ernest Jones, 'Complex and ... fundamental emotions are at work in the construction and maintenance of the vampire superstition. It is ... [a] product of the deepest conflicts that determine human development and fate – those concerned with the earliest relationships to the parents ... repressed desires and hate and guilt derived from early incest conflicts.'[2]

This curious mythical character continues to resurface in various times and cultures, and in many ways, to reflect the sexual taboos of particular cultures in a sublimated form.

Human sexuality certainly did survive in the Victorian age, in spite of strict obscenity laws, censorship, and the prudery of the dowager queen. It manifested itself in literature in many symbolic forms, and in society as a kind of mass hypocrisy, for example the pretended idealization of woman while the reality was often contempt and exploitation. The surface of prudery, and the 'dirty secret' beneath the appearance, is one form of social decadence.

Victorian writers, unless they went underground, could not write graphically about sex: it had to be camouflaged as something else. Since dead persons do not literally engage in sexual intercourse, there is nothing specifically prurient with which to reproach the writer. When a vampire drinks blood, he is engaging in a sex act without the embarrassments of nudity, genitals, pregnancy, or various other unmentionable aspects, and thus the writer can revel in any number of taboo subjects with impunity. Ernest Jones remarks on the subconscious equation of blood with semen: 'A nightly visit from a beautiful or frightful being, who first exhausts the sleeper with passionate embraces, and then withdraws from him a vital fluid ... can only point to nocturnal emissions accompanied by dreams of ... [an] erotic nature.'[3] Drinking blood is also a satanic parody of the Eucharist, the sacrament of the blood of Christ. Communion wine is a promise of eternal life; human blood bestows eternal life on the vampire. Blood and food, eating and sex, are poetic metaphors that become literal in the vampire myth.

In my reading of vampire literature I find four categories which can be grouped chronologically, generically, and thematically. The first stage is the origin of the vampire myth in the folklore of many cultures; the second is its transformation by the English Romantic poets into a symbol of the outcast artist and sexual adventurer; third is its metamorphosis into a sublimated symbol of sexual perversion on the nineteenth-century English, French, and American stage; and last is the vulgarization and decline into parody that we know today. This paper will briefly chart the first two stages to show how the vampire evolved from its primitive origins in myth into the great stage figure of Count Dracula, and then consider in detail how the vampire was the ideal anti-hero of melodrama because of his association with evil, and the forbidden games of deviance and eroticism.

In almost every culture there is a fear of dead bodies. It is natural and understandable that at some point in the process of separation and grieving, the mourner becomes alienated from the physical body of the deceased and fixes on the spirit, or soul, which we imagine to have departed from the body and either gone elsewhere or ceased to exist. The 'uninhabited' body becomes increasingly alien, and as we observe the changes and deterioration brought on by decay, the corpse takes on an increasingly frightening aspect. Prostrated by sorrow, exhaustion, and loss, and unable to sleep, we lie awake trying to picture what the newly buried loved one is actually doing as he 'sleeps' under the ground. A sleeper eventually awakes. The story of the Resurrection of Christ is the joyous interpretation of this reawakening; the vampire is the nightmare version.

All cultures have customs which suggest a need to placate the dead. The universal ancient practice of burying precious objects in the tomb, All Hallows Eve and All Souls Day in Catholic countries, flowers at funerals – these are bribes to the dead to stay in their graves and let us live. The ancient Greeks are thought to have poured blood on graves to keep the dead from rising. The original function of the tombstone may well have been to hold the monster down. What other reason is there to nail a coffin shut?

One shocking, unassimilable aspect of death is that the body is cold: so the vampire seeks warmth, the blood of living humans. The dead are lonely, so he seeks to drag us down into darkness with him. Early folk vampires all prey on members of their own families. They are not the sophisticated continental gentlemen in evening dress of the Victorian stage: they are monstrous walking corpses.

In his book, *Vampires, Burial and Death: Folklore and Reality*,[4] Paul Barber makes the fascinating point that the vampire superstition of eastern European peasants has a somewhat logical basis. When people die from unknown causes which are mysterious to them, such as viruses or bacteria, one likely explanation is that death is a contagion that comes from the dead. Is it surprising then, that where there is fear and ignorance, every exhumation yields a vampire? *Rigor mortis* was not understood to be a temporary condition until the late eighteenth century, nor was it commonly known that a corpse's rate of decomposition is related to the amount of moisture in the soil; in certain climatic conditions the blood will not congeal for months. Hair and nails continue to grow after death. Small wonder the bodies seemed alive. Most gruesomely, Barber even has an explanation for the wooden stake:

> The peasants of Medvegia assumed that if the corpse groaned, it must still be alive. But a corpse does emit sounds, even when it is only moved, let alone if a stake were driven into it. This is because the compression of the chest cavity forces air past the glottis, causing a sound similar in quality and origin to the groan or cry of a living person ... A corpse that did not emit such sounds when a stake was driven into it would be unusual.[5]

These superstitions spread westward in the eighteenth century when Serbia and Wallachia were acquired by Austria in the Treaty of Passarowitz (1718). The word 'vampire' is first entered in the *Oxford English Dictionary* with a 1734 citation.

Perhaps inspired by such late eighteenth-century German poems as Goethe's 'The Bride of Corinth' and Bürger's 'Lenore', the English Romantics transformed this figure of eastern folklore into a seeker after forbidden knowledge, an outcast wanderer and heroic defier of God, an awakener, as exciting, tragic, and attractive as the Satan of *Paradise Lost*. One concern of the Romantic poets was the predatory nature of human relationships: man and woman, parent and child, philosopher and madman, artist and subject, all feed on one another's souls. Although the Victorian stage vampires are rigidly heterosexual, the myth of the vampire can be used to express almost any devouring human relationship: incest (Byron's 'Manfred'), lesbianism (leFanu's *Carmilla*), sadism and child abuse (Shelley's and Artaud's *The Cenci*), female domination (Strindberg's *The Father*), romantic love (Keats's 'Eve of St Agnes'), male homosexuality and pedophilia (Anne Rice's *Interview with the Vampire*), and nymphomania (Dumas père's *La Tour de Nèsle* and Bram Stoker's *other* novel, *The Lair of the White Worm*).

In June 1816 at the Villa Diodati on Lake Geneva, Lord Byron, Percy Bysshe Shelley, Mary Shelley, Claire Claremont, and John Polidori each agreed to contribute a gothic tale to an informal literary contest, a sort of horror decameron. The progeny of this group were monstrous: Count Cenci, Manfred, the Giaour, Dr Frankenstein's Monster. The vampire in his modern form was actually created by the least of these literary lights: John Polidori, who was Byron's physician, wrote a twenty-page short story, 'The Vampyre', based on an abandoned fragment of Byron's. It was published in the *New Monthly Magazine* with a false attribution to Byron which was later retracted. In many ways it can be taken as a portrait of Byron, perhaps satirizing his affair with Lady Caroline Lamb. The vampire's name, Lord Ruthven (pronounced 'rivven') is taken from her novel *Glenarvon*.

Ruthven is the paradigm for almost all nineteenth-century stage vampires. Within a year of publication he made his first appearance on the French stage in an adaptation by Nodier, Jouffrey, and Carmouche. Of these, the best known is Charles Nodier, one of the fathers of French Romanticism, much influenced by Goethe. *Le Vampire*[6] opened on 13 June 1820 at the Théâtre de la Porte-Saint-Martin, which specialized in gothic horror. It had been closed in 1807, and, obtaining the rights to stage *mélodrame*, it reopened under J. T. Merle, specially equipped with extensive spectacle machinery and the services of the designer Ciceri.[7] After *Le Vampire*, which barely qualifies as a *mélo-drame* since it contains only one musical number, they prospered with such horror specialties as *Le Doge de Venice* (1821), *Chateau de Kenilworth* (1822), *Frankenstein* and *Le Monstre et le magicien* (1826), and Nodier's only other play, *Faust* (1828).

Although the 1820 edition lists a Monsieur Philippe as the first Lord Ruthven (Ruthwen), according to Stephen Wischhusen, the vampire was played by an English actor, T. P. (Thomas Potter) Cooke, who repeated the role in London in an English adaptation, as well as directing the production.[8] Cooke became a well-known star of the English stage, playing the heroic sailor William in Jerrold's nautical melodrama *Black-Eyed Susan* 785 times, and Vanderdecken in *The Flying Dutchman*, which he also directed.

The French play follows Polidori's plot, shifting emphasis from Aubrey (Aubray) to his sister Malvina, and adding a juvenile couple, and an elaborate ballet–prologue set in Fingal's Cave in the Hebrides, haunted by phantoms with names taken from MacPherson's *Ossian*. There the vampire has hidden his coffin. Ituriel, benevolent spirit of the moon, attempts to warn Malvina of her danger, but she is prevented by Oscar, another spirit, and vanishes in a cloud. Lord Ruthwen (sic) is an aristocratic Scotsman – cold, world-weary, moody, amoral, and fatally attractive to women. Events in the short story which take place in Greece – Ruthwen's murder there by bandits, the vow he extracts from his friend Aubray that his death not be revealed – are related as narrative by Aubray who, in loving memory of this lost friend, has promised his sister Malvina to Ruthwen's younger brother, whom he has never met. To his horror, Ruthwen himself appears to claim the girl as his bride, and Aubray is silenced by his inconvenient oath, while the vampire proceeds to debauch a servant girl in the compulsively womanizing manner of the French. The marriage is about to be performed, Aubray and Ruthwen are at swordpoints, when the floor opens beneath the vampire's feet and he is dragged by demons to eternal torment, crying 'Le néant! Le néant!' (Nothingness, annihilation).

Amazingly, within two days of the premiere, Eugene Scribe and his female collaborator 'Mélesville' had a parody on the boards, a one-act vaudville with music featuring an English vampire named Ruthven.[9]

Ambrose Bierce's *Devil's Dictionary* defines 'dramatist' as 'one who adapts from the French', and two months later the prolific James Robinson Planché, author of *Charles VII*, *The Merchant's Wedding*, and *The Brigand*, had a version on the stage in London. *The Vampire, or The Bride of the Isles*[10] opened at the English Opera House, Strand, on 9 August 1820, billed as 'a new Romantic Melodrama partially taken from a celebrated Piece which has for some weeks past attracted all Paris ... The effect produced on crowded audiences by *The Vampire* is perfectly electrical. The publick demand will be answered by a repetition every evening.'[11]

It again starred T. P. Cooke as Lord Ruthven, and Unda, Spirit of the Flood, was played by Miss Love, who became a popular singer at Covent Garden. The announcement on the play bill, 'The action of the Melodrama under the direction of Mr T. P. Cooke', is highly unusual for the early nineteenth century.

Planché's version adds nine musical numbers, including Scottish love ballads and drinking songs. Much stage time is consumed by unbearable Scottish low-character comedy – the hen-pecked, heavy-brogued

THE VAMPIRE;

OR, THE BRIDE OF THE ISLES:

A ROMANTIC MELO-DRAMA,

En Two Acts,

BY J. R. PLANCHÉ,

Author of Charles the XII. The Merchants' Wedding, A Woman Never Vext,
The Mason of Buda, The Brigand, A Daughter to Marry, &c.

PRINTED FROM THE ACTING COPY, WITH REMARKS,

BIOGRAPHICAL AND CRITICAL, BY D—G.

To which are added,

A DESCRIPTION OF THE COSTUME,—CAST OF THE CHARACTERS,
ENTRANCES AND EXITS,—RELATIVE POSITIONS OF THE PER-
FORMERS ON THE STAGE,—AND THE WHOLE OF THE STAGE
BUSINESS.

As performed at the

THEATRES ROYAL, LONDON.

EMBELLISHED WITH A FINE ENGRAVING,

By Mr. BONNER, from a Drawing taken in the Theatre, by
Mr. R. CRUIKSHANK.

LONDON:

JOHN CUMBERLAND, 6, BRECKNOCK PLACE,
CAMDEN NEW TOWN.

23 Title page of *The Vampire* (1826)

drunkard McSwill; Effie, the soubrette part, with little plot function but many songs; and Robert, the proletarian hero, who actually subdues the vampire. Malvina has become Lady Margaret; Aubray has become Lord Ronald and is now her father. In the masque–prologue spirits warn Margaret of the vampire's designs:

> Death binds them not – from form to form they fleet,
> And though the cheek be pale, and glaz'd the eye,
> Such is their wondrous art, the hapless victim
> Blindly adores, and drops into their grasp,
> Like birds when gaz'd on by the basilisk.

(Prologue)

Ruthven has evolved from the blood-sucking beasts of European folklore. The French play adds sexual attractiveness; the English play adds a tragic sense of sin. The vampire has become a passionately romantic seducer consumed by a guilty conscience. In remorseful soliloquy (with what Stephen Sondheim would call a remarkable amount of sympathy for his meal), he declaims:

> Demon as I am, that walk the earth to slaughter and devour! The little that remains of heart within this wizard [sic] frame, sustained alone by human blood, shrinks from the appalling act of planting misery in the bosom of this veteran chieftain. Still must the fearful sacrifice be made, and suddenly, for the approaching night will find my wretched frame exhausted, and darkness – worse than death – annihilation is my lot! Margaret! Unhappy maid! Thou art my destined prey! Thy blood must feed a vampire's life, and prove the food of his disgusting banquet. (I, ii)

Quite a sentimental fellow compared with the master of evil, Dracula, who was to come after him, Ruthven's *modus operandi* is to marry an innocent girl and slowly drain the life from her over a year's time, a kind of supernatural serial killer. The marriage vow has importance for him. It is his license to do as he will with Margaret since, after all, a wife is a man's property. He rises from the dead when revived by moonlight, and Margaret is saved by the timely setting of the moon.

T. P. Cooke as Ruthven appears to have had an acting triumph. The *New Monthly Magazine* critic wrote, 'Mr T. P. Cooke, whom we have long regarded as an actor of unappreciated talent, has secured a high place in the public esteem, by his performance of the Vampire. In his fearful action – his triumphant smiles – and his very assumed softness of tone and demeanor – he gives us the idea of being not of this world.'[12] He goes on to state that *The Vampire* is 'one of the best *mélo-drames* we have ever seen ... The idea itself has so much of the disgusting, that there appeared considerable hazard in its representation ... however ... we feel throughout only a pleasing horror.'[13] No less a critic than William Hazlitt also approved: '[It] is, on the whole, the most splendid spectacle we have ever seen ... A little shocking to the senses ... notwithstanding the repugnance

R. *Cruikshank, Del.*   G. *W. Bonner, Sc.*

The Vampire.

Lady Margaret.   Hold! hold! I am thine;—the moon has set.

Act II. Scene 4.

24 Engraving by G. W. Bonner from drawing by R. Cruickshank of *The Vampire*

of every circumstance and feeling, this melodrama succeeds very well: and it succeeds in spite of Mr Kean's last nights.'[14]

The 1820 production featured an innovation in stagecraft, the vampire trap; two doors on springs which allowed the actor to disappear almost instantly. It has been in use in plays dealing with the supernatural ever since. The first edition of the play contains a description of the costumes, also designed by Planché. All characters were in Scottish kilts and tragedy plumes.

The success of the play was enormous. It toured extensively and was revived with much profit by the same company in 1829. Other productions of Planché's *Vampire* played the Theatre, Durham, in 1821, the Park Theatre, New York, in 1837, and the Theatre Royal, Liverpool, in 1839.

The Royal Coburg Theatre mounted a rival vampire play in 1823, *Thalaba the Destroyer* by E. Ball, based on Robert Southey's poem. This play also begins with a semi-masque, but it is set in the mysterious orient. Stage effects included a winged serpent, a colossal statue that comes to life, and a giant war elephant. Thalaba is a warrior who discovers that his true love, Oneiza, who died on their wedding day, is a vampire. With Oneiza's father, Moath, Thalaba descends into her tomb, where the vampire bride is dispatched in customary fashion with a stake through the heart. On the bill with *Thalaba* at the Royal Coberg was a short version of *Frankenstein*, subtitled *The Demon of Switzerland*.

In 1828 a German opera, *Der Vampyr* by Heinrich Marschner, made its appearance. Marschner was a pupil of Weber, admired by Schumann and also by Wagner, who modelled many aspects of *Der Fliegende Holländer* on *Der Vampyr*, and in 1833 contributed an aria for Ruthven of his own composition, 'Ha, welche lust'.[15] The libretto, by Marschner's brother-in-law Wilhelm August Wohlbruck, is an interesting example of early German romanticism with a psychologically divided protagonist. It is based on Polidori but owes something to the Faust legend as well. Lord Ruthven (bass) is given three years of life by his master the devil in exchange for the souls of three sopranos. Ianthe and Emmy are easy prey, but Malvina is faithful to Aubrey (tenor, now her fiancé). As usual, just as the marriage is to be solemnized, Ruthven's time is up; he is struck by a bolt of lightning and descends into the fiery pit.

The opera premiered in Leipzig on 29 March 1828. Malvina was sung by the composer's wife, Marianne Wohlbruck. It was an immediate success in Germany, and opened in London at the Lyceum on 25 August 1829, where it had an extraordinary run of sixty consecutive performances.

In 1845 the penny-dreadful serial, *Varney the Vampire, or The Feast of Blood*, by either James Malcolm Rymer or Thomas Pecket Prest (who also wrote a serial version of *Sweeney Todd*), further popularized the vampire

Theatre Royal, English Opera House, Strand.

This Evening, SATURDAY, August 19th, 1820;

Will be presented (FIFTEENTH TIME) an entirely new OPERATICK DRAMA, in Three Acts, called

Woman's Will—A Riddle!

WITH ENTIRELY NEW MUSICK, SCENERY, DRESSES AND DECORATIONS.
The OVERTURE and MUSICK composed by Mr DAVY, with the exception of Two Songs by Mr. PINDAR, of Bath.
The SCENERY designed and executed by Mr. CAPON, Mr. A THISELTON, Mr. GILL, and Assistants.
The DRESSES by Mr. HEAD, Mrs. BROOKES, &c. &c.

Duke of Milan,   Mr. ROWBOTHAM,   Count Vitaldi,   Mr. BARTLEY,
Cæsario,   Mr. PEARMAN,   Corvino,   Mr. HARLEY,
1st Lord, Mr. WEBSTER,   2nd Lord, Mr. LOUCE,   Officer, Mr. MINTON,
Principal Priest. Mr Moss,   Attendant Priests, Mr. FISHER. Mr. KENNETH,
Children of the Chapel, Master COOTE, Miss E. LANCASTER,
Nobles of the Court, Messrs Boreman, Collingsworth, Kinmore, Jenkins, Lovs, Nichols, H. Phillips, R. Phillips,
Proud, Shaw, Spratley, &c. &c.

Duchess of Mantua, Mrs. W. S. CHATTERLEY,
Princess Clementine, Miss KELLY,   Isabel, Miss CAREW,
Ladies of the Court, Mesdames & Misses Holtin, Jerrolda, Lancaster, Lodge, Manuall, Mears, Miller, Newton, Shaw, Tokely, Webster.

The EPILOGUE, in Character, by Miss KELLY.

In the course of the Opera, the following new Scenes will be exhibited.
An ANTI-CHAMBER of the DUCAL PALACE. (Gill)   SALOON and BANQUET HALL (A Thiselton.)
An ANTIENT STREET of POINTED ARCHITECTURE, selected entirely from remains of the middle ages. (Capon.)
ANTI CHAMBER adjoining the PALACE CHAPEL. (A Thiselton)

To which will be added (NINTH TIME) a NEW ROMANTICK MELODRAMA, (partly taken from a celebrated Piece which has for some Weeks past attracted all Paris) in THREE PARTS, founded on THE CELEBRATED TALE, called

"THE VAMPIRE"

The OVERTURE from OSCAR & MALVINA, composed by the late Mr. REEVE.
The INCANTATION and CHARM in the INTRODUCTORY VISION, be Mr. M. MOSS.
The VOCAL MUSICK selected from the SCOTTISH MELODIES——The Melodramatick Musick composed by Mr. HART.
The SCENERY, including correct Views of The BASALTICK COLUMNS of The ISLAND of STAFFA, with The
GROTTO and CAVE of FINGAL, entirely new, by Mr. A THISELTON, Mr SMITH, and Assistants.
The ACTION of the MELODRAMA under the direction of Mr T. P. COOKE.

Characters in the Introductory Vision.

The Vampire, Mr. T P. COOKE,
Lady Margaret,   Mrs. W. S. CHATTERLEY,
Unda, (Spirit of the Flood) Miss LOVE,   Ariel, (Spirit of the Air) Miss WORGMAN.

Characters in the Drama.

Ruthven, (Earl of Marsden) Mr. T. P. COOKE, Ronald, (Baron of the Isles) Mr. BARTLEY,
Robert, (a Retainer of the Baron) Mr. PEARMAN, Mc.Swill, (Henchman to the Baron) Mr. HARLEY,
Andrew, (Steward to the Earl of Marsden) Mr. MINTON,   Father Francis, Mr. SHAW.
Lady Margaret, (Daughter to Lord Ronald) Mrs. W. S. CHATTERLEY,
Bridget, (Housekeeper to Lord Ronald) Mrs. GROVE,
Effie, (Daughter to Andrew, and betrothed to Robert) Miss CAREW.

THIS PIECE IS FOUNDED ON
the various Traditions concerning THE VAMPIRES, which assert that they are Spirits, deprived of all Hope of Futurity, by the Crimes committed in their Mortal State—but, that they are permitted to roam the Earth, in whatever Forms they please, with Supernatural Powers of Fascination—and, that they cannot be destroyed, so long as they sustain their dreadful Existence, by imbibing the BLOOD of FEMALE VICTIMS, whom they are first compelled to marry.

The effect produced on crowded audiences by THE VAMPIRE is perfectly electrical. The applause at the conclusion of each performance has lasted for several minutes, and its success is nightly testified by shouts of approbation.—The publick demand will be answered by a repetition, every evening.

The highly successful Opera of WOMANS WILL—A RIDDLE, will be repeated this evening, and twice next week.

THE SPACIOUS SALOON
Has been again tastefully fitted up, with a NEW DESIGN, representing
An ILLUMINATED ORIENTAL GARDEN
and will be opened as usual at EIGHT o'Clock, for the admittance of the SECOND PRICE, which commences at NINE.
Stage Manager, Mr. BARLEY.   Leader of the Band, Mr. MOUNTAIN.

Boxes 5s Second Price 3s. Pit 3s. Second Price 1s 6d. Lower Gallery 2s. Second Price 1s. Upper Gallery 1s. Second Price 6d.
PRIVATE BOXES may be had nightly of Mr. S. EVESON, of whom Places are to be taken, at the Box Office, Strand Entrance,
from Ten till Four; also at PEARMAN's Library, 170, New Bond Street.
Doors open at half-past Six, the Performance to begin at Seven —No Money returned—Lowndes, Printer, Marquis Court, Drury Lane

On Monday will be produced (First Time) a new ex-tempore, temporary, Sketch, to be called

"PATENT SEASONS."

The Characters by   Mr. WRENCH,   Mr. HARLEY,   Mr. WILKINSON,   Mr. PEARMAN,
Mrs CAREW,   Miss KELLY.

After which (16th time) The VAMPIRE: to which will be added (First Time) an entirely NEW FARCE, in Two Acts, which has been some time in preparation, to be called

WHANG FONG:
OR
HOW REMARKABLE!

The Musick composed by Mr. PINDAR, of Bath.
Principal Characters by Mr. PEARMAN. Mr. HARLEY, Mr T.P. COOKE, Mr. WILKINSON, Mr. LANCASTER.
Mrs. ROVE, Miss LOVE.
Mrs. PINDAR, (from the Theatre Scarborough, being her first appearance on a London stage.)

25   Play bill for *The Vampire* (1820)

myth and seized the public imagination. The first mass-market serial shocker, *Varney the Vampire* is an epic of 868 pages crammed with carnage, sex, violence, and 'godalmighty muckamuck'. Sir Francis Varney has killed his wife and son and turned vampire after being hanged during the Restoration. He was the first vampire to wear a black cape. No woman is immune to his power of seduction. Suavely sophisticated, impeccably mannered, he is a genius of hairbreadth escapes, and like Ruthven is killed many times but revives by moonlight. A romantic hero in the Byronic mold, he suffers guilt and self-loathing, and longs to destroy himself to escape his destiny, which is to devour women. His suicide is quite dramatic:

> You will make what haste you can, from the mountain, inasmuch as it is covered with sulphurous vapours, inimical to human life, and when you reach the city ... you will say that you accompanied Varney the Vampyre to the crater of Mount Vesuvius, and that, tired and disgusted with a life of horror, he flung himself in to prevent the possibility of a reanimation of his remains.[16]

Meanwhile in Paris, Alexandre Dumas père brought his formidable skills to bear in creating a new version of Ruthven (Ruthwen). By curious coincidence, the first play Dumas saw when he came to Paris as a young man was *Le Vampire*.[17] The gentleman seated beside him in the audience who was busily hissing the actors turned out to be none other than Charles Nodier, one of the play's three authors, who became Dumas's patron and friend.

Dumas wrote a number of popular and successful historical dramas that were romantic in style, mostly in prose, and ignoring the Unities. *Kean* and *La Tour de Nèsle* are outstanding examples. With his occasional collaborator, Auguste Maquet, who usually contributed plots and historical research, he wrote *Le Vampire*,[18] 'drame fantastique' in five acts and ten tableaux. Maquet later sued to prove his co-authorship. Dumas, desperate for money to pay his debts, claimed sole credit for the piece. Critics ever since have tried to argue the opposite and lay the play entirely in Maquet's lap.[19]

Dumas's *Vampire* follows the main outlines of the Polidori original but switches to new and exotic locales – Spain, Brittany, and a palace in Circassia. He attempts to place the main focus on the Aubrey character, here called Gilbert, a romantic hero who valiantly attempts and fails to save a Spanish lady, Juana, and his sister Hélène from the vampire's embrace. In the last scene set in a cemetery, 'sinister and fantastic, snow on the ground, red moon in the sky' (v, xv), Gilbert and his fiancée Antonia are saved when a female ghoul, in love with Gilbert (who has shadowed and protected him throughout the action), defies Ruthwen and sacrifices her immortal life by revealing the secret of how to kill the vampire, who then curses God and dies. The sky fills with angels, including the ghosts of the three murdered women, who bless the happy couple, saying 'Soeur, sois heureuse!' (Scène unique, 535).

Also featured is a finely written comedy part, the servant Lazare, who is suborned with vampire gold but later repents and saves the day.

Of interest in this as yet untranslated play is a ballet–masque in which the figures of a tapestry come to life to warn Gilbert of Hélène's danger. The masque featured 'sweet, pale' Isabelle Constant, with whom Dumas fell in love, as the mystical fairy Melusine. She speaks (or sings) this lovely verse:

> Même pour nos regards, sa nuit est trop profonde.
>   Dans quel morne dessein
> Le Seigneur permet-il qu'il demeure en ce monde,
>   Immortel assassin?
>
> Nul ne le sait; Dieu met ses plus blanches colombes
>   Dans se fatale main,
> Et l'on retrouverait sa trace par les tombes
>   Qu'il sème en son chemin.
>
> Nulle vierge n'échappe aux meutres qu'il entasse;
>   Le hideux oppresseur
> Brave les éléments et commande à l'espace . . .
> (*Gilbert.*) O ma soeur! O ma soeur!
>   . . .
> Prions, pour qu'à Gilbert Dieu tout-puissant inspire
>   Un généreux effort.
> Rutwen est un démon, Ruthwen est un vampire:
>   Son amour, c'est la morte!
>
>   (II, ii)

Ruthwen was played, 'enthrallingly' according to Dumas, by a Monsieur Arnault. The classic scene of recognition with Hélène, played by Jane Essler, contains this marvelous bit of dialogue:

Ruthwen. How pale you are!

Hélène. Less than you, milord.

Ruthwen. Less than I? You know, Hélène, that this pallor is habitual to me, and it's simply that I lost so much blood the day your brother tried to kill me.

Hélène. Excuse me, Georges, but such pallor is more like a corpse than a living person.

Ruthwen. What are you trying to say, Hélène?.

Hélène. I am saying that I am of a valiant race; I am saying that I have never been afraid; I am saying that you horrify me!

Ruthwen. You too, Hélène? Ah, this is what comes of having left you alone: the solitude, the silence, the shadows have excited your imagination. The shadows . . . But I left lights in this chamber, did I not?.

Hélène. In your absence they went out.

Ruthwen. Ah, how strange! . . . All by themselves?

Hélène. By themselves!

Ruthwen. You are trembling, Hélène.
Hélène. I have told you! I'm afraid! I'm afraid!
Ruthwen. Your hand, my beloved. (*He takes her hand.*)
Hélène. Cold as a corpse!
Ruthwen. Yes, cold, Hélène, because your doubt freezes me ... Oh come, come
    my betrothed! Come, come my wife! Come to my breast, come to my heart!
Hélène. Ah, leave me! It seems to me your breast is not alive, that your heart
    does not beat!

$$(\text{IV}, \text{V})^{20}$$

Le Vampire was written shortly after the fall of the Second Republic, and played at the Ambigu-Comique, opening 18 December 1851. It was Dumas's last play before leaving Paris.

A spectacular entry in the lists of English vampire melodramas was made in 1852 with *The Vampire: A Phantasm Related in Three Dramas* by Dion Boucicault.[21] Also billed as 'A Spectral Drama in Three Acts', the premiere was a benefit night for Charles Kean and the role was written for him. The great actor declined, and it was played instead by Boucicault himself, who was not previously known as an actor. It opened on 14 June 1852, at the Princess Theatre.

The action is shifted to Wales, the ruins of Raby Castle in the peaks of Snowden, and 'the ruins of the Clock Tower'. No less than seven sets employing three designers were constructed for this extravaganza, 'an altogether weird and dreadful thing', which turned the theatre into 'a chamber of horrors'.[22] Despite a critical panning, it packed in audiences for many nights.

Boucicault was intrigued by the vampire's immortality, and his three acts take place respectively in 1660, 1760, and 1860 (which was in the future when the play was written). This device allowed him to have three leading ladies, one of whom, playing Alice Peveril in the second act, was the nineteen-year-old Agnes Robertson, Charles Kean's ward, whom Boucicault later married and made his leading lady. She received very bad reviews for this performance: 'Not exactly suited to her character, convulsive, spasmodic, and unintelligible in her efforts to be forceful', wrote *Era*'s critic.[23] Boucicault's acting drew great praise: 'He looked the Vampire to perfection, and spoke and acted it exceedingly well. His deathly hue and rigid cast of countenance, his high and bald forehead and spare figure, his measured accents and grave demeanor, were all in keeping, and his "make-up" in each act quite a study.'[24] Even Queen Victoria was amused: '[He] is very handsome and has a fine voice, acted very impressively. I can never forget his livid face and fixed look ... It quite haunts me.' She recanted a week later: 'It does not bear seeing a second time, and is, in fact, quite trashy.'[25]

Before international copyright laws came into effect, dramatists borrowed so freely and openly from each other that it was not even considered theft. It is carrying matters quite far, however, to steal from oneself: ten years later, in a bit of thrifty recycling, Boucicault presented a shortened version of his own play, retitled *The Phantom*, 'a new romantic drama with all new scenery'. It opened 28 August 1862 at the Theatre Royal, New Adelphi, having been tried out in America in Philadelphia and at Wallach's Theatre in New York.

The vampire, again played by Boucicault, is now named Sir Alan Ruthven, Lord of Lochiel (Scottish or Welsh, he nevertheless spoke in a broad Irish brogue), and Agnes Robertson's character became Ada Raby. The two acts take place 100 years and many miles apart – first we are in the Scottish highlands, the ruins of Ravensleigh, and 'the Wolf's Craig [sic]'. It features a spectacular storm and burial scene on the peak of Ben Nevis. The second act is again on Mount Snowden in Wales, where the resurrected vampire, now calling himself Rookwood, in a Svengali-like seduction scene, causes Ada to jilt her fiancé Edgar:

> *Alan.* Ada, my soul, are you not mine – are you not she whom I snatched from the jaws of death? I love you, your young life shall revive me, and for this end I bade you live.
> *Ada.* What power is this which oppresses me?
> *Alan.* It is my will: mine eyes fix upon thy heart as if with fangs, while my soul like a serpent entwines thine within its folds, and crushes thee to my will ... Tonight, ere the moon rises, a new life drawn from the pure heart of a maiden must enter this form. Ada shall be the victim – her life for mine!
>
> (II, V)

In 1862 *Vampire! Or The Spectre of Mount Snowden* starring Annie Senter and Harry Langdon, was probably a version of Boucicault's play with added music.

In September 1863 the Barnum Museum Theatre of New York presented *Brunhilda, or Wake Not the Dead*, 'altered and adapted by E. F. Taylor from *The Vampire Bride*'[26] by Ludwig Tieck. Refreshingly, this vampire is a female. The play is set in Thurswalden, Germany, and completely departs from Polidori in every respect except for the beneficial effect of moonlight upon vampires. Lord Walter begs a reluctant sorcerer to revive his dead wife Brunhilda, who proceeds to run amok. The dialogue, in surprisingly passable blank verse, is heavily larded with symbolic imagery of sexual starvation. In this riveting scene between husband and vampire, the author, like Dumas, plays ironically with the sexual double-entendres of cold and heat:

> *Brunhilda.* Thou broughtst me back to life, but thought not of
>   The means whereby on earth I was to live.
>   All I now possess is an existence, chilled
>   And colder than the snake. Give me thy hand.
>   Am I not cold?
> *Walter.*   Colder than death!

Brunhilda. A living statue, and 'twas requisite
           A vital draught should animate the dull
           Slow current in my veins – and wake me to
           The glow of life – the flame of love! A draught
           Of cursed abomination unto all save me –
           Human blood! Warm, fresh from the veins,
           This is the hellish drink for which I've thirsted,
           And even when beside thee I have laid,
           And thou been wrapped in so sweet a slumber
           As sleeps an infant at its mother's breast,
           I have longed to taste of thine.

                                                      (ii, i)

Walter's second wife Swanhilda is abandoned and commits suicide after her children are devoured by the vampire. She returns as a ghost. The low-comedy character, appropriately named Kibitz, lightens the atmosphere with such remarks as 'Lady Brunhilda may pop up from the ground and down upon me like a fire extinguisher!' (ii, iii) The play ends with a witches' sabbath 'production number'.

Lord Ruthven was killed many times on stage, but only Bram Stoker's *Dracula* could keep him in the grave. Superseding all vampires that came before him and the model for all that came after, Count Dracula transcends the work in which it is presented – one of Jung's archetypal patterns of the subconscious and a powerful poetic image of Freud's 'primal hoarder'. Dracula, 'the Dragon', has tremendous intelligence, grace, and strength, an aristocratic manner, an ironic sense of humor, a commanding presence, a contempt for mankind, and a hypnotic power over women. His nocturnal habits, his sudden reversions to animal form and ability to fly through the air, his association with forbidden, unclean, and dangerous sex, make him one of the great fictional creations of Victorian literature.

Dracula's bite is a sexual violation which brings death but also sexual arousal beyond the ordinary senses. The erotic imagery in the novel and the play is unmistakable to us today, the vampire's kiss being a thinly veiled reference to oral sex. On one level the plot is an interracial sexual competition, a story of how stalwart Englishmen succeed in preventing a swarthy European degenerate from introducing repugnant continental sex practices to British womanhood, who, it is to be noted, quickly develop a taste for Dracula's technique and forgo it only with great reluctance. In addition to oral sex, there are references to voyeurism, necrophilia, pedophilia, nymphomania, incest, rape, nocturnal emissions, venereal disease, sadism, bestiality, menstruation, and group sex. This passage is typical:

The fair girl went on her knees and bent over me, fairly gloating. There was a deliberate voluptuousness which was both thrilling and repulsive, and as she arched her neck she actually licked her lips like an animal, till I could see in the moonlight the moisture shining on the scarlet lips and red tongue as it lapped the white sharp teeth. Lower and lower went her head as the lips went below the range of my mouth ... Then she paused and I could hear the churning sound of her tongue ... and feel the hot breath on my neck. Then the skin of my throat began to tingle as one's flesh does when the hand that is to tickle it approaches nearer – nearer. I could feel the soft, shivering sound of the lips on the supersensitive skin of my throat, and the hard dents of two sharp teeth, just touching and pausing there. I closed my eyes in a langourous ecstasy and waited – waited with beating heart.[27]

With charming innocence Victorian critics failed to pick up on the erotic content of *Dracula*, and although several critics branded it 'ghoulish' and 'disgusting', not one questioned its moral or sexual content, which is amazing in view of the hullaballoo that Ibsen's *Ghosts* had caused only a few years earlier with the mere mention of venereal disease.

The simple plot of Stoker's novel sends Jonathan Harker, a young British lawyer, to Transylvania with the deed to an English estate which Count Dracula wishes to purchase. Dracula imprisons Harker and gives him to his vampire harem to feed on while he travels to England, where he mentally enslaves the madman Renfield and makes a vampire of the young aristocratic Lucy Westenra, whose father and three suitors summon the Dutch doctor Van Helsing to save Lucy's life. Lucy dies, but walks by night, seducing and preying on young children. The men open her tomb, impale her and behead her corpse. Harker's wife Mina is then besieged by Dracula, but he is destroyed by Van Helsing at the climax of the novel and Mina is saved.

Bram Stoker had read and been influenced by Abbé Calmet's *Dissertation on Vampires* and *The Phantom World*, as well as Matthew Lewis's *The Monk*, *The Castle Spectre*, and *The Mysteries of Udolfo*, but Dracula owes the specific features of his personality to the great Shakespearian actor Henry Irving, on whose charismatic personality it was based. Stoker was Irving's business manager and had known him for ten years before he wrote *Dracula*, actually modelling many facets of the character, including physical characteristics, on the actor. Irving was tall, thin, of a saturnine appearance. His voice was hypnotic – it had a metallic, sibilant quality. Many critics, including Bernard Shaw and Gordon Craig, commented on his rather curious pronunciation: a lisp, almost a foreign accent. His great roles were in spine-tingling melodramas such as *The Bells* and *The Flying Dutchman*, roles verging on the demonic and the supernatural. His portrayal of Mephistopheles in *Faust* made a deep impression on Stoker, who had been involved in some of the research in Nuremburg in preparation for this production. One of Irving's greatest gifts was his ability to strike terror into an audience. His great Shakespearian roles, as Eric Bentley notes, were those that could be interpreted simply melodramatically,[28] and had an element of the demonic – Shylock, Richard III, and most importantly for Bram Stoker, Macbeth. The great 1888 Lyceum production had a profound influence on Stoker, who was deeply involved in Irving's preparation of the role. They spent many hours discussing its finer interpretive points, and Stoker travelled to Slains Castle on Cruden Bay, a desolate, remote, and deeply superstitious part of Scotland, to soak up atmosphere for the production.

Under the spell of this performance, Stoker wove the vampire theme around the structure of *Macbeth*: the bumbling, disorganized forces of good, like a gang of boys, finally succeed in banding together to kill the evil father figure which has been devouring them.

The first dramatic version of *Dracula* was read on the stage of the Lyceum on 18 May 1897. It had been quickly adapted by Stoker to protect the copyright. Irving pronounced it 'Dreadful!' and that was the end of that.

1897 was a year of disaster for Irving. He had been knighted in the previous year, the first actor to be so honored, but in 1897 he fell down a flight of stairs, injured his leg permanently, and had to close the theatre for several weeks. Then fire consumed a Lyceum storehouse and scenery and costumes for most of the repertory were destroyed. The damage was estimated at £60,000; the insurance reimbursement was one tenth that amount. The subsequent forced closing and the emergence of rival companies bankrupted the Lyceum and Irving was forced to sell to a syndicate, which collapsed in its turn. But the major catastrophe of 1897 was his failure to recognize in Dracula the role of a lifetime. Among other things, it would have made him rich. Ill with pneumonia and pleurisy, he blamed his manager for his misfortunes and broke with Stoker.

Irving's grandson Laurence Irving sums up the relationship as follows:

> Stoker, inflated with literary and athletic pretensions, worshipped Irving with all the sentimental idolatry of which an Irishman is capable, revelling in the patronage which, as Irving's manager, was at his disposal, and in the opportunities which this position gave him to rub shoulders with the great. This weakness and his emotional impetuosity handicapped him in dealing with Irving's business affairs in a forthright and sensible manner. Irving needed, though he might not have tolerated, a partner of financial and executive ability who would keep a stern check upon the extravagances and irregularities to which a theatrical organisation of his kind was peculiarly prone. Stoker, well-intentioned, vain, impulsive, and inclined to blarneying flattery, was perhaps the only man who could have held his position as Irving's manager for so many years; from him Irving got the service he deserved but at a cost that was no less fatal because it was not immediately apparent.[29]

Perhaps Irving was embarrassed or subconsciously repulsed by the sexual content of *Dracula*. At any event he never played it, and the role has never had a great interpreter.

Dracula was successfully adapted for the stage in 1924 in Derby, England, by the actor Hamilton Deane, who perversely chose the role of Van Helsing, the Dutch scientist and the play's *raissoneur*. His version is set entirely in England, the parts of the story which transpire in Transylvania related as narrative. It was Deane's idea that the Count should appear in full evening dress. The first Dracula was Edmund Blake, but Raymond Huntley took over the role when it opened in London on 15 February 1927 at the Little Theatre, and despite tepid reviews, played 391 performances. *Era* said, 'One doubts if such a story can ever be as successful on stage as it is in print . . . It was only a tiny step from the devilish to the ridiculous . . . It is remarkably well acted, with Raymond Huntley in a terrifyingly sinister make-up as Dracula.'[30] 'A play full of incident, at times even powerful. Mr R. Huntley is capital as Dracula', said *Stage*. 'The locales have been changed from a wild continental district to more prosaic London. This . . . lessen[s] the effectiveness.'[31]

It was produced in America the same year, and Hamilton Deane acquired a co-author, John Balderson, who updated the action to the 1920s. Dracula now crosses Europe overnight in a plane to avoid sunlight. The stage play, in both the British and American versions, alters the novel by reversing the characters of Lucy and Mina, and eliminating all but a few references to the latter, who is already dead as the action begins. Harker now becomes Lucy's fiancé, saving her for the life of a proper British wife by the sincerity of his love, assisted by Van Helsing's practical know-how with garlic, holy wafers, and whatnot.

The American production, which opened on 5 October 1927 at the Fulton Theatre, starred the Hungarian actor Bela Lugosi, who would ever afterward be associated with the role, playing it more than 1,300 times, in addition to the first film version, numerous sequels, and as he fell on hard times, burlesque parodies including one with the Three Stooges. Despite his classical stage training in Hungary, Lugosi was a stiff, graceless, unimaginative actor who was made by the role rather than the reverse. American critics seemed to enjoy the play more than the British, but Lugosi's performance was universally condemned: 'Mr Lugosi performs Dracula with funereal decorum, suggesting little more than an operatically inclined but cheerless mortician than a blood-sucking fiend.'[32] 'It was a rigid hobgoblin presented resembling a wax man in a shop window [rather] than a suave ogre bent on nocturnal mischief-making.'[33] 'Westward the course of vampires makes its way . . . ye who have fits prepare to throw them now . . . A fairly callous audience quaked delightedly last night at the Fulton. Your correspondent shook like an aspen.'[34]

The great scenes of the play are the duel of wills between the doctor and the vampire, whose line, 'You are very clever, Doctor, for a man who has lived only one lifetime',[35] is the most famous of the play; Renfield's spider-eating mad scenes; Dracula's materialization in Lucy's bedroom, first as a bat, then arriving via trap-door in a puff of smoke: Lucy's metamorphosis into a 'vamp' and lunge at Harker's throat; and finally the discovery and destruction of Dracula in his coffin in a secret underground vault. It's all great hokum, and very thrilling it must have been when first shown to the world.

Judged as dramatic literature, it is a thin and plodding piece of stage-craft, fatally overburdened with three dull straightmen – the old doctor, the father, and the juvenile – who expound endlessly on their own virtue and consume stage time by eternities while we wait in near catatonic state for the interesting characters, the vampire or the girl, to appear. The structure is creakily mechanical, and the dialogue irritating in its hoked-up, commercialized religiosity. (One of Anne Rice's amusing notions in her vampire novels is that only those vampires who were devout Catholics during their mortal lives are afraid of the cross.)

There have been several revivals in America – *Dracula Sabbat* by Leon Katz in 1970, and in 1977, Bill Hall and David Richmond's *Passion of Dracula* starring Christopher Bernau at the Cherry Lane Theatre, playing concurrently with the Broadway *Dracula* with Frank Langella as the count and evocative black-and-white sets by Edward Gorey. All attempted to take the story seriously but were ultimately defeated by their own scripts.

After so much recent mauling and trivializing, especially in the movies, it is extraordinary to discover a really powerful new version of *Dracula*[36] by the Scottish poet and playwright Liz Lochhead, which opened at the Royal Lyceum Theatre in Edinburgh on 14 March 1985. Although critics complained of the three-and-a-half-hour length, they were full of admiration for Lochhead's ambitous achievement: '[She] handles the story with an almost disturbing emotional directness. Its mood emphasises the pure tragedy of Dracula's exile from human happiness, and Stoker's powerful intuition – expressed here through the atmosphere of Seward's horrible Victorian asylum – that the cruelty, bloodthirstiness, and arrogance of the vampire underworld reflect human life.'[37] Some scenes are seen through the eyes of the madman Renfield, who functions as a kind of chorus. The writing is brilliantly theatrical, even expressionistic, going below the surface of the prudish Victorian novel and the well-made prison of the melodramatic plot to the psycho-sexual truth that lies beneath. More than an *homage* to the Stoker novel, it is a penetrating and poetic meditation on his dream of Dracula. The women are drawn with great individuality, particularly the poor servants and the mad patients. Lochhead's Dracula in many ways surpasses the original. In this scene she plays deftly and poetically with 'Romanian' English:

(*A howling of wolves.*)
Dracula. Listen. Listen to the children of the night. What music they make.

Jonathan. Mus-ic?

Dracula. Ah yes, music. Not a true soul but knows its melody. By heart. The first time he hears it.

Jonathan. They curdle my blood.

Dracula. Come, come, Mr. Harker, blood is not so easily curdled. In milksop kindergartens perhaps, tales of the Big Bad Wolf might – what do you say – scare the pretty children witless? But a man whose heart has wintered enough for him to be worth something, he hears the wolf sing to the moon his own sometime desolation and it quickens the hunter in him so in his mind he runs with that grey pack in the night. Can't you see them, flowing like a ragged wind over Russia, pouring lower than the blown grasses over the steppes? Outside, in that black forest, their eyes are more than the stars and twice as secret.

. . .

Jonathan. Ordog, Pokol, Stregioca, vrolok, vlkoslak ... werewolf.

Dracula. 'Satan', 'hell', 'vampire' ... Ah, my friend, girlish superstition. I am sure your reason tells you so? I can assure you: these outside you hear howling are real wolves. All animals. Were-wolves, are-wolves, and ever-more-shall-be-wolves. (*Pause.*) Ah, Jonathan, I make a joke. Is good. No?

(i, vii)

Lochhead's Dracula is destroyed by the light of the rising sun, and the end of the play is pure surrealism: '*Shrieks and hammer blows. As it dies away with our lovers entwined on Dracula's cloak, white snow begins to fall, then blush-pink petals like apple blossoms and confetti, darker pink and finally red, red petals as the curtain falls*' (ii, xvii).

The vampire myth has a resonance, a depth of symbolism and meaning, that can still chill the spine and heat up the libido in the hands of a good writer. The vampire of today's films and television is vulgar, adolescent, and boring. The creature has forgotten its mystery and become hopelessly debased. But the vampire on stage, the black villain of melodrama, had a power to him. He was a primordial nightmare of evil – sinister, soulless, decadent – an embodiment of our ancient terrors.

When we think of the vampire today, we are more inclined to snicker than to shudder. We know everything; we have no need of images of sexual sublimation; the trashy take-offs have, vampire-like, sucked out the blood and potency of the original myth until it has finally succumbed, like the dinosaur, to the ultimate insult – it has been made cute. But, as Lochhead's new *Dracula* shows, there is something buried under all the trash that is very interesting: why are we afraid of the dead? And why, when sex is linked with death, is it so compelling?

A tall figure ... fingernails ... intense fear ... That one shriek is all that she can utter ... a heart beating ... wildly ... bosom ... eyes ... window ... she waits, frozen with horror ... long arms moving ... It is too dreadful – she tries to move ... hoarse ... whisper cry – Help – help – help – help! ... the tall gaunt figure in hideous relief ... a long gaunt hand which seems utterly destitute of flesh ... long nails that literally appear to hang from the finger

ends ... The figure turns half round ... It is perfectly white – perfectly
bloodless. The eyes look like polished tin ... the fearful-looking teeth ...
glaringly white and fanglike ... no sound comes from its lips ... But her eyes
are fascinated ... What was it? – what did it want ... Her bosom heaves ...
He advances. God of Heaven! Is it real or some dream ... a sudden rush ...
Then she screamed ... The bed-clothes fell in a heap ... Her beautiful
rounded limbs quivered ... He drags her ... forces [her head] back by the
long hair ... he seizes her neck in his fang-like teeth – a gush of blood, and a
hideous sucking noise follows. *The girl has swooned, and the vampire is at his hideous
repast!*[38]

NOTES

1 Eric Bentley, *The Life of the Drama* (New York: Atheneum, 1967), p. 176.

2 Ernest Jones, *On The Nightmare* (New York: Liveright, 1951), quoted in *The
Vampyre: Lord Ruthven to Count Dracula*, ed. Christopher Frayling (London: Gol-
lancz, 1978), pp. 323–4.

3 Ibid., p. 330.

4 Paul Barber, *Vampires, Burial and Death: Folklore and Reality* (New Haven: Yale
University Press, 1990).

5 Paul Barber, 'The Real Vampire', *Natural History* (October, 1990), pp. 79–80.

6 Pierre Carmouche, Achille Jouffrey, and Charles Nodier, *Le Vampire* (Paris: J.
N. Barba, 1820).

7 Marvin Carson, *The French Stage in the Nineteenth Century* (New York: Scarecrow,
1972), pp. 50–1.

8 Stephen Wischhusen, *The Hour of One: Six Gothic Melodramas* (London: Gordon
Fraser, 1975), pp. 167–8.

9 Ronald McFarland, 'The Vampire on Stage: A Study in Adaptations', *Comparative Drama*, 21 (1987), 21.

10 James Robinson Planché, *The Vampire: or, The Bride of the Isles* (London: John
Cumberland, 1826) reprinted in *The Hour of One: Six Gothic Melodramas*, ed.
Wischhusen.

11 *The Vampire*, play bill, 19 August 1820, Billy Rose Theatre Collection, Lincoln
Center Library for the Performing Arts, New York.

12 'The Drama', *New Monthly Magazine*, 14: 8 (1 September 1820), 321–2.

13 Ibid., p. 321.

14 William Hazlitt, 'The Drama', *The London Magazine*, 9 (September 1820), in
Victorian Dramatic Criticism, ed. George Rowell (London: Methuen, 1971), p.
204.

15 *The Simon and Schuster Book of the Opera*, ed. Arnoldo Mondadori (New York:
Simon and Schuster, 1977), pp. 1827–8.

16 Thomas Pecket Prest (or James Malcolm Rymer, authorship is disputed),
Varney the Vampire, or The Feast of Blood (1845), reprinted (New York: Dover
Publications, 1970), p. 868.

17 Arthur E. Davidson, *Alexandre Dumas: His Life and Works* (Philadelphia: J. B.
Lippencott Co., 1902), pp. 47–8.

18 Alexandre Dumas père, *Le Vampire*, in *Théâtre Complet*, vol. xi (Paris: Michel Lévy frères, 1863–74).

19 See, among others, Herbert Gorman, *The Incredible Marquis: Alexandre Dumas* (New York: Ferrar and Rinehart, 1929).

20 My translation.

21 Dion Boucicault, *The Vampire*, later shortened and retitled *The Phantom* (New York: French's Standard Drama, 1856).

22 Quoted in Walsh Townsend, *The Career of Dion Boucicault* (New York: Benjamin Blom, 1915), p. 46.

23 Quoted in Richard Fawkes, *Dion Boucicault* (London: Quartet Books, 1979), p. 75.

24 Ibid., p. 74.

25 Ibid., pp. 74–5.

26 E. F. Taylor, *Brunhilda, or Wake Not the Dead*, unpublished manuscript, Billy Rose Theatre Collection, Lincoln Center Library.

27 Bram Stoker, *Dracula* (Westminster: Constable, 1897), p. 30.

28 Bentley, *The Life of the Drama*, p. 177.

29 Laurence Irving, *Henry Irving: the Actor and his World* (London: Faber and Faber, 1951), p. 453.

30 Play review, *Era*, London, 16 February 1927.

31 Play review, *Stage*, London, 17 February 1927.

32 John Anderson, *New York Post*, 6 October 1927.

33 Percy Hammond, *New York Herald Tribune*, 6 October 1927.

34 Alexander Woolcott, *New York World*, 6 October 1927.

35 Hamilton Deane and John Balderson, *Dracula* (New York: Samuel French, 1927).

36 Liz Lochhead, *Mary Queen of Scots Got Her Head Chopped Off and Dracula* (London: Penguin, 1989).

37 Joyce McMillan, *Guardian*, 16 March 1985, in *London Theatre Record*, 5, 6.

38 Prest (or Rymer), *Varney the Vampire*, condensed and quoted in Leonard Wolf, *A Dream of Dracula: In Search of the Living Dead* (Boston: Little, Brown and Co., 1972), p. 250.

Dionysus in the afternoon: bullfighting as ritual sacrifice and tragic performance

EILEEN FISCHER

> *Pentheus.* And you – you are a bull
> who walks before me there. Horns have sprouted
> from your head. Have you always been a beast?
> But now I see a bull.
> *Dionysus.* It is the god you see.
>
> (*The Bacchae*)

America's famous *aficionado*, Ernest Hemingway, calls his informative yet artless book on bullfighting *Death in the Afternoon*. That is like calling a Greek tragedy *Clytemnestra Axes Husband in Tub*. Hemingway's emphasis on death side-steps the inherent tragic nuances of bullfighting and blunts the beauty of its Dionysian dance of death. To appreciate the tragic agony and exhilaration of an afternoon of bullfighting, spectators must accept bullfighting as an art, a performing art. Neither a sport nor a barbaric exhibition of macho man's cruelty to innocent animals, bullfighting shares its origin, structure, tragic vision, and performance significance with ancient sacrificial rituals and Greek tragedies.

Most theatre historians agree that the drama originated and evolved from sacrificial rituals. These rituals served – and serve – numerous functions: the sharing of knowledge, the influencing of weather and wombs, the appeasement of gods, the glorification of gods, heroes, and totemic animals, along with the giving of pleasure. The ritual tearing of wild animals to pieces, *sparagmos*, afforded spectators pleasurable participation through a union or communion with primal needs. In fact, members of the cult of Dionysus enjoyed, as early as the thirteenth century BC, intoxicating sacrificial rites wherein the women wore bull horns themselves.

Dionysus, the god of wine and fertility, alternately adopted the forms of a goat, lion, snake, tiger, and bull. According to Jan Kott's recounting of the myth in *The Eating of The Gods*, 'while he [Dionysus] was in the last disguise, the Titans tore him to pieces and consumed his raw flesh. Zeus killed the Titans with a flash of lightning, and of the soot that remained of the fire that burned them, men were created.'[1] This primal bullfight

26

creates humanity. Quite like the contemporary *corrida de toros* (the running
and fighting of bulls), the original Olympian bullfight gives us ourselves.

When the Greeks were no longer content to sing choral *dithyrambs* in
honor of Dionysus, they built an open-air theatre, the Theatre of Dionysus
in the city of Dionysia, for their sacrificed and sanctified bull god. There,
they reserved a special throne as altar for Dionysus and dramatized ritual
sacrifices with increased sophistication and aesthetic formality. The tragic
trilogies, presented in festival competitions, inverted the Dionysian signs
through the representation of primarily human sacrifices, rather than
those of animals. 'There is no essential difference between animal sacrifice
and human sacrifice', René Girard suggests in *Violence and The Sacred*, 'and
in many cases one is substituted for the other'.[2] From this perspective,
pagan Greek tragedies reverse the primal bullfight, while Catholic
Hispanic bullfighting retains and re-presents the manual sacrifice of Dionysus, the bull god who was also part man. In both cases, man's tragedy
emerges. Then and now, in the theatre or the *plaza de toros*, warring
elemental passions and civilization's necessities remain essentially
constant.

During festivals at the Theatre of Dionysus, competing playwrights
presented trilogies followed by satyr plays. The *archon* served as judge and
awarded the prizes. Similarly, bullfights have a tri-part or three-act structure per fight with two or three rival matadors alternately fighting two or
three bulls. The *presidente*, a festival official, orchestrates and recognizes

27

the fights' winners, and he determines their awards from his 'throne'. In a sense, the *presidente* acts like Tadeusz Kantor during a performance, for the *presidente* directs the play and players' fates without truly participating in the on-stage action.

The Greek *orchestra* (dancing–playing place) corresponds to bullfighting's sand covered *arena*. All the dramatic action happens here. A *barrera*, a four-foot or so high maroon, wooden fence, encircles the *arena*. Behind the *barrera*, a circular passageway, *callejon*, permits the players their entrances and exits. Interspersed at regular distances in front of the *barrera*, wooden squares – roughly five feet by five feet – called *burladeros* protrude and function like *skene*. The audience witnesses this theatre in the round from a wooden amphitheatre.

Quite like the Greek *parados*, the entrance of the chorus and the chorus leader, bullfighting begins with the *paseo*, the ritual entrance of the *cuadrillas*, fight teams, and their leading actors, the *matadors*. The *cuadrilla* enters to much fanfare. Trumpets blow. Drums beat. And the crowd cheers, jeers, and watches the *matador* pay homage to the *presidente* who is surrounded by the musicians and local 'dignitaries'. With a flick of his white hankerchief, the *presidente* signals the official start of the performance.

Each competing *cuadrilla* consists of the *matador* – the actual killer of the bull, a *picador*, a man on horseback who pics and stabs the bull according to the matador's instructions, and a few *banderilleros*, usually four, quick-footed men, also obedient to the matador's dictates, who tire the bull with

28

their uninspired capework and place colorful beribboned *banderillas* (yard-long harpoons) in the bull's neck and shoulders. Like actors in a subplot, the *picadors* and *banderilleros* antagonize the bull in the first and second acts of the fight before the matador comes in for the dramatic kill in the third and final act. The team also employs an *arenero*, a nearly comic, young servant boy, who has the odious job of sweeping up the bullshit. Literally.

The *toreros* (a general term applied to *all* the performers in the arena) wear spectacular brocade and sequinned costumes that glitter beneath the lighting system of the powerful sun. Far harsher, in effect, than the glare of Richard Foreman's naked on-stage light bulbs, the sun – according to a Spanish proverb – 'es el mejor torero'. Furthermore, the sun certainly ignites the *cerveza* and *tequila* which the audience drinks throughout the hot afternoon in Greek or Brechtian style.

Audience participation persists as a standard performance value in bullfighting. Some matadors, like many actors, play directly to 'the house' on occasion and very consciously seek to please the voluble audience with well-known *muleta* (red cape) tricks, favorite passes, and *veronicas* – slow, classical, and very dramatic *muleta* moves. Spectators spontaneously shout both approval and disdain for the matadors' work. Not surprisingly, Spanish *aficionados* use the word *espontáneo* to refer to the over-zealous spectator who, in Living Theatre fashion, chooses to scale the *barrera* and foolishly attempts to fight the bull and become a part of the scripted performance. 'To really start to see the bullfights, a spectator,' Hemingway claims, 'should go to the *novilladas* or apprentice fights ... At a *novillada* the spectator may see the mistakes of the bullfighters.'[3] To which we can add, there one also experiences the mistaken responses of the spectators. Cancun, Mexico offers a small-scale *novillada* or minor league bullfight with two matadors working two bulls apiece. Misguided and melodramatic identification with the bull prompts overly sentimental and probably anti-theatrical *turistas* to leave the *plaza de toros* at the first jet of bull's blood. More to the aesthetic point, spectators should respect the ritualistic tragedy unfolding and unfurling from the man's *muleta faena* (work). Or, in Eric Bentley's words, we should uncover 'the idea behind the idea'.

A bull performs once – never more. Matadors, when they are lucky, talented, and in audience demand, reappear in arenas regularly throughout the fighting season and repeatedly confront *symbolically interchangeable bulls*. Yet bulls and men both prepare and train, for years, for this one and only particular performance *agon*. The frenzied if not hysterical entrance of the wild bull into the arena signifies a virgin's ritual debut. Dancing initiation rites follow while the man instructs, inflames, tames, and finally sacrifices the virgin. The 'signifiers' mysteriously shift and 'float' during the three acts of the fight. At once, it is a cruel and phallic imitation of cruel and phallic action; it is history, Aristotelian tragedy, a 'cock-fight' of sorts, and a realization of Artaud's sensually assaulting theatre.

Hispanics call the acts of the fight of each bull *los tres tercios de la lidia*, the three thirds of combat. In the first act, the virgin bull, with unbridled Dionysian energy and ignorance of the ways of man, bursts into the arena chaotically. The Apollonian matador, on the other hand, calmly appraises his virgin and patiently waits. The matador knows that the bull will charge the *picadors* and their horses. In this scene, the bull – as quadruped – attacks the other quadruped in the arena, not the bipedal man. In a *gestus* of Sadean foreplay, the *picador*, poised on a tall horse, pierces the bull's hide without true or full penetration. At the same time, the bull gores the horse's protective padding and quickly learns the dramaturgical rules of the game. The unprotected bull, filled with animal exuberance and primitive powers, must contend with cunning men who manipulate tools of civilization – domesticated animals and weapons – during combat. Nonetheless, the bull clearly wins the first act or trial run. Here, without technology and artifice, man remains impotent in *praxis* and can not impose order upon the violent bull. The *presidente*, as performance director, decides when to close the first act.

The second act of combat, sometimes called 'the sentencing', offers thrill-seeking spectators their spectacle, the *mise en scène* of bullfighting, or

29

what Aristotle considers 'the crudest tragic element least akin to the art of poetry'. This quick act lasts for only about five spectacular moments. It begins with the bull, alone, enraged, and slightly wounded, wandering about the arena in search of his *querencia* – the spot where the bull feels most comfortable. Freedom and peace now elude the doomed bull. Necessity, Might, and Violence usurp the stage in the controlling *personae* of the *banderilleros*. These darting men enter with gaily colored harpoons and try to jab these pics in the top of the bull's neck. The pics lower the bull's head for Inevitability, personified by the matador. Without the great honor and respect bestowed upon matadors, the not very dignified *bandilleros* provide a touch of 'comic relief' while they play a sometimes laughable game of hide-and-seek with the bull. They stab the bull, occasionally miss their target, fearfully run behind the *burladeros* for safety to the hoots of the audience, and slither around the bull. Although this scene delights and invigorates the audience, it teases yet sobers the bull. When the *banderilleros* pic off-target, their *hamartia* seems comic rather than tragic; for at this point in the performance, we await and require the tragic *peripeteia*, the reversal of fortune, which the matador discloses in the third and final act of the fight. At the close of the second act, the bull receives a sacrificial death sentence.

The sacrifice of the bull promises to transform and satisfy the increas-

30

ingly violent emotions and primitive desires of the now orgiastic and bull-
like audience. 'As soon as we human beings give rein to animal nature',
George Bataille notes in *Death and Sensuality*, 'in some ways, we enter the
world of transgression forming the synthesis between animal nature and
humanity through the persistence of the taboo; we enter a sacred world, a
world of holy things.'[4] In one voice, a communal prayer and petition, the
audience cries out, begs, for the matador. Only the matador – as artist,
sacrificer, scapegoat, and savior – can protect the audience from its own
violent instincts and prevent a virtual regression to our baser, ancestral
quadrupedal selves. Wisely exercising choral moderation, then, the
presidente cuts the second act short and responds to the audience's demand.
We get the matador and realize that the role of the sacrifice, as Girard
explains, 'is to stem the rising tide of indiscriminate substitutions and
redirect violence into "proper channels"'.[5]

Performed in the sacred domain of transgressions, the third and final
act of bullfighting 'channels' tragic agony and ecstasy. Hemingway calls
this act 'the execution' and finds death in the afternoon when he
improperly ascribes the tragedy to the bull. Misreading the performance

script, Hemingway believes that 'the spectators pay to see the tragedy of the bull, not the man'.[6] By focusing on the bull's tragedy – which is not necessarily tragic – instead of man's tragic choice and the spiritually ennobling denouement of the act, Hemingway (ever visionless and *mucho macho* man that he was) overlooks the 'resurrection' at the threshold of life and death.

With his scarlet *muleta* and finally his sword, the matador works the bull in the last act. The word *faena* encompasses all the fancy cape, foot, and sword co-ordination of the third act. Slowed and wounded, the bull charges the *muleta* which the matador skillfully weaves through the air. At this point, the matador drives the bull as well as the audience wild with graceful moves and expertly calculated risks. Each pass tires and exasperates the bull who now charges, if the matador performs courageously, closer and closer to the man's belly. Often, the bull's blood from the pic wounds of act ɪɪ stain the matador's midriff. When the matador executes a visibly dangerous pass, the audience gasps and sighs as one. The inevitable *peripeteia* occurs when both the matador and bull, along with the audience *aficionados*, 'know' that the man will soon 'have' and control the virgin bull. Wordlessly, the reversal of fortune and *anagnorisis*, or recognition scene, come together. No longer impelled with seemingly boundless energies, the bull now obeys the matador. As performance artist, the matador milks this episode for as much drama as possible.

The recognition scene conforms to Aristotle's tragic requirements, for the man and bull find themselves in an altered relationship. The change, using Aristotle's words from the *Poetics*, 'from ignorance to knowledge of a bond of love or hate' proceeds by 'virtue of blood ties'. Smeared with his antagonist's blood, the matador recognizes that the noble bull deserves love and respect – not death. But it is too late. The sword has been drawn. Even though the bull possesses complementary strengths, performing abilities, courage, and phallic vitality, the matador must kill him. The matador must kill the animal god who mirrors man's image of himself. Girard's thought pertains: 'The sacrificer and his victim are recognized as doubles.'[7] They discover that their tragic bond will unify and liberate them through the sword's inter-penetration.

At the performance threshold of life and death, man and bull prolong their dance of death. Their beautiful duet expresses agony and tragic exhilaration. Should the matador momentarily become clumsy, display *hubris*, or thrust off-target, the bull can kill or, more likely, gore the man. But this is not probable. In bullfighting as performance, Hemingway correctly notes that it is 'the only art in which the artist is in danger of death ... and the degree of brilliance in the performance is left to the fighter's honor'.[8] *Honor* sounds like a well-chosen word in this context.

With signs reversed and doubles disclosed, an honorable kill becomes a performance necessity. Sensitive to each other's moving bodies and cues, the man and bull proudly show the audience their concerted physical and technical virtuosity. In the highly theatrical pass *cambio de rodillas*, the matador kneels on one or both knees while the bull rushes the *muleta*. This genuflecting pass overwhelms the spectators. *Tremendum*, the apprehension or revelation of the sacred commingling with death and sensuality, descends upon the arena and respectfully hushed amphitheatre. The spectators await 'the *faena* that takes a man out of himself and makes him feel immortal ... that gives him an ecstasy, that is, while momentary, as profound as any religious ecstasy; moving all the people in the ring together and increasing emotional intensity as it proceeds'.[9] Given such a transporting *faena*, the dancers, the dance, and the audience converge.

When the sacrifice can no longer be postponed, when the tragic agony and pathos grow unbearably intense, the matador acts upon his tragic choice. The 'moment of truth' comes through the sword's fatal, yet oddly loving, thrust. If performed ideally, the final stroke enables the matador to levitate, like Grotowski's actors, over the bull's horns. This entrancing thrust, known as *volapié*, unites the flying man and the dying bull. The penetrating sword connects the sacrificer and his victim: the double. One ascends when the other falls. As tragic performance rite, the mystically achieved and transferred resurrection at the moment of sacrifice 'is directed toward order and tranquility, not violence. It strives to achieve violence solely in order to eliminate it.' Girard continues, 'to see these rites as expressions of man's pathological morbidity is to miss the point'.[10] Performance, however, illuminates the point.

On stage, all we can do with death is re-present and theatricalize it. In performance spaces such as theatres and *plazas de toros*, actors, matadors, and bulls continually re-enact primal sacrifices for us. In theatrical performance, death remains repetitive. Dionysus as bull, man, and god lives, dies, and survives death in the afternoon.

NOTES

1 Jan Kott, *The Eating of The Gods*, trans. Boleslaw Taborski (New York: Vintage Books, 1974), p. 196.

2 René Girard, *Violence and The Sacred*, trans. Patrick Gregory (Baltimore: Johns Hopkins University Press, 1977), p. 10.

3 Ernest Hemingway, *Death In The Afternoon* (New York: Charles Scribner's Sons, 1932, 1960), p. 17.

4 George Bataille, *Death and Sensuality* (New York: Ballantine Books, 1962), p. 79.

5 Girard, *Violence and the Sacred*, p. 10.

6 Hemingway, *Death in the Afternoon*, p. 96.

7 Girard, *Violence and the Sacred*, p. 132.

8 Hemingway, *Death in the Afternoon*, p. 91.

9 Ibid, p. 206.

10 Girard, *Violence and the Sacred*, pp. 132 and 103.

Modern melodrama: the living heritage in the theatre of John Arden and Margaretta D'Arcy*

ELIZABETH HALE WINKLER

1. The melodramatic heritage

As every critic of theatre knows, the traditions of Victorian melodrama never disappeared entirely in the twentieth century, in spite of the advent of realism in drama. Playwrights such as George Bernard Shaw, Sean O'Casey and Bertolt Brecht retained many elements of melodramatic technique and passed them on to generations of artists after World War II. Of all the various elements of melodrama, two in particular have appealed to dramatists of the middle and late twentieth century: firstly the use of music (which gave the genre its name) as one of the many elements of non-realistic staging; and secondly the characteristically simplified world of values, in which all judgments are clearcut, characters are two-dimensionally good or evil, and, in Michael Booth's words, 'dream justice' prevails at the end.[1]

The first characteristic, music, in association with other elements such as dance, or emblematic staging, proves to be useful to all those trying to escape the confining conventions of realism, those trying to re-establish a more exciting, perhaps sensational, form of total theatre, regardless of their political ideology. The second characteristic, the use of absolute, uncomplicated, clearcut value judgments, appeals to committed drama-tists, especially to those working within political alternative theatre, to those who wish to create a form of political drama without wasting time with complications, doubts and ambiguities. James L. Smith distinguishes between problem plays, which try to present all sides of an issue sympathetically, and protest theatre, which has always used a 'melodram-atic structure of experience' to drive home political points.[2] Both tendencies survive in postwar British theatre, and both can be well illustrated in the work of the dramatists John Arden and Margaretta D'Arcy. Arden's early work, as well as the later collaborations of Arden and D'Arcy, provide some of the best examples of melodrama in the

* A draft of this paper was read at the *Themes in Drama* International Conference held at the University of California, Riverside, in February 1990.

contemporary period of British theatre. The playwrights draw not only on Brecht and O'Casey but also on their own extensive knowledge of theatrical and musical traditions, especially from the nineteenth century. They have helped to create a climate of experimentation from which many younger dramatists have profited.

Arden, in a 1975 essay on Sean O'Casey, reflects on some of the traditions which he has inherited through O'Casey. Arden points out that the pictorial, symbolic style of O'Casey's later plays is derived ultimately, via Dion Boucicault and John Bunyan, from Shakespeare and the Morality tradition. Arden argues that O'Casey's 'dramatic iconography' should be translated into stage images of the type of the Victorian Toy Theatre, clearly emblematic, in primary colors, with firm outlines. However he emphasizes that such emblems are used by O'Casey not with any implications of Victorian morality, but in the interests of a progressive world view:

> O'Casey constructs an entire world, seen in primary colours and arranged in long-established traditional images, in order to present a new analysis of society.[3]

Arden's own development also shows experimentation with theatrical vocabulary, first to create more poetry, excitement and anarchy in theatre, then, in the later phase of his development and in collaboration with his wife Margaretta D'Arcy, in the interests of their own Marxist socialism. The musical element is present from the very beginning of Arden's career; in his pieces created together with D'Arcy both the musical and political aspects of melodrama become intensified. There is scarcely any Arden play which does not contain some song or music, and several are predominantly musical. Several of the dramas are subtitled 'melodramas' and make considerable use of both on-stage song and background musical accompaniment. The works bearing the generic designation 'melodrama' include one of Arden's earlier plays, *The Workhouse Donkey* (1963), one early Arden and D'Arcy collaboration, *The Hero Rises Up* (1968), and two of the later collaborative political pieces, *Vandaleur's Folly* and *The Little Gray Home in the West* (both 1978).

Some of Arden's early plays, for example *Serjeant Musgrave's Dance* or *Armstrong's Last Goodnight*, contain an intense lyricism which has attracted much critical praise. An equally important vein in his early work, one which not all critics appreciate as much as the poetic lyricism, is the melodramatic vein of spectacular staging, especially the use of pictorial and musical elements to create his brand of what Arden calls 'Dionysian' or 'vital' theatre, in other words a form of total theatre. None of these early works, however, approaches the melodramatic mindset of black-and-white judgments. In fact the early Arden plays and the early collaborations are characteristically complex, ambiguous, and morally undecided. Michael Cohen convincingly demonstrates that the political tendencies in Arden's earlier work must be seen as anarchic pacifism.[4] The music in Arden and D'Arcy's earlier drama functions primarily as either disruptive force or as ironic, critical commentary; this contrasts to the music of melodrama, which is used to intensify emotional situations and even supplant dialogue.[5]

As the dramatists become more clearly committed to their own socialist ideal, their use of the melodramatic tradition shifts somewhat. The moral and political world portrayed becomes increasingly clearcut, seen in the mental dimensions of melodrama. Javed Malick demonstrates that *The Island of the Mighty*, a vast and elaborate trilogy which the playwrights worked on for a good decade before it was finally performed in 1972, is the first major work which embodies a polarized universe, clearly divided into antithetical groupings of oppressors and oppressed.[6] This trilogy, although not called a melodrama by the authors, exhibits many features of the genre in its extensive use of song and background music, and also in its antithetically ordered universe.

Of course the issues in all the later works are radically different from those of nineteenth-century melodrama. Like O'Casey, Arden and D'Arcy use long-established traditional techniques to convey new progressive political views. Whereas traditional melodrama tended to be romantic and escapist, Arden and D'Arcy's political melodrama confronts contemporary realities, especially the conflict in Northern Ireland. The similarity between the traditional and modern political melodrama lies in the fact that the issues are clearcut in both, seen in terms of good and evil. In some respects political melodrama here approaches agit-prop. The movement towards more consciously political playwriting in the later collaborations intensifies the political thrust of the music. Here the message of the lyrics and the overall intention of the authors dominate the play; both the dramatic form and the music serve as vehicles for the transmission of the political message.

A recent West German dissertation by Michael Göring examines the function of music and other elements of traditional melodrama in the work of Arden and D'Arcy. Göring attempts to integrate the methodology of structuralist genre criticism into a new theory of melodrama. He discusses Tzvetan Todorov's distinction between theoretical genres and historical genres, and draws in part on Klaus Hempfer's structuralist theory of genre which differentiates between unchanging structures or generic invariants and changing historical variants.[7] Göring isolates what he terms the underlying structural patterns of melodrama: the pattern of conflict (by which he means the externalized conflict of melodrama as compared to the internalized conflict of tragedy); pattern of action (polarized, antithetical clash of good and evil); moral pattern (the perfect system of rewards and punishments); emotional pattern (singleness of feeling); and lastly performance pattern (techniques designed to intensify the emotional effect). Ironically, Göring concludes that musical background, the element which provided Arden with his initial access to the melodramatic tradition, is not in fact a generic invariant of the genre but merely one of the possible historical techniques for intensifying its emotional reception. Göring does, however, concede that it is the music which proves Arden's most consistent link to melodrama.[8]

Arden may be seen as a seminal influence in passing on earlier traditions of music in drama to the postwar generations of playwrights. Katharine J. Worth comments:

> A thoroughgoing musical style didn't really emerge in the postwar theatre ... until writers like Arden appeared on the scene. So far as form is concerned, he was the great revolutionary among the playwrights of the 1956 burst, the one who made the most sustained and radical break with realism.[9]

Arden's early interest in music in drama is intimately related to his plea for poetry in the theatre. Arden is perhaps the most articulate advocate of poetic drama in the contemporary British theatre. For Arden, poetic theatre means essentially a non-realistic, non-psychological form of theatre, a popular theatre which is openly and unabashedly aware of its own artificiality:

> The essential artificiality of the public stage will become apparent again ... People must want to come to the Theatre *because* of the artificiality, not despite it ... I am pleading for the revival of the Poetic Drama.[10]

Arden wishes to engage his audience not just in an intellectual manner but to appeal to the emotions and all the senses as well:

> Vital Theatre consists of plays which must be organic events – to get hold of their audiences by laughter, by pain, by music, dancing, poetry, visual excitement, rhythm: and occupy not merely the minds of the people ... but their stomachs and their loins as well.[11]

As Arden explains in his famous introduction to *The Workhouse Donkey* he ideally envisions a form of theatre which is loosely structured, musical, comic, and engages the audience in a more active fashion than 'legitimate' twentieth-century proscenium arch theatre:

> I would have been happy had it been possible for *The Workhouse Donkey* to have lasted, say, six or seven or thirteen hours ... and for the audience to come and go throughout the performance ... A theatre presenting such an entertainment would, of course, need to offer rival attractions as well, and would in fact take on some of the characteristics of a fairground or amusement park ... I am convinced that if what we ... call 'vital theatre' is ever to live up to its name, some such casual or 'prom-concert' conception must eventually be arrived at.[12]

Musicality is an essential part of Arden's attempt to recreate 'vital' or 'Dionysian' theatre, a theatre of 'disorder', 'corruption' and 'fertility', to name a few of the attributes he lists in his introduction to the play. The music is one of the primary means of creating disorder and anarchy in the traditional dramatic structure.

As Arden and D'Arcy elucidated in a personal interview with me in 1984, they draw inspiration for their work, musically and theatrically, from the folk and ballad heritage, from the traditions of eighteenth-century ballad opera, nineteenth-century opera and melodrama, and the classical choral societies which are strong in the north of England and Wales. The ballad opera provides the model for *The Hero Rises Up*. Opera is seen by Arden and D'Arcy as 'musical melodrama', and they emphasize the popular appeal of opera outside of London. From the standpoint of their later, radically political consciousness, Arden and D'Arcy have come to see these popular theatrical and musical traditions as models for the celebration of working-class culture. With respect to melodrama the dramatists value the strong, black-and-white character portrayal, the heightened cultural expression, and the sense of dignity. They feel that they are carrying on a working-class tradition ignored by other left-wing dramatists such as John McGrath. After a visit to India in 1969, Arden and D'Arcy have also come to favor a driving, rhythmic percussion accompaniment derived from Indian folk plays and Indian film music.[13]

11. Dionysian theatre

The Workhouse Donkey is Arden's most thoroughly musical early play, and the first one which he calls a 'Vulgar Melo-drama'; he explains his use of the concept as 'a term I intend to be understood in its original sense of a play with a musical accompaniment'.[14] Arden adds: 'It's not a musical by any manner of means, but it has this integrated music with it.'[15] By 'not a musical' he is both emphasizing its difference from the more superficial entertainment of this kind and pointing out the primary importance of the text over the music. By calling it a 'melodrama' on the other hand, he wishes to call attention to the crucial role of the musical accompaniment and the songs. He continues:

> I'm also using some shreds from English music-hall and pantomime tradition, which are more apparent when the play's staged than when you read it because there is a sort of running musical background ... which sometimes becomes the accompaniment to songs and sometimes is just played behind speech.[16]

It is important to note that a loose dramatic structure and an extensive use of theatrical music are already characteristics of Arden's early work. Although these elements increase in the later collaborative plays, they are not entirely due to Margaretta D'Arcy's influence, as some critics claim.

Reminiscent of melodrama, Arden's characterizations in *The Workhouse Donkey* are larger than life. The major figure of the play, local Labour politician and ex-Mayor Charlie Butterthwaite, represents not just vulgarity, anarchy, and corruption, but also lust, good humor and zest for life; in addition he is a scapegoat and Christ parody. He clashes with the newly appointed Chief of Police, Feng, a man of unbelievable integrity and moral principles, until finally both are destroyed. But Arden's moral universe is not that of melodrama; each man commands an amount of sympathy and even respect. As in most of Arden's early plays, there are no heroes or villains in *The Workhouse Donkey*. Arden himself explains his method of characterization in words which make his distance from the easy judgments of melodrama quite clear:

> If you dramatize a conflict and you say, one side . . . is white, the other side is black . . . then you will give your side an easy walkover . . . Why not be fair?[17]

Arden uses elements of melodrama not just in music and song and in the larger-than-life character portrayal but also in the emphasis on visual aspects of performance. The style of staging in *The Workhouse Donkey* demands broad, melodramatic strokes. The play has dozens of characters and a labyrinthine plot, and demands to be played at a swift pace. Song, dance, comic turns and sensational revelations all follow one another quickly, and need to be staged, as John Russell Taylor rightly points out, with 'a few incisive strokes of bright colour to indicate what the main focuses of attention should be'.[18] Arden emphasizes that the decor should be kept to a minimum, and that 'both costumes and settings may have a certain air of caricature'.[19] In a 1963 interview concerning *The Workhouse Donkey* Arden says:

> Of course I am influenced by the nineteenth century theatre to some extent; I don't mean so much the plays as the approach to the theatre, the type of staging, the strong lines of character drawing and plot.[20]

For the first time in his work, Arden here calls for a band to play the musical accompaniment. In the original production, this was placed 'on an upper balcony of the stage and remained in view of the audience throughout the action', very much in the Brechtian manner.[21] Thus Arden combines nineteenth-century tradition with distinctly modern distancing techniques. The actors would signal to the band when they wanted a tune. Except for a few traditional tunes, the songs and the background music were written by the theatrical composer John Addison.

Addison's musical score, which I have examined, demonstrates many uses of music which are similar to nineteenth-century melodrama.[22] Music is not only frequently used during scene changes but also to cover over transitions within scenes. We often find musical accompaniment to particularly significant speeches. In most cases the music emphasizes moments of heightened dramatic tension or satirical climax. In *The Work-house Donkey*, however, most of the musical climaxes are comic, rather than sentimental or terrifying as in nineteenth-century melodrama. The primary function of the music in this play is not emotional but satiric or ironic.

The Workhouse Donkey uses not just background musical accompaniment in the manner described, but also introduces many songs sung on stage. These tend strongly to stylization and theatricalism, and are employed in a variety of introductory, explanatory and commentary functions. Band and song contribute to the comic theatrical ritual when Butterthwaite makes his processional entrance to the saloon bar of the Victoria and Albert. Butterthwaite's final exit is also accomplished in a ritual procession. Arrayed as a carnival Lord of Misrule, costumed in a tablecloth and paper chain with a ring of flowers on his head, he is carried out forcibly through the aisle singing 'Out He Goes the Poor Old Donkey'. The processional songs here create a formal musical framework for the play, spanning a bridge between beginning and end, and emphasizing the theatrical opening and closing of the action. The melodramatic elements are thus paired with a decidedly anti-illusionistic, ironic consciousness.

Such writing indicates the liveliness, musicality, and humor of Arden's performance imagination. These are essential to the vitality of his theatre on the stage. In a melodrama such as *The Workhouse Donkey* the reader must necessarily exercise his or her theatrical, visual and musical imagination in order to appreciate the effect. In this type of theatre there really is no substitute for live performance.

The first full-fledged collaboration between Arden and D'Arcy for professional theatre, *The Hero Rises Up*, is subtitled 'A Romantic Melodrama'. Like *The Workhouse Donkey*, it is related to the nineteenth-century tradition in its constant use of music and its spectacular staging, but not in its moral universe. As in the former play, the major figures are psychologically complex rather than two-dimensional. The conception of *The Hero Rises Up* is based on contradictions and ironies, contradictions in the character of the hero, Admiral Lord Nelson, and ironies concerning the whole idea of romantic heroism. Albert Hunt comments:

> Into the melodrama has been injected a detached and ironic intelligence, which uses the form both to celebrate and to question an English myth ... On the one hand there's all the genuine panache and extravagance of a heroic melodrama: and on the other hand, there's the cool, ironic distancing of the events shown.[23]

Nelson is similar to Butterthwaite in *The Workhouse Donkey* in that he is boldly drawn, both attractive and repulsive at the same time. He is heroic and imaginative, but also trivial, weak, and adulterous. The ironic distancing of characters and events is achieved in part through the figure of Nelson's step-son Nisbet who acts as a commentator. But much of the distancing is achieved by musical means: discrepancy between tunes and texts, discrepancy between original words and new words, ironical musical quotations and satiric musical thrusts.

In *The Hero Rises Up* the musical element is as important as the dramatic; indeed, it could be called semi-operatic. Its nature is determined by its music to a greater extent than even *The Workhouse Donkey*. At first entitled *Trafalgar*, it was conceived of as a musical to which American composers were to write the song music. In the end, it turned out to be a play firmly based in English, rather than American traditions of musical theatre. When the Broadway arrangements fell through, Arden and D'Arcy decided to turn the piece into an eighteenth-century-type ballad opera. The drama achieves much of its special flavor through traditional eighteenth-century tunes. The play thus represents an amalgamation of the musical and dramatic traditions of the ballad opera, opera and melodrama.

The final chorus is melodramatic and ironic simultaneously. The title song of the drama, 'The Hero Rises Up', is sung to an eighteenth-century patriotic air. The resurrected hero ascends to heaven in a chariot shaped like a sea shell, with his wife on one arm, his mistress on the other, and a mermaid at the front. Suddenly, the singing players become 'conscious of their own artificiality', but they rally to complete the 'fa la la' chorus in unison.[24] Göring calls this ending a parody of the traditional melodramatic happy end; conventional elements such as 'poetic justice', elaborate costuming, music and concluding tableau are consciously used to anti-illusionistic effect.[25] Altogether we may say that the musical elements emphasize both the romantic, emotional and the critical, ironic aspects of the play. *The Hero Rises Up* is in effect a most extraordinary mixture of elements: it is a play which draws much of its material dramatically and musically from the eighteenth century, treats this material in a theatrical manner derived from both eighteenth-century ballad opera and nineteenth-century melodrama, and achieves in the end a distinctively twentieth-century critical and ironic perspective.

III. Political melodrama

Corresponding to the shift in political consciousness of Arden and D'Arcy to radical Marxism in the late 1960s we may observe a shift in their melodrama towards a more radical political intention. In the period beginning in the early 1970s they produced several pieces which can be termed political melodrama. Most of the dramatic works which they wrote during this period are set in Ireland and are concerned with Irish themes. In part this new focus is also due to the renewal of political violence in Northern Ireland during the same period. The musical and melodramatic elements remain strong, as can be seen in the subtitle, 'Anglo-Irish Melodrama', given to two of these works, *Vandaleur's Folly* and *The Little Gray Home in the West*. The latter is a revision of the earlier *The Ballyqombeen Bequest* (1972), which had to be withdrawn from performance due to a libel suit. The tunes in these Irish plays are drawn from traditional sources, mostly music hall and folk song, and the dramatists call for unaccompanied singing in the traditional manner. In addition, there is some improvised, rhythmic music for which the inspiration came from far-eastern, specifically Indian theatre and film. This improvised percussion music is designed, according to the playwrights, to guide the audience's emotions and to mold them into a collective.

In contrast to the earlier plays discussed, the melodramatic heritage is now also seen in the black-and-white method of characterization. This borders on caricature in the case of some of the politically undesirable, i.e. villain, figures. The political views of the authors have crystallized; the stylization of characters is far more extreme than in the earlier plays. The ideology of these political melodramas, with their clearcut distinctions between right and wrong, is much closer to the mentality of traditional nineteenth-century melodrama than to the mindset of the anarchic, ambiguous melodramas discussed earlier.

The Little Gray Home in the West concerns the exploitation of the Irish by English absentee landlords and the collusion of some Irish men and women with the English establishment. (The libel suit was brought against Arden and D'Arcy by a landlord specifically named in a theatrical handout.) Essentially, the play shows a world in which the rich exploit the poor. It is difficult to see any good in the class enemy, the capitalist–exploiter–businessman–landlord named Baker-Fortescue. Still, plot, action and style remain quite complex. Albert Hunt comments:

> If the world-view of the play is simple, the detailed analysis – the way in which [the dramatists] show the tangled structures of Irish society – is both subtle and masterly.[26]

In spite of the serious political and didactic content of these Anglo-Irish melodramas, the spirit of comedy and even farce is constantly present throughout. This combination of simplified world view and comic dramatic manner is, in my judgment, problematic. Baker-Fortescue is treated realistically to the extent that he survives to continue his exploitation elsewhere. But he is also seen farcically and subjected to a great deal of ridicule. The entire play ends with a non-realistic resurrection scene, followed by a farcical custard pie fight. On this level, there is hope for eventual socialist justice, as the capitalist villain 'makes his exit in a grotesque tumble', slipping on a custard pie.[27] There is some doubt in my mind, however, whether this farcical treatment of the melodramatic villain really achieves the critical purpose the playwrights intend.

This fusion of politics, theatrical spectacle, farce and music is a visual and aural expression of Arden and D'Arcy's deeply rooted conviction that political drama must be theatrically entertaining or it has failed its purpose. The combination of stylized comedy with a serious and critical political intention is reminiscent of the dramatic method of the later O'Casey, for example in *Purple Dust*, which combined song, music, dance, and comedy with socialist purpose. In O'Casey, however, the positive forces of innovation and renewal are generally given greater imaginative and lyrical expression, and there is a certain sympathy with many of the figures of outmoded life about to be swept away. The ridicule is tempered with human pity. In Arden and D'Arcy the humor seems more forced and sterile, and somewhat out of place where the characters are portrayed as thoroughgoing villains. A villain demands to be taken seriously and fought with bitter energy.

Vandaleur's Folly, like the other Irish plays, embodies a wide variety of disparate theatrical elements. Its political content is entirely serious: it is the examination of a real event, an early historical experiment in communal farming in the west of Ireland inspired by Robert Owen. The experiment collapsed suddenly 'just like the denouement of a melodrama of the same period', as the dramatists comment in their preface.[28] Arden and D'Arcy's political position is clear: the experiment was admirable and should not have been allowed to fail merely because one landlord, Vandaleur, was weak and irresponsible. The major villain figure is again called Baker-Fortescue, and is again an absentee landlord. He is a malicious, vicious political plotter and even a rapist. The dramatical treatment, however, is once again oddly mixed: he is caricatured and ridiculed mercilessly – at one point his pants are shot off – but at the end he is forced to commit suicide. At times the farcical treatment of his character distracts from the more important issues, even more crucially than in *The Little Gray Home in the West*. The villain of melodrama at least was generally taken seriously and was opposed in a series of traumatic and violent struggles.

The manner of presentation includes multiple incongruous elements: music and song as integral parts of the drama; farcical moments; exaggerated, type characterization; a complex plot; and multiple ironies. It is written in a totally theatrical convention. Two reviewers complain:

> The play that is produced from this fertile ground is a confused and over-long burlesque melodrama, the style of which is ridiculously at odds with much of the serious subject matter.[29]

Indeed, the humor is applied indiscriminately to all characters and actions.

Although the dramatists have subtitled their piece 'An Anglo-Irish Melodrama' and the setting and main lines of the plot are Irish, they have introduced several fictional threads of subplot which are American and which give the play as a whole, musically and theatrically, a distinctly American touch. It might more accurately be termed an 'Irish-American Melodrama'. The combination does not work as well in *Vandaleur's Folly* as it does in *The Little Gray Home in the West*. Nor is *Vandaleur's Folly* as effective as *The Non-Stop Connolly Show*, a more serious, though equally musical and spectacular six-part epic treatment of the great labour leader, James Connolly. Perhaps, in addition to the indiscriminate and unsympathetic humor, the major difficulty in *Vandaleur's Folly* is the introduction of the American component which seems to confuse the issue both politically and musically.

Arden and D'Arcy's experimental style has proved influential particularly for younger playwrights working within political alternative theatre. John McGrath, for example, acknowledges the inspiration of the early Arden's musicality, and later Arden and D'Arcy collaborated with McGrath's 7:84 Theatre Company. Playwrights such as Steeve Gooch, David Edgar, Caryl Churchill, Barrie Keeffe, or Alan Plater and political or feminist companies such as 7:84, Belt and Braces, Red Ladder, or Monstrous Regiment almost routinely came to integrate music and song into their performances, partly due to the climate of theatrical and musical experimentation encouraged by Arden and D'Arcy.

While the dramatists are not the only forces at work in musical theatre – directors such as Joan Littlewood must obviously also be recognized – they are among the most diversified writers in the contemporary period. Their labyrinthine plots and multiple layers of irony are combined with a variety of musical forms derived from ballad opera, opera, melodrama, the choral tradition, music hall, and last but not least traditional English and Irish folk music. Albert Hunt claims:

> No other British playwrights have the ... breadth of historical vision, the dramatic inventiveness and the sheer theatrical *knowledge* of D'Arcy and Arden.[30]

In spite of their clear-cut political views and their melodramatic confrontation of good and evil, the later work of Arden and D'Arcy is dramatically seldom simplistic in the way that political alternative theatre sometimes tends to be. Arden and D'Arcy continually surprise with the inventiveness of their theatrical and musical imagination. Needless to say, none of this is easy to put on stage, especially since the artists have very precise ideas about the style of production they want: not just the general thrust of the political message but also the details of kind of music and the type of costumes and staging. The continuous history of production problems in England is symptomatic of their innovative dramatic style.

Critical responses to Arden and D'Arcy's later melodramatic style have been sporadic and often influenced by political likes and dislikes.[31] Due to the writers' withdrawal from the professional London theatre, the performance evidence is scanty. I believe that it would require a melodramatic imagination to stage these plays adequately. Even so, perhaps the diffuse aim of the comedic element and the lack of musical focus might create problems. Nineteenth-century melodrama was nothing if not coherent; the music indicated to the audience exactly what to feel at the appropriate moments, and the relaxation of comedy was seldom allowed when the villain was on stage. In spite of such reservations the fact remains that Arden and D'Arcy have done much to restore to the theatre its older variety of idiom. Many younger dramatists have learned from them the excitement of total theatre and the usefulness of political melodrama for the present day.

NOTES

1 Michael R. Booth, *English Melodrama* (London: Herbert Jenkins, 1965), p. 14.
2 James L. Smith, *Melodrama* (London: Methuen, 1973), p. 72.
3 John Arden, 'Ecce Hobo Sapiens: O'Casey's Theatre', in *Sean O'Casey: A Collection of Critical Essays*, ed. Thomas Kilroy (Englewood Cliffs, NJ: Prentice Hall, 1975), pp. 73–4.
4 Michael Cohen, 'The Politics of the Earlier Arden', *Modern Drama*, 28: 2 (June 1985), 198–210.
5 On the music of melodrama see especially David Mayer, 'The Music of Melodrama', in *Performance and Politics in Popular Drama*, ed. David Bradby, Louis James and Bernard Sharratt (Cambridge University Press, 1980), pp. 49–63 and Booth, *English Melodrama*, pp. 36–9.
6 Javed Malick, 'The Polarized Universe of "The Island of the Mighty": The Dramaturgy of Arden and D'Arcy', *New Theatre Quarterly*, 2: 5 (February 1986), 38–53.
7 See Tzvetan Todorov, *The Fantastic: A Structural Approach to a Literary Genre*, trans. Richard Howard (Cleveland: The Press of Case Western Reserve University, 1973), p. 13; and Klaus W. Hempfer, *Gattungstheorie: Information und Synthese* (Munich: Fink, 1973).
8 Michael Göring, *Melodrama Heute: Die Adaption melodramatischer Elemente und Strukturen im Werk von John Arden und Arden/D'Arcy* (Amsterdam: Grüner, 1986), pp. 73–90 and 194. See also Thomas G. Winner, 'Structural and Semiotic

Genre Theory', in *Theories of Literary Genre*, ed. Joseph P. Strelka (University Park: Pennsylvania State University Press, 1978), pp. 254–68.

9 Katharine J. Worth, *Revolutions in Modern English Drama* (London: Bell, 1972), p. 126.

10 John Arden, 'The Reps and New Plays', *New Theatre Magazine*, 1: 2 (January 1960), 25.

11 John Arden, 'Correspondence' to the Editor, *Encore*, 20 (May–June 1959), 42.

12 John Arden, 'Author's Preface' to *The Workhouse Donkey*, in Arden, *Plays: One* (London: Methuen, 1977), p. 113.

13 Most of the information summarized in this paragraph was provided by Arden and D'Arcy in an unpublished interview with me on 9 May 1984.

14 'Author's Preface' to *The Workhouse Donkey*, p. 112.

15 'Arden of Chichester: John Arden talks to Frank Cox about *The Workhouse Donkey* at Chichester this month', *Plays and Players* (August 1963), p. 18.

16 Ibid.

17 John Arden, 'On Comedy', *Encore* (September–October 1965), p. 15, as quoted in Albert Hunt, *Arden: A Study of His Plays* (London: Methuen, 1974), pp. 80–1.

18 John Russell Taylor, 'Back to Melodrama', *Plays and Players* (September 1963), p. 36.

19 'Author's Preface' to *The Workhouse Donkey*, p. 112.

20 'Arden of Chichester', p. 18.

21 'Author's Preface' to *The Workhouse Donkey*, p. 112.

22 I have consulted the score of Addison's music, which is available on request from the composer's agents at London Management, 235–41 Regent Street, London W1A 2JT.

23 Hunt, *Arden: A Study of His Plays*, pp. 128 and 132.

24 John Arden and Margaretta D'Arcy, *The Hero Rises Up* (London: Methuen, 1969), p. 102.

25 Göring, *Melodrama Heute*, pp. 232–4.

26 Hunt, *Arden: A Study of His Plays*, p. 155.

27 Margaretta D'Arcy and John Arden, *The Little Gray Home in the West* (London: Pluto, 1982), p. 72.

28 Margaretta D'Arcy and John Arden, 'Preface' to *Vandaleur's Folly* (London: Eyre Methuen, 1981), p. v.

29 Tony Allen and Mary Ann Lysaght, 'Vandaleur's Folly', *Plays and Players* (February 1979), p. 33.

30 Albert Hunt, 'Passions and Issues', *New Society* (18 January 1979), p. 151.

31 The most balanced view of the dramatists' later work is provided by Henry I. Schvey, 'From Paradox to Propaganda: The Plays of John Arden', in *Essays on Contemporary British Drama*, ed. Hedwig Bock and Albert Wertheim (Munich: Hueber, 1981), pp. 47–70.

Structure of melodrama

WILLIAM SHARP

Most modern critics who have concerned themselves with melodrama have been primarily concerned with effect. When structure is explored as Heilman does, his primary concern is to compare the tragic hero to the melodramatic hero and to describe the kind of things that happen to each kind of hero.[1] His major distinction, and certainly a useful one, between tragic and melodramatic heroes, is that the former are concerned with inner struggles and the latter with outer ones. Hamlet's problems, for example, are centered in his own duality of conscience, as Heilman would say a 'dividedness'. Melodramatic heroes are not bothered by their conscience but by outside forces. Maurya, in *Riders to the Sea*, for example, is forced to face the death of her last son, and with no particular debate in her conscience she accepts this death and comes to terms with the world she lives in without him. And so she is a melodramatic heroine.

Clearly, if we are to consider a play like *Riders to the Sea* as Heilman and Smith do, we are not talking simply about the clichéd description of a form which limits itself to mustache-twirling villains who tie innocent maidens to railroad tracks but are foiled by virtuous heroes who untie them.[2] The melodramatic form, as I see it, is at least as old as *The Oresteia* of Aeschylus and for me includes Shakespeare's *Macbeth*. I think the lack of structural discussion is primarily due to critics' refusal to take the world that melodrama presents seriously. This leads to the assumption that heroes in that world cannot be taken seriously and so melodrama cannot be taken seriously. The biggest problem with such a position is the large body of excellent drama that gets ignored. I think drama can be structurally limited to three forms – comedy, tragedy, and melodrama; and I think any producer of a play can help the shaping of his production greatly by recognizing the kind of play he is dealing with.

Let me start with some simple definitions of dramatic forms that include some description of the worlds, the society, that they assume. In tragedy there is a corrupt society (*Lear* or *Hamlet*), a scared one (*Oedipus*) or at least one incapable of doing anything (*Antigone*) in which some kind of action must be taken. Our hero is the one who acts. Since, however, society (the world) doesn't change because of his action, he must leave it, usually by death, sometimes as in *Oedipus* by being turned out of it. Our empathy may go to Hamlet or Antigone, but our body and soul, thank you very much, stay here on earth. We may admire the tragic hero's action, but we do not, nor would we if we were faced with his decision, necessarily accept it as our own. We learn from tragedy what a single human is capable of, but we remain Fortinbras or the elders of Thebes. And that means that we accept this society, this world, rotten as we may think it to be.

In comedy there is a similar kind of problem, but here the hero is worse than the society around him, and he is finally either excluded by his own choice, as is Harpagon in Molière's *The Miser*, or forced to leave it by a slow moving arm of that society like the law, as are Volpone and Mosca in Ben Jonson's *Volpone*. In such a play we laugh at the fool and remain with the society convinced that its foolishness is better than his. In a comedy of manners the situation is somewhat different. Our heroes here, the Milla-mants and Mirabels, heroes better than the society around them, are forced by that society, at least until the final curtain, to remain outside of it. Finally the obstacles that stand in their way are overcome, and they join that society in a wedding dance to which we are all invited. Be it noted, however, that they join a society in no way changed by them. In comedy one feels that the social bond society represents is a better bond than the anti-social position of Harpagon or Volpone, or the unwed condi-tion of Mirabel and Millamant. Finally we laugh at the greed of Harpa-gon, the over-cleverness of Volpone, and we are happy when Millamant and Mirabel can join the society no matter how fully we may recognize its limitations.

In tragedy we accept the social bond and recognize how much we cheat our best selves to do it. In comedy we accept the social bond recognizing the foolishness of pretending we can live without it. They are really two sides of the same coin, and the coin is our need for an absolute social bond of some kind in order to live. We cannot tolerate total isolation, no matter how distasteful the society we insist on joining appears. Structurally this means that tragedy focuses on a hero who is better than society, who rises above the social bond, but finally must accept the price of such behavior which is either death, or disgrace and expulsion from that society. Com-edy focuses on the foolishness of the hero who thinks he can live outside of society and laughs at him for his presumption. It is called dark comedy when we recognize the rottenness of the society he would escape, and yet are willing to accept his decision to join it. We may not laugh at this kind of comedy, but in its depiction of society as essential to our lives no matter how rotten it is, it remains comedy. Melodrama is different from both comedy and tragedy. It focuses on the nobility of a hero who would change society, not his foolishness. Unlike tragedy in which society rejects such a hero, melodrama reclaims him, either because he is willing to change or because society realizes it must change, or at least must try. In melodrama one has either a rotten society that must somehow be cleansed or an inadequate hero that must somehow change his behavior to conform to that society. The social bond is still crucial, but unlike tragedy and comedy it is not absolute in its claims. Social change is possible in melodrama as is change in its hero. There are no such possiblities in tragedy or comedy. Indeed because of this possibility melodrama is the form used for those plays that push for social change or reform, from *Everyman* to *Waiting for Lefty*, or more subtly, from *Ghosts* to a movie like *The Accused*.

It is not fair, I think, to dismiss melodrama as if its proper home were the snarling villains and unconquerable heroes in *Batman* or *Superman* cartoons, descended as they are from such nineteenth-century plays as *The Drunkard* or *The Gambler*. Certainly such plays are melodramas. The villains, representative of society here as surely as Edmund and Goneril are in *King Lear*, are finally killed or foiled – often only foiled, the Simon Legrees don't always die any more than the Joker does, but he is foiled and society is rid of him, and our hero, the reformed drunkard, for example, re-emerges as a reformed citizen who can now live in the world. It is true that the villains in tragedy die as often as those in melodrama do, but there is no hint that their moral point of view has been changed or that a new society will emerge that will insist on such change. In melodrama such change is at least suggested. Occasionally, as in the nineteenth-century melodrama, *The Gambler*, our hero dies magnificently while killing the villain and saving his family in a glorious visualization – a cabin engulfed in flames, high atop a mountain, the child saved so that the new society can emerge, the father, a victim of his diseased gambling, lost in the flames. We may not take such plays seriously any longer, but that is not the fault of the form, that is simply the clichéd and sentimental way it is used. *A Man for All Seasons* may present a more sentimental view of the world than *King Lear*, but that doesn't mean it isn't a tragedy.

We tend sometimes to use the term tragedy for a good serious play and melodrama for a bad one, and that can be very misleading. The elements that make plays melodrama, the misled hero, the selfish society that can work on him for its own gains but be changed, the big climactic visual scene which has become so much a part of the form, and the surge of hope at the curtain that things can be changed, are as certain in *The Gambler* as in *The Accused*, where a misled heroine will finally get her day in court. The big scene here is not her death in flames, but her rape, yet it leads to that hopeful curtain as surely as does that cabin in flames. Her lawyer will take the case to trial, as we want her to, because we have seen the violence and viciousness of that rape. The structure of the two works is similar. The danger of that big scene, so often visual so seldom verbal, is that it leads to a conclusion that we accept without much exploration. After all in *Lear* in that big climactic scene (IV, vi) we get a detailed description of Lear's view of society and why he would leave it, from the 'simpering dame who goes to't with a more riotous appetite than the soiled horse' to 'the great image of authority; a dog's obeyed in office'. Of course Shakespeare won't let him have his escape from that world without paying a price. Even if the world is rotten you must live in it in tragedy or else leave it altogether. The price of Lear's 'No, no, no, no. Come let's away to prison' is the death of Cordelia with whom he would escape alive. In melodrama where change is possible we can't afford such close and sensitive analysis of our world, because such sensitive analysis leads to a complexity which makes change impossible. Lear's world cannot be changed, nor can a sensitive person living in it find any means within himself to change in such a way to accommodate it.

The world of melodrama is a simpler one, where change of either the protagonist or the society he must struggle with is possible. For this to happen we are usually given a visual picture or a rhetorical speech that asks us not to think but to respond. It is difficult to quote good modern, theatrical melodramas because movies have so completely taken over the form, but if one goes back before the movies it is easy to see how simply the theatre fed the cinema when it arrived. Let me quote but two. Here is Laura in *The Easiest Way* by Eugene Walters, first produced in New York in 1908.[3] She is a heroine who cannot change her convictions and so will continue to exist in a society that she doesn't like. Incidentally the major point of the play, and the reason I define it as melodrama not comedy, is that we are not to like the society either, because of what it does to the Lauras of this world, and we are certainly asked to change it and to believe in that possibility. Here is the final curtain.

> *Laura.* (*who is arranging her hair*) Doll me up Annie.
> *Annie.* You goin' out Miss Laura?
> *Laura.* Yes, I'm going to Rector's to make a hit, and to hell with the rest. (*At this moment the hurdy-gurdy in the street, presumably immediately under the window, begins to play the tune of 'Bon-bon Buddie. My Chocolate Drop'. There is something in this ragtime melody which is particularly and peculiarly suggestive of the low life, the criminality and prostitution that constitute the night excitement of that section of New York City known as the Tenderloin. The tune, its association, is like spreading before Laura's eyes a panorama of the inevitable depravity that awaits her. She is torn from every ideal that she so weakly endeavored to grasp, and is thrown into the mire and slime at the very moment her emancipation seems to be assured. The woman, with her flashy dress in one arm and her equally exaggerated type of picture hat in the other, is near prostrated by the tune and the realization of the future as it is terrifically conveyed to her. The negress, in the happiness of serving Laura in her questionable career, picks up the melody and hums it as she unpacks the finery that has been put away in the trunk.*)

Laura. (with infinite grief, resignation and hopelessness.) O God – O my god. (*She turns and totters toward the bedroom. The hurdy-gurdy continues with the negress accompanying it. A SLOW CURTAIN.*)   (p. 225)

One can see why the movies liked melodrama so much.

A similar effect can be achieved with language, or I should say could be achieved in 1906. Listen to the final curtain of Moody's *The Great Divide*.[4] Ruth is finally discovering her New England prudery and throwing it away.

> *Ruth.* Another woman would have gone straight to her goal. You might have found such a one. But instead you found me, a woman in whose ears rang night and day the cry of an angry heaven to us both – 'Cleanse yourselves!' And I went about doing it in the only way I know – (*she points to the portraits on the wall*) the only way my fathers knew – by wretchedness, by self-torture, by trying blindly to pierce your careless heart with pain. And all the while you – Oh, as I lay there and listened to you, I realized it for the first time – you had risen, in one hour, to a wholly new existence, which flooded the present and future with brightness, yes, and reached back into our past, and made of it – made all of it – something to cherish! (*She takes the chain and comes closer*) You had taken the good of our life and grown strong. I have taken the evil and grown weak, weak unto death. Teach me to live as you do! (*She puts the chain around his neck*)
>
> *Ghent. (Puzzled and yet realizing the full force of her words)* Teach you – to live – as I do?
>
> *Ruth.* And teach him!
>
> *Ghent. (Unable to realize his fortune)* You'll let me make a kind of happy life for – the little rooster?
>
> *Ruth. (Holds out her arms, her face flooded with happiness)* And for us! For us!
>
>   (p. 315)

Hardly cinematic, but a very similar effect. Not an effect that modern theatre has found a vocabulary for. When we sound like that today the effect is not melodramatic but comic. We laugh at such language, and since we haven't found another, melodrama has left the stage and found itself comfortably housed in the movie theatre.

We have ended up with either comedy or tragedy on the stage, primarily comedy. In my sense that in tragedy society must lose the people we admire, I think both *Death of a Salesman* and *Streetcar Named Desire* are tragedies. We may find Willy stupid to believe in the kind of success he believes in, but we do it enough ourselves to recognize him. We may not die for it as he does, but then we don't go through Hamlet's hell toward death either. And certainly if we are moved by Blanche – and I am – it is her desire for a world where some relation between man and woman beyond simple lust is possible. Again, not finding it, we may not go insane, but our recognition of the validity of her need is certainly what connects us to her. If the society depicted by Miller and Williams recognized the need to accommodate Willy's dream and Blanche's gentleman we would have melodrama. Because neither of them do we have tragedy. So too *The Glass Menagerie* is certainly a sentimental comedy not a melodrama. There is no call for social change here. Tom's change is that he grows up as we all must. Our mothers and our sisters, much as we may miss them, leave us, or we leave them, and we become what is called an adult. We join a larger society than our family. Even Albee's *Who's Afraid of Virginia Wolf*, excruciating as it may be, is not a melodrama but a comedy of manners. A married couple who want a child and can't have one may lead a sour existence as husband and wife, but in no way does that play ask for social change. The focus is on the relation of the couple, not the society that crushes two good people and must change. Nor do George and Martha change; they simply recognize, finally, the lie they have been living.

But even if my thesis that melodrama has left the stage is true, the question still is why. Our difficulty in taking the language seriously may be part of the problem, but there is also the problem of the kind of statement melodrama wants to make. The possibility of change in society, or of change in the hero or heroine who lives in that society, is a necessity for melodrama. Unlike comedy or tragedy where society remains the same and we join it or leave it, melodrama at least implies a change in conviction, and a positive change at that, in either the protagonist (our hero) or the antagonist (society). To believe in this possibility takes both an original mind and a society that wants to believe in that mind. Ibsen may have shocked his audience in *Ghosts*, but there was certainly an audience there that wanted that shock. I am not at all sure that we do, except in the easy sentimentalized versions that movies give us. What most intelligent playwrights are describing at the moment is our poverty of thought, our poverty of expression, and the inadequacy of any of our attempts at understanding even ourselves, much less the world we live in. Such a concern is the province of comedy.

In this context let me look at typical plays of two playwrights who are sometimes looked on as melodramatists, David Rabe and Sam Shepard. David Rabe is probably the easier of the two. In *Hurlyburly*, for example, we have a play about Eddie's attempt to deal with two contradictory aspects of his existence: one, the recognition and the will to act on it, that man is basically rotten as is life, and a cynical dismissal of anything meaningful is necessary to live in the world; and two, that there is a wild, mad, original, creative, and positive impulse which cannot be defined or acted upon in this way. These two states, as Rabe himself says, are most clearly shown in Mickey and Phil: Mickey as the cynic who lives and Phil as the madman who kills himself. To quote Rabe the story of the play is 'how Eddie, through the death of Phil, was saved from being Mickey'.[5] This potential salvation is most clearly seen in the note Phil leaves: 'The guy who dies in an accident understands the nature of destiny', or as translated finally by Eddie 'If you die in a happening that is not expected, foreseen, or intended, you understand the inevitable or necessary succession of events.' Or to put it in an active state, which Eddie never does in the play, 'act as impulsively and uncynically as you can while recognizing that there is no order in your life and its movement is at best an accident'.

A melodrama would have had its hero recognize this at the climax of the play and the curtain would be the act that proved he could live in such a way. In *Hurlyburly* Eddie tries to join these two extremes in the last act, first in his dialogue with Johnnie Carson on his television set, a comic and necessarily inconclusive discussion since Johnnie obviously can't hear him, and secondly in the following speech to Donna about Phil's funeral.

> *Eddie. (with a shrug. Eddie gets through it quickly not seeming to care at all.)* You know everybody wears the suits, you do things. Everybody's there; you hang around, you know. The cars. Everybody gets to the church. So the priest is there, he blah-blah, blah-blah-blah, some guy singing ... mmmmmmmmmm ... mmmm, you drive to the cemetery, right. Everybody's in a line, cars all in a line. Brmmm, brmmm. Everybody's in the cars; blah-blah, blah-blah-blah. So we get to the cemetery, the priest's got some more to say, rapateta, rapateta. So there's the hole, put him in. Blah-blah, blah-blah-blah.
> *Donna.* Was it sad?
> *Eddie. (Somewhere here it hits him, a grief that, though there are tears, is beyond them: it is in his body which heaves and wracks him):* There in the church we were all like a bunch of dogs. This guy would sing with his beautiful voice. He had this beautiful high voice. All alone. No organ or anything. Just his voice. And we would all start to cry. The priest could say anything, a lot of nice things, sad things. Nothin'. But then this guy from way in the back of the church would sing, and you couldn't hear the words even, just this high, beautiful, sad, sound, this human sound, and we would all start to cry along with him. *(He gasps, tries to breathe.)* (p. 165)

But lest we think this feeling of Eddie's can lead anywhere the next line is Donna's: 'You know somethin', Eddie. I didn't really go to all these actual places on my clothes.' She is pointing to emblems of cities and parks around the country. The fact that she can ignore what moves Eddie, and indeed force Eddie to ignore it, puts us in a comic world not a melodramatic one. Donna is the representative of that cynical and meaningless society that man must change, or at least make hear, if we are to have melodrama, but note how the play moves from here to its curtain. The conversation moves on to her travels which go from Hollywood to Oxnard, a few miles north of Hollywood, and finally to the curtain:

> *Donna.* I'm gonna sleep here if you don't mind. You got room?
> *Eddie.* I'm gonna be up for a while.
> *Donna. (Standing up, looking around.)* Oh, I don't care. I'm just happy to get off the streets at the moment. The desperation out there is paranormal.

Eddie. I don't know if I'm going to sleep ever again. I might stay awake
  forever.
Donna. That's okay; should I lay down on the floor?
Eddie. No, there's room here.
  (*Eddie slides to the end of the couch, while Donna, carrying her coat, settles up against
  him, covering herself with her coat, then she looks at him*)
Donna. You wanna fuck me or anything Eddie, before I go to sleep?
Eddie. No.
Donna. Great. Not that I don't want to, I'm just sleepy.
Eddie. You want a lude or anything?
Donna. No. (*Turning back to sleep*)
Eddie. Valium?
Donna. No. 'Night.
Eddie. Goodnight.
Donna. Pleasant dreams. (*He holds her*) *BLACKOUT CURTAIN.*   (p. 167)

With whatever comfort or discomfort Eddie finally holds Donna, the
gesture is certainly a return to the social norm. Eddie may consider never
sleeping again, but no matter what his thoughts are he is literally holding
the world that he would have to change, and certainly Donna has given no
hints of such a possibility. Rabe may have hoped for Eddie's salvation in a
different kind of world, but he doesn't cheat him or us and give it to him.
That is not to say that the play couldn't be pushed toward melodrama.
Think, for example, of how different that final curtain is with a change in
that last stage direction. If, for example, instead of holding Donna Eddie
were to rise, stare at Donna with a smile of dismissal and then, after
shaking his head at her insensitivity, walk to the door, turn and laugh at
her once more, and then walk out and leave her there. This would suggest
the possibility of change, if not in Donna, at least in Eddie. In the play as
published, however, no new directions are even suggested, and we are in
the world of comedy – black comedy and not very funny, but comedy not
melodrama.

The more difficult of the two playwrights to define, however, is certainly
Sam Shepard. There is a violence in his plays that suggests melodrama,
and serious struggle for what seems, at first glance, to be new ground. The
world of *Buried Child* is basically one of family.[6] There are three generations in the house, Hallie and Dodge, their son Tilden, and Tilden's son
Vince. The story is built around Vince's return to his grandparent's farm
in Illinois on his way from somewhere to New Mexico where he had hoped
to visit his father, Tilden. By the end of the play his grandfather is dead
and the farm is Vince's. Shelley, Vince's girlfriend, will go to Hollywood,
her home and up to now Vince's as well, but Vince will stay in Illinois, on
what is now his farm. He is forced through the play into a number of
confrontations, mostly to do with his attempts to convince his father and
his grandfather that he is indeed their son and grandson. When Dodge,

near the end of the play, prepares for his own death by announcing his last will and testament and leaves the farm to Vince, we have on the surface his recognition of Vince, and, with Vince's acceptance of the property, a new beginning. On the surface we have melodrama, our hero is finally recognized and with his acceptance of the farm a new social order will emerge in the new management of the farm. Vince's final speech even sounds like melodrama:

> This is my house now y'know? All mine. Everything. Except for the power tools and stuff. I'm gonna get all new equipment anyway. New plows, new tractors, everything. All brand new. Start right off on the ground floor.
>
> (p. 131)

The trouble is we are not allowed such a simple reading of the play.

What we have in the body of the play is not the mismanagement of a farm that needs correcting. It is true that no one can account for the crops that appear, but according to Tilden who appears loaded with fresh ears of corn from the farm on his first entrance, 'There's tons of corn', even though Dodge insists he hasn't planted any since 1935. And on Tilden's next entrance in act II he appears loaded with carrots. The farm seems to supply food abundantly, and no one is starving. In fact the issues that we are continually asked to deal with in the play are confrontations between fathers and sons who don't know one another, not the management of the farm. If Vince has a problem in the play it is getting someone, his father or his grandfather, to recognize him. Here is Shelley in act II:

> *Shelley.* You really don't recognize him? Either one of you? (*Tilden turns and stares at Shelley's hands as she cuts and scrapes the carrots.*)
> *Dodge.* (*Watching TV*) Recognize who?
> *Shelley.* Vince.
> *Dodge.* What's to recognize. (*Dodge lights a cigarette, coughs slightly and stares at TV, smoking.*)
> *Tilden.* I thought I recognized him. I thought I recognized something about him?
> *Shelley.* You did?
> *Tilden.* I thought I saw a face inside his face.
> *Shelley.* Well it was probably that you saw what he used to look like. You haven't seen him in six years.
> *Tilden.* I haven't?
> *Shelley.* That's what he says. (p. 100)

And so the conversation drifts, getting nowhere, but certainly making confusion of any sense of family relations. The major focus is on Tilden who keeps circling Shelley, staring at her hands and finally asking if he can touch her coat, a rabbit skin coat which she finally gives him. He continues the scene by walking around the room stroking it; and one has the eerie feeling that one is not in a real farmhouse at all, but in a strange remake of *Of Mice and Men* in which Tilden is Lennie and Shelley the girl he accidentally murders.

It is this strange creation of the movies that first tells us about the dead child, the buried child of the title, a child Dodge, at least so says Tilden, killed and buried, a charge which scares poor Shelley and which Dodge nowhere denies. And this sense of threat is continued with the entrance of another son of Dodge's, Bradley, who arrives out of the rain, his squeaking wooden leg and its thump heard in silence before his entrance and during it as he takes off his wet slicker before his first line 'What's going on here?' Again we're in a bad remake of a horror movie. One can almost hear the clichéd voice. 'It was a dark and rainy night when my car broke down. There was no place in sight but this strange castle, and so I went there for help.' Of course Bradley doesn't come to help, he comes to threaten and appears more the monster in the castle than the outsider entering. After scaring poor Tilden from the room and ignoring Dodge's coughing he ends the act with a brutal gesture at Shelley:

> Bradley. (*To Shelley, motioning her to open her mouth.*)
> Shelley. What?
> Bradley. Open up. (*She opens her mouth slightly.*) Wider. (*She opens her mouth slightly.*) Wider. (*She opens her mouth wider.*) Keep it like that. (*She does. Stares at Bradley. With his free hand he puts his fingers into her mouth. She tries to pull away.*) Just stay put. (*She freezes. He keeps his fingers in her mouth. Pause. He pulls his hand out. She closes her mouth, keeps her eyes on him. Bradley smiles. He looks at Dodge on the floor and crosses over to him. Shelley watches him closely. Bradley stands over Dodge and smiles at Shelley. He looks down at Dodge and then drops the coat so that it lands on Dodge and covers his head. Bradley keeps his hands in the position of holding the coat, looks over at Shelley and smiles. The lights black out.*)   (p. 107)

The hand in the mouth is like a rape, and it makes a very strong and terrifying curtain, but we find Shelley in the next act acting not only comfortably but very much as if it were her own house – she even says it feels like hers – we are in a very different world, a world in which life is defined by role playing. Shelley, Hollywood child that she is, now plays the role of wife mastered by Bradley's force. Of course we realize that the force is a joke, since Bradley plays the entire third act on the couch unable to move without his wooden leg. We are in a world of worn out movie plots. Even Vince finally gets his inheritance not through his blood line, but by attacking the farm à la John Wayne as a Green Beret. Throwing whiskey bottles like hand grenades he attacks the house until Dodge finally yells 'Go ahead! Take over the house! Take over the whole god-damn house! You can have it! It's yours!' The new ownership is established not by inheritance but by Vince playing the role of military conqueror and winning it in battle, at least mock battle, and we are again in the movies. Richard Gilman is probably right when he describes Shepard's search for self in the introduction to *Seven Plays*.

Might not the true question in putting forth the self, certainly in the theatre but also in life with its theatrical hunger, be 'Who do I seem to be?' and 'what am I taken for?' And might not the quest for identity really be a quest for a *role.* (p. xviii, Introduction)

It is true that this search goes on in the play in a melodramatic fashion. The problem is that the roles sought and played are such clichés that it is hard to take them other than ironically. We laugh, finally, however bitterly, at the roles played; and the apparent melodrama becomes self-parody. There is no hint of real social change in the play nor does Vince in any way have a new view of who he is. When at the end of the play we see Vince lying on the floor, his position imitating precisely that of the previous owner, Dodge, who lies next to him, and at the final curtain see Tilden going up the stairs carrying the moldy remains of the dead corpse of the 'buried child', what we see is that Vince is simply his grandfather, the child murderer, all over again. His feeling in that trip to buy whiskey that he is part of a family – has a father, a grandfather, and generations before that, a family, as he says, that he followed 'clear into Iowa. Every last one of them. Straight into the corn belt and further. Straight back as far as they'd take me' has indeed, as he says 'dissolved'; and he is now nothing more than himself unrelated to anything but the latest movie role that attracts him. It is no accident, I think, that he goes back from Illinois to Iowa, from east to west, not as one would expect if this were a real trip back to one's forbears from west to east. It is as if he got only part of the movie right. When we see this picture of Vincent against the dead child carried up the stairs by Tilden, we see the refusal of fathers to recognize a connection between generations. We don't feel the joyous surge of melodrama's happy ending, or even the possibility of one in the future, but the return to the same society of which Dodge was a part, a society that refuses to see anything resembling a connection between generations, who at best recognize social bonds through the movies they have seen and the roles they want to play. We are in a world of comedy, dark though it may be. Hallie's last speech which comes from upstairs, off stage, as Tilden comes on with the moldy corpse in his arms and slowly climbs the stairs toward her is anything but the hopeful note one seems to hear in it. She has just discovered the field of corn that Tilden had picked from in act 1, and she is explaining to a Dodge we know to be dead how it must have happened.

Good hard rain. Takes everything straight down deep to the roots. The rest takes care of itself. You can't force a thing to grow. You can't interfere with it. It's all hidden. It's all unseen. You just gotta wait until it pops up out of the ground. Tiny little shoot. Tiny little white shoot. All hairy and fragile. Strong though. Strong enough to break the earth even. It's a miracle Dodge. I've never seen a crop like this in my whole life. Maybe it's the sun. Maybe that's it. Maybe it's the sun. (*Tilden disappears above. Silence. Lights go black.*) (p. 132)

Even if the 'sun' 'son' pun is accidental one can't help feeling the irony of the situation. Everything including the dead child 'pops up'. 'You can't interfere with it. It's all hidden', including the need for connection between generations, a connection that clearly in its reappearance here can't be hidden forever, even though it's dead. The pity, of course, is that there is no sense, especially with Vince lying on the floor so exactly like his grandfather, that any such birth is about to take place in Vince. It is, I think, a very bitter and hopeless curtain, not one with the melodramatic assumption of the possibility of change.

To insist on such definitive distinctions between the two forms may seem simply carping. After all, what difference does it make? It seems to me that in a production of the play quite a bit. To begin with if we recognize the comic form of the play we emphasize the cinematic parody wherever we see it. For the actor playing Tilden or Bradley or Vince or Shelley I think there is a very different way of acting John Wayne or Boris Karloff in a movie role than acting the same part as if it were real. I would also emphasize and point to the waste in such a world. In production, for example, the husking of the corn and the paring of the carrots can appear very like masturbating. If I felt the piece were melodrama I would certainly hide that appearance if I could, just as I would push for realistic acting with no sense of the movie roles the parts seem to come from. Instead of the irony of that last speech I would play for hope; and though I know such direction would be wrong, it is structural definition that helps me realize it.

NOTES

1 Robert Heilman, *The Iceman, the Arsonist and the Troubled Agent: Tragedy and Melodrama on the Modern Stage* (Seattle: University of Washington Press, 1973).
2 James I. Smith, *Melodrama* (London: Methuen, 1963).
3 Eugene Walter, 'The Easiest Way', in *Chief Contemporary Dramatists. Second Series*, ed. T. R. Dickinson (New York: Houghton Mifflin Co., 1921).
4 W. V. Moody, 'The Great Divide', in *Chief Contemporary Dramatists. First Series* ed. T. R. Dickinson (New York: Houghton Mifflin Co., 1915).
5 David Rabe, *Hurlyburly* (New York: Grove Press, 1985), p. 175. All quotations from the play are from this edition.
6 Sam Shepard, *Seven Plays* (London: Bantam Books, 1981). All quotations from the play are from this edition.

Defending melodrama*

IRA HAUPTMAN

In the late nineteenth century, so the histories go, the European and American stages moved away from an infatuation with sensation and crude moralism – melodrama – and toward an appreciation of quiet truthfulness and more or less disinterested social analysis – realism. Although melodrama is, properly speaking, a dramatic genre, while realism is an amalgam of ideology and style, still the tendencies they represent seem so totally opposed that the attempt to link them in dialectic is understandable. Customary definitions tend to reinforce the feeling of strict opposition. We can start with:

> Melodrama is a form of dramatic composition in prose partaking of the nature of tragedy, comedy, pantomime, and spectacle, and intended for a popular audience. Primarily concerned with situation and plot, it calls upon mimed action extensively and employs a more or less fixed complement of stock characters, the most important of which are a suffering heroine or hero, a persecuting villain, and a benevolent comic. It is conventionally moral and humanitarian in point of view and sentimental and optimistic in temper, concluding its fable happily with virtue rewarded after many trials and vice punished. Characteristically it offers elaborate scenic accessories and miscellaneous divertissements and introduces music freely, typically to underscore dramatic effect.[1]

We need merely reverse this to arrive at a traditional definition of the realist theatre of middle Ibsen, some Strindberg, and total Zola: a drama presenting psychologized characters formed by heredity and environment instead of heroes and villains, and more interested in analyzing the relationships of these characters with each other than in hustling them through a ramshackle plot; a drama whose morality is crusading and concerned with social institutions; a drama which is conventionally pessimistic, concluding its fable with a perception of human unhappiness in which virtue and vice may be irrelevant; and a drama which offers no scenic accessories, divertissements, or musical accompaniments that are not part of the social milieu of its characters, which it renders as

* A draft of this paper was read at the *Themes in Drama* International Conference held at the University of California, Riverside, in February 1990.

accurately as possible. All of this is what is generally implied in the term 'realism', which I will put in quotes from now on because, as Vladimir Nabokov said of 'reality', it is one of the few words that make no sense without them.

This idealized opposition of melodrama and 'realism' informs most histories of the theatre. But there is a typically cryptic utterance by Northrop Frye that clamors for attention at this point:

> As tragedy moves over towards irony, the sense of inevitable event begins to fade out, and the sources of catastrophe come into view. In irony catastrophe is either arbitrary and meaningless, the impact of an unconscious (or, in the pathetic fallacy, malignant) world on conscious man, or the result of more or less definable social and psychological forces.[2]

It doesn't seem unreasonable to locate the first of Frye's sources of disaster (the 'world') within the melodramatic vision, and to locate the second ('social and psychological forces') within the 'realistic'. The sense of irreconcilable difference between melodrama and 'realism' then 'begins to fade out', and a relation between them as deepening forms of irony becomes possible. Irony to Frye involves the sense of man's lost freedom and the increase of the world's power, and it is apparently of little consequence to him if art decides to internalize this worldly power within the hero according to the laws of psychology. The 'realistic' forces within the hero's psyche are no more accessible to his conscious control than are the floods and avalanches of melodrama.

So melodrama and 'realism' come closer here as complementary forms of irony. If we adopt a larger historical perspective now and consider that Euripides is commonly given credit for being the first 'realist' in drama as well as being the most melodramatic of the Greek tragedians, and if we consider also that Menander presumably introduced both 'realism' and melodrama into comedy, and if we consider further that this sort of comedy was the basis of the chief comic tradition in Europe, then it may indeed begin to seem that the relation of melodrama and 'realism' is not at all one of mutual exclusivity in a streamlined historical dialectic.

At any rate, we may begin to suspect that the 'progression' from tragedy to melodrama to 'realism' that is conveniently signified by the names Racine, Hugo, Zola is most likely misleading in some important way, and that the actual relationships among these three kinds of drama are more delicate than the great partisans of any of them are usually willing to admit.

In this spirit of perhaps forced reconciliation, I would like to discuss some of the characteristics of melodrama that are hardest for us to take and briefly to suggest ways to reconsider them in light of the practices of both tragic and 'realist' theatre.

Melodrama is too moralistic. Of course. But if moralism is an objectionable quality, then 'realism' with its seemingly endless round of thesis plays designed for the betterment of society is even more unbearable in its moral earnestness than bumbling old melodrama. Shaw's description of the progress of literature in the nineteenth century, in his preface to three plays by Brieux, almost equates 'realism' with moralism:

> In this new phase we see the bourgeoisie, after a century and a half of complacent vaunting of its own probity and modest happiness (begun by Daniel Defoe in Robinson Crusoe's praises of 'the middle station of life'), suddenly turning bitterly on itself with accusations of hideous sexual and commercial corruption ... the bourgeois was depicted as a thief, a tyrant, a sweater, a selfish voluptuary whose marriages were simple legalizations of unbridled licentiousness. Sexual irregularities began to be attributed to the sympathetic characters in fiction not as the blackest spots in their portraits, but positively as redeeming humanities in them.[3]

The difference of course is that melodrama's morality is derived from a system of spiritual values beyond the world of the senses – that is, it is a kind of religious drama – while 'realism's' morality is totally of this world, and in fact of this society. Melodrama is symbolic drama. It sees life as a field for the struggle of eternal impulses of good and evil. The variety of dramatic patterns possible is limited, and the same moments keep recurring from play to play as the same conflict works itself out. Good does not always win, self-pity sometimes getting so out of hand that it demands the defeat of innocence, but in the original, 'classical' melodrama created by Pixérécourt in France at the end of the eighteenth century, virtue generally reigned triumphant in a self-renewing myth of promise and encouragement born of the Revolution. Pixérécourt's theatre was one of sheer wish-fulfillment. The victory of virtue in his plays, its power to make savages drop their weapons in admiration just by revealing itself in their beautiful civilized victims, is a kind of completely unironic *deus ex machina* without a visible *deus*.

I have to admit that seeing the world as a battleground for good and evil may not be acceptable metaphysics any longer, but as a theme of western literature it is certainly more enduring than the moral themes – such as the unfairness of inheritance laws – that were bequeathed us by the 'realistic' thesis plays of Dumas *fils* and Augier, and then of Becque and Brieux, and perhaps of Shaw himself some of the time. The moral purpose of theatre had changed, and the 'realist' intention of defining human beings by their relation to other human beings rather than by their place in the spiritual order of the universe was supposed to produce an art of description, not classification, in which the moral categories of melodrama were to become meaningless. But to describe almost inevitably means to strip and expose, and melodrama's 'villain' came back, as the Shaw quote suggests, as the entire bourgeois way of life itself.

Another of our problems with melodrama is that its characters are too simple, to put it mildly. The most common way for a work of art to achieve form, as Susan Sontag has pointed out, is by doubling, and clearly characters are among the things that plays and novels double. But we are likely to be critically resentful if a writer reverses this process and achieves form by splitting character and endowing more or less trivial fragments with autonomy. It is this process that we are bemoaning when we reject the hero–victim–villain makeup of the melodramatic world.

Robert B. Heilman makes character the central issue in his book *Tragedy and Melodrama*:

> In the structure of melodrama, man is essentially 'whole'; this key word implies neither greatness nor moral perfection, but rather an absence of the basic inner conflict that, if it is present, must inevitably claim our primary attention . . . It is in tragedy that man is divided; in melodrama, his troubles, though they may reflect some weakness or inadequacy, do not arise from the urgency of unreconciled impulses. In tragedy the conflict is within man; in melodrama, it is between men, or between men and things.[4]

This is a dangerous notion, I think, first because of the large number of tragic characters from Prometheus to the Trojan women who are not at war with themselves, second because the idea of a divided self suggests the sort of love versus honor conflicts that fill heroic drama of the later seventeenth century more than it suggests anything crucial about *King Lear*, and finally because melodrama of Pixérécourt's variety is a continual display of inner conflict of the kind in which a virtuous maiden thrown out of the house after a false accusation must stifle all thought of vindicating herself out of deference to the authority of her father. With regard to the tragedies of Aeschylus, it is almost safe to say that it is not character but the world which is divided against itself when, as is customary, it presents the hero with a grim choice between two contradictory divine imperatives. The main reason that such heroes as Agamemnon, Orestes, and Pelasgus are divided is that they are weighing the relative disasters that each course of action promises.

But perhaps the best answer to Heilman is that the most profoundly split character in all of tragedy, Pentheus in Euripides' *Bacchae*, is divided into components so elemental and so irreconcilable that they are in purest essence melodramatic. Pentheus, at the mercy of Dionysus, the god whose power it is in the play to reverse nature, passes from pure rationality to pure sensuousness, from sovereign to animal, and is destroyed because there is no accommodation possible within the human form. We may remind ourselves that this sort of division of human nature into battling halves is of course the starting point of melodrama, which, from this point of view, takes tragedy's awesome conclusions as exciting givens, objectifies the split in human nature by creating a villainous new character to harass the hero, and rubs its hands in anticipation of a thrilling time.

Perhaps this merely shows that melodrama isn't a negation of tragedy but a debasement of it. Melodramatic villains, after all, are pretty ridiculous. But some remarks by Lionel Trilling may help restore our respect for this character type. Trilling is discussing 'the literary culture of the post-Victorian age':

> The diminished credibility of the villain, the opinion that he was appropriate only to the fantasy of melodrama, not to the truth of serious novels or plays, may in part be explained by the modern tendency to locate evil in social systems rather than in persons. But it is worth considering whether it might not also have come about because the dissembling which defined the villain became less appropriate to new social circumstances than it had been to preceding ones ... There is ground for believing that the villain was once truer to life than he later became ... A salient fact of French and English society up to a hundred years ago is the paucity of honourable professions which could serve the ambitious as avenues of social advancement. To a society thus restricted, the scheme, the plot, do not seem alien; the forging or destroying of wills is a natural form of economic enterprise.[5]

And of course villains become less preposterous as characters the farther back we reach. Nobody dismisses Jacobean drama because of its schemers.

To conclude this partial vindication of 'stock' characters I would like to quote something from Jacques Barzun which has the effect of redefining melodrama as a kind of drama of manners. And manners are a much more acceptable thing for drama to be about than morals.

> ... the villain in these conventional pieces usually came to grief before the final curtain, [but] it was clear in retrospect that his aims were precisely the same as the hero's: he wanted the girl and the money. The difference which marked him off as evil was a matter of style. He was not fastidious enough in the means he employed to gratify his otherwise natural desires ... the essence of melodrama appears as a deep conviction that certain expressions of human feeling are evil because they are deformed, and that this evil is positive and must be resisted.[6]

With this emphasis on attractive as opposed to 'deformed' ways of revealing oneself on stage, melodrama in fact becomes more a mode of estheticism than of morality. The opposite of the villain, if we carry this argument through, would then not be a stiff, virtuous hero but an amoral dandy. That doesn't sound much like the melodrama we know, but if we turn to the almost amoral detective and western heroes of Hollywood – say Humphrey Bogart and the James Stewart of the 1950s – we may get an idea of the way melodrama actually can be defined in terms of style and manners.

Is there anything to be said for melodramatic acting – all of those rolling eyes and sweeps of the arm to make sure that everyone in the tenth balcony had a clear idea of who was being evil and when? After all, every

theatrical reformer from young André Antoine to old August Strindberg –
'realist', symbolist, or expressionist – began by calling for a smaller house
so that the actors could relax and start acting. When D. W. Griffith
developed the close-up shot in the movies he was taking dissatisfaction to
its logical conclusion by bringing the audience right up to the actor.

But we don't do nineteenth-century acting justice unless we at least
acknowledge its power to take paltry plays and fill them with enough
refined energy to create theatrical events. Audiences didn't attend the
theatre because they couldn't wait until Sunday to hear a sermon, and it's
possible to argue that the rise in importance of scenic surprise as
melodrama developed was at least in part the result of a shortage of actors
who could live excitingly on the melodramatic stage. We must remember
that the great Romantic critics, Coleridge and Hazlitt, were electrified
when they saw Edmund Kean, a great actor of melodrama, embody
Shakespeare's characters. Eric Bentley quotes a description of impressive
melodramatic acting from Laurence Irving's life of Sir Henry Irving. The
play is *Louis XI* by Dion Boucicault, and this is what Irving did with it.

> But never was there such a picture of moving prostration and animated
> decay. The back of a couch lost hold of for a moment, and the tottering form
> stumbles forward in a manner which sends a painful start through the whole
> audience. The sceptre drops, after being used head downwards as a staff, and
> is forgotten. Then the king is induced to be seated on a couch, and with
> extraordinary elaborated graduations of sensibility, violently interrupted by
> spasms of vigour, he gradually loses his consciousness. No physical detail is
> neglected that can help to realize a sinking of mind and body into annihilating
> death. The voice and articulation have the weird, half-drunken thickness of
> paralysis. Even the effect observable in age and sickness of drawing the
> retreating lips over the sunken teeth is somewhat simulated ... Mr. Irving ...
> gives a picture of gradual and placid yet horrible death such as we believe has
> never been achieved before. Perhaps the greatest success of all is the still and
> silent impassibility into which the king sinks so absolutely that the courtiers
> and his son suppose it to be death. The actual death is not placid ...[7]

Bentley speaks this way about an actor's use of his power of presence:
'The extreme case of such use would be that an actor should literally
hypnotize his audience ... I would not say that acting is good to the extent
that it is hypnotic, but only that it is *melodramatic* to the degree that it is
hypnotic ... Baffling as is Richard III's scene with Lady Anne to victims
of modern Naturalism, it is a characteristically hypnotic piece of
melodrama.'[8]

A 'star' is an actor whose own presence overwhelms that of the mere
character he inhabits, and this was the great melodramatic actor. That
did not mean that he was in competition with the plays he acted in,
because the plays were not offering him characters to act so much as roles
to play, to use a Bentleyesque distinction. The subordination of the actor

to the character in 'realism' is equally arbitrary and, what's worse, runs the risk of untheatricality.

What about the excesses of melodramatic language? An interesting perspective emerges from perhaps an unlikely source, de Tocqueville's *Democracy in America*. This excerpt is from a chapter entitled 'Of the Inflated Style of American Writers and Orators'.

> The cause of this may be pointed out without much difficulty. In democratic communities each citizen is habitually engaged in the contemplation of a very puny object, namely himself ... When he has been drawn out of his own sphere, therefore, he always expects that some amazing object will be offered to his attention; ... The authors, on their part, do not fail to obey a propensity of which they themselves partake; they perpetually inflate their imaginations, and expanding them beyond all bounds, they not infrequently abandon the great in order to reach the gigantic.[9]

One of the problems of the early American theatre, with regard to *comedy*, is that because of this inflation of style, rhetoric was not recognized as rhetoric, and so distinctions among characters on the basis of how natural or sanctimonious they *sounded* – the distinction between Charles and Joseph Surface in Sheridan's *The School for Scandal* – became impossible. In Royall Tyler's famous old American play *The Contrast*, strongly influenced by Sheridan's play, the patriotic American hero sounds just like a Sheridan hypocrite. Rhetoric apparently sounded on this side of the ocean like the language of the heart. The point here is that in America, and among much of the European audience of the nineteenth century as well, melodramatic verbal excess seemed, oddly enough, natural. It seemed so, probably, exactly because it was so unnatural – not the normal language of society but the language that gives elemental expression to the feelings that society helps us conceal – rage, terror, helplessness. To us, of course, this language is close to totally opaque, almost non-existent as a medium of perception. And yet the pretense of 'realistic' dialog to be not dialog but actual speech seems pretty ludicrous to us now too.

It's essential also not to overlook the importance of non-verbal means of communication to the actor of melodrama. The description of Henry Irving's acting quoted earlier suggests how language could give way to mime. Melodrama did in fact cultivate a language of the entire theatre, uniting words, music, spectacle and gesture. The grand aim of this theatre, whose sensuous ambitions were a match for Antonin Artaud's, was to reproduce the physical world – mountain passes, caverns, ice floes – and make it vibrate to human sentiment and concerns. If words failed, it was at least partly because they tried to do more than their fair share in accomplishing this task.[10]

Do we object that melodramatic plots, with all of their absurd coincidences, are just too much to take? Most Greek tragedies are as bad.

Aristotle says that there is something wondrous about coincidence. The reason, I would say, is that coincidence is the dramatic technique of the powers of the universe. It seems to be mere accident only to those who don't understand those powers. Coincidence is one way of asserting that there is form in the world that is independent of human will. In the nineteenth century the plot of coincidence takes its place on equal esthetic terms with the plots of the well-made play and with the episodic formlessness of avant-garde naturalism.

I'd like to end with some further references to tragedy. Northrop Frye reminds us that the righting of the world's balance that is accomplished in tragedy when the world swoops down on the erring hero is unaffected by the moral quality of the hero's motivation when he disturbed that balance. In melodrama, by contrast, there is no such thing as a morally neutral wrong like Oedipus's. Crime occurs because there are criminals. Melodrama is concerned with poetic justice, with characters getting or failing to get what they deserve, while in tragedy the hero gets not what he 'deserves' but what he brings on himself.

I think, though, that it's possible to use the restorative movements of tragedy for a final vindication of melodrama. Think of the melodramatic play in which the hero has become a drunkard, and his desperate, weeping wife comes to the saloon to show him their helpless little baby. And the hero sees the baby and melts and gives up his terrible life. Now consider: from the point of view of the baby this is not melodrama but *The Eumenides*. By his mere puny aliveness the baby causes the world to become a better place. His needful existence puts a new moral responsibility on his parent-gods and, wondrously, inexplicably, they reconcile themselves to each other to meet it. To an audience of Titans the struggle in *The Eumenides* between gods and furies and the transformation of the furies into benevolent deities is pure melodrama. But the play is not written for them. To an audience of implacably adult adults the transformation of drunkard into caring father in the barroom is also pure melodrama. But if we think of it as addressed to the child within them it's joyous and mysterious.

NOTES

1 Frank Rahill, *The World of Melodrama* (University Park and London: Pennsylvania State University Press, 1967), p. xiv.
2 Northrop Frye, *The Anatomy of Criticism* (Princeton University Press, 1957), p. 285.
3 George Bernard Shaw, Preface to *Three Plays by Brieux* (London: A. C. Fifield, 1911), pp. x–xii.

4 Robert B. Heilman, *Tragedy and Melodrama* (Seattle: University of Washington Press, 1968), p. 79.

5 Lionel Trilling, *Sincerity and Authenticity* (Cambridge, MA: Harvard University Press, 1972), pp. 14–16.

6 Jacques Barzun, *The Energies of Art* (New York: Harper, 1956), pp. 229–30.

7 Eric Bentley, *The Life of the Drama* (New York: Atheneum, 1974), p. 174.

8 Ibid., p. 176.

9 Alexis de Tocqueville, *Democracy in America*, trans. Henry Reeve (New Rochelle, NY: Arlington House, 1966), vol. II, p. 82.

10 Peter Brooks's *The Melodramatic Imagination* (New Haven: Yale University Press, 1976) has a chapter on mute characters that also invokes Artaud and 'total' theatre.

Index